Financial Futures

Fundamentals,
Strategies,
and Applications

Financial
Futures

Fundamentals, Strategies, and Applications

Edward W. Schwarz
Joanne M. Hill
Thomas Schneeweis

1986

DOW JONES-IRWIN
Homewood, Illinois   60430

Classroom edition of this book is available through
Richard D. Irwin, Inc., under the same title.

ISBN 0-256-03005-7
Library of Congress Catalog Card No. 84–71299

Printed in the United States of America

3 4 5 6 7 8 9 0 ML 2 1 0 9 8 7 6

To Shirlee, Joe, and Alison
for their patience and support and to Pat
for bringing us together for this project

Preface

This book is a primer on the fundamentals, strategies, and applications of financial futures contracts. Since the introduction of GNMA financial futures contracts in October 1975, the financial futures markets have grown significantly. Over a brief period, financial futures have become an accepted part of corporate and investment management. For professional traders, financial executives and investors, an understanding of financial futures is necessary in helping them meet their financial objectives.

This book grew out of an earlier work of Ed Schwarz, *How to Use Interest Rate Futures Contracts*. This new book contains material and adaptations related to the evolution of financial futures markets. In the first section, fundamentals of financial futures, we describe the structure of the financial futures exchanges and the characteristics of futures contracts themselves. In addition we present the basis for valuing financial futures and their associated cash markets. We also explain the use of financial futures to hedge the risk of unexpected price changes. In the second section, entitled strategies and applications, we present alternative uses of financial futures in banking, pension and insurance management, portfolio management, and real estate and investment banking. In addition, corporate financial management applications are discussed. Arbitrage and speculative strategies for the individual trader are also reviewed. In the final section special topics pertaining to financial futures, options, and options on futures are explored.

The purpose of this book is to provide a source of information on the theory, applications, and strategic uses of financial futures.

The reading audience is intended to include practitioners and students. The topics covered do not demand an extensive background in mathematics or statistics.

We would like to thank all of those individuals who have helped in this endeavor. We also extend our appreciation to those who in countless discussions and writings have helped us in our understanding of the futures markets. We expressly extend our thanks to the following individuals.

Lloyd Besant; Stuart McCrary; Lawrence Leuzzi; Jerome Lacy; Bill DeRonne; Gail Gordon; Arthur Rebell; Warren E. Lebecki; Leslie Rosenthal; Richard L. Sandor; Kenneth J. Thygerson; Ronald F. Young; Mark Zurach; Larry Larkin; Andrew Harmstone; Robert J. Corcoran; Mike Phillip; Steve Figlewski; Gerald Gay; Jerome Stein; Dennis Draper; Ben Branch; Robert Kolb; Bob Daiger; Ann Peck and participants at Chicago Board of Trade Research Seminars.

We would like to convey a special thanks to Patricia Pembroke, of the Chicago Board of Trade, who was instrumental in bringing us together to work on this project.

Finally we wish to thank those who helped to put this book together. The manuscript was typed by Becky Baldwin. Anshu Jain helped to compile the bibliography. The views expressed here are those of the authors alone and any remaining errors are our responsibility.

Edward W. Schwarz
Joanne M. Hill
Thomas Schneeweis

Contents

PART 1

Fundamentals of Financial Futures

The first section of this book covers the creation and development of financial futures markets, and the pricing fundamentals of futures and their underlying cash securities. Chapter 1 describes the evolution of commodity markets and financial futures markets. In Chapter 2 the operation of a futures exchange is described and the differences between forward and futures markets are examined. In addition to the internal mechanism of the markets, government regulation relating to futures markets are detailed. The actual futures contract specifications on fixed income securities and stock indexes are presented in Chapters 3 and 4. Since futures prices are based on their underlying cash instruments, an understanding of the pricing fundamentals of short- and long-term fixed income and equity securities is also required. In Chapters 5 and 6, the pricing fundamentals of fixed income, equity securities, and futures are developed. In Chapter 7 the various methods used to determine the number of futures contracts required to hedge uncertain cash price movement are analyzed. The material in Chapters 1–7 thus provides an understanding of the fundamental structure of the financial futures markets and contracts.

1

Introduction to Futures Contracts and Markets

Over 100 years ago, the desire to transfer risk associated with unexpected commodity price changes was primarily responsible for the formation of the Chicago Board of Trade. Today, financial markets experience severe price volatility over short periods of time. Financial futures markets make possible the transfer of risk associated with unexpected price changes in financial markets. They also serve the functions of providing liquidity and continuous forward price information.

HISTORY OF COMMODITY TRADING

In the mid-1840s, Chicago became the market center for products from the farmlands of Illinois, Michigan, Indiana, and Wisconsin.[1] Marketing, however, was erratic and seasonal. In the autumn, large quantities of grain arrived in loaded carts that sometimes stretched for miles. Grain was normally cheap in the fall and expensive in the spring when supplies were depleted. The price of bread could triple between October and February. There were few storage facilities in Chicago to alleviate this feast-to-famine cycle. There was a need for an organized market to attract capital for developing storage facilities and to ensure a dependable grain supply. In 1848, local grain merchants formed the Board of Trade of the City of Chicago. With the availability of an organized central marketplace to sell commodities, individuals with capital invested in storage facilities. The Board of Trade itself used the aggregate political influence of its membership to work toward improving transportation and creating laws that would facilitate trade. Order began to replace chaos. Surplus grain, which earlier would have been dumped rather than returned unsold to farms, was stored in available space. Merchants and speculators were willing to bear the cost of storing grain, because they knew it would be needed later when orders would be forthcoming.

During this period, a particular trading practice developed which is used both inside and outside the exchange. It was called forward contracting. A producer would agree to sell grain to a buyer for a date following the harvest. In times of surplus or shortage, and corresponding low or high prices, defaults became common. To resolve this problem, buyers and sellers developed the practice of depositing money with a third party as a performance bond. This evolved into the current margin concept required of all buyers and sellers of future contracts. Deposits were recorded by clerks of the various trading firms and later by a department of the exchange known as the clearinghouse.

As trading volume increased, the mechanisms of delivery had

to change. Initially, a contract was traded through a chain of buyers and sellers, and the last buyer took delivery from the first seller. To simplify the delivery process, a third-party practice developed. Each buy-and-sell transaction was recorded by the clearing department of the exchange. At the time of delivery, the clearing office issued warehouse receipts which were used to document delivery by the sellers to the outstanding buyers. In addition to simplifying the delivery process, this clearing mechanism facilitated interchangeability and the offsetting of futures contracts. A contract could be offset by buying or selling another contract for the same delivery month. A trader's position then became net zero with the clearing office. This offset capability allowed people to trade who did not want to make or take delivery of the actual commodity. It attracted an increasing amount of speculative venture capital to the marketplace and created the liquidity necessary for increasing the use of futures markets by hedgers. Today, most trades are settled by offsetting transactions.

By the early 1870s, the elements of a futures market were in place:

1. A standard quantity with quality determined by inspection and grading.
2. Payment of premiums or discounts for grain of greater or lesser than standard quality.
3. Payment by buyers and sellers of performance bonds held by a third party.
4. Established future delivery dates.
5. The interchangeability of futures contracts of the same delivery month and the ability to offset.
6. Prices negotiated by open outcry in the marketplace.

HEDGING AND SPECULATION

As the experience with futures trading developed, market participants began to note a fundamental aspect of price movement in futures markets that supports the basic premise of hedging. Cash prices and futures prices tended to move in the same direction as they responded to underlying conditions of supply and demand. When supplies are perceived to be relatively scarce compared with demand, prospective sellers tend to raise their offering prices. Conversely, when supplies are felt to be relatively large compared with demand, prospective commodity buyers tend to lower their bids. Cash and futures prices naturally tend to rise and fall in roughly parallel movement as they respond to an underlying common set of supply and demand factors. Once this aspect of price movement was noted by market participants, they realized that action could be taken in futures contracts to minimize their risks of financial loss due to sharply rising or falling prices.

At the beginning of the season, a grain farmer risks receiving a price for grain at harvest time that does not cover the cost of production or return a profit. This risk can be minimized by selling the appropriate grain futures contracts in an amount that approximates the expected production of grain. The selling price of the futures contract is then the price at which the farmer will be able to sell his or her harvest. This action came to be known as hedging.

A theoretical hedge and its results are illustrated in Exhibit 1–1. The example used is highly simplified; the loss resulting from the cash sale of wheat is matched exactly by earnings on futures contracts. This rarely happens. Usually cash and futures prices tend to move in parallel fashion but not in equal amounts. Exhibit 1–1 illustrates a short, or selling, hedge. It provides the means of controlling or minimizing the risk of financial loss due to lower cash prices in the future.

Consumers of basic commodities also face price risks. Flour millers are expected to provide a steady supply of flour to their customers at stable prices. The miller is called upon to quote selling prices for flour that will be delivered many weeks or months in the future. Often the miller is unwilling or unable to buy the wheat for milling until just before the flour is processed. In the meantime, there is nothing to prevent wheat prices from rising to an extent that will either erase the projected profit or produce a loss on the forward sale of flour.

These experiences taught the millers that by buying wheat fu-

---

EXHIBIT 1–1
Short Hedge

	Cash Market	Futures Market
May	Expects to harvest wheat in August with price objective of $3.35 per bushel	Sells September wheat futures at $3.37 per bushel
August	Sells wheat at $3.28 per bushel in the cash market	Buys September wheat futures at $3.30 per bushel
Result	Receives 7 cents per bushel less than expected in May	Earns 7 cents per bushel on hedge

$3.28 per bushel cash income
.07 per bushel earned on hedge
$3.35 per bushel—objective price

tures contracts equal in volume to their commitments to sell flour for future delivery, protection could be purchased against rising wheat prices. This is called a long hedge and is illustrated in Exhibit 1–2.

This, too, is a highly simplified example and is an almost perfect hedge. Price changes in the cash market and in the futures market often move in different magnitudes over time.[2]

In addition to providing a means of minimizing price risk, a futures hedge provides a second benefit. A sound hedging program improves the prospects of the producer for acquiring needed capital. Producers of hedged commodities are often able to borrow as much as 90 percent of the market value of a commodity. Lenders understand that hedged loans contain significantly less risk than loans against unhedged crops. Warehouse managers and merchandisers of commodities who hedge, such as grain elevator companies, can more easily obtain the large amounts of capital needed to finance costly physical plants and ongoing purchases of grain. Users of basic commodities who process refined products and hedge are able to reduce their cash expenditures substantially through hedging.

The first cost associated with hedging is a performance bond, the initial margin deposit. Initial grain margins normally range from 2 to 10 percent of the actual market value of the commodity represented by the futures contract. Margins are subject to exchange-established minimum requirements and are kept consistent with the prevailing price risk.

An additional contribution of the futures market is its value as a price reference. Users of futures markets quickly found that commodity contract prices in actively traded markets served as

---

EXHIBIT 1–2
Long Hedge

	Cash Market	*Futures Market*
October	Agrees to deliver flour in January based on expected cost of wheat of $3.30 per bushel	Buys March wheat futures contracts at $3.28 per bushel
January	Buys cash wheat at $3.35 per bushel	Sells March futures contracts at $3.32¾ per bushel
Result	Pays 5 cents higher price for wheat	Earns 4¾ cents per bushel on hedge

$3.35   cash cost for wheat
 .04¾ earned on hedge
$3.30¼ actual cost of wheat

good indicators for the value of a commodity in the future. As an example, the wheat contract price represents the best-informed judgment of numerous buyers and sellers as to its relative supply and demand plus the carrying costs associated with the transaction. Wheat futures contract prices are used worldwide to establish prices on export transactions.

Speculative Trading

The term *speculation* is used in futures markets to represent trades initiated for profit purposes over short periods of time. Similar goals may trigger stock and bond transactions. However, these trades are normally classified as investments, since most public trades do not involve margins and are open for extended periods of time. In addition, a futures contract is not an asset, since it only represents a contractual obligation. Stocks are associated with ownership, and bonds are collateralized debts.

The process of short-selling is also simplified on a commodity exchange. The initial margin required to sell what one does not own is no greater than the initial margin associated with a buy or long position. Since these margins are usually between 2 and 10 percent of the contract value, the transaction is readily classified as speculative.

As we shall see in further discussions, the lines of distinction between hedging, speculation, and investment are quite blurred. Participation in futures markets may be motivated by several different considerations, including:

1. The desire to hedge the risk of a cash position with an opposite position in futures (hedging).
2. A perceived temporary discrepancy between cash and futures prices, or a set of futures prices that can be exploited with little risk.
3. The desire to profit from price movement in the underlying instrument using no leverage or large amounts of leverage over very short or long periods.
4. The desire to diversify a portfolio of securities providing a lower level of overall risk.
5. The desire to adjust the average maturity or duration of a position in fixed-income securities.

Traditionally, only the first item in the above list has been called hedging, and the rest must fit under the umbrella of speculation. We will abide by the use of these terms because of their wide acceptance in the futures industry.

In an important case involving the Chicago Board of Trade before the U.S. Supreme Court in 1905, Chief Justice Oliver Wendell Holmes held that "people will endeavor to forecast the future and to make agreements according to their prophecy. Speculation of this kind by competent men is the self-adjustment of society to the probable."[3] The similarities between speculation and investment are much more important than the differences.

Since at any moment an equal number of long and short hedgers are often not present, futures speculators provide a vital economic function. Professionals who seek to minimize risks through hedging in futures have a need to transfer that risk to others who are financially capable of bearing that risk with the hope of profiting in the process. Speculators in futures possess capital that they hope to increase by using price forecasting and analysis to serve as a basis for buying and selling futures contracts. The speculative demand for futures contracts is much greater in volume and frequency than the hedging demand. Speculators, therefore, provide the liquidity (the continuous presence of buyers and sellers) that helps to make futures markets efficient hedging mechanisms. See Exhibit 1–3 for a brief profile of a commodity speculator.

EXHIBIT 1–3
Profile of a Commodity Speculator

— Approximately 200,000 active speculators.
— 50% of speculators are over 50 years of age; 14.9% of speculators are less than 35 years old.
— 73% of speculators use a different broker for futures trading than for other investments.
— 36% of traders have been active in commodity markets for more than six years; 21% of all traders have traded for more than 10 years.
— The total investment portfolios of 19% of investors exceed $500,000; 61% exceed $100,000.
— The average annual household income of commodity traders is higher than the national average: 61% have incomes greater than $50,000, and 21% have annual incomes in excess of $100,000.

Source: CBOT 1983 Retail Profile Survey.

DEFINITION OF A FUTURES AND A FORWARD MARKET

Since forward markets also provide a means of hedging against unexpected price risk, futures must be unique to exist as distinct financial instruments. A detailed comparison is provided in Chap-

among commodity traders who embraced the contract. The primary hedgers using the Treasury bill contract were government security dealers who bore the risk of large inventories of Treasury bills. In early 1983, the Treasury bill contract was the second most actively traded commodity contract on the floor of the Mercantile Exchange.

In August of 1977, the Chicago Board of Trade introduced the U.S. Treasury bond contract. The Treasury bond market was dominated by government dealers much like the Treasury bill market. Dealers found the futures market attractive as a hedging vehicle. The bond contract also presented new opportunities for arbitraging cash bond positions. During 1979 and 1980, trading volume expanded rapidly (Exhibit 1–5) as interest rate volatility became even greater with the post October 1979 noninterventionest policy of the Federal Reserve in credit markets.

The next major landmark for financial futures occurred in the spring of 1982. The Kansas City Board of Trade introduced a stock index futures contract based on the value of the Value Line Stock Index. This offering was quickly followed by the introduction of the S&P 500 Index futures contract on the Chicago Mercantile Exchange and the New York Stock Exchange Composite Index traded on the New York Futures Exchange. All of these contracts provided for cash deliveries. The cash value was a multiple of the respective index.

The introduction of these futures contracts was rapidly followed by a major bull market in equities. Stock prices rose by 60 percent between August 1982 and April 1983. The stock index contracts became an immediate success. During the last half of 1982, over 2 million S&P 500 Index contracts and 1 million New York Futures Exchange contracts were traded. Their combined total exceeded the daily trading volume of such established financial futures contracts as the Swiss Franc, copper, and GNMA CDRs. Their trading volume made a meaningful contribution toward the continued growth of futures trading in the United States. During 1984, a total of 149,372,225 contracts were traded on all regulated commodity exchanges. This may be compared to 139,924,940 in 1983 and 112,400,879 in 1982. The five most active traded contracts in 1984 were:

1. Treasury bonds   29.96 million
2. S&P 500   12.36 million
3. Soybeans   11.36 million
4. Gold (100 ounces)   9.11 million
5. Corn   9.10 million

SUMMARY

The development of the centralized trading exchanges in the 1800s was the result of a need by farmers and merchants to facilitate commercial exchange. The exchanges soon developed into a means of forward contracting to reduce the risk of price and delivery uncertainty. Over time the exchanges developed into an arena where buyers and sellers could minimize their price rise by taking opposite positions in the futures market with the exchanges acting as a third party in every trade. Since cash and futures prices rise and fall together in response to similar sets of supply and demand conditions, sellers could simply close out their futures positions and sell their cash products or securities in the spot market. Any gain or loss in the spot market could be offset by a gain or loss in the futures market. Through self and government regulation, the futures exchanges gained the traders confidence necessary for a free and open market.

The evolution of financial and currency contracts is similar to other established commodity contracts. The cost of money is as important to the financial industry as the cost of wheat is to the food industry. The development and growth of financial and currency futures markets in the 1970s was the result of a need by financial managers and investors for a means of reducing the risk of price uncertainty. The wide range of actively traded financial futures contracts attest to their success. As subsequent chapters will show, their application and strategies provide a necessary tool in the management of financial resources.

APPENDIX

Overview of Actively Traded
Financial and Currency Contracts

U.S. Treasury Bond Contract

This contract began trading during September 1977. It has become the most successful interest rate futures contract on any exchange when measured by daily trading volume and open interest. The U.S. Treasury bond contract is used to hedge exposures related to government auctions, hedge the value of Treasury and corporate bond portfolios, and execute numerous arbitrage strategies.

A holder of a contract must be willing to take or make delivery of a $100,000, 8 percent coupon Treasury bond, whose maturity date is at least 15 years beyond the expiration date of the futures contract against which delivery is made. If it has a call feature, the call date must be 15 years from expiration on the delivery date. Other coupons may be substituted on a yield maintenance basis.

GNMA Collateral Depository Receipt Contract[7]

This contract began trading in October 1975. It is used to hedge mortgage assets and mortgage commitments. The contract requires the holder to make or take delivery of an 8 percent GNMA security whose original face value was $100,000, plus or minus 2½ percent. Other GNMA coupons are also eligible for delivery on a price maintenance basis. Equivalent balances are computed by using constants provided by the CBOT. All values are calculated on the assumption that the remaining life of a mortgage-backed security is 12 years, regardless of its issue date or experience factor.

These contract conditions make the GNMA CDR futures contract more difficult to understand than bonds, since the subtleties of premium bond pricing, fast paying pools, and FHA rate changes can have a significant impact on the implied value of a GNMA contract. These variables will be discussed in later chapters.

10-Year Treasury Note Contract[8]

With increasing price volatility, both investors and issuers are desirous of shortening investment maturities. This has the effect of reducing price exposure and generally increasing liquidity. As of June 1982, new corporate issues rated "investment grade," with maturities from 5 to 12 years, represented more than 50 percent of the 1982 corporate calendar. In 1978, corporate debt with intermediate maturities represented less than 25 percent of the new issue calendar. Simultaneously with these changes in the corporate debt markets, the Treasury stepped up its issues of intermediate-term marketable securities. The 10-year maturity is now a frequent issue in the quarterly refinancing package. By June 1982, the public held a supply of Treasury notes that exceeded $30 billion.

To enable professional traders and investors to hedge intermediate term debt with less reliance on basis trading, the CBOT posted the 10-year Treasury note futures contract on May 3, 1982. On its first day of trading, the daily volume was fabulous: it exceeded a record 30,000 contracts. Currently, it is averaging 8,000 round turns per day and is used primarily by arbitrageurs and professional hedgers.

90-Day Treasury Bill Contract

This $1 million face value contract is being used to hedge all types of money market exposures. The results of these hedge programs are satisfactory, where strong correlations exist between the instrument being hedged and a 90-day Treasury bill.

A thrift liability hedging application uses these contracts to hedge yield levels on 180-day money market certificates. Due to the poor correlations between the prime rate and 90-day Treasury bills, the use of the Treasury bill futures to hedge variable rate loans tied to prime have been less successful.

Currently, this contract enjoys significant participation among speculators since it is easily understood and very liquid.

90-Day Certificate-of-Deposit Contracts (CD)

Large negotiable CDs became popular in the 1960s when loan demand at money center banks exceeded their lending abilities. To compete with the government for surplus corporate cash, commercial banks issued "jumbo" CDs. Rapidly, this form of liability became a major source of funds for lending institutions. The yield on these obligations varied widely with international and domestic uncertainties. When a significant crisis occurs, money flows into treasury obligations, and the yield on CDs increases rapidly.

To improve the ability to hedge nongovernment money market risks, the IMM designed and posted a $1 million, 90-day Certificate-of-Deposit contract in July 1981. The contract has proven itself useful for hedging CDs, commercial paper, banker's acceptance, and variable rate loans tied to prime. Due to its limited liquidity, care must be used in executing orders.

Three-Month Eurodollar Time Deposit Contracts

To provide the buyer and seller of Eurodollars an accurate hedging vehicle, the IMM also designed and posted a $1 million Eurodollar contract. Currently this contract enjoys a large commercial following. It can be traded throughout the day and night since the contract is also posted on the London International Financial Futures Exchange and the new Singapore International Monetary Exchange. During 1984 the trading volume of Eurodollar contracts increased by 360% over 1983. The correlation between a 90-day CD and a 90-day Eurodollar futures contract is often strong.

Stock Index Contracts

In addition to these financial contracts, a new breed of commodity contracts called stock index contracts have recently begun to trade. In February of 1982, the Kansas City Board of Trade commenced trading the first stock futures contract based on the Value Line Index. The IMM and the New York Futures Exchange have the most actively traded contracts based on the S&P 500 and NYSE composite indexes. In July 1984 the CBOT began to trade the Major Market index futures contract. Its value is based on 20 stocks, 15 of which are also part of the Dow Jones Index. The similarities between all stock index contracts are more significant than their differences. Each contract permits the trader to buy or sell a market basket of stocks. The contents of the baskets differ with the composition of each index. Their price movement is affected by the weighting of specific stock within an index and the movement of the component stocks. Weights on the two most actively traded contracts are based on the market value of outstanding shares.

The cash value of the S&P 500 and NYSE Composite Index contracts at delivery are 500 times the value of the index. Prices are quoted on a comparable basis to that of the cash value of the index.

Equity futures contracts differ in volatility in accordance with the volatility differences of the indexes they represent. The S&P 500 has the largest weighting of highly capitalized stock. The Value Line Index is the broadest and thus would be expected to be the most volatile. A complex weighting scheme serves to reduce the level of its fluctuations in value. It most closely represents a change in value of lesser capitalized stocks.

Summary of Actively Traded Financial Futures Contracts

	U.S. Treasury Bond	GNMA Collateral Depository Receipt Contract	10-Year Note	90-Day U.S. Treasury Bills	90-Day Domestic Certificate of Deposit	90-Day Eurodollar Time Deposit	S&P 500 Stock Index	NYSE Composite Index (NYFE)
Size	$100,000	$100,000	$100,000	$1 million	$1 million	$1 million	$500 times value of index	$500 times value of index
Ticker symbol	US	GM	TY	TB	DC	ED	SP	YX
Minimum price fluctuations (points)	$1/32$	$1/32$	$1/32$	.01 (one basis point)	.01 (one basis point)	.01 (one basis point)	.05	.05
Dollar value of minimum fluctuations	$31.25	$31.25	$31.25	$25.00	$25.00	$25.00	$25.00	$25.00
Limit move (points)	2	2	2	.60	.60	.60	5.00—except during delivery month	—
Last day of trading	Business day prior to last 7 business days of delivery month			2d day following 1st day of delivery month	Day prior to last business day of month	2d London business day before 3d week	3d Friday of delivery month	Business day prior to last business day in delivery month
Original margin (speculative)	$3,000	$3,000	$3,000	$2,500	$2,500	$2,500	$6,000	$3,500
Maintenance margin	$2,000	$2,000	$2,000	$2,000	$2,000	$2,000	$3,000	$1,500
Averaged daily volume* (contracts)	80,000	3,000	7,000	7,000	3,000	12,000	60,000	15,000
Exchange	CBOT	CBOT	CBOT	IMM	IMM	IMM	IMM	N.Y. Futures Exchange

	Value Line Index	Major Market Index	Pound Sterling	Canadian Dollar	Deutsche Mark	Japanese Yen	Mexican Peso	Swiss Franc	French Franc
Size			$25,000	$100,000	$125,000	$12 million	$1 million	$125,000	$250,000
Ticker symbol	KV	CBT	BP	CD	DM	JY	MP	SF	FR
Minimum price fluctuations (points)	.05	⅛	$2.05	$10.00	1	1	1	1	5
Dollar value of minimum fluctuations	$25.00	$12.50	$2.50	$10.00	$12.50	$12.50	$10.00	$12.50	$2.50
Limit move (points)	—		500	75	100	100	150	150	500
Last day of trading	Last business day of delivery month	Third Friday of contract month	2 days before 3d Wednesday	1 day before 3d Wednesday	2 days before 3d Wednesday	2 days before 3d Wednesday	1 day before 3d Wednesday	2 days before 3d Wednesday	2 days before 3d Wednesday
Original margin	$6,500	$2,300	$1,500	$1,500	$1,500	$1,500	$4,000	$2,500	$1,500
Maintenance margin	$2,500	$500	$1,000	$1,000	$1,000	$1,000	$3,000	$2,000	$1,000
Average daily volume (contracts)	4,000	18,000	14,000	6,000	25,000	15,000	1,000	12,000	6,000
Exchange	Kansas City Board of Trade	Chicago Board of Trade	IMM	IMM	IMM	IMM	IMM	IMM	IMM

The S&P 500 contract has the largest daily volume and more than four times the open interest of the NYFE, Value Line, and Major Market contracts. All are highly liquid and viable markets.

Currency Futures

To help meet investor and corporate concerns related to foreign exchange uncertainties, currency futures were established at the IMM in 1971. The International Monetary Market division of the CME quotes currencies in terms of the U.S. dollar. All quotations are prices per unit of the foreign currency. Possible uses of futures markets for hedging, speculating and arbitraging are endless. Companies borrowing or investing abroad, manufacturers exporting or importing goods or raw materials, investors selling or purchasing foreign securities can all use currency futures contracts.

NOTES

[1] For further information on the history of commodity futures, see the *Commodity Trading Manual,* Chicago Board of Trade, 1982, and Proceedings of the History of Futures Seminar in *Review of Research in Futures Markets* 2, no. 2 (1983).

[2] Later chapters will provide examples of how long and short hedges can be used in financial markets to reduce risks associated with price changes.

[3] Oliver W. Holmes, 198. *U.S. Board of Trade vs. Christie Gram and Stock Co.,* 245, October Term 1904.

[4] Minimum customer margins are assigned by Future Commission Merchants who carry customer accounts. They can raise these minimums as volatility increases.

[5] Currency futures are generally discussed separate from financial futures. The growth in foreign currency futures trading indicates that the IMM has filled a need from those who have found the interbank market impractical. Hedging examples used for financial futures can also be applied to currency futures. For other examples, see Raul Chalupa, "Foreign Currency Futures: Reducing Foreign Exchange Risk," *Economic Perspectives,* Winter 1982, pp. 3–11.

[6] Stanford Research Institute, (1978) *Preliminary Findings on Hedging Demand for Domestic Interest Rates and Foreign Currencies,* 1978.

[7] A new GNMA II contract reflecting the price of current coupons began trading on the CBOT during 1984. This contract is discussed in greater detail in Chapter 3. As of April 1985, this contract has little liquidity.

[8] Chicago Board of Trade, *Introduction to Ten Year Treasury Futures,* April 1982.

SELECTED REFERENCES

Arak, Marcell, and Christopher McCurdy. "Interest Rate Futures." *Quarterly Review* of the Federal Reserve Bank of New York, Winter 1980, pp. 44–66.

Besant, Lloyd, and Thomas Schneeweis. "Financial Futures Markets." In *Handbook of Modern Finance,* ed. D. Logue. New York: Warren, Gorman, and Lamont, 1984.

Burns, Joseph M. *A Treatise on Markets, Spot, Futures and Options.* Washington, D.C. ATI Institute for Public Policy, 1979.

Fitzgerald, M. Desmond. *Financial Futures.* London: Euromoney, 1983.

Gay, Gerald, and Robert Kolb. *Interest Rate Futures: Concepts and Issues.* Richmond, Va.: Robert F. Dame, 1981.

Gray, Roger W., and David Rutledge. "The Economics of Commodity Futures Markets: A Survey." *Review of Marketing and Agricultural Economics* 39, no. 4 (1971), pp. 57–108.

Khoury, Sarkis. *Speculative Markets.* New York: Macmillan, 1984.

Kolb, Robert. *Interest Rate Futures: A Comprehensive Introduction.* Richmond, Va.: Robert F. Dame, 1982.

Loosigian, A. *Interest Rate Futures.* Homewood, Ill.: Dow Jones-Irwin, 1980.

Peck, Ann, ed. *Selected Writings on Futures Markets: Explorations in Financial Futures Markets.* Chicago Board of Trade, Forthcoming.

Powers, Mark, and David Vogel. *Inside the Financial Futures Markets.* New York: John Wiley & Sons, 1981.

Rebell, Arthur, and Gail Gordon with Kenneth B. Platnick. *Financial Futures and Investment Strategy.* Homewood, Ill.: Dow Jones-Irwin, 1984.

Rothstein, Nancy, ed. *The Handbook of Financial Futures.* New York: McGraw-Hill, 1984.

Sandor, Richard. "The Interest Rate Futures Markets: An Introduction." *Commodities* 5, no. 9 (September 1976), pp. 14–17.

Schwarz, E. W. *How to Use Interest Rate Futures Contracts.* Homewood, Ill.: Dow Jones-Irwin, 1979.

Telser, Lester G., and H. N. Higinbotham. "Organized Futures Markets: Costs and Benefits." *Journal of Political Economy* 85 (1977), pp. 969–1000.

CHAPTER 2

Financial Futures Exchanges and the Mechanics of Trading

Financial futures are traded on a regulated exchange. The exchange establishes rules which provide assurances of proper and consistent performance. Exchange members who are brokers, scalpers, day traders, and position traders all act to insure a liquid and efficient market system. At the heart of the exchange is the exchange clearinghouse. The clearinghouse is a third party to all transactions. The clearinghouse operations insures the integrity of the market place.

Due to the existence of the clearinghouse, buyers and sellers of contracts need not concern themselves about each other's identity or financial integrity. Instead, the trader of financial futures can concentrate on the daily operational aspects of trading. Types of traders and customer orders are described in this chapter to provide the background necessary to understand the daily trading operations of the markets. To insure the proper functioning of the exchange, both the exchanges themselves and governmental regulatory bodies (e.g., CFTC) monitor daily operations. Through their efforts, new contracts are formed and the proper functioning of old contracts insured. The information in this chapter offers the reader understanding of both the internal and external environment governing futures markets.

THE EXCHANGES

As of December 1984, there were six actively traded interest rate futures contracts in the United States. The Chicago Board of Trade (CBOT) has achieved dominance in trading U.S. Treasury bond, GNMA, and 10-year note contracts. The Chicago Mercantile Exchange, often referred to as the Merc or the International Monetary Market (IMM), has achieved supremacy in contracts reflecting shorter maturities. The 90-day Treasury bill, 90-day Certificate-of-Deposit, and 90-day Eurodollar contracts are representative of these maturities. The trading of stock indexes commenced in 1982. Currently, the S&P 500 Composite Index at the IMM, the New York Stock Exchange Composite Index traded on the New York Futures Exchange (NYFE) and the Market Index contract traded on the CBOT, are the most frequently traded futures contracts suitable for hedging. For purposes of this book, the term *financial instrument futures* refers to both fixed income and equity futures. Both debt and equity are sources of financing for economic enterprises and this fits the definition of financial instruments.

EXCHANGE MEMBERS

Futures contracts have a tradition of trading by open outcry whereby the members of an exchange buy and sell contracts to one another in a trading pit. To the casual observer, this process may appear chaotic and unorganized. Traders use elaborate physical gestures to attract attention to their bid and offering prices. Many trades are made simultaneously. In reality, the futures pit has very definite formal and informal rules of operation that make it function as an orderly and efficient market.

Each trader has his or her own set of signals and body language with which other traders are familiar. Even the pit location in which a trader stands may alert another member to the type of trading pattern an individual will follow. Many futures traders do not hold trading positions overnight. They open and close positions frequently within one market session. The price volatility and leverage in these markets is great. Therefore, there can be large risks in carrying a position overnight.

On a continuous basis, recorders employed by the exchange keep track of all pit trades, transmitting immediately the prices of consummated transactions to an overhead price quotation display. Trade confirmations are recorded on trading cards by both the buying and selling broker and matched daily by computer. Seats on a futures exchange are held by individuals. Brokerage or commodity firms are permitted to buy seats but must select a nominee to trade for them. The latter must meet all the membership qualifications of an exchange. Individual members are responsible for posting funds to cover trading losses with a clearing firm. A member may be guaranteed by his employer for such losses.

Members who trade on the floor of the Exchange can be classified into three major categories. The first category is the floor broker, who is sometimes called a commission broker. This person executes orders written by an account executive or a registered commodity representative located in distant branch offices. Floor brokers receive their instructions by telephone or teletype. Orders are then recorded and time stamped before they are executed. Floor brokers can be self-employed, or employees of a brokerage firm or commission merchants. A floor broker can talk directly to customers from the exchange floor. A broker normally limits this activity to a few clients since it reduces the executing efficiency for other customers. A floor broker may trade for his personal account. If the floor broker desires to take a position, he or she must exercise great care that all customer orders are filled at an equal or better price before executing a proprietary order.

The second type of member who trades in a commodity pit

is a scalper, who is often called a "local." This individual provides instant liquidity for customer orders by buying from or selling to floor brokers wishing to execute public orders. As soon as a scalper opens a new position, in a futures contract, he or she will attempt to close out the position at a favorable price. Scalpers are the most active pit traders and hold their positions for the shortest period of time. At the conclusion of the trading day, scalpers hope to be without an open position. This is referred to as being flat. The more scalpers that function in a trading pit, the greater is the contract liquidity. Contract liquidity means that large orders can be executed without significantly affecting the execution price. Some scalpers position only nearby contracts, while others specialize in trading spreads between two futures contracts.

Traders who trade for their personal accounts in response to technical and/or fundamental signals are position traders. They may also represent one side of an arbitrage account. Their positions are generally open for longer periods of time than those of the scalper. It is often more prudent for position traders to close out a position at the end of a trading session and reopen it again the following morning, than to take a price risk and post initial margins associated with overnight positions. In commodity trading, there is no tax advantage to holding a position for a specific time period. All profits and losses on regulated (exchange-traded) futures contracts are treated as 60 percent long term and 40 percent short term for tax purposes, regardless of the length of time the futures position is open.[1] The expenses of a pit trader represented by brokerage costs and exchange fees are minimal. Trading can usually occur for less than $2 a round turn for an exchange member.

An inexpensive way for a beginner to learn pit trading as a local is to purchase or lease a special exchange membership or permit. These are generally issued by an exchange when a new contract is posted. During 1982 and 1983, several opportunities existed in Chicago and New York enabling a person with $20,000 of expendable working capital to lease a seat or to become a permit holder for a monthly fee of approximately $200. Other floor traders did their apprenticeships as runners or clerks for an exchange while learning the intricacies of markets.

THE ROLE OF THE EXCHANGE CLEARINGHOUSE

The integrity of the American commodity industry is assured through the existence of a clearing corporation associated with every exchange. The slogan of the Chicago Board of Trade Clearing

Corporation, "A Party to Every Trade," describes the function of these institutions. A clearinghouse is party to every trade since neither the buyer nor seller of a contract knows the identity of the opposite party to a transaction. This is unnecessary since the clearinghouse guarantees the integrity of each transaction, eliminating the need for credit checks. Clearinghouse assets are available to back a member default.[2] During the first quarter of 1985 a clearing member of the COMEX failed. The customers of Volume Investors, Inc. were made whole by the clearing system. This was the first failure of a clearing member since 1925.

To assure continued success, membership in a clearing corporation is limited to organizations and individuals who meet financial and professional criteria established by a board of directors. In addition to determining the clearing margin requirements that pertain to all members, the corporation also adjusts the monetary value of open positions to reflect settlement prices. Daily variation or maintenance margin calls are made to clearing members whose balances reflect a debit. If a member fails to meet a margin call by 9:15 A.M., all open positions of the firm are assigned to other clearing members in a predetermined manner. If the open positions on the books of a clearinghouse member reflect a net gain, the credit balance is available for withdrawal that morning.

If a seller of a contract chooses to settle contractual obligations by making delivery, the clearing corporation selects the clearing member who will receive the delivery. The selling member is then notified of the name of the buying member. The final invoicing and payment procedures are conducted between the buyer and seller under the rules of the clearing corporation.

TYPES OF ORDERS FREQUENTLY USED

Market Order. The most frequently used order is a market order. This instructs a floor broker to promptly execute an order at the most favorable price available. The broker is prohibited from using any discretion in executing this transaction.

Limit Order. A buy limit order prohibits the floor broker from paying more in the execution of a buy order than the limit set by the customer. If it is a sell limit order, the broker cannot sell for an amount less than that stipulated on the ticket. A limit order may be used to establish a new position or to liquidate an old one. If the price is touched, but the order cannot be executed, it does not become a market order. This can happen often in commodity trading, because price moves are rapid, and numerous floor brokers may have open orders to fill at an identical level.

If there is only one seller of 10 contracts at a price of 97–00, and there are four buyers wishing to fill 10 contracts at 97–00, it is possible that only one order will be filled. If the following sale takes place at 97–01, the buy limit orders that were unfilled at 97–00 may never get filled. This is a significant difference from the stock market, where all orders are channeled to one specialist and recorded in a time-received sequence that assures a buyer that the oldest buy order at a price of 97–00 is the first one filled. Under commodity trading rules, the investor cannot be assured that an order has been filled just because a price is displayed on a tape or on an inquiry station.

Stop Orders. Stop orders are executed differently than limit orders. A buy stop order is usually placed above the current market price and will become a market order if the price is touched.

Its use is illustrated by a client who determines that a technical buy signal exists for the March 1983 bond contract at 78–16, although currently it is trading at 78–00. A buy stop order is entered at 78–16. The broker is now directed to buy one March 1983 bond contract if the price is touched at any time that day. This order can be executed at, below, or above 78–16.

Straight Cancel Order. This will cancel an order in the pit. If a client forgets to cancel or replace an order before entering a new one, both the old and the new order could get executed.

Open Orders—Good Till Cancelled. Order placed by a customer that will continue to be good until the order is executed or is cancelled by the customer. Open orders can exist until a contract expires. The burden is on the initiator of the order to keep track of open limit orders that are placed.

Spreads. The simultaneous purchase and sale of one commodity of different option months. Intermarket, or intercommodity, spreads are also used.

There are other ways of entering orders into the system, but those reviewed should satisfy the needs of most hedgers and speculators. Beginning speculators will find choosing a trend sufficiently challenging without compounding the chore by selecting specific execution prices. Market, limit, and stop orders make up the largest percentage of transactions.

THE ORDER–PROCESSING CYCLE

Once a futures order is entered by a customer, the responsibility of the broker is to get the instruction to the trading floor of the appropriate exchange. Transmitting through either automated equipment, phones, or clerks in back offices, the branch sends commodity orders to the appropriate order desk. Large customers may be allowed to call directly to an order desk to ensure expeditious executions. Arbitrageurs commonly use this practice. When an order is received on the floor of an exchange, it is recorded and time stamped. A copy of the order is rushed into the pit and given to a floor broker for execution. On some exchange floors, orders are flashed by hand signals. This practice is risky and usually conducted only by individuals trading for their own accounts.

A market order is filled immediately. Other orders are held by the pit broker for the appropriate execution. Until an order is cancelled, the broker assumes responsibility for its proper execution. When the order has a "price limit," the phone clerk or floor broker files it in his or her deck. Limit orders are filed by price, with the transaction being completed as the market moves within the parameters designated by the customer. If a broker holds more than one order at the same price, the orders must be executed in the sequence received. Because of varying degrees of efficiency on the part of brokerage firms, orders are not necessarily received by floor brokers in the same time sequence that they are entered by customers. Thus, the sequence in which orders are filled on the floor may not always reflect the pattern in which they were received from customers.

HOW TO BEGIN TRADING

To bridge the gap between a classroom environment and the trader's circle, some simulations of actual trades will now be presented. These examples will also include a description of administrative events that accompany these trades. Practical applications have been selected that demonstrate the use of currently active interest rate contracts. A cash retail trade of a Treasury bond has also been included, since some readers may never have bought a bond.

A Cash Treasury Bond Transaction

On August 10, 1983, I. M. Sure asks a broker to select an appropriate bond investment that will produce income, safety, and retain liquidity for at least 10 years. The broker is aware of an upcoming government auction that will include a long-term bond and suggests that Sure purchase 10 bonds at a noncompetitive bid. This will minimize the acquisition cost and guarantee Sure of a successful bid. The coupon of the bond will not be known until the auction takes place, since coupons of new issues reflect current market yields.

Step 1.   I. M. Sure agrees to bid for 10 bonds in the upcoming government auction. These will represent a face value of $10,000.

Step 2.   A margin deposit of 10 percent is requested by the broker.

Step 3.   Sure is notified by the broker on August 18 that the auction took place, and he bought 10 bonds with a coupon of 12 percent and a maturity date of 2013 for $10,000. The remaining payment of $9,000 is now requested for a settlement date of August 25. Frequently, this could be a next-day settlement.

Step 4.   I. M. Sure receives a trade confirmation and a request for the remaining funds.

Step 5.   On August 25, Sure pays the remaining $9,000, plus any accrued interest.

    The investor now owns 10 U.S. Treasury bonds that will pay 12 percent interest, annually. Interest payments of 6 percent are made semiannually, and the government will repay the principal on August 15, 2013.

    On Monday, September 7, 1983, I. M. Sure is confronted with an unexpected expense and decides to sell the bonds. The broker informs Sure that the current yield for the 12 percent bond is 12.50 percent. The bonds are sold for a price of 96.00, which reflects the higher yield levels now in existence. The actual price of this bond at a yield to maturity of 12.50 percent was obtained from a bond yield book.[3]

Step 6.   On September 12, 1983, Sure receives $9,600 for each bond sold plus any earned prorated interest not yet paid out.

    There are no commissions charged for a fixed-income transaction. The brokerage firm makes its profit from this transaction by reselling those bonds to another party at a lower yield. The difference between the purchase and sales price of a secondary market transaction is called a bid-asked spread.

Trading Interest Rate Futures

Commodity contracts for interest rate futures behave in the same manner as bond and Treasury bills: when yields fall, prices rise. Before N. O. Cash, our trader, can execute a hedging strategy using interest rate futures, Cash must open a commodity account. This requires different customer agreements than those demanded for an equity account in which both stocks and bonds are traded. In

---

EXHIBIT 2-1

INDEX FUTURES GROUP, INC.
☐ BOARD OF TRADE BUILDING, 141 WEST JACKSON BLVD., CHICAGO, ILLINOIS 60604   (312) 663-0310
☐ 30 BROAD STREET, NEW YORK, N.Y. 10005   (212) 747-0290

COMBINED COMMODITY STATEMENT

DATE

MAR 14, 1985

ACCOUNT NUMBER

12345 67890

MICHAEL SMITH

Retain for tax records.

DATE	BOUGHT	SOLD	COMMODITY OPTION DESCRIPTION	TRADE PRICE	AMOUNT DEBIT	CREDIT
SEGREGATED ACCOUNT						
3/12/85 ACCOUNT BALANCE - SEGREGATED FUNDS					291.25	
			CONFIRMATION		,	
WE HAVE MADE THIS DAY THE FOLLOWING TRADES FOR YOUR ACCOUNT AND RISK.						
	1		JUN 85 S&P INDEX	183.05		
	1		JUN 85 S&P INDEX	183.15		
		1	JUN 85 S&P INDEX	183.15		
		1	JUN 85 S&P INDEX	183.25		
	2*	2*				
			PURCHASE & SALE			
3/14/85	1		JUN 85 S&P INDEX	183.05		
3/14/85	1		JUN 85 S&P INDEX	183.15		
3/14/85		1	JUN 85 S&P INDEX	183.15		
3/14/85		1	JUN 85 S&P INDEX	183.25		
	2*	2*	P&S			100.00
			COMM		2.50	
			TOTAL COMMISSIONS & FEES		2.50*	
			NET PROFIT OR LOSS FROM TRADES			97.50*
CURRENT ACCOUNT BALANCE SEGREGATED FUNDS					193.75*	

Grains in 000's   Confirmation, Purchase & Sale Statements, Account Statements, and Open Positions shall be deemed accurate unless you object. Customer should immediately notify Index Futures Group, Inc. at the office where your account is maintained (141 West Jackson Blvd., Chicago, Illinois 60604 (312) 663-0310 or
30 Broad Street, New York, N.Y. 10005 (212) 747-0290) by telephone. If immediate objection is not made, then this statement shall be deemed accurate.

addition, the broker may insist that the initial commodity transaction be accompanied by a minimum dollar deposit. Once an account has been opened, commodity business can be conducted. Regardless of which contract is traded, it is essential that the customer become acquainted with the initial margin requirements of the member firm.[4]

The initial margin is considered a security deposit which guarantees the performance of a customer when a margin call is made. Margins and commissions may differ slightly among brokerage houses. They are also different for hedgers and speculators. Commissions and exchange fees charged are normally similar; therefore, confidence in one's broker should determine the firm with which your business will be conducted. Ideally, no more than 50 percent of the initial margin should be absorbed by the opening speculative trade. This will give N. O. Cash the ability to withstand temporary market reversals without being exposed to additional margin calls.

Once a trade is executed, a verbal confirmation is received, which will be followed by a trade confirmation. (See Exhibit 2–1.) Monthly statements with year-to-date profit and loss statements are mailed. A purchase and sale statement, reflecting the profits and losses of a specific transaction, is also sent if an open position is offset. This P&S statement will show the remaining open equity positions in the account and the commissions charged. (See Exhibit 2–1.)

Although margin calls have been mentioned repeatedly, their trigger mechanisms have not been clarified. When the available balance in a commodity account is reduced below the maintenance margin level, an account representative contacts the customer by phone and asks that the available balance in the account be restored to the required initial margin level. This verbal notification is followed by a mailed margin notice (see Exhibit 2–2). Computa-

---

EXHIBIT 2–2

88138   47606   8/16/83
              SALESMAN   DATE

CONFIRMATION OF MARGIN REQUEST

AS OF THIS DATE YOUR COMMODITY ACCOUNT
WAS UNDERMARGINED BY A TOTAL OF
REQUESTED $8,625.00

FIRST S & L OF BIG SPRING
600 MAIN ST   BOX 325
BIG SPRINGS   TX   79720

PLEASE DEPOSIT THIS AMOUNT **IMMEDIATELY**
IN ORDER TO MAINTAIN YOUR ACCOUNT.
FAILURE TO MAINTAIN ADEQUATE MARGINS
MAY RESULT IN THE LIQUIDATION OF YOUR
POSITIONS WITHOUT FURTHER NOTICE. IF
THE TOTAL FUNDS AS REQUIRED ABOVE HAVE
BEEN SENT PLEASE DISREGARD THIS NOTICE.
YOUR PROMPT ATTENTION IS APPRECIATED.

tions are based on the previous night's closing prices. A margin call must be made even if prices have readjusted in favor of the customer when the contract begins trading the next morning. The customer is obliged to meet a margin call by mail or federal wire transfer. If a customer fails to respond within a reasonable amount of time, a position can be sold out, and any loss sustained is deducted from the remaining balance. If a contract has increased in value, the investor can withdraw the surplus balance above the initial margin amount by simply requesting a check or using the federal funds wire transfer system.

A Retail Long Trade. On January 7, 1984, N. O. Cash, a speculator, decides to take a position in the GNMA market, because Cash believes that mortgage rates will improve shortly (i.e., yields will go down). If this happens, prices of GNMA futures contracts will go up. Therefore, Cash buys one March 1984 GNMA CDR contract at 70–16. Yields improve, and the contract is offset on January 14, 1984, at 71–20. The administrative steps illustrating this transaction are:

Step 1.   The available balance in the commodity account is increased to $5,000 on January 5, 1984. This is the minimum balance required by the broker to open a commodity account. It may be greater than the initial margin required by an exchange to trade one contract.

Step 2.   On January 7, 1984, N. O. Cash buys one March 1984 GNMA at 70–16. This requires an initial margin of $3,000 and reduces the available balance, or open trade equity, to $2,000.

Step 3.   On January 12, 1984, the March 1984 GNMA contract closes at 70–24, and the account is credited with 8 × $31.25, or $250.00. The $250 could be withdrawn by the client. On the morning of January 13, the available balance in this account is ($2,250).

Step 4.   On January 14, the contract is sold at 71–20. The trading profit is credited to the account. The open GNMA positon is offset. All funds, less commission and exchange fees, can be withdrawn the next day.

A Limit Market Move. Encouraged by this profitable GNMA trade, N. O. Cash now decides to tackle the bond contract. Cash carefully studies available economic data, listens to business associates, reads *The Wall Street Journal,* and reviews several charts. Cash comes to the conclusion that long-term Treasury bonds are likely to move to higher yields and lower prices. On January 17,

Cash redeposits a minimum of $5,000 in the account. On January 18 he sells a March 1984 contract for 77–10. At this time, the bond speculative initial margin is $3,000 and the maintenance margin $2,000.

At the close of trading, at 3 P.M., EST January 19, Cash is pleased since bonds closed at 77–02. At 4:15 P.M., EST, the Federal Reserve announced a ½ percent reduction in the discount rate. The next morning, the market opens at 79–02, limit up, and remains there for the day. The government cash markets continue to trade on the upside during the afternoon of January 20. March bond futures open at 79–18 on January 21. Cash closes out the short position at 11 A.M. at 79–18.

Step 1.   On January 17, a $5,000 deposit is made into the commodity account, and a March 1984 Treasury bond is sold at 77–10 on January 18.

Step 2.   On the morning of January 20, the account had a credit balance of $5,250 and an available balance of $2,250.

Step 3.   On the morning of January 21, the credit balance was reduced by the 2-point limit move to $3,250. No margin call was made since the maintenance level for one bond contract was $2,000.

Step 4.   On January 22, the contract was bought back at 79–18. Cash experienced a loss of $2,250 on this trade. The available balance was now $2,750.

Step 5.   On January 25, Cash closed his account and received a check for $2,750, less commission and exchange fees.

Investing a Future Cash Flow

On June 25, 1984, C. Fast, a portfolio manager for a pension fund, is informed that $1 million will be available for investment on July 1 for a six-month period. Two sample alternatives are examined. The first is to invest the funds in a six-month Treasury bill to be purchased at a Monday acution. It is estimated that the discount yield for a six-month bill will be 12.50 percent. This is equivalent to a price of 87.50 (100.00 − 12.50) for a Teasury bill futures contract. Another alternative is to deposit these funds in a money market account and buy a 90-day September 1984 Treasury bill contract. The latter is trading at 87.60 and current money market rates are 13.50 percent. Since market opinion remains bearish, Fast believes that the 100 basis-point premium is sufficient reason to select the money market–Treasury bill futures approach. For purpose of this illustration, it is assumed that money market rates remain stable throughout the first 90 days.

On June 29, the hedge initial margin for a 90-day Treasury bill contract is $2,000, and the maintenance margin is $2,000. Initial margins for hedgers are generally lower than those for speculators. For hedgers the maintenance margin levels are often the same as the initial margins.

Step 1.   On June 30, deposit $5,000 into commodity account.

Step 2.   On July 1, deposit $1 million in a money market account. Simultaneously purchase one 90-day September Treasury bill contract at 87.60. On the first day in September on which a 13-week Treasury bill is issued and a one-year Treasury bill has a remaining life of thirteen weeks to maturity, liquidate money market account to pay for Treasury bill delivery in two days.

Step 3.   On the 2d day of the delivery cycle in September, the September 90-day Treasury bill contract closes at 87.25. The commodity account is debited for a loss of $875. The account is notified that the open position will be closed out by a delivery of a $1 million Treasury bill with a remaining life of 90 or 91 days. The cash Treasury bill will also be invoiced at 87.25, or 12.75 percent.

Step 4.   Delivery and payment of the 90-day Treasury bill takes place on the next day. A $1 million 90-day Treasury bill at a discount yield of 12.75 percent is invoiced at $968,125. A comparison of the simulated results obtained from each of the strategies is illustrated.

Step 5.   The 90-day Treasury bill will mature in December.

Alternative A. Buy six-month Treasury bill at 12.50. The invoice price for the transaction would be $937,500. Fast would have earned $62,500 over a six-month period.

Alternative B. Invest in a money market fund for 90 days at 13.50 percent and purchase a 90-day Treasury bill contract for the last 90 days at 12.40 percent.

A deposit of $1 million for 90 days earning 13.50 percent, compounded daily, will earn $33,500. The 90-day $1 million Treasury bill invoiced at 12.40 percent has an invoice price of $968,125. Upon maturity, Fast will have earned $31,875 from the 90-day Treasury bill investment. The combined profit from this strategy is $65,375. The futures trading loss of $875 must be subtracted from $65,375 before comparing the final results of these two trading strategies. Alternative B has an income advantage of $2,000, less a commission for the commodity transaction. The latter should be between $20.00 and $100.00, depending on the customer classification of C. Fast.

Before a transaction is made on behalf of a regulated institution, it is necessary for management to become acquainted with current rules and regulations governing such trades. In the United States, regulated institutions are national and state banks, thrift institutions, insurance companies, federal pension funds, and credit unions. Accountants and auditors should also be notified of impending trades to assure that the proper accounting treatment has been established to record a gain or loss from a futures trade.

LEGISLATIVE AND REGULATORY ENVIRONMENT

Federal regulation of financial futures follows a long tradition of federal oversight of commodity trading. Federal regulation of futures trading was initiated in 1922 with the Grain Futures Act. In 1936, the Commodity Exchange (CE) Act replaced the Grain Futures Act. The CE Act itself was amended in following years as newly discovered needs arose. The increasing use of commodity markets and the problems surfacing in the 1972 Russian grain purchase led Congress in 1974 to drastically amend the 1936 Commodity Trading Act.[5] The 1974 amendments authorized the establishment of the Commodity Futures Trading Commission (CFTC). The commission is responsible to Congress for the functions previously assigned to the Department of Agriculture in the CE Acts. Financial futures contracts traded in the United States on a commodity exchange are regulated by Exchange rules which have been approved by the CFTC. The rules and regulations clearly define the size of a contract, what is eligible for delivery, where delivery must take place, how a contract is priced and invoiced, and when trading begins and stops. After a contract is posted and trading has commenced, the rules and regulations cannot be changed without CFTC approval. All contracts traded can be closed out or offset at anytime before their expiration date. Current rules are always available at the Office of the Secretary of each exchange.

Following the 1974 amendments, the CFTC had regulatory authority over almost anything which is or which can be the subject of a futures contract. As new product areas (e.g., options on futures) developed, however, a further distinction was necessary between the SEC and CFTC on areas of regulation. In adopting the Economic Recovery Act of 1981, Congress took special note of the rapid growth of the commodity industry. The act clarifies the jurisdictional prerogatives of the Commodities Futures Trading Commission and the Securities Exchange Commission. It provided four more years of funding for the CFTC and established an industry self-regulatory agency, the National Futures Association (NFA). This agency would assume the responsibility of licensing and regulating individuals and corporations that participate in soliciting public orders. Under an 1982 act, the CFTC regulates (1) all futures contracts, (2) broadly based stock and bond index futures, (3) options on futures contracts (including financial futures), and (4) options on foreign currencies trading on commodity markets. The SEC regulates (1) all options directly on securities (stock as well as bonds, bills and stock indexes) and (2) options on foreign currencies trading on stock exchanges.

The principal concerns of the CFTC are the safeguarding of funds, the control of monopoly, and the prevention of price manipulation.[6] A cursory view of the structure of the CFTC will permit a better view of its regulatory directions and remedies. CFTC's organizational chart is given in Exhibit 2–3. The principal regulatory divisions of the CFTC include the Division of Enforcement, Division of Economics and Education, Division of Trading and Marketing, and the Office of the General Counsel.

The commission's division of Enforcement takes responsibility for investigation and prosecution of the Commodity and Exchange Act and commission regulations. The division is divided into two sections: (1) customer protection and (2) market integrity. The customer protection section investigates and litigates alleged violations of the sale of regulated instruments to the investing public. The market integrity section investigates possible violations directly in the exchanges.

The Division of Economics and Education is responsible for the daily analysis of market conditions to ensure against price manipulation and/or exchange disruptions. The division is also in charge of reviewing new futures contracts. In addition to the CFTC's own surveillance programs, the exchanges themselves are responsible for self-monitoring. The commission's Division of Trading and Marketing determines how the exchanges are meeting their market surveillance and enforcement responsibilities. The division also reviews exchange applications for contract market designation. The unit also considers exchange requests to implement new or revised rules; drafts regulations governing the operations of registration, surveillance, and auditing entities regulated by the commission.

EXHIBIT 2–3
Commodity Futures Trading Commission Organizational Chart

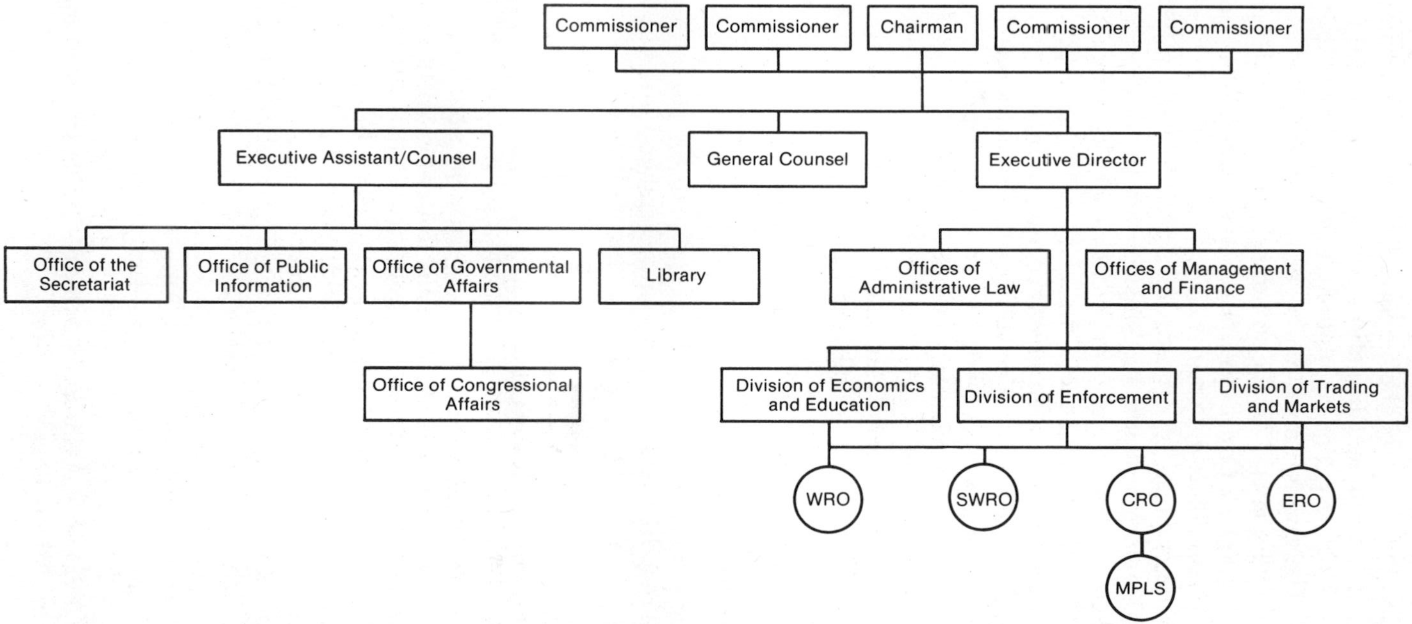

Source: Commodity Futures Trading Commission Annual Report, 1982.

Lastly, the Office of the General Counsel is the commission's chief legal advisor and litigation counsel. The counsel's office is a reviewer of all major regulatory legislative and administrative matters. The counsel also acts as advocate with the cooperation of the solicitor general for the commission before the U.S. Supreme Court and the U.S. Court of Appeals, and defends the commission against actions brought against it.

This description of division directives covers only a few of the CFTC major regulatory responsibilities. In addition to monitoring and correcting past grievances, the CFTC is a regulator of last resort.[7] The CFTC will avoid direct government intervention as long as the exchanges themselves are attempting to deal effectively with the problem. Only when self-regulatory activities are incapable of solving the problem will the agency suspend trading, impose margins, or force liquidation. In response to the increased sophistication of users and sales personnel, the Federal Home Loan Bank and state insurance regulators have also eased their restrictions. The following summary of current-rules and regulations is illustrative of this attitude.

Federal Reserve Board

The Federal Reserve Board (FRB) is contributing to the breakdown of traditional barriers between commercial and investment banks. On July 1, 1982, the FRB approved the application of J. P. Morgan & Co., Inc. (J. P. Morgan), to establish an operating subsidiary, Morgan Futures Corporation (Morgan Futures), which will act as a futures commission merchant (FCM). J. P. Morgan sought permission for the subsidiary to deal in futures markets involving bullion, foreign exchange, U.S. government securities, domestic money market instruments, and Eurodollar Certificates of Deposit.

In reviewing J. P. Morgan's application, the FRB had to determine that a Morgan Futures' operation as a futures commission merchant (FCM) was a proper addition to banking. This meant considering whether its "performance as an affiliate of a holding company can reasonably be expected to produce benefits to the public, such as greater convenience, rising competition, or gains in efficiency, that outweighs possible adverse effects, such as undue concentration of resources, lowering or unfair competition, conflicts of interest, or unsound banking practices." 12 U.S.C. 1843 (c) (8).

The FRB found the FCM activity incidental to banking and gave approval to the application.

Comptroller of the Currency

The comptroller of the currency is likewise relaxing prohibitions against national banks acting in the futures field. On April 7, 1982, the comptroller granted preliminary approval to the North Carolina National Bank to operate an FCM subsidiary. That approval was conditioned upon the bank: (1) developing internal standards concerning the type of contracts dealt with, positions taken, and the type of customer solicited and serviced; (2) developing supervisorial standards on churning, best execution, customer fund segregation, employee trading, employee compensation, transactions for portfolios of affiliated organizations, customer credit, and internal audit and reporting system; and (3) obtaining CFTC registration for all bank employees accepting or soliciting customer orders for futures transactions. A detailed description of these requirements are in Banking Circular, no. 79, 2d revision (March 9, 1980).

Federal Home Loan Bank Board

On July 2, 1981, the FHLBB greatly expanded the range of savings and loan activities in securities and futures. This action was in response to increased pressure by the savings and loan industry.

Savings institutions have recently been vigorous lobbyists because of the devastating effect of long-term fixed loan assets and short-term rate sensitive liabilities.

Specifically, the FHLBB fashioned amendments permitting expanded trading of financial futures as follows:

1. Permitted hedging in all interest rate futures in which an S&L association can legally invest and eliminated the requirement that each futures position be directly matched to cash transactions.
2. Position limits should be set by the savings and loan board of directors and not the FHLBB.
3. Adopted a system of hedge or deferral accounting rather than requiring savings and loans to utilize the mark-to-market system required by some other financial institutions.
4. Authorized the use of long futures in connection with forward commitments to sell mortgages not yet originated.
5. Extended the FHLBB's regulations regarding interest rate futures to cover state-chartered institutions as well as federal associations.

The details of the changes are in 12 CFR, parts 545 and 563.

New York State Insurance Department

The New York State legislature amended the state's insurance law in July 1983 to permit New York insurers to employ "noninterest bearing and nonincome paying investments." This would enable insurance companies licensed to conduct business in New York State to incorporate the use of futures markets in their hedging and investment strategies. Selected instruments must be traded on regulated domestic exchanges. All transactions should be associated with a hedge strategy and will be limited in size to 2 percent of the total admitted assets of the insurer.

Pension funds and other trust arrangements managed by insurance companies are held in separate accounts. The new law also lifts existing prohibitions against futures trading in relationship to managing these assets. Insurance company pension managers can now begin to use futures and options contracts to increase portfolio performance and reduce market risks when interest yield levels begin to climb.

SUMMARY

In this chapter we described the primary differences between forward and futures markets. In contrast to forward markets, futures are traded on an open exchange. The exchange establishes rules which provide assurances of proper and consistent performance. The various exchange members, brokers, scalpers, and day traders all act to ensure a liquid and efficient market system. At the heart of the exchange is the exchange clearinghouse. The clearinghouse is a third party to all transactions. The clearinghouse operations ensure the integrity of the marketplace. Through its actions, the trader on one side need not be concerned about the identity of the other trader.

Due to the existence of the clearinghouse, most users of the futures markets need not concern themselves about exchange operations. Instead, the trader of financial futures can concentrate on the daily operational aspects of trading. These everyday aspects of trading (e.g., types of orders, types of traders) were described in order to give the reader the background necessary to understand the daily trading operations of the markets. To insure the proper functioning of the exchange, their surveillance organizations and governmental regulatory bodies (e.g., CFTC) monitor daily operations. Through both their efforts, new contracts are posted and the proper functioning of old contracts is assured. The information in this chapter offered the reader understanding of the internal and external environment that governs futures markets.

APPENDIX

How to Read Futures Quotations

Price is the key statistic generated by futures markets, although the volume of trade and the number of outstanding contracts (open interest) are also important. Prices are available from a variety of sources, including the daily newspapers. Many papers also report volume and open interest.

The policies of the wire services and of newspapers vary, so this publication will describe price tables in general terms from which the reader can select those that apply to any publication's system of reporting.

Column Designation. Across the top of most price listings will be some combination of these words or their abbreviations:

Open. The price or range of prices for the day's first trades, registered during the period designated as the opening of the market or the opening call. Many publications print only a single price for the market open or close regardless of whether there is a range with trades at several prices. For exchanges with split openings and closings, a commission house or exchange will be the accurate price source.

High. Highest price at which the commodity sold during the day.

Close. The price or range of prices at which the commodity sold during the brief period designated as the market close or on the closing call.

Settlement Price. Some tables report settlement price rather than closing price. In commodity markets, every trade is "marked to the market" each day—in other words, the gain or loss from that day's trading is computed and posted or charged to each trader's account. If a market closes on a range of prices, a settlement price is determined and used for the computation. The settlement price is a figure determined by formula from within the closing range, or it is the closing price if there is a single price. For some publications or markets, settlement price is used as a column heading; other tabulations use a small *s* to designate the settlement price.

Yield, Yield Close, Yield Settlement, Yield Change. Any of these or some combination of like words may appear for financial instruments. These columns translate the futures quotations into the annual return of the futures contract.

Season or Lifetime High-Low. The highest and lowest prices recorded for each contract maturity from the first day it was traded to the present.

Open Interest. The outstanding contracts are reported in different ways, and the custom of each publication must be studied to determine the data that applies. Some publications show the open interest for each maturity month of each contract; others show the open interest for all maturities combined plus the amount of increase or decrease from the last previous report; and some do not report this number. The number represents the quantity of open long positions at the Exchange clearinghouse for each contract.

Volume. Shortly after the market closes, exchanges report the number of contracts traded on that day. Some report an estimate as well as a final figure for the previous session.

Commodities/Exchanges/Prices. Most publications identify each commodity, the exchange on which it is traded, the size of the contract, and the way in which prices are quoted.

Following is a key to what the price numbers mean. Some tables do not include decimal points.

GNMAs, Treasury Notes, and Bonds. Percentage of par. Minimum change may be $\frac{1}{32}$ of 1 percent, equal to $31.25 per contract, or $\frac{1}{64}$ of 1 percent, equal to $15.625 per contract.

$$96 - 00 = .96 \times \$100,000 = \$96,000$$
$$96 - 09 = .96\frac{9}{32} \times \$100,000 = \$96,281.25$$

Treasury Bills, Commercial Paper. The quote is an index rate computed by subtracting the annual discount rate from 100. Minimum change is .01 percent or $100 per contract per year (360 days); $25 for 90 days. As as example: 94.03 = 5.97 percent yield (100 − 94.03) times $1 million, divided by 4 = $14,925. $1 million minus $14,925 = $985,075. This is the 90-day Treasury bill price at an annual yield of 5.97%. An index rate of 94.00 = 6 percent yield or $15,000 per quarter.

Contract Maturities. In virtually all commodity price tables, the left hand vertical column will be a series of months. These designate the maturities at which time deliveries are made or taken unless the contract has been offset by an opposite transaction. It is normal that commodities will be traded for at least a year into the future, and some commodities will have prices extended for more than two years.

Example of Treasury Bond Futures Quotations, August 30, 1984*

	Open	High	Low	Settle	Chg	Settle Yield	Yield Chg	Open Interest
Sept	65.10	65.20	65.06	65.19	+6	12.808	−.037	85,431
Dec	64.19	64.30	64.16	64.29	+6	12.945	−.038	73,430
Mar 85	64.01	64.12	63.31	64.12	+6	13.053	−.038	9,691
June	63.20	63.30	63.18	63.30	+6	13.143	−.039	6,264
Sept	63.08	63.18	63.05	63.18	+6	13.221	−.039	5,564
Dec	62.27	63.08	62.27	63.08	+6	13.286	−.040	7,032
Mar 86	62.21	62.31	62.21	62.31	+6	13.346	−.039	4,944
Jun	62.14	62.23	62.13	62.24	+6	13.392	−.040	4,540
Sept	—	—	—	62.18	+6	13.432	−.040	853
Dec	—	—	—	62.12	+6	13.472	−.041	84
Mar 87	—	—	—	62.07	+6	13.506		21

* Treasury bonds ($100,000 principal) points 32ds of 100 percent.

This example shows September 1984 as the nearby future. During September, that maturity will also be called the "spot" or nearby month. Trading takes place for 11 different maturities stretching to March of 1987—the most "distant" or "deferred" maturity.

These columns show a settlement price and a yield, in addition to the change in the settlement price and yield. The far right column shows the outstanding contracts (open interest) for each maturity as of the previous trading session.

There was no trade in the September, December 1986, or March 1987 maturities, but a settlement price was computed for accounting purposes. Since there were not actual transactions, some publications might key the figures with an *n* to show they have been computed and are "nominal."

NOTES

[1] The Economic Recovery Tax Act of 1981.

[2] *A Party to Every Trade,* Chicago Board of Trade, 1980.

[3] "High Coupon Bond Yields," Semiannual Coupon Publications, no. 354 (Boston: Financial Publishing Company).

[4] A clearing member may require customer initial margins in excess of the minimum amounts specified by an exchange.

[5] Howard Schneider and Fred M. Santo, "Regulation of Futures Trading," in Frank J. Fabozzi and Frank C. Zarb's *Handbook of Financial Markets: Securities, Options and Futures,* 2d ed., Homewood, Ill.: Dow Jones-Irwin 1986), presents a detailed discussion of regulation in futures trading. The CFTC Annual report also reviews present and anticipated regulatory procedures.

[6] For the interested reader, the *Journal of Futures Markets* Summer 1981 issue contains a series of articles on "Regulation of Futures Markets."

[7] While the principal concerns of regulatory action are the safeguarding of funds, the control of monopoly, and the prevention of price manipulation, all regulation involves a potential to redistribute wealth. Unfortunately, no standards exist on how an action will affect social welfare. Research results (e.g., Robert Verrecchia, "The Use of Mathematical Models in Financial Accounting," *JAR* Supplement, 1982, indicate that maximum disclosure may not maximize social or individual welfare.

SELECTED REFERENCES

Anderson, Ronald W. "The Industrial Organization of Futures Markets: A Survey." CSFM, no. 66 (July 1983).

Commodity Futures Trading Commission. 1982 Annual Report. *Commodity Trading Manual.* Chicago: Chicago Board of Trade, 1982.

Edwards, Frank. "The Clearing Association in Futures Markets: Grantor and Regulator." *Journal of Futures Markets*, Winter 1983, pp. 369–92.

Edwards, Franklin. "Futures Marketing Transition: The Uneasy Balance Between Government and Self-Regulation." CSFM, no. 46 (January 1983).

Houthaker, H. "The Regulation of Financial and Other Futures Markets." *Journal of Finance*, May 1982, 481–91.

Kilcollin, Thomas. "Different Systems in Financial Futures Markets." *Journal of Finance*, December 1982, pp. 1183–98.

Kyle, A. S. "A Theory of Market Manipulations." CSFM, no. 64 (July 1983).

"Regulation of Futures Markets." Proceedings of CSFM Conference. *Journal of Futures Markets*, Summer 1981.

Schneider, Howard, and Santo, Fred M. "Regulation of Futures Trading." In *Handbook of Financial Markets: Securities, Options and Futures*, 2d ed., ed. Frank J. Fabozzi and Frank C. Zarb. Homewood, Ill.: Dow Jones-Irwin, 1986.

Schwarz, Edward. *How to Use Interest Rate Futures*. Homewood, Ill.: Dow Jones-Irwin, 1979.

Telser, Lester G. "Why There Are Organized Futures Markets." *Journal of Law and Economics*, 24 (1981), pp. 1–22.

Futures on Fixed-Income Securities

The Chicago Board of Trade opened trading on the GNMA CDR contract in October of 1975. In January of 1976, the Chicago Mercantile Exchange began trading futures on 90-day Treasury bills. Since that time, other successful contracts have been introduced, and volume in futures on fixed-income securities has grown sharply to the point where the daily principal value of Treasury bill and bond futures traded exceeds the volume of trading in the dealer markets for cash securities. At major security dealers, fixed-income futures traders work side by side with cash market traders in order that hedging and arbitrage between the two markets can be implemented effectively. Many fixed-income traders use both cash and futures markets simultaneously to construct the position they desire in the cheapest and most effective manner. Fixed-income futures have become an integral part of financing and investment and have, in a sense, transformed the whole process of interest rate risk management.

In this chapter, we will learn about the features of actively traded futures contracts on fixed-income securities. A fixed-income security is defined as a debt contract that calls for repayment of principal or interest in fixed dollar amounts at specific points in time. We also provide an overview of the uses of fixed-income futures for increasing and reducing exposures to the risk of changing interest rates. The first section of the chapter covers futures on underlying instruments of less than a year in maturity when issued. These include Treasury bills, Certificates of Deposit, and Eurodollar futures. These short-term fixed-income futures are all traded at the Chicago Mercantile Exchange. Futures on longer term fixed-income securities—U.S. Treasury bonds, U.S. Treasury notes, and GNMA securities—are covered in the second section. The Chicago Board of Trade has been most successful in the development of these long-term fixed-income futures markets. Stock index futures are covered in Chapter 4.

FUTURES ON SHORT–TERM FIXED-INCOME SECURITIES

Treasury Bill Futures

The futures contract on Treasury bills was among the first financial instrument futures to be traded. The Treasury bill futures market opened on January 2, 1976, at the International Monetary Market (IMM) of the Chicago Mercantile Exchange. The contract calls for delivery of bills with 13 weeks (91 days) remaining to maturity.

Other 91-day Treasury bill futures contracts were eventually offered by the AMEX and COMEX, and a 1-year contract was offered by the IMM, but these were not successful. Our discussion will concentrate on the IMM 91-day Treasury bill contract. On a typical day, volume in this contract is around 10,000–15,000 contracts representing $10–$15 billion of Treasury bills—roughly four times the typical volume of $4 billion in the secondary market for Treasury bills.

90-Day Treasury Bills—The Underlying Instrument. The 90-day Treasury bill is the major instrument traded in the U.S. money market. This market consists of securities maturing in under one year. A Treasury bill represents a direct obligation of the U.S. government and is the most widely used security for the financing of the federal government. Primary issues of both 91- and 182-day bills are sold in weekly auctions held on Mondays. Minimum denominations are $10,000 with multiples of $5,000 acceptable. The volume of the offering of both 91- and 182-day bills is currently between $6 and $7 billion each week. As of the end of 1984, there was $374.4 billion in Treasury bills outstanding. A very high degree of liquidity is available in the Treasury bill market. Treasury bills are widely used as collateral for borrowings via repurchase agreements, because they have essentially no risk and are highly liquid.

The Federal Reserve (Fed) is also active in the Treasury bill market in carrying out its open market operations. The degree of Fed intervention to influence the level of Treasury bill rates has varied over the years. In October of 1979, Fed Chairman Paul Volcker indicated that the Fed would tolerate larger fluctuations in interest rates and would focus on money supply data to control monetary policy. Treasury bill rate volatility increased as a result of this action, leading in part to the greater use of the Treasury bill futures to speculate on interest rate movements and to hedge the increased interest rate risk. In the late fall of 1982, the Fed Chairman declared a change in this noninterventionist policy, precipitated by difficulties in monitoring actual money flows due to banking deregulation. The Federal Reserve now sets targets for both money supply and interest rates and regularly intervenes in both the federal funds and Treasury bill market to moderate destabilizing fluctuations in rates and to achieve its monetary objectives.

Exhibit 3–1 shows the Treasury bill quotations as they appear in the financial press. The maturity dates of the bill are shown in the first column. Next, the annualized "bid" and "asked" discount rates appear. These are computed as follows:

EXHIBIT 3–1
Quotations of U.S. Treasury
Bill Prices and Yields
(August 1, 1984)

U.S. Treas. Bills Mat. date	Bid	Asked Discount	Yield		Mat. date	Bid	Asked Discount	Yield
1984-					**-1984-**			
8- 9	10.02	9.96	10.12		12-13	10.40	10.34	10.90
8-16	9.60	9.50	9.67		12-20	10.38	10.34	10.92
8-23	9.82	9.76	9.95		12-27	10.38	10.34	10.94
8-30	9.46	9.40	9.60		**-1985-**			
9- 6	9.97	9.91	10.14		1- 3	10.45	10.39	11.02
9-13	9.86	9.80	10.05		1-10	10.52	10.46	11.12
9-20	9.93	9.87	10.14		1-17	10.60	10.54	11.24
9-27	9.70	9.66	9.94		1-24	10.61	10.55	11.27
10- 4	10.21	10.17	10.50		1-85	10.64	10.60	11.35
10-11	10.23	10.17	10.52		2-21	10.61	10.55	11.31
10-18	10.33	10.27	10.64		3-21	10.63	10.57	11.36
10-25	10.38	10.32	10.72		4-18	10.69	10.63	11.47
11- 1	10.43	10.41	10.84		5-16	10.72	10.68	11.59
11- 8	10.42	10.34	10.78		6-13	10.72	10.68	11.66
11-15	10.24	10.18	10.73		7-11	10.72	10.70	11.75
11-24	10.40	10.36	10.85		Source–	Federal Reserve
11-29	10.41	10.37	10.88		Bank.			
12- 6	10.39	10.33	10.86					

Source: Reprinted by permission of
The Wall Street Journal, © Dow Jones &
Co., 1984. All rights reserved.

Annual discount rate

$$= \frac{(\text{Face value} - \text{Price})}{\text{Face value}} \Bigg/ \frac{\text{Number of days to maturity}}{360} \quad (3\text{–}1)$$

Treasury bills are traded on a discount basis with the holder receiving the difference between the price paid and selling price or face value as interest. The annual discount rate of a bill maturing in 42 days and selling for 99 percent of face value asked would be 8.57 percent, or

$$8.57\% \text{ or } .0857 = \frac{100 - 99}{100} \Bigg/ \frac{42}{360}$$

The discount rate does not properly represent the actual interest return, called the *yield.* Yield measures the return based on the actual price paid. Since this price is less than the face value, the yield will always exceed the quoted discount rate. The formula for the yield uses the average of the bid and asked prices and is based on a full 365-day year as below:

$$\text{Yield} = \frac{(\text{Face value} - \text{Price})}{\text{Price}} \Bigg/ \frac{\text{Number of days to maturity}}{365} \quad (3\text{–}2)$$

For a Treasury bill in the above example, the annual yield would be 8.78 percent versus a discount rate of 8.57 percent.

$$8.78\% \text{ or } .0878 = \frac{100 - 99}{99} \Bigg/ \frac{42}{365}$$

Futures Contract Characteristics. Treasury bill futures call for delivery of $1 million in face value of 91-day bills and are available for delivery dates in March, June, September, and December for up to two years from the current date. Open interest in the two near-term contracts generally represents over half of total open interest. The last day of trading is the day before the first day of the delivery month when the Treasury bill issued as a one-year bill has 13 weeks remaining to maturity.

A sample of Treasury bill futures contract price quotations is shown in Exhibit 3–2. For each delivery date, the opening, high, low, and settle price are shown as well as the change in price from the settlement price of the previous day. The annualized discount rate and the change in this rate are also given. Open interest (number of contracts outstanding) and daily volume figures are shown.

EXHIBIT 3–2
Quotations of Treasury Bill Futures
Prices (August 1, 1984)

TREASURY BILLS (IMM) – $1 mil.; pts. of 100%

						Discount		Open
	Open	High	Low	Settle	Chg	Settle	Chg	Interest
Sept	89.45	89.53	89.30	89.34	– .12	10.66	+ .12	21,050
Dec	88.95	89.12	88.93	88.94	– .05	11.06	+ .05	13,460
Mar85	88.59	88.74	88.56	88.58	....	11.42	....	4,742
June	88.28	88.45	88.28	88.30	+ .02	11.70	– .02	1,657
Sept	88.14	88.23	88.10	88.10	+ .03	11.90	– .03	891
Dec	87.94	88.09	87.94	87.96	+ .03	12.04	– .03	763
Mar86	87.88	87.95	87.86	87.86	+ .05	12.14	– .05	499
June	....	....	....	87.78	+ .07	12.22	– .07	320

Est vol 14,544; vol Tues 10,560; open int 43,382, – 865.

The discount rate as defined in (3–1) is subtracted from 100 to determine the futures price quotation. The actual price to be paid at delivery for a 91-day bill will be based on an adjustment of the trading price to reflect the 91-day maturity:

Price paid $= 100 - (\text{Discount rate} \times 90/360)$
at delivery
(as a percent of   or
face value)   (3–3)

$$= 100 - [(100 - \text{Price quoted})\, 90/360]$$

Treasury bill futures trading is done in terms of prices; yields are the basic unit of the Treasury bill cash market. The use of prices allows the future to be put on the same price basis as futures on other deliverable instruments. The minimum price index change (or discount rate change) is 0.01 percent of the price index, or one basis point. This corresponds to a $25 change in the actual value of the futures contract. If the discount rate in the near Treasury bill future in Exhibit 3–2 changed from 8.25 to 8.26, the value of the futures contract will drop $25 from $979,375 to $979,350, or:

$$97.937 = 100 - 8.25 \ (90/360)$$
$$97.935 = 100 - 8.26 \ (90/360)$$

The maximum price fluctuation is set at 60 basis points, or $1500 (60 × 25). This limit can be expanded in the event of unusual circumstances by the exchange. The mechanics of delivery for Treasury bill futures are covered in Chapter 15.

Uses of the Treasury Bill Futures Market. Theoretically, any individual or institution exposed to short-term interest rate risks or wishing to profit from correct forecasts of short-term rates would be motivated to participate in the Treasury bill futures market. In practice, the major users of the market have tended to be institutions that are experienced in short-term lending or borrowing, such as banks, brokerage houses, and securities dealers. Other major participants include those who have a significant stake in movements of short-term interest rates. The latter include business and governmental units who maintain large positions in cash-equivalent securities, who engage in large and frequent issues of commercial paper, and who rely on short-term lending from bankers at variable lending rates. Individuals who speculate on movements of Treasury bill rates or on the relation of Treasury bill rates to other short-term securities, foreign and domestic, are also users of this market.

One can broadly describe the different types of Treasury bill futures transactions as arbitrage, speculation, or hedging activity. One group that has been an extensive user of the Treasury bill futures market is the government securities dealers. Most large money center and investment banks in addition to brokerage firms have dealer operations in which traders make active markets in government bonds.

Most bond dealers describe their activity as a strategy called interest rate arbitrage. Dealing in government securities involves constantly buying and selling large amounts of Treasury bills and engaging in repurchase agreements to finance security inventories. Dealers are in an excellent position to analyze Treasury bill futures prices by considering whether they are out of line with forward interest rates or the cost of carrying their security inventory. In circumstances where observed price discrepancies exceed transaction costs, the dealers will engage in arbitrage: buying in the cheaper market and selling in the more expensive market. They thus help perform the very important function of keeping prices in the Treasury bill futures market in their proper relationship to those in the cash market. These relationships and the concepts of forward rates and carrying charges are discussed in a later chapter.

Individual investors and institutions with sufficient risk capital to trade in futures will often use Treasury bill futures to speculate on short-term interest rate movements. Because of the great leverage associated with futures and the requirement to mark-to-market, the risks of speculation are substantial. Most Treasury bill futures floor traders (except for brokers) would describe their activity as speculation. They do a large portion of their speculation on price movements within the day. A smaller group of floor traders called position traders maintain speculative positions over periods of several days or weeks.

A large amount of hedging activity occurs in the Treasury bill futures markets. Most of this is initiated by major financial and non-financial corporations. The side of the market they are in (buy versus sell) depends on whether they are hedging an existing investment in a portfolio of money market securities, an anticipated future investment, or a short-term security issue. Careful Treasury bill futures hedgers monitor their *net* short-term cash position at various maturities and place the hedging trades accordingly. Most large institutions have sizable amounts of both short-term liquid assets and liabilities. Their exposure to interest risk will depend on the gap between the amounts and maturities of their short-term position. Some institutions prefer to hedge only specific positions in short-term investments or borrowings because of the greater ease with which they can define their interest rate risk exposure and thus reduce it with specific futures contracts.

Some applications of hedges involving the sale of Treasury bill futures are identified below:

1. *Corporation or municipality* expects to issue commercial paper or other short-term securities and hedges against an increase in interest costs.
2. *Bank* hedges the cost of future certificate of deposit issues, money market deposit account inflows, money market certificate issues, and repurchase agreements.

3. *Any financial or non-financial institution* protects the value of Treasury bill or other money market assets with maturities in excess of 90 days from increases in short-term interest rates.
4. *Financial institutions* adjust the maturity gap between assets and liabilities.
5. *Underwriters* protect the value of a short-term security issue they are in the process of selling.
6. *Insurers* hedge the cost of policy loans extended at fixed rates from rising interest rates.
7. *Bond issuers, pension funds, and insurers* hedge the risk of lower selling prices (higher rates) for short-term securities that will be sold to meet coupon payment obligations or pension benefits or insurance payments.

Some applications involving the purchase of Treasury bill futures are identified below:

1. *A financial or non-financial institution or investor* expects to purchase money market securities in the near future and wishes to hedge against a decline in short-term rates when the purchase is made (anticipatory hedge).
2. *Securities dealers or banks* hedge against falling rates as they restock their securities inventories or roll-over their short-term securities portfolios.
3. *Banks and insurers* seek to offset lower interest proceeds from variable rate loans as interest rates fall.
4. *Investors or pension funds* fix returns on investment of anticipated interest (coupon) income.
5. *Financial institutions* adjust the maturity gap between assets and liabilities.
6. *Foreign investors* can acquire a position in Treasury bills with only a small portion of the cost needed to be converted to dollars.
7. *Investors* create a synthetic money market security by holding Treasury bill futures instead of a short-term security.

Certificate of Deposit Futures

In July 1981, three futures contracts on negotiable bank certificates of deposit were introduced by the New York Futures Exchange (NYFE), the IMM, and the Chicago Board of Trade (CBT). It was the intention of the regulators to give all three futures markets a chance at establishing a successful contract. The winner was clearly the IMM, which already had a successful short-term security futures contract trading. Floor traders who had the interest and knowledge to trade financial futures on short-term securities were located at the IMM. "Spreading" between Treasury bill and CD futures was also easier with the IMM CD futures contract. Volume in the CD futures is less than the volume on the Treasury bill futures, reflecting in part the greater breadth of the underlying Treasury bill cash market.

90-Day CDs—The Underlying Instrument. Negotiable certificates of deposit issued by large "money center" banks are an important part of the U.S. money market. These short-term securities represent a key source of short-term funds for these banks. Negotiable CDs tend to be more expensive than other types of bank deposits but are more discretionary in the sense that they can be quickly issued to secure funds for a lending opportunity that the bank does not want to miss. Many banks, in fact, regularly price their short-term business loans in accordance with their desired spread and the cost of funds in the CD market.

These CDs are typically issued in denominations of $1 million by large banks or more, although the minimum denomination is $100,000. The negotiable CD has a preset maturity date and interest rate with interest paid to the holder of the CD at maturity. The rate and maturity date are based on negotiation between the bank and depositor at time of issue. Maturities must be at least 14 days at issue. Because they are issued in bearer form, there is a secondary market in CDs of the largest regional and money-center banks.

Rates on bank CDs are higher than those on Treasury bills because of the greater risk associated with issuance by a private institution (see Exhibit 3–3). The yield spread relative to Treasury bills is usually in the range of one to two percent and tends to increase in periods of tight short-term credit such as in 1974 and early 1982. Any crisis in the banking industry—such as the default of Drysdale Government Securities' Dealer and Penn Square Bank in 1982, or the loan repayment problems of the Less Developed Countries in 1983—increases the perception of risk of all bank CDs among investors. Such events are often associated with a rise in CD rates in general relative to Treasury bills and, in particular, a rise in CD rates for those banks experiencing the losses associated with the debt crisis.

CD rate differentials are also common between CDs of large regional banks and those of "top-tier" money center banks. The actual rate on a particular bank's CD will depend on the credit

EXHIBIT 3–3
Money Market Rates

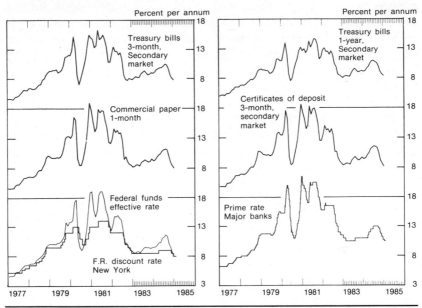

Source: *Federal Reserve Chart Book,* Board of Governors of the Federal Reserve System.

standing of the bank and the liquidity of the CDs it issues. The secondary market for CDs is sufficiently large, over $100 billion, and the CDs of the top-tier banks so homogenous in terms of quality that the conditions necessary for a successful futures market do exist for negotiable CDs.

The size of the cash market has been affected by the recent introduction of two other high-cost sources of funds for banks: the money market certificate, MMC, and the money market deposit account, MMDA. MMCs are actually nonnegotiable small denomination ($10,000) CDs with a rate tied to the Treasury bill rate. MMDAs are the banks' answer to competition from the money market funds, and offer depositors variable money market rates on even smaller deposits with limited check-writing privileges. The initiation of these new types of accounts has attracted new funds to time deposit accounts of banks but has also encouraged the switching of funds from lower interest deposit accounts such as passbook accounts. The high interest cost of these new funds and their variable rate structure have significantly changed the nature of the banking business. Banks are much more sensitive to short-term fluctuations in interest rates and, because of the greater proportion of deposits concentrated in these high cost funds, have a much narrower spread between interest earned on assets and their cost of funds. Therefore, interest rate risk management has taken on greater importance for banks. Negotiable CD futures along with Treasury bill futures are important tools in the risk management process.

Futures Contract Characteristics. The denomination and contract months for the CD futures are identical to those for the Treasury bill futures. The CD contract at the IMM will serve as the basis for our discussion, because it is the only one of the CD contracts that remains active. The delivery calls for "no-name CDs" that mature between the 16th and last day of the month that follows three months after the delivery month. The identity of the particular bank's CDs that will be accepted is not announced until two business days before the first day that they can be delivered into the contract. CDs considered for delivery must have no more than 199 days of accrued interest. Delivery specifications are discussed in more detail in a separate chapter of this book.

Prices for CD futures are quoted in a similar fashion to those of Treasury bills as shown in Exhibit 3–4. The price quotes are based on indexes calculated by subtracting the annual interest rate from 100. A price move of .01 represents $25 of contract value. The maximum or limit move is .80 or $2,000 (80 × 25). Interest on CDs is add-on rather than on a discount basis as with Treasury bills. Therefore, the price paid at delivery equals $1 million.

EXHIBIT 3–4
Quotations of CD Futures Prices
(August 1, 1984)

```
BANK CDs (IMM) - $1 million; pts. of 100%
Sept    88.43 88.58 88.40 88.42   ....  11.58   ....  11,743
Dec     87.95 88.17 87.90 88.02 +  .07  11.98 -  .07   9,393
Mar85   87.61 87.81 87.52 87.67 +  .11  12.33 -  .11   3,370
June    87.36 87.55 87.22 87.42 +  .15  12.58 -  .15   2,286
Sept    87.35 87.35 87.02 87.16 +  .12  12.84 -  .12   1,212
Dec     ..... ..... ..... 86.98 +  .12  13.02 -  .12     569
  Est vol 3,853; vol Tues 2,107; open int 28,573, -208.
```

Uses of the CD Futures Market. The most common use of CD futures is to fix the interest cost of bank funds for a period longer than the 90-day maturity of the typical negotiable CD issue.

This is important when a bank makes a commitment to lend funds raised by a negotiable CD issue at a fixed rate for a period longer than the maturity of the CD, e.g., a year. By using CD futures, the bank can approximately determine its cost of funds over the year prior to extending the one-year loan. This is done by selling CD futures for each of the three 90-day periods that the 90-day CD will need to be rolled-over to provide financing for the loan. The greater volume and open interest in longer-term delivery CD futures versus Treasury bill futures reflects this particular hedging strategy. An illustration of the application follows.

On December 10, 1984, a medium-sized, regional bank extends a $10 million one-year loan at a fixed rate of 12 percent to one of its corporate customers. The bank simultaneously issues a 90-day CD at a 10¾ percent annual rate and sells CD futures with a contract value of $10 million in each of three different delivery months: March, June, and September of 1985. These futures are available in December at rates of 10.34 percent, 10.70 percent, and 10.97 percent, respectively. The sale of CD futures reduces the risk exposure of the bank to higher future CD rates. The bank knows that when it rolls over the CDs in March, June, and September, the effect of any increase in issue costs will be moderated by profits from the repurchase of these CD futures at prices below those at which they were sold in December. If CD rates fall, the bank will not profit as much as if it had remained unhedged. However, management feels the risk associated with the rise in rates is sufficient to make it appropriate to secure a profit margin upfront on this loan.

The full description of interest revenue, interest expenses, and profits for both a hedged and unhedged position is shown in Exhibit 3–5. In the example, the CD rate for the bank increases from 10.75 percent to 12.75 percent between December 1984 and September 1985. Interest expenses reduce the total spread below the 12 percent loan rate to 0.125 percent for a net profit on the loan of only $12,500. If rates had remained at 10.75 percent, the spread would have been 1.25 percent and net profit 10 times that actually earned, or $125,000. Hedging with CD futures earns the bank $87,250 which considerably augments the $12,500 profit.

The futures profit along with the net interest revenue of $12,500 allows the bank to realize roughly a 1 percent spread on the loan—only 0.25 percent less than if rates had not changed at all (12.0% − 10.75%).

The bank will not make up the full 1.25 percent original spread via a CD futures hedge. The expectation of an increase in CD rates was already reflected in the futures prices available on December 10. The implied rates in the CD futures were 10.34 percent, 10.7

EXHIBIT 3–5
Hedging a One-Year Fixed-Rate Loan with CD Futures

Size of loan	$10 million
Loan rate	12 percent or .12
Term	1 year
90-day CD rate	Bank's rate 10.75%; Money Center Bank Rate 10.00%
Expected profit spread 1.25% (12 − 10.75)	

Results of Unhedged Loan Financing

Interest revenue ($10 million × 12%)	= $1,200,000
Interest expense	= 1,187,500
(10 CD futures contracts sold in March, June, and September)	

CD issues:

Dec 10—Mar CD $10 million × 10.75% × 90/360	= $ 268,750
Mar 10—Jun CD $10 million × 11.50% × 90/360	= 287,500
Jun 10—Sep CD $10 million × 12.50% × 90/360	= 312,500
Sep 10—Dec CD $10 million × 12.75% × 90/360	= 318,750
	$1,187,500
Net interest revenue (unhedged)	$ 12,500
Effective profit rate on assets (loan)	.125%

Results of CD futures hedge

CD Futures Dec 10, sell 10 Mar at −89.66 (10.34%)		
sell 10 Jun at −89.30 (10.70%)		
sell 10 Sep at −89.03 (10.97%)		
. Mar 10, buy 10 Mar at −88.75 (11.25%)	+	22,750
Jun 10, buy 10 Jun at −88.00 (12.00%)	+	32,500
Sep 10, buy 10 Sep at −87.75 (12.25%)	+	32,000
Net interest revenue (unhedged)	$	12,500
Net interest revenue (hedged)		99,750
Effective profit rate on assets (loan)		.997%

---

percent, and 10.87 percent versus the current CD rate for large money-center banks of 10 percent. There is also no assurance for the bank that CD rates on which futures prices are based will move in exactly the same direction and the same amount as CD rates in the example. This is called the "basis risk" of hedging, which will be explained in more detail in the Chapter 7. CD futures would not, for example, protect a particular bank against any increased costs associated with a large increase in the perceived risk of its loan portfolio. The rise in CD issue rates for the bank would not necessarily be reflected in CD futures prices unless all banks were experiencing the same increase in risk.

It is useful to note that the hedging of loans backed by funds raised in money market rate deposit accounts would provide similar benefits in terms of protecting a bank against increasing deposit interest rates. Treasury bill futures are usually used to hedge money market deposit account costs, because the rates in these accounts are tied to changes in Treasury bill rates.

Another use of the CD futures market would be the purchase of CD futures by corporations or municipalities who anticipate having excess cash which they intend to use to purchase CDs at some future date. Rates as reflected in CD futures prices may be attractive at a time when there is concern about lower short-term rates as the cash becomes available for short-term investment.

For example, in June 1982, CD futures were available for delivery in December 1982 at an annual rate of 15 percent. A corporate treasurer at a retail firm expected a large inflow of cash in December as Christmas sales occur and felt rates were more likely to fall than increase over the next six months. This cash is usually invested in short-term funds until late spring, when inventories will again be acquired for the 1983 Christmas season.

The treasurer bought December CD futures in an amount equivalent to the minimum forecast for cash inflows in the fourth quarter of 1983. (She does not want to be "overhedged" and find that she does not need to buy as many CDs come December as she has purchased futures.) In December, the CD futures have risen in price to reflect a rate of only 10 percent. By using futures, the retail firm will have earned an additional 5 percent (1.25 percent for 90 days) on its funds, compared to what it would have earned as interest over the first quarter of 1983 if it had bought CDs at the 10 percent rate prevailing in December 1982.

Another application of CD futures strategies would be their sale as cross-hedges for issuers of commercial paper by bank holding companies or other financial and nonfinancial institutions. This strategy would be appropriate in periods of rising interest rates. The effectiveness of the hedge would depend on the stability of the spread between commercial paper rates and rates in the CD futures markets. If commercial paper rates increase faster than CD rates, the gains on the short CD futures position will not be sufficient to compensate for the higher short-term borrowing costs.

Eurodollar Futures

In December 1981, Eurodollar deposit futures contracts began trading at the IMM in Chicago. A very similar contract is also traded on the London International Financial Futures Exchange (LIFFE). Volume in Eurodollar futures on the IMM has grown dramatically over the last few years and is now typically in the range of 40,000–50,000 contracts per day. The Eurodollar future is now the most actively traded futures contract on short-term securities. The contract is similar to the CD contract in that it represents $1 million of bank deposits. However, these dollar-denominated deposits are located in banks outside the United States, primarily in London and other European financing centers. Another unique feature of the Eurodollar future is that settlement is in the form of cash rather than the deposits themselves.

Three-Month Eurodollar Time Deposits—The Underlying Instrument. Dollar-denominated deposits outside the United States are the basic short-term security in the international money market. The market for these deposits grew most rapidly in the mid-60s and early 70s when lenders and borrowers used it as a means to circumvent the reserve requirements and interest rate ceilings to which U.S. deposit accounts were subject. The effect of these regulations has diminished, but the market has survived as a means for short-term investment and borrowing of dollar balances outside the U.S. banking systems. The rate in the Eurodollar market is called the London Interbank Offer Rate (LIBOR). This is the rate at which top-tier banks in London are willing to borrow and lend deposits among themselves. The LIBOR rate is very similar to the prime rate in the United States in the sense that actual lending rates involve a premium over LIBOR based on the particular circumstances of the loans and the credit quality of the borrower.

Because of lower overhead on deposit accounts and higher credit standards on lending policy, Eurodollar borrowing can be done at rates competitive with U.S. short-term loan rates. Eurodollar deposit accounts tend to earn higher interest rates than those available in the U.S. bank CD market. Many of these Eurodollar deposits are nonnegotiable and thus less liquid than bank CDs. There is always the possibility that those deposit holders who are not citizens of the country in which the deposits are located will not have their property rights respected in an international crisis. Finally, because a large proportion of the market is an interbank market, rates must be high enough to provide a premium to a bank for holding the nonnegotiable CD of another bank.

The spread between CD, Treasury bill, and Eurodollar deposit rates is not constant over time. There appears to be a tendency for these spreads to be related to the general level of short-term Treasury bill rates and to the value of the dollar. When interest rates are high, the LIBOR rate increases relative to the Treasury bill rate, reflecting the willingness of investors to pay a premium for the lower risk of a government security during such periods. The particular segment of the Eurodollar deposit market on which the future is traded is the three-month Eurodollar time of deposit.

EXHIBIT 3–6
Quotations of Eurodollar Futures
Prices (August 1, 1984)

EURODOLLAR (IMM)–$1 million; pts of 100%

	Open	High	Low	Settle	Chg	Yield Settle	Chg	Open Interest
Sept	87.99	88.13	87.94	87.96	– .01	12.04	+ .01	38,372
Dec	87.52	87.72	87.45	87.56	+ .06	12.44	– .06	32,035
Mar85	87.13	87.34	87.07	87.20	+ .09	12.80	– .09	14,326
June	86.91	87.07	86.78	86.93	+ .11	13.07	– .11	5,801
Sept	86.60	86.85	86.57	86.72	+ .12	13.28	– .12	2,809
Dec	86.40	86.66	86.39	86.55	+ .13	13.45	– .13	1,723

Est vol 25,866; vol 19,457; open int 95,066, +100.

Futures Contract Characteristics. The delivery value of a Eurodollar futures contract, like the CD and Treasury bill futures, is $1 million. Contracts call for delivery in March, June, September, and December of each year. The features of the Eurodollar futures contract traded at the IMM and LIFFE are very similar. Prices are quoted in terms of an index basis as 100 minus the annualized Eurodollar futures rate. (Exhibit 3–6.)

The final settlement is made in cash directly through the IMM Clearinghouse based on the LIBOR rate on the last trading day. The last trading date is the second London business day before the third Wednesday of the month. The LIBOR rate on which settlement for the IMM contract is based is the average three-month time deposit rate quotes on a random selection of 12 banks from the top 20 banks in the London Eurodollar market. Quotes at the termination of trading on this day and a quote collected at a randomly selected time in the last 80 minutes of trading are averaged to determine the settlement rate.

The last trading day of the LIFFE contract is roughly one week prior to the termination of the IMM Eurodollar contract. Trading ceases at 11 A.M. The settlement price is based on the average of a random sample of offered rates taken between 9:30 and 11 A.M. on this last trading day. The smallest trading unit on both markets is one basis point or $25, with a limit move set at 100 basis points or $2,500. The wider range of limit moves for Eurodollars versus Treasury bill futures reflects the higher volatility of the Eurodollar rates.[1]

Uses of the Eurodollar Futures Market. Eurodollar futures can be used in ways very similar to CD futures for hedging the cost of loans financed by Eurodollar deposit issues. Lenders can buy Eurodollar futures to protect their loan income from an unexpected drop in rates. Banks that expect to be net issuers of Eurodollars in the future may wish to sell the futures to guard against higher interest costs associated with a rise in rates. The market also provides another vehicle in which arbitrageurs can profit from price discrepancies in related forward and cash markets.

The supply and demand forces in the Eurodollar loan and deposit market are sufficiently unique to warrant a contract separate from other short-term money market futures. The size of the market is great, rate volatility is higher than on other short-term instruments, and there is more participation among large international banks and multinational corporations than in the negotiable CD market.

Many multinational corporations are large holders of Eurodollar deposits. These firms may use this market to reduce fluctuations in their short-term capital income over a planning period. They may also wish to buy Eurodollar futures in anticipation of expected cash flows which they intend to convert into Eurodollar deposits at some future date. Multinationals also tend to use the lending capacity of the Eurodollar market and thus have considerable short-term financing costs linked to the movements of Eurodollar rates. They may wish to use the market to hedge the possibility of higher future financing charges.

An interesting opportunity is the possibility of combining foreign currency futures (also traded at the IMM) with Eurodollar futures to create a simulated hedge for a deposit denominated in another currency such as marks or yen.[2] One can capitalize, in effect, on any discrepancy between local currency deposit rates, currency futures prices, and Eurodollar futures rates in a kind of three-way arbitrage. A summary of the characteristics of short-term, fixed-income futures is given in Exhibit 3–7.

FUTURES ON LONG–TERM SECURITIES

This section is concerned with financial futures calling for delivery of long-term fixed-income securities. A summary of characteristics of long-term, fixed-income futures is given in Exhibit 3–8. Presently, these futures contracts all call for delivery of securities either issued or guaranteed by the U.S. government (i.e., U.S. Treasury bonds, U.S. 10-year Treasury notes, and mortgage pass-through certificates guaranteed by the U.S. government (GNMAs)). Futures

EXHIBIT 3-7
Summary of Characteristics of Short-Term Fixed-Income Futures

	90-day U.S. Treasury Bill	*90-day Domestic Certificate of Deposit*	*90-day Euro$ Time Deposit*	*90-day U.K.$ Time Deposit*
			Contract	
Exchange	IMM	IMM	IMM	LIFFE
Size	$1 million	$1 million	$1 million	$1 million
Hours	8:00 A.M.–2:00 P.M. (Chicago)	7:30 A.M.–2:00 P.M. (Chicago)	7:30 A.M.–2:00 P.M. (Chicago)	8:30 A.M.–3:00 P.M. (London)
Minimum price change	.01 ($25)	.01 ($25)	.01 ($25)	.01 ($25)
Limit move	.60 ($1,500)	.80 ($2,000)	1.00 ($2,500)	1.00 ($2,500)
Initial margin	$1,500	$1,500	$1,500	$2,000
Last trading day	Day before delivery day	Last business day before last delivery day	2d London business day before the 3d. Wednesday in delivery month	2d business day before 2d Wednesday of delivery month
Delivery months	March, June, September, December			
Delivery day	1st day of delivery month when Treasury bill issued as 1 year bill has 13 weeks to maturity	15th through last day of month	Last trading day	2d Wednesday of delivery month

EXHIBIT 3–8
Summary of Characteristics of Long-Term Fixed-Income Futures

	U.S. Treasury Bonds	U.S. Treasury Notes	GNMA CDR
Date trading began	8/22/77	3/3/82	10/20/75
Exchange		Chicago Board of Trade	
Trading unit		$100,000 face value of securities	
Hours (Chicago time)		8:00 A.M.–2:00 P.M.	
Minimum price change		⅟₃₂ or $31.25	
Limit move		⁶⁴⁄₃₂ or $2,000	
Initial margin		$3,000*	
Maintenance margin		$2,000*	
Hedging margin		$2,000*	

* Subject to change.

contracts on other fixed-income securities and indexes, such as municipal bonds and corporate bonds, are in the planning stages.

The existing fixed-income futures markets developed well before cash settlement was a possibility. The most successful contract—futures on U.S. Treasury bonds introduced in August 1977—has a deliverable instrument with a very liquid market, dealer positions are easily financed by repurchase agreements, and default risk is nonexistent.

In 1984, Treasury bond futures were the largest volume futures contracts traded. This was a significant development for the financial futures market, which is less than 10 years old. Typical volume is now over 100,000 contracts or $10 billion per day. Fixed-income portfolio managers and security dealers are most concerned about ways to reduce the impact of shifts in the general level of interest rates on their portfolios and inventory. The Treasury bond future has been effective in fulfilling this need. Futures on corporate and municipal bond indexes may be on the horizon. The diversity among issues in the corporate and municipal bond market and the thinness of these bond markets for arbitrage-trading will make the Treasury bond futures hard to displace as the most widely traded financial future.

GNMA (CDR) futures were the first financial instrument futures to trade on an exchange when they were introduced by the Chicago Board of Trade in October 1975. Their acceptance in the mortgage financing business grew rapidly, with over 2.13 million contracts traded in 1980. Since that time, trading volume in this contract has declined due to a number of factors. The severe recession in the housing finance business in the early 1980s and the introduction of variable rate mortgages to reduce the exposure of mortgage issuers and holders to interest rate movements are part of the explanation of the lower volume. Probably more important is the awkward delivery mechanism of GNMA futures, the CDR—Collateralized Depository Receipt. The use of the CDR has hampered the delivery process because of the uncertainty facing GNMA futures traders regarding the composition of the GNMAs backing the CDR. This has led many participants to seek other ways of speculating on and hedging the risk of changing mortgage rates.

Futures on 4–6-year Treasury notes were introduced in June 1979 but had little success. In May 1982, the Chicago Board of Trade began trading a new note contract calling for delivery of Treasury obligations maturing in 6½ to 10 years from contract delivery. This contract has been more successful, yet still has a volume of only 5,000–10,000 contracts per day.

U.S. Treasury Bond and Note Futures

U.S. Treasury bond futures have become an integral part of the financial markets in debt instruments. The growing size of the Treasury debt in the credit markets and the great increase in interest rate volatility that occured in the late 70s has stimulated interest and participation in Treasury bond futures markets. The Treasury bond future has become the most actively traded futures contract. It is not unusual for 150,000 contracts to trade each day, representing $15 billion in principal value. The value of long-term, fixed-income securities is highly sensitive to changing interest rates. Many investors buy fixed-income securities for the stable high coupon income and do not wish to be subject to these wide swings in value caused by short-term changes in interest rates. Dealers in long-term bonds also bear considerable risk of changes in the value of their inventory from shifting interest rates.

Hedging strategies with Treasury bond and note futures can provide profits and losses that partially or fully offset these short-term changes in value. Bond dealers and traders now consider these futures a regular part of the techniques they use in managing their long-term bond positions. Many investment banks are active participants in both the Treasury bond and Treasury bond futures markets. They also use futures as a part of strategies designed to capitalize on shifts in interest rates. Considerable profits are available to those who have the expertise and capital to trade in these markets. Large positions can be acquired and unwound cheaply. Interest rate movements on a short-term basis have been large enough for traders to profit handsomely on correct forecasts of intraday, daily, or weekly price swings.

Large institutional investors, such as pension funds, insurance companies, endowment funds, and the like, have been slower to utilize Treasury bond futures in management of their fixed-income portfolios. This reticence is primarily due to legal and procedural barriers, lack of knowledge about the instruments, and the simple resistance to change. The legal barriers to hedging by private pension funds have been removed, and most state regulations regarding the use of futures in the insurance industry are presently undergoing revision. New York State, a leader in insurance regulation, recently gave the insurance companies under its jurisdiction permission to use futures to hedge a portion of their general account assets.[3] All of these factors point toward further growth for Treasury bond futures as portfolio managers and traders become more sophisticated in the use of these instruments.

Long-Term Treasury Bonds and Notes—The Underlying Instruments. Treasury bonds are marketable obligations of the U.S. government. They are typically issued in the refunding cycles which occur quarterly in February, May, August, and November. Most quarterly refunding issues contain a note of 3 to 4 years in maturity, another note in the 7 to 10-year range, and a long-term bond with a maturity of 20 to 30 years. In November 1984 quarterly financing, for example, $8.1 billion of 3-year notes, $6.6 billion of 10-year notes, and $6.0 billion of 30-year bonds were issued.[4]

The secondary Treasury bond markets are highly liquid and broad. The U.S. government is the largest borrower in the world. The dollar is an important currency, and the risk of its default is negligible. The markets consist of dealers who provide bid-and-ask prices on outstanding securities. As of December 1984, $705 billion of Treasury notes and $167 billion of Treasury bonds were outstanding.[5] As seen in Exhibit 3–9, the holders of this debt include financial institutions, individuals, corporations, state and local governments, and foreign investors.

The bid-and-ask quotes for Treasury notes and bonds are shown in the daily financial press based on mid-afternoon quotes in the dealer market. (See Exhibit 3–10.) Most dealers in the mar-

EXHIBIT 3–9
Estimated Ownership of U.S. Debt by Private Investors
(December 1984)

Owner	Percent	$ Billions
Commercial banks	16.0	185.5
Individuals	12.5	145.3
Insurance companies	6.4	73.9
Money market funds	22.4	26.0
Corporations	4.3	50.2
State local governments	14.2	165.0
Foreign and international	16.7	193.1
Other investors	27.6	319.4
(thrift includes institution, broker		
and dealers, pension funds)		

Source: Treasury Bulletin, Department of Treasury, Winter Issue, 1984.

kets rely on continuously updated quotes communicated via a computer communication system called *Telerate*. The quotes in *The
Wall Street Journal* include the coupon rate, maturity year or years
over which the issue can be called, the maturity month, and a
designation *n* indicating whether the security is a note. Bid-and-
ask prices are given in units of 32ds. The yield quoted is the yield
to maturity or first call if the issue is selling at a premium based
in the ask price.

The secondary market for notes and bonds is a dealer rather
than an exchange market.[6] In this market, round-lot transactions
occur in units of $100,000 face value. This is also the contract
size for Treasury bond futures. Bid-ask spreads are the compensation the dealers receive for making the market in these securities.
These bid-ask spreads vary depending on the financing costs of
the dealers, liquidity, and volatility of particular issues. Spreads
are usually around 0.25 percent of par value, or $250. In contrast,
the transaction cost on a Treasury bond futures contract is considerably less—under $20 for most market participants.

Government security dealers are important participants in
both the cash and futures markets for Treasury bonds. They operate with a small amount of capital in proportion to the size of
their positions, financing their inventory using repurchase agreements. In addition to profiting from the bid-ask spread, dealers
also profit when the coupon interest earned in their inventory
plus any price appreciation is higher than the financing charges.
When the yield curve is upward sloping, the carry (interest re-
ceived-financing charges) is positive. Thus, the incentive to reduce

EXHIBIT 3–10

Treasury Issues/*Bonds, Notes & Bills*

Wednesday, August 1, 1984

Representative mid-afternoon Over-the-Counter quotations supplied by the Federal Reserve Bank of New York City, based on transactions of $1 million or more.

Decimals in bid-and-asked and bid changes represent 32nds; 101.1 means 101 1/32. a-Plus 1/64. b-Yield to call date. d-Minus 1/64. n-Treasury notes.

Treasury Bonds and Notes

Rate	Mat. Date	Bid	Asked	Bid Chg.	Yld.
6 3/8s,	1984 Aug	99.27	100.3	+ 2	3.43
7 1/4s,	1984 Aug n	99.28	100		7.01
11 5/8s,	1984 Aug n	100.2	100.6		8.71
13 1/4s,	1984 Aug n	100.3	100.7		6.22
12 1/8s,	1984 Sep n	100.5	100.9		9.91
9 3/4s,	1984 Oct n	99.23	99.27	+ 1	10.16
9 7/8s,	1984 Nov n	99.19	99.23	+ 1	10.59
14 3/8s,	1984 Nov n	100.27	100.31		10.52
16s,	1984 Nov n	101.11	101.15		10.29
9 3/8s,	1984 Dec n	99.9	99.13	+ 1	10.80
14s,	1984 Dec n	101.2	101.6		10.82
9 1/4s,	1985 Jan n	99	99.4	+ 1	11.12
8s,	1985 Feb n	98.9	98.13	+ 1	11.16
9 5/8s,	1985 Feb n	98.30	99.2	+ 1	11.35
14 5/8s,	1985 Feb n	101.18	101.22	+ 1	11.28
9 5/8s,	1985 Mar	98.22	98.26	+ 1	11.54
13 3/8s,	1985 Mar n	101.2	101.6	+ 1	11.46
9 1/2s,	1985 Apr n	98.16	98.20	+ 1	11.48
3 1/4s,	1985 May	94.31	95.31	- 3	8.67
4 1/4s,	1975-85 May	95.1	96.1		9.62
9 7/8s,	1985 May n	98.18	98.22	+ 2	11.58
10 3/8s,	1985 May n	99.2	99.6	+ 2	11.49
14 1/8s,	1985 May n	101.23	101.27	+ 1	11.60
14 3/8s,	1985 May n	101.28	102	+ 1	11.64
14s,	1985 Jun n	101.27	101.31	+ 2	11.66
10s,	1985 Jun n	98.15	98.19	+ 3	11.67
10 5/8s,	1985 Jul n	98.27	98.31	+ 2	11.76
8 1/4s,	1985 Aug n	96.20	96.24	+ 3	11.68
9 5/8s,	1985 Aug n	97.24	97.28	+ 2	11.87
10 5/8s,	1985 Aug n	98.19	98.23	+ 2	11.93
13 1/8s,	1985 Aug n	101.1	101.5	+ 3	11.90
10 7/8s,	1985 Sep n	98.24	98.28	+ 2	11.94
15 7/8s,	1985 Sep n	103.27	103.31		12.11
10 1/2s,	1985 Oct n	98.7	98.11	+ 3	11.97
9 3/4s,	1985 Nov n	97.4	97.8	+ 3	12.12
10 1/2s,	1985 Nov n	97.29	98.1	+ 3	12.15
11 3/4s,	1985 Nov n	99.17	99.21	+ 3	12.05
10 7/8s,	1985 Dec n	98.10	98.14	+ 4	12.11
14 1/8s,	1985 Dec n	102.9	102.13	+ 1	12.22
10 5/8s,	1986 Jan n	97.30	98.2	+ 3	12.08
10 7/8s,	1986 Feb n	98.2	98.6	+ 4	12.17
13 1/2s,	1986 Feb n	101.18	101.22	+ 2	12.26
9 7/8s,	1986 Feb n	96.21	96.25	+ 4	12.24
14s,	1986 Mar n	102.9	102.13	+ 4	12.35
11 1/2s,	1986 Mar n	98.20	98.24	+ 5	12.36
11 3/4s,	1986 Apr n	98.29	98.31	+ 6	12.43
7 7/8s,	1986 May n	92.28	93.4	+ 4	12.28
9 3/8s,	1986 May n	95.6	95.10	+ 6	12.38
12 5/8s,	1986 May n	100.5	100.7	+ 5	12.49
13 3/4s,	1986 May n	101.31	102.3	+ 5	12.41
13s,	1986 Jun n	100.26	100.28	+ 5	12.47
14 7/8s,	1986 Jun n	103.31	104.7	+ 4	12.33
12 5/8s,	1986 Jul n	100.8	100.10	+ 5	12.44
8s,	1986 Aug n	92.7	92.11	+ 6	12.37
11 3/8s,	1986 Aug n	98.6	98.10	+ 8	12.34
12 1/4s,	1986 Sep n	99.19	99.23	+ 7	12.40
6 1/8s,	1986 Nov	90.9	91.9	+ 3	10.52
11s,	1986 Nov n	97.5	97.9	+ 8	12.40
13 7/8s,	1986 Nov n	102.18	102.26	+ 5	12.42
16 1/8s,	1986 Nov n	106.30	107.6	+ 7	12.42
10s,	1986 Dec n	94.29	95.1	+ 7	12.45
9s,	1987 Feb n	92.20	92.24	+ 7	12.42
10 7/8s,	1987 Feb n	96.16	96.20	+ 8	12.47
12 3/4s,	1987 Feb n	100.16	100.20	+ 6	12.45
10 1/4s,	1987 Mar n	94.30	95.2	+ 8	12.49
12s,	1987 May n	98.24	98.28	+ 4	12.49
12 1/2s,	1987 May n	99.25	99.27	+ 7	12.57
14s,	1987 May n	103.8	103.12	+ 8	12.53
10 1/2s,	1987 Jun n	95.2	95.6	+ 9	12.52
13 3/4s,	1987 Aug n	102.29	103.1	+ 8	12.52
11 1/8s,	1987 Sep n	96.8	96.12	+ 7	12.55
7 5/8s,	1987 Nov n	87.10	87.26	+ 9	12.24
12 5/8s,	1987 Nov n	100.2	100.6	+ 8	12.55
11 1/4s,	1987 Dec n	96.11	96.15	+ 8	12.55
12 3/8s,	1988 Jan n	99.12	99.20	+ 6	12.51
10 1/8s,	1988 Feb n	93.1	93.9	+ 8	12.54
12s,	1988 Mar n	98.2	98.4	+ 5	12.66
13 1/4s,	1988 Apr n	101.27	102.3	+ 4	12.53
8 1/4s,	1988 May n	87.11	87.19	+ 4	12.46
9 7/8s,	1988 May n	91.20	91.28	+ 8	12.64
13 5/8s,	1988 Jun n	102.27	102.29	+ 7	12.66
14s,	1988 Jul n	104.2	104.10	+ 10	12.58
10 1/2s,	1988 Aug n	93.6	93.14	+ 10	12.63
15 3/8s,	1988 Oct n	108.6	108.14	+ 11	12.72
8 3/4s,	1988 Nov n	87.24	88	+ 10	12.45
11 3/4s,	1988 Nov n	96.31	97.7	+ 10	12.61
14 5/8s,	1989 Jan n	106.10	106.18	+ 11	12.65
11 3/8s,	1989 Feb n	95.19	95.27	+ 9	12.61
14 3/8s,	1989 Apr n	105.19	105.27	+ 9	12.69
9 1/4s,	1989 May n	88.11	88.19	+ 11	12.49
11 3/4s,	1989 May n	96.20	96.24	+ 12	12.68
14 1/2s,	1989 Jul n	106.3	106.11	+ 13	12.73
13 7/8s,	1989 Aug n	104.3	104.5	+ 13	12.72
11 7/8s,	1989 Oct n	96.28	97.4	+ 14	12.65
10 3/4s,	1989 Nov n	92.20	92.28	+ 12	12.64
10 1/2s,	1990 Jan n	91.9	91.17	+ 12	12.70
3 1/2s,	1990 Feb	89.19	90.19	+ 1	5.49
10 1/2s,	1990 Apr n	90.30	91.6	+ 15	12.72
8 1/4s,	1990 May	83.5	83.21	+ 15	12.28
10 3/4s,	1990 Jul n	91.22	91.30	+ 11	12.72
10 3/4s,	1990 Aug n	91.19	91.27	+ 15	12.73
11 1/2s,	1990 Oct n	94.18	94.26	+ 14	12.73
13s,	1990 Nov n	100.31	101.7	+ 16	12.71
11 3/4s,	1991 Jan n	95.18	95.22	+ 12	12.75
12 3/8s,	1991 Apr	98.6	98.10	+ 16	12.76
14 1/2s,	1991 May n	107.11	107.19	+ 18	12.79
13 3/4s,	1991 Jul n	104.7	104.9	+ 14	12.80
14 7/8s,	1991 Aug n	109.7	109.15	+ 17	12.79
14 1/4s,	1991 Nov n	106.10	106.18	+ 16	12.84
14 5/8s,	1992 Feb n	108.7	108.15	+ 15	12.84
13 3/4s,	1992 May n	104.6	104.14	+ 19	12.83
4 1/4s,	1987-92 Aug	89.22	90.22		5.71
7 1/4s,	1992 Aug	74.11	74.27	+ 18	12.26
10 1/2s,	1992 Nov n	88.9	88.17	+ 17	12.78
4s,	1988-93 Feb	90.1	91.1	+ 5	5.32
6 3/4s,	1993 Feb	70.25	71.9	+ 15	12.27
7 7/8s,	1993 Feb	75.15	75.31	+ 18	12.54
10 7/8s,	1993 Feb n	89.31	90.3	+ 19	12.82
10 1/8s,	1993 May n	85.28	86	+ 21	12.83
7 1/2s,	1988-93 Aug	73.7	73.23	+ 27	12.42
8 5/8s,	1993 Aug	78.1	78.9	+ 17	12.74
11 7/8s,	1993 Aug n	94.30	95.6	+ 20	12.79
8 5/8s,	1993 Nov	77.27	78.3	+ 18	12.71
11 3/4s,	1993 Nov	94.4	94.8	+ 19	12.83
9s,	1994 Feb	79.17	79.25	+ 19	12.72
4 1/8s,	1989-94 May	89.17	90.17	+ 1	5.38
13 1/8s,	1994 May	101.24	101.28	+ 19	12.78
8 3/4s,	1994 Aug	77.22	77.30	+ 20	12.70
10 1/8s,	1994 Nov	85.6	85.14	+ 23	12.70
3s,	1995 Feb	89.24	90.24	+ 4	4.09
10 1/2s,	1995 Feb	87	87.8	+ 24	12.73
10 3/8s,	1995 May	86	86.8	+ 23	12.76
12 5/8s,	1995 May	99.4	99.12	+ 25	12.73
11 1/2s,	1995 Nov	92.10	92.18	+ 22	12.76
7s,	1993-98 May	64.13	64.29	+ 15	12.37
3 1/2s,	1998 Nov	89.20	90.20		4.39
8 1/2s,	1994-99 May	71.30	72.14	+ 19	12.67
7 7/8s,	1995-00 Feb	67.15	67.23	+ 20	12.68
8 3/8s,	1995-00 Aug	70.13	70.21	+ 18	12.70
11 3/4s,	2001 Feb	92.8	92.16	+ 11	12.85
13 1/8s,	2001 May	102.14	102.22	+ 26	12.73
8s,	1996-01 Aug	67.12	67.28	+ 16	12.63
13 3/8s,	2001 Aug	103.19	103.27	+ 23	12.81
15 3/4s,	2001 Nov	120.13	120.21	+ 1	12.76
14 1/4s,	2002 Feb	109.22	109.30	+ 23	12.81
11 5/8s,	2002 Nov	91.6	91.14	+ 13	12.85
10 3/4s,	2003 Feb	85.3	85.11	+ 18	12.84
10 3/4s,	2003 May	85.3	85.11	+ 18	12.83
11 1/8s,	2003 Aug	87.21	87.29	+ 13	12.84
11 7/8s,	2003 Nov	93.2	93.10	+ 21	12.82
12 3/8s,	2004 May	96.23	96.31	+ 26	12.80
13 3/4s,	2004 Aug	106.12	106.14	+ 21	12.84
8 1/4s,	2000-05 May	67.27	68.11	+ 17	12.57
7 5/8s,	2002-07 Feb	63.2	63.10	+ 14	12.54
7 7/8s,	2002-07 Nov	64.11	64.19	+ 5	12.62
8 3/8s,	2003-08 Aug	67.25	68.1	+ 10	12.64
8 3/4s,	2003-08 Nov	70	70.8	+ 8	12.74
9 1/8s,	2004-09 May	72.21	72.29	+ 13	12.75
10 3/8s,	2004-09 Nov	82	82.8	+ 16	12.74
11 3/4s,	2005-10 Feb	92.7	92.15	+ 19	12.75
10s,	2005-10 May	79.13	79.21	+ 24	12.70
12 3/4s,	2005-10 Nov	99.17	99.25	+ 14	12.78
13 7/8s,	2006-11 May	107.19	107.27	+ 18	12.80
14s,	2006-11 Nov	108.20	108.28	+ 16	12.79
10 3/8s,	2007-12 Nov	81.22	81.30	+ 16	12.75
12s,	2008-13 Aug	94.1	94.5	+ 19	12.77
13 1/4s,	2014 May	103.29	104.1	+ 16	12.71

Source: Reprinted by permission of *The Wall Street Journal* © Dow Jones & Co., 1984.

inventory levels is not great. By contrast, when short-term rates are above long rates, dealers are paying to carry inventory and therefore try to keep that inventory as low as possible.

Shifts in long-term or short-term interest rates are a source of risk to government bond dealers. They try to manage this risk via hedging transactions in both the cash and futures markets. For example, dealers holding a large inventory in Treasury bonds have a choice of reducing their interest rate risk exposure by selling off some of their inventory or selling Treasury bond futures. The latter route is often attractive, because it allows the dealer to maintain inventory levels. The size of the futures position can be readily and cheaply adjusted as inventories are sold. In addition, they can finance their inventory via repurchase agreements from which they receive funds while, in effect, using their securities as collateral for very short periods. Some dealers also "short" Treasury bonds and notes. This is usually done by borrowing a bond from another dealer and selling it to raise funds with the idea of repurchasing it at a lower price when the funds are no longer needed. In contrast to the "shorting" of Treasury bond futures, sellers of Treasury bonds must pay interest to the lender.

The invoice amount paid for a Treasury bond or note includes accrued interest since the last coupon date. Purchasers of Treasury bonds pay the price plus accrued interest as defined below:

$$\text{Accrued interest} = \frac{n \times \begin{array}{c}\text{annual}\\\text{coupon}\\\text{rate}\end{array} \times \begin{array}{c}\text{face}\\\text{value}\end{array}}{365} \qquad (3\text{--}4)$$

where n = the number of days since the last coupon payment.

Invoice amounts in delivery of securities into futures contracts are also adjusted to account for any accrued interest.

Futures Contract Characteristics. Treasury bond futures call for delivery of Treasury bonds with $100,000 face value at any time during the delivery period. These bonds must have a maturity date or call date no sooner than 15 years from the delivery date. There are always several bonds acceptable for delivery. For example, any bond maturing or callable after September 1999 would be acceptable for delivery into the September 1984 futures contract. Treasury note futures are also based on $100,000 face value per contract. Deliverable notes are those maturing no less than 6½ years and no more than 10 years from the delivery date.

Price quotations in the Treasury bond futures market are based

---

EXHIBIT 3–11
Quotations for Financial Futures on
Long-Term Securities—August 1, 1984

```
TREASURY BONDS (CBT) – $100,000; pts. 32nds of 100%
Sept      64-09  65-14  64-09  64-27  +   11  12.958  −  .070  130,642
Dec       63-21  64-26  63-21  64-07  +   11  13.085  −  .071   23,308
Mar85     63-06  64-10  63-06  63-24  +   11  13.182  −  .071    6,538
June      62-29  64-00  62-29  63-12  +   11  13.260  −  .072    5,354
Sept      62-28  63-20  62-28  63-02  +   11  13.326  −  .073    5,173
Dec       62-05  63-11  62-05  62-26  +   11  13.379  −  .073    5,574
Mar86     63-01  63-05  62-19  62-19  +   11  13.425  −  .074    4,961
June      62-15  62-30  62-13  62-13  +   11  13.466  −  .074    4,787
Sept       ....   ....   ....  62-08  +   11  13.499  −  .075      866
Dec       62-10  62-21  62-04  62-04  +  .11  13.526  −  .075       86
Mar        ....   ....   ....  62-01  +   11  13.547  −  .075       10
     Est vol 200,000; vol Tues 130,643; op int 192,299, +4,664.
TREASURY NOTES (CBT) – $100,000; pts. 32nds of 100%
Sept      75-06  76-03  75-06  75-22  +   12  12.289  −  .081   29,926
Dec       74-21  75-16  74-21  75-03  +   10  12,417  −  .067    6,178
Mar85     74-27  74-30  74-16  74-19  +   10  12.525  −  .068      353
June       ....   ....   ....  74-01  +   10  12.648  −  .069        3
     Est vol 10,000; vol Tues 6,097; open int 36,460, +466.

GNMA 8% (CBT) – $100,000 prncpl; pts. 32nds. of 100%
Sept      65-31  66-23  65-31  66-13  +    9  13.981  −  .068   10,795
Dec       65-06  65-23  65-06  65-14  +   11  14.218  −  .085    4,700
Mar85     64-15  63-20  64-15  64-16  +   12  14.452  −  .095    1,739
June      63-24  63-28  63-24  63-24  +   12  14.643  −  .096      455
Sept       ....   ....   ....  63-06  +   12  14.788  −  .098      178
Dec        ....   ....   ....  62-24  +   12  14.903  −  .099      348
Mar86      ....   ....   ....  62-13  +   12  14.993  −  .100      352
June       ....   ....   ....  62-05  +   12  15.060  −  .100      515
     Est vol 5,500; vol Tues 2,181; open int 19,082, +456.
```

---

on a bond with an 8 percent coupon rate and a 20-year maturity. The actual amount paid or received at delivery will be determined by this price, accrued interest, and a *conversion factor* which adjusts the futures price for the characteristics of the particular bond being delivered. These conversion factors are equal to the ratio of the price of a deliverable bond, assuming an 8 percent yield, to the delivery price of the futures contract. A detailed discussion of conversion factors and the delivery process is contained in Chapters 6 and 15.[7]

The actual invoice price at delivery is determined as a function of the conversion factor applicable to the bonds delivered.

Invoice Amount

$$= \left(\$100,000 \times \begin{matrix} \text{Settlement price} \\ \text{of futures} \end{matrix} \times \begin{matrix} \text{Conversion} \\ \text{factor for} \\ \text{bonds delivered} \end{matrix} \right) \quad (3\text{–}5)$$

+ Accrued interest

Bonds may sell in the cash bond market at prices above or below the converted price of the futures contract (futures price

× conversion factor). The bond that is "cheapest to deliver" (i.e., for which the difference between the invoice price and the market price is the most positive) is the bond that Treasury bond futures traders focus on in making their transaction decisions. As an example we show invoice prices (ignoring accrual interest) for two bonds acceptable for delivery into the September 1983 future.

In Exhibit 3–12 based on July 20, 1983, prices, the bond which is cheapest to deliver at the invoice price is the 7⅝ percent coupon. Both bonds would be delivered at a loss at this point in time. The loss of 1$\frac{3}{32}$ associated with the 7⅝ percent coupon is the lowest.

The same procedure is used in invoicing Treasury note contracts. Here an 8 percent, 10-year note is used as the standard note for exchange futures price quotations. Knowing the "cheapest-to-deliver" Treasury bond or Treasury note at any point in time is critical to constructing trading strategies for Treasury bond futures, speculators and arbitrageurs analyze the cash-futures relative prices using the cheapest-to-deliver bond as the benchmark for the cash market price.

Uses of the Treasury Bond and Treasury Note Futures Markets

Potential participants in these markets include any economic units that are exposed to the risk of short-term fluctuations in interest rates and wish to reduce that risk. Participants also include investors who are looking to profit from shifts in long-term rates. In reality, futures traders are limited to those institutions or individuals with sufficient capital to absorb the risk of futures price volatility, given the minimum contract size of $100,000. Other limiting factors are the legal constraints facing a particular financial institution with interest rate exposure. Alternative investment strategies are available to manage the risk of interest rate volatility. These strategies are always considered as competing options to use of the futures market.

Another factor influencing participation is the trading or investment horizon of the participant. Government security dealers, arbitrageurs, and speculators are very short-term oriented in their trading strategies. They are, therefore, the groups most attracted to the fixed-income futures markets because of their cheap entry and exit costs, liquidity, and rapid response to financial news. A large percentage of the sales volume in these markets comes from these three groups. Their domination of these futures markets also stems from the fact that they tend to be very knowledgeable about the cash and futures markets in these long-term instruments. Dealers and speculators or arbitrageurs typically specialize in a particu-

EXHIBIT 3-12
Comparison of Invoice Prices of Deliverable Treasury Bonds

Bond	(1) Price	(2) Time to First Call‡	(3) Conversion Factor	(4) Invoice Price*	(4) − (1)
7⅞ 2002–07 February†	71¹⁴/₃₂	18 years, 8 months	.9641	70¹¹/₃₂	− 1³/₃₂
7⅞ 2002–07 November	73¹⁰/₃₂	19 years, 5 months	.9878	72³/₃₂	− 1⁷/₃₂

Invoice price* = Futures settlement × Conversion factor price

As of July 20, 1983   72.969 × .9641 = 70.344
(Future = September 1983)   72.969 × .9878 = 72.079

* Ignores accrued interest differences.
† Cheapest to deliver—delivery occurs at loss of 1³/₃₂ versus loss of 1⁷/₃₂ with other bond.
‡ The time to first call is rounded to the nearest quarter in determining the conversion factor.

lar type of security and quickly develop considerable expertise from the rigors of surviving the short-term trading process.

Another group of participants are managers of portfolios, holding either intermediate or long bonds, and issuers of these bonds. Intermediate-term bank lenders and borrowers also have an interest in using these futures markets. Bond portfolio managers may have a mix of corporate, U.S. agency, and Treasury bonds in their holdings. They may also be the holders of tax-exempt (municipal) fund portfolios. These fixed-income portfolio managers usually have a set of investment horizons extending anywhere from one month to as long as 10 years over which they are concerned with performance. Treasury bond or Treasury note futures are of value to these portfolio managers as tools for reducing the sensitivity of the market value of their portfolios to shifts in the long end of the yield curve.

For example, a bond portfolio manager with a portfolio that has an average maturity of 10 years may wish to shorten the maturity of the portfolio based on an expectation of a rise in short-term rates relative to long-term rates. Normally, he or she would do this by selling some bonds with intermediate maturities and buying some short-term securities. In the process, a switch would be made from higher to lower yielding securities (assuming an upward sloping yield curve). If, instead, Treasury note futures were sold, losses to the portfolio caused by a rise in rates would be partially offset by profits on the futures position. The profits on the futures hedge could be thought of as a reduction in the cost basis of the intermediate bonds.

The *cross-hedge* is used for introducing a short futures position into a portfolio consisting of securities that are not acceptable for delivery into the future. The effect of selling Treasury bond futures continuously against such a bond portfolio would be to reduce the volatility of its market value over time without disturbing the income flow from coupon interest. Capital changes would still occur to the extent the securities in the portfolio changed in value independently of the Treasury bond future.

Treasury bond and Treasury note futures can also be purchased as temporary or permanent substitutes for fixed-income securities as a means to alter the maturity of a portfolio. If a lengthening of maturity is desirable because of prospects for downward yield curve shifts, one could buy Treasury bond futures instead of long maturity bonds. After the rate drop, one could then either accept delivery of the Treasury bonds at the price set in the futures contract or sell the Treasury bond futures at a profit. This profit plus the interest earned on the cash that would have been invested in long-term bonds would make up for the higher price that would be paid for the bonds acquired as a permanent part of the portfolio. Should the yield curve shift upward instead of in the anticipated direction, the futures position can be closed out quickly for a limited loss.

Certain investors may wish to continuously use Treasury bond or Treasury note futures as a substitute for government bonds. The additional risk of this strategy would be the assumption of basis risk. The tax status of the portfolio would be affected, because 60 percent of the profits or losses from futures trades are treated as long term for tax purposes. This would be an advantage for the taxable portfolio if coupon income represented, on average, more than 40 percent of the realized return. On the other hand, only 40 percent of realized losses on futures could be used to offset realized gains.

Issuers of liabilities may find the sale of Treasury bond and Treasury note futures attractive to reduce the impact of rising borrowing costs over the period during which the debt issue is being evaluated and executed. For example, a corporate or municipal treasurer expecting to issue bonds in six months time can sell Treasury bond futures calling for delivery in at least six months. In this way, he or she will be partially protected from the additional cost of unanticipated upward interest rate swings.

A similar opportunity to reduce losses associated with unanticipated upward shifts in the yield curve would exist for banks or finance companies managing term loan positions. Here the Treasury note future is most similar to the position being hedged. However, the choice between a Treasury note or Treasury bond future will also depend on the liquidity of each futures market. A crosshedger usually prefers to avoid delivery and closes out the positions in the futures market at a later date.

It should be noted that the opportunity to use financial futures to hedge bond portfolios tends to be most attractive when the future direction of rate changes is very uncertain to the investor or when the investor feels a rate rise is imminent but cannot liquidate bonds in the portfolio for tax or other reasons. In normal circumstances, a bond manager would simply reduce the maturity of the portfolio when rates are expected to rise more than the rate implied in the yield curve.

GNMA CDR Futures

The GNMA CDR futures contract was the first financial instrument future traded when it was offered by the Chicago Board of Trade in October 1975. Since 1980, the volume of trading in this future has dropped from an annual volume of about 2 million contracts sold, or roughly 7,000 contracts per day to under 1,000 contracts per day. There has always been an active forward market in GNMA pass-through certificates among mortgage bankers and holders of mortgage securities. Terms in this forward market are not standard and no performance guarantee is made. Thus, the shift to futures trading was easy and had the advantage of greater liquidity and more contract integrity, given the guarantee of the clearing corporation in the futures market.

GNMA CDR futures are more complex than other financial instrument futures because of the lack of familiarity most people have with GNMA securities themselves and also because the delivery instrument, a collateralized depository receipt, a CDR, is one step removed from the actual GNMA security. Let us begin our study of GNMA futures with a discussion of the characteristics of mortgage pass-through securities.

Mortgage Pass-Through Certificates. A pass-through certificate consists of a share in a pool or portfolio of mortgage loans.[8] These shares are often called participation certificates. Mortgage originators, usually mortgage bankers or thrift institutions, assemble individual mortgages in a pool and turn the title over to a trustee. The originators continue to service (collect payments on) the loans, but in effect, they have sold the mortgages to the holders of the mortgage pass-through certificates. The servicer monitors the properties involved, helps keep track of payments and prepayments, and carries out the pass-through of the mortgage income to holders of the certificates.

GNMA pass-through securities are different from U.S. Treasury bonds in their method of interest and principal repayment. GNMAs pass through principal and interest to the holder on a monthly basis. Most other government, agency, and corporate bonds pay interest semiannually and repay the principal amount of the bond on its maturity date. The mortgage pass-through securities pay an income return quoted in terms of a coupon rate that is based on the mortgage rates in the underlying pool. Differences between the mortgage rate and the GNMA coupon rate are allocated to servicing the mortgage. Unlike the cash flows associated with bonds, in which the principal is generally not repaid until maturity, mortgage securities include prepayment of principal in their periodic payments. This means there exists an opportunity to reinvest principal value over the life of the security and the associated risk of changing interest rates at which the principal can be reinvested.

This opportunity to reinvest principal has advantages and disadvantages to holders of GNMA securities. On the plus side, cash flows are more evenly distributed throughout the life of the security, making them attractive to investors preferring an annuity-like investment. The disadvantage is that the actual yield earned may differ considerably from the promised yield based on prices when the securities are purchased, because investment income and prepayment of principal will be reinvested at whatever rate of return is available when the cash flows occur. Further, gains on amortized or prepaid principal are usually treated as ordinary income unlike the case of bonds in which gains are treated as capital income. If a security was purchased at a premium, the investor would experience a loss on principal prepaid before twelve years.

Mortgages in the Pool and Maturity. The characteristics of the mortgages in the pool backing the pass-through certificate are important factors in determining the actual cash flows to investors. Even though the mortgages in a particular pool may all be the same stated maturity, say 30 years, the actual life of the pass-through certificate will depend on the rate at which the loans are repaid. This can occur at any time prior to maturity for a particular mortgage. Thus, mortgage pass-throughs have an uncertain life that will depend on the characteristics of the underlying mortgages. Delinquencies and defaults will also affect the life and payment levels of any pass-through certificates not guaranteed by the U.S. government.

GNMAs have yields and prices quoted based on an average 12-year prepayment and 30-year mortgage term. As mentioned above, prepayment experience will vary from pool to pool and will depend on the characteristics of mortgages in the pool.

1. The coupon rates of securities.
2. The number of mortgages in a pool.
3. The number of subsidized loans in a pool.
4. The geographical characteristics of the mortgages.
5. The type of mortgage—graduated payment versus fixed payment.

Generally, the higher the mortgage rate of the underlying securities, the greater the risk of prepayment. Prepayments also tend to increase when current mortgage rates drop significantly below those of the securities in the GNMA pool. The smaller the face value of the mortgages and the larger the number of these in a pool, the more predictable is the pool life. Prepayment experience also differs across regions, depending on the mobility of the population and housing market in a particular area.

GNMA Issuers and Certificate Characteristics. The Government National Mortgage Association is the primary guarantor of mortgage pass-through certificates representing more than 75 percent of the outstanding certificates. These securities are the basis for delivery in the futures contract. GNMA was created in 1968 by an act of Congress and charged with responsibility of providing federal support to the mortgage market. In 1970, GNMA initiated the mortgage-backed securities program. Through this program, mortgage lenders who are authorized to make Federal Housing Administration (FHA) and Veterans Administration (VA) loans can pool a minimum of $1 million of FHA and VA loans with an approved custodian bank. The custodian bank certifies to GNMA that all mortgages in the pool are properly executed and calculates the face amount of the combined mortgage balances. Upon receipt of this certification, GNMA gives its approval for the mortgage lender to issue a GNMA pass-through security for a value equal to the mortgage balance of the collateralized loans.

A large amount of GNMA securities have been issued since the program began in 1970. At the end of 1983, about $140 billion in GNMAs were outstanding as compared to only $80 billion in 1980. This represents almost 10 percent of all mortgage debts outstanding. The increasing reluctance of thrift institutions to hold the long-term mortgages they originate has contributed to the growth of the secondary market in mortgage securities and in GNMA pass-throughs in particular. Volume of the GNMA's transferred from one investor to another in the secondary market has been growing as well. (Exhibits 3–13 and 3–14.)

These trends reflect the shift of the primary holders of mortgage securities away from banking institutions and toward institutions with longer-term liabilities such as pension funds and insurance companies.

Other issuers of mortgage pass-through certificates, including other government-sponsored agencies and private financial institutions, are becoming a larger part of the mortgage backed security market. All mortgages in GNMA pools are FHA insured or VA guaranteed. They have double protection: government insurance plus the GNMA guarantee. Prepayment risk rather than default risk is the only uncertainty facing GNMA holders. Each pool is at least $1 million in size with minimum denomination for the

EXHIBIT 3–13
GNMAs Issued ($ billion)

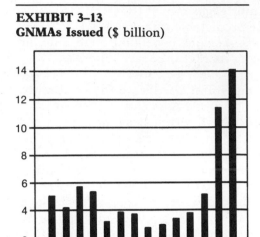

Source: Chicago Board of Trade, *GNMA II Futures,* and Government National Mortgage Association.

certificates of $25,000. Usually, a pool consists of 50 or fewer mortgages from a single originator and is geographically homogenous.

The actual delivery instrument in the GNMA futures is a CDR-collaterialized delivery receipt. This is a document prepared and signed by a bank certifying that it has received on deposit the equivalent of $100,000 principal balance GNMA 8 percent certificates. These CDRs pay a fixed rate of interest and are redeemable for GNMAs. CDRs can be acquired by those wishing to deliver into a GNMA futures contract by originating a new CDR or by purchasing one from another originator. All CDRs must be registered with the Chicago Board of Trade. Time must be allowed for the approval process when a new CDR is originated.

Futures Contract Characteristics. The GNMA CDR futures contract is traded at the Chicago Board of Trade. The prices quoted are based on $100,000 of principal balance with an 8 percent coupon. As with Treasury bond and Treasury note futures, GNMA pools can be delivered at other coupon rates via adjustment of the principal balance by a conversion factor. For the GNMA CDR contract, the invoice amount is fixed, and the principal balance of the GNMAs backing the CDRs is adjusted via a conversion factor.

The GNMA CDR has developed a market itself. High coupon GNMAs (when available) have been the cheapest to deliver into

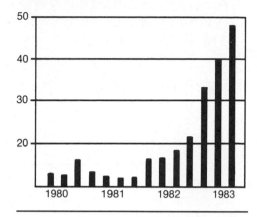

EXHIBIT 3–14
GNMAs Transferred in Secondary
Market ($ billion)

Source: Chicago Board of Trade, *GNMA II Futures,* and Government National Mortgage Association.

the GNMA CDR contract. Thus, the GNMA CDR futures prices have tended to be based on prices of higher coupon GNMAs. In practice, these GNMAs are very short in maturity, because borrowers repay the high coupon mortgages as quickly as possible when interest rates drop. The relationship between the price of new issues of GNMAs and this GNMA CDR future has been unstable.

Since the drop in interest rates in the summer of 1982, peculiarities in the delivery method of this GNMA future have reduced its effectiveness as a hedge for "current production" GNMA securities. Instead, the GNMA futures have become a vehicle for hedging or speculating in price changes of GNMA CDRs and/or high coupon GNMA certificates. As a result, the Chicago Board of Trade has introduced a new GNMA future in an attempt to fulfill the need that the CDR future was originally intended to serve.

The new GNMA future, called GNMA II, calls for direct delivery of actual GNMA certificates (not CDRs). The acceptable GNMAs must have a coupon rate at or below the coupon rate which was in effect on new GNMAs issued during the period six months prior to the delivery date. In addition, there is a ceiling on the invoice price (conversion factor × principal amount) of $102,500. This means that the GNMA II futures price will reflect GNMA certificates that meet these criteria.

The advantage of this new contract is a relationship between currently issued GNMAs and GNMA II futures prices that should be more stable and predictable than was the case with the GNMA CDR contract. The hope of the exchange is that the GNMA II futures contract will be a superior hedging tool and will be easier to arbitrage than the GNMA CDR futures. As of December 1984 this goal has not been achieved since speculators continue to prefer trading the GNMA/CDR contract.

Use of the GNMA Futures Market. GNMA futures provide a similar function for the mortgage market as Treasury bond futures do for the corporate and government bond market. The GNMA certificate is considered to be a "bellweather" secondary market mortgage security with a price that is highly correlated with other mortgage-backed securities. Thus, GNMA futures can be used by issuers, dealers, and holders of mortgages to hedge the risk of changing mortgage rates over the period in which they have a position or forward commitment in a mortgage security. In addition, investors who wish to speculate on mortgage rates and arbitrageurs who attempt to profit from price differentials in two related mortgage markets would have a use of GNMA futures.

Some highlights of hedging and speculative strategies with GNMA futures are covered here. More detail on the use of futures in mortgage finance is covered in Chapter 12. Mortgage bankers originated the forward market in GNMA certificates that laid the groundwork for the futures market. They can use GNMA futures to attempt to lock in a price for the sale of mortgages they will be issuing upon future completion of a financed construction project. The hedging of the risk of increases in mortgage rates over the construction periods allows a mortgage banker to secure the short-term commercial bank financing needed to underwrite the real estate development project.

Dealers in the secondary market for GNMAs also can sell GNMA futures to hedge their existing inventory in order to reduce losses of rising rates. They may also wish to purchase GNMA futures as an anticipatory hedge against mortgage rate reductions not already reflected in futures prices. A dealer can acquire inventory for sale to pension funds or other institutions over a future period of high anticipated GNMA demand. He or she can do so by purchasing GNMA futures calling for delivery on a date closest to the point at which he or she wishes to increase inventory holdings.

Several different types of financial institutions are purchasers or holders of mortgage-backed securities or mortgages. These include pension funds, bank trust departments, thrift institutions, and commercial banks. Any of these mortgage holders can use GNMA futures as protection against a drop in the value of their mortgage holdings from rising mortgage rates. The sale of GNMA futures with a contract value equivalent to the mortgage holding (after adjustments for differing maturities) will effectively convert the long-term holdings into a fully hedged position with a return close to that short-term interest rate. Additional profits and losses may occur because of changes in the relative prices of the particular mortgages held and those on which the GNMA futures price are based.

By selling varying amounts of GNMA futures against the mortgage holdings, one can easily change the maturity of the hedged position. This allows mortgage holders to purchase mortgage securities at maturities with the most attractive relative prices, and then use futures to adjust the maturity risk exposure to desired levels.

The availability of GNMA futures also benefits mortgage portfolio managers by permitting them to reduce the risk of increasing rates without shifting funds directly out of long-term and into short-term securities. This shift is often costly in terms of trading costs and potentially disadvantageous tax consequences. Moreover, large cash flow additions or withdrawals in the mortgage position can be managed more efficiently with GNMA futures. A sale of futures can help secure a selling price for mortgage securities that will be converted into cash for a withdrawal of funds from the portfolio.

Because the GNMA CDR futures prices have recently had a weak correlation with newly issued GNMAs, many mortgage dealers and issuers have used either the GNMA forward market or the Treasury bond and note futures markets as hedging vehicles. The latter strategy involves a cross-hedge but can be effective as long as there is sufficient correlation between Treasury security rates and mortgage rates. It is too early to tell whether the new GNMA II contract will be as successful as the GNMA CDR once was to financial institutions involved in the mortgage market.

Speculation and arbitrage are other strategies that involve the trading of GNMA futures. Speculators use both GNMA contracts to attempt to profit from forecasted changes in mortgage rates. Some traders buy and sell the spread between GNMA futures and Treasury bond futures, between GNMA and Treasury bill futures, and between futures prices in different delivery months. These spread relationships are volatile and can be analyzed in terms of the fundamental factors affecting both sides of the spread. Normally the spread can be traded with less risk exposure than an outright position in the future itself.

Arbitrageurs will attempt to exploit price differentials between equivalent positions in two markets. The basic arbitrage relationship depends on the factors in the valuation of the future and deliverable security covered in Chapters 5 and 6. With respect to GNMA futures, an arbitrageur will buy (sell) the cheapest-to-delivery GNMA or GNMA CDR and sell (buy) the GNMA future when the future is overvalued (undervalued) relative to the cash market GNMA securities. Usually, the arbitrageur finances his or her position by borrowing funds using a long cash market position as collateral; if the trade involves the sale of cash and purchase of the future, the arbitrageur will borrow the cash market GNMA securities and hope to repay them with GNMAs purchased at a cheaper price via the GNMA futures contract.

SUMMARY

Futures on fixed-income securities are widely used as instruments for speculating on and hedging price volatility associated with interest rate changes. Contracts on short-term securities include Treasury bill futures, Certificates of Deposit futures, and Eurodollar futures. Futures on long-term securities include U.S. Treasury bonds, U.S. Treasury notes, GNMA CDR, and GNMA II contracts. While each of these futures contracts differs in certain aspects, similar characteristics and uses are evident.

All the financial futures contracts are traded in open outcry exchanges, require variation margin, and face limits on daily price movements. In addition, while the specifics of delivery differ among contracts, actual delivery of the underlying cash securities (or in the case of Eurodollars futures the cash equivalent) ensures a close association between the price movements of the futures contract and the price movements of the underlying cash instrument. As a result of this close relationship, each market permits the trader to hedge some of the price uncertainty of fixed income securities, to arbitrage price differentials between cash and futures, and to speculate on interest rate changes.

NOTES

[1] Brief mention should be made of the new short-term financial futures on UK three-month time deposits which are traded on the LIFFE. These are designed to provide an opportunity for arbitrage, speculation, and hedging of interest rate movements and relationships in the UK. Uses of the UK deposit futures market

would be similar to those for Treasury bill and CD futures. These contracts would be specifically designed for those institutions that participate in the London money market either in a borrowing or lending capacity. These futures can also serve as a vehicle for UK-US interest rate arbitrage between spot, forward, and futures markets. The three-month Sterling Deposit futures call for delivery of £250,000. The settlement price is based on the average of rate quotes of a random sample of designated banks with delivery occurring on the second Wednesday of the delivery month.

[2] For a more detailed example of such a hedge, see *Inside Eurodollar Futures* (Chicago, Ill.: International Monetary Market, 1981).

[3] The enabling legislation was passed in late June 1983.

[4] *Treasury Bulletin*, U.S. Government Department of Treasury, Winter, 1984.

[5] *Treasury Bulletin*, U.S. Government Department of Treasury, Winter, 1984.

[6] There are also a few bank dealers in Treasury securities that do not carry inventories but rather execute transactions for a fee.

[7] For a full exposition of delivery details for all financial futures covered in this chapter, see *Financial Futures: The Delivery Process in Brief*, published by the Chicago Board of Trade.

[8] For a comprehensive survey of mortgage pass-throughs, see Dexter Senft, "GNMA Pass-Through Securities," in *Fixed Income Securities*, ed. F. M. Fabozzi and I. M. Pollack (Homewood, Ill.: Dow Jones-Irwin, 1983).

SELECTED REFERENCES

Bacon, P. W., and R. Williams. "Interest Rate Futures: New Tool for the Financial Manager." *Financial Management* 5 Spring 1976, pp. 32–38.

Capozza, D. R., and B. Cornell. "Treasury Bill Pricing in the Spot and Futures Markets." *Review of Economics and Statistics* 61 November 1979, pp. 513–20.

Ederington, L. H. "The Hedging Performance of the New Futures Markets." *Journal of Finance* 34 March 1979, pp. 157–70.

Franckle, C. T. "The Hedging Performance of the New Futures Markets: Comment." *Journal of Finance* December 1980, pp. 1273–79.

Gay, G. D., and R. W. Kolb. "The Management of Interest Rate Risk." *Journal of Portfolio Management* 9 Winter 1983, pp. 65–70.

Hill, J., and T. Schneeweis. "Risk Reduction Potential of Financial Futures for Corporate Bond Positions." In *Interest Rate Futures: Concepts and Issues*, eds. G. D. Gay and R. W. Kolb. Richmond, Va.: Robert F. Dame, 1982.

Kolb, R. W. *Interest Rate Futures: A Comprehensive Introduction*. Richmond, Va.: Robert F. Dame, Inc., 1982.

Kolb, R. W., and R. Chiang. "Improving Hedging Performance Using Interest Rate Futures." *Financial Management* 10 Winter 1981, pp. 72–79.

Lang, R. W., and R. H. Rasche. "A Comparison of Yields on Futures Contracts and Implied Forward Rates." *Federal Reserve Bank of St. Louis Review*, December 1978, pp. 21–30.

McEnally, R. W., and M. L. Rice. "Hedging Possibilities in the Flotation of Debt Securities." *Financial Management* 8 Winter 1979, pp. 12–18.

Merrick, J., and S. Figlewski, "An Introduction to Financial Futures." *Occasional Papers in Business and Finance,* Salomon Brothers Center for the Study of Financial Institutions, 1984, No. 6.

Poole, W. "Using T Bill Futures to Gauge Interest Rate Expectations." *Federal Reserve Bank of San Francisco Economic Review,* Spring 1978, pp. 7–19.

Puglisi, D. J. "Is the Futures Market for Treasury Bills Efficient?" *The Journal of Portfolio Management,* Winter 1978, pp. 64–67.

Rendleman, R. J., Jr., and C. E. Carabini. "The Efficiency of the Treasury Bill Futures Market." *The Journal of Finance* 34 September 1979, pp. 895–914.

Trainer, Francis H. "The Uses of Treasury Bond Futures in Fixed-Income Analysis." *Financial Analysts Journal,* January–February 1983, pp. 27–34.

Futures on Stock Indexes

The year 1982 marked two important financial developments: the beginning of a major bull market in equities and the successful introduction of futures contracts on stock indexes. The first equity futures contract based on the Value Line Stock Index began trading on February 24, 1982, at the Kansas City Board of Trade. Soon to follow in April of that year were futures contracts on the Standard & Poors 500 index, traded at the Chicago Mercantile Exchange. Futures contracts on the NYSE Composite Index, commenced trading in September of 1983 at the New York Futures Exchange, a unit of the NYSE. The entry of the NYSE, the largest and most established stock exchange, into the futures business was especially significant. The establishment of a stock index futures market in New York City within easy access of the major stock exchanges, investment banking houses, brokerage firms, and investment advisors provided the investment industry with a showcase from which they could view firsthand the operations of a futures market. The latest entry is futures on the Major Market Index (MMI) which began trading in July of 1984 at the Chicago Board of Trade. This future is based on an index which is very similar in construction to the Dow Jones Industrial Average. The next stock index futures offerings are likely to be contracts on indexes of stocks traded over the counter. Since the summer of 1982, volume in stock index futures has quickly grown (Exhibit 4–1) to a point where it approximates and often exceeds the volume in equity share value on the NYSE itself.

The S&P 500 futures contract traded at the Chicago Mercantile Exchange has been by far the most successful of the three equity contracts with volume running four to five times that of the NYSE and MMI futures and greatly in excess of that of the Value Line future. All four stock index futures represent unique index portfolios in terms of coverage and weighting. This chapter is devoted to a presentation of the most important features of stock index futures and the indexes on which they are based. An overview of the uses and users of stock index futures markets is also included.

The development of stock index futures markets is particularly significant, because it represents an integration of equity and futures trading. This integration has important implications for both branches of the investment business. Brokerage firms and investment banks have been quick to incorporate equity futures into their market operations. Along with the floor traders at the exchange, they are the most active participants in the markets, using stock futures to hedge their inventories and to conduct arbitrage with their own investment capital. They have helped to bring to

EXHIBIT 4-1
S&P 500 Futures: Daily Volume, April 1982 through March 1985

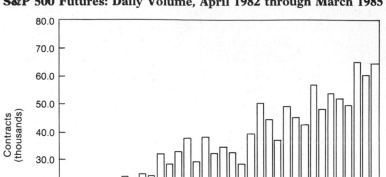

the stock index futures markets the liquidity and pricing efficiency that is so essential for the success of a contract.

Now that the stock futures market has proven itself as a permanent part of the investment scene, other financial institutions and individuals involved in equity management, such as pension funds, pension sponsors, insurance companies, and wealthy investors, are looking at applications of stock index futures that fit into their own investment strategies and objectives. Many existing and potential applications of stock index futures are covered in this and other chapters of this book.

STOCK INDEXES—THE UNDERLYING INSTRUMENT

Stock market indexes are designed to reflect overall movements in a large group of equity securities. The performance of an equity index is important, because it represents the performance of a broadly diversified stock portfolio and gives insight into the returns of an average risk stock in the market. Index performance is also important as a benchmark against which the results of alternative investment strategies can be judged. To be viewed as successful, an investment strategy must demonstrate risk-adjusted performance in excess of a market index over time.[1] Investors who wish to perform in line with the equity market as a whole can try to structure portfolios equivalent to stock indexes.

Stock indexes differ from one another with respect to the range of stocks covered, stock weighting, and index computation. The most widely followed index, the Dow Jones Industrial Average, consists of the stocks of only 30 large companies, weighted by their relative prices, and added together (a divisor is used to incorporate the impact of stock splits).

The range of stocks covered in different indexes can vary considerably. The Dow Jones Industrial Average contains only 30 stocks, while the Value Line and NYSE indexes contain over 1,500 different issues. Indexes differ in composition because of the need to measure the price movements of segments of the overall equity market. These segments range from narrow to broad. Even though returns on indexes are often highly correlated over time, relative index performance can vary sharply over short periods such as a month or quarter.

The weighting of stocks in an index is a very important factor in determining index value. Most stock indexes are either equal-weighted or market value-weighted. The most common weighting scheme is market value weighting, used in both the S&P 500 and NYSE indexes. The prices of each issue included are weighted by the number of shares outstanding divided by the aggregate number of shares outstanding of all stocks in the index. This means that the changes in the index reflect changes in the aggregate equity value of the stocks included in that index. In addition, stock splits do not affect the value of market value-weighted indexes. Mergers or divestitures also should not have an impact as long as all of the old and new companies are included before and after the corporate restructuring.

Finally, the method of averaging influences the index value. Most market value-weighted indexes represent arithmetic averages. The Major Market Index and the Dow Jones Industrial Average are arithmetic averages of stock prices (adjusted for stock splits). Another averaging technique is the use of a geometric mean or the nth root of the product of the individual stock prices, returns, or value relatives. This method of index construction is used in the Value Line Index.

A geometric mean index differs from an arithmetic mean index if there are changes over time in the value of items making up the index. In terms of percentage changes in value, an index based on a geometric mean will increase and decrease more slowly than one based on an arithmetic mean. This is illustrated in Exhibit 4–2 which shows the return of an index consisting of two stocks that initially have the same price. The arithmetic index increases 10 percent versus 9.5 percent for the geometric index in the first period. In the second period of declining prices, the geometric

---

EXHIBIT 4–2
Comparison of Geometric and Arithmetic Mean Indexes

Stock	Period 0	Period 1	Period 2
A	100	120	100
B	100	100	110
Index value			
Arithmetic	100	110	105
Geometric	100	109.5	104.88
Return			
Arithmetic		10.0%	−4.5 %
Geometric		9.5%	−4.2 %

---

index registers a −4.2 percent return compared to −4.5 percent for the arithmetic index.

The S&P 500 Index is the key index in terms of institutional investment management. Introduced in the 1930s, this index is broad in its coverage and weights stocks by aggregate market value. It includes most of the largest industrial service, utility, and transportation companies in the U.S. Percentage increases in the index represent equivalent percentage increases in the aggregate market value of the stocks included. Companies such as IBM, AT&T, Exxon, and General Motors, have large weights in the index as compared to small capitalization companies.

Since stock prices change daily, the market value weights also automatically change over time. The aggregate market value is easy to calculate as the sum of the price of each of the 500 stocks multiplied by the number of the shares outstanding. Standard & Poor's provides current information on the timing of dividends and weighting for all the stocks in the index. *The NYSE Index* is also market-value weighted but is broader than the S&P 500, including all stocks listed on the NYSE. The number of exchange-listed stocks varies over time but is around 1,700. The S&P 500 represents about 75 percent of the value of NYSE stocks.

The success of futures on the S&P 500 index is not surprising. The S&P 500 Index is the most important index for investment managers of institutional investment funds. The Dow Jones Industrial Average is the index given more attention by the media. However, because of the narrow coverage of the Dow Jones Industrial Average of only 30 "blue-chip" companies, this index is too narrow to serve as an indicator of the performance of the overall equity market.

Pension funds and other institutional investors often judge the performance of their money managers relative to a benchmark index. The returns of this benchmark index should represent returns of an unmanaged or naive investment strategy. This strategy can best be applied to those stocks in the equity market that have sufficient volume to facilitate trading by holders of large pools of funds. If a "managed" stock portfolio does not consistently perform over long periods above such an index (on a risk-adjusted basis), one may choose the alternative of directly investing the funds in a portfolio closely resembling an index. This type of portfolio is often called an index fund and is designed to mirror the performance of an index.

Stock brokers and dealers are also concerned with movements in the overall equity market, because their inventories consist of holdings in a wide range of stocks that the customers have traded or may wish to trade. Stock index futures contracts can be valuable to these institutions because these futures can serve as hedges to reduce the risk of value changes in the stock inventory position. Here, also, a broadly based index that comes closest to reflecting the combined inventory positions of the broker or dealer firm is the most suitable.

Finally, arbitrageurs who attempt to profit on the mispricing of futures relative to their underlying instrument tend to prefer the S&P 500 to the NYSE futures. These arbitrageurs do not hold portfolios of all 500 or all 1,700 NYSE stocks when the index becomes "cheap" relative to the future. Instead, they try to identify portfolios of roughly 30 to 60 stocks that will track most closely in value to the index. Because the S&P 500 represents less than one third of the issues in the NYSE, it is often easier to successfully identify it as "arbitrage portfolio" based on the S&P 500 and successfully carry out such arbitrage.

The Value Line Index is based on an equal-weighted return average of the approximately 1,500 stocks covered by the Value Line Investment Services. Compared to the other indexes on which futures are traded, the equal-weighting of the Value Line Index results in a relatively larger weighting for the returns of smaller capitalization companies. The method used to average the returns is also unique: the calculation is based on a geometric rather than arithmetic average. This method of averaging tends to reduce the volatility of the index. The greater weight given to smaller companies in this index contributes to higher volatility levels, but the effect of this is somewhat offset by the method of index construction.

The *Major Market Index* is a price-weighted index of 20 blue-chip stocks. It was first constructed as a basis for an index option that was introduced in September of 1983 by the American Stock

Exchange. This exchange entered an agreement with the Chicago Board of Trade to permit the CBT to use the index as a basis for a financial futures contract.

The index is constructed by adding up the prices of the component stocks and dividing the sum by a number reflecting stock splits, deletions, and additions. Fifteen of the 20 stocks in the MMI are also in the Dow Jones Industrial Average. The total capitalization of the two indexes, based on prices as of the end of July 1984, is very close, implying that the average stock in the MMI is actually larger than that of the Dow Jones. This newest stock index future is particularly suitable for stock and futures arbitrage. Because the index is so narrowly based, arbitrageurs can easily and cheaply construct cash market positions of the stocks included.

The correlations between the indexes on which futures are traded is of importance in seeing the extent to which they move together over time. As with most broad-based equity indexes, the daily percent price changes of these particular indexes are highly correlated with one another, as shown in Exhibits 4–3 and 4–4. The degree to which they move together can be quite variable within short periods, however. It is not uncommon for indexes like the Dow Jones Industrial Average and NYSE to show differences in return of a percent or more in any given month. Exhibits 4–4 and 4–5 include a fifth index, the S&P 100. This index is a subset of the S&P 500. It is the underlying instrument for the most actively traded index options contract.

Futures contracts have also been proposed based on indexes representing particular industries or specialized subgroups of stocks. These "subindex" stock futures call for delivery of cash representing the value of an index of stocks covering a particular industry. In January 1984, the CFTC voted to restrict subindex futures to indexes composed of at least 25 companies, each with a minimum of $75 billion in stock outstanding. The intent of these

---

EXHIBIT 4–3
Correlations of Stock Market Indexes (based on daily percent price changes), January 1978–December 1983

	S&P 500	S&P 100	NYSE	DJIA
S&P 500	1.00			
S&P 100	0.98	1.00		
NYSE	0.99	0.96	1.0	
DJIA	0.95	0.96	0.95	1.0

Source: New York Stock Exchange.

EXHIBIT 4–4
Values of Stock Market Indexes, 1978–1983

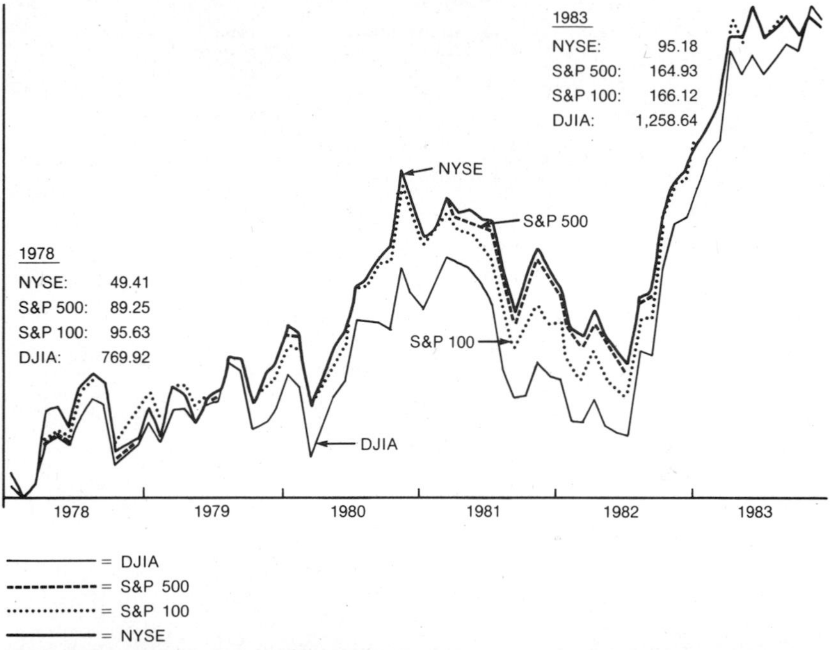

1983	
NYSE:	95.18
S&P 500:	164.93
S&P 100:	166.12
DJIA:	1,258.64

1978	
NYSE:	49.41
S&P 500:	89.25
S&P 100:	95.63
DJIA:	769.92

———— = DJIA
---------- = S&P 500
·············· = S&P 100
———— = NYSE

Source: New York Stock Exchange.

guidelines is to reduce the potential for manipulation of index values by parties with large holdings in particular stocks in the index.

FUTURES CONTRACT CHARACTERISTICS

Futures on stock indexes represent a contractual obligation to have sufficient funds on deposit at delivery to buy or sell the stocks in the index at a predetermined price. This price is the value of the futures contract when the futures position was initiated. The value of stock futures contracts is a multiple of their quoted price. The contract value is 500 times the quoted price except for Major Market Index futures which use a multiplier of 100.

A sample of price quotations for futures and their underlying indexes is shown in Exhibit 4–5. The minimum trading increment is .05 point or $25 (.05 × 500). Other contract specifications are shown in Exhibit 4–6. Unlike most other futures contracts, stock index futures settle in cash rather than in delivery of the stocks

EXHIBIT 4–5
Stock Futures and Index Quotations (August 1, 1984)

S&P 500 FUTURES INDEX (CME) 500 Times Index								
Sept	152.80	155.20	152.65	154.85	+ 2.60	178.15	148.45	30,974
Dec	155.40	157.75	155.40	157.40	+ 2.50	179.20	150.70	2,894
Mar85	158.00	160.00	158.00	159.90	+ 2.50	180.25	153.00	90
June	....	....	....	162.35	+ 2.45	180.70	155.70	9
Sept	....	....	....	164.80	+ 2.40	173.40	158.10	4
Est vol 53,156; vol Tues 44,606; open int 33,971, +904.								
S&P 500 STOCK INDEX (Prelim.)								
	151.68	154.08	150.66	154.08	+ 3.42	....	....	....
MAJOR MARKET INDEX (CBT) $100 Times Index								
Aug	220 7/8	224 3/4	220 7/8	224	+ 3 1/2	217 3/8	214 1/4	4,175
Sept	222 1/4	226 1/4	222 1/4	252 1/4	+ 3 3/8	218 1/2	215 1/2	1,233
Oct	226 5/8	226 3/4	226 1/4	226 3/8	+ 3 1/4	219 1/2	217 5/8	2
Dec	226 1/2	229 1/8	226 1/2	228 1/2	+ 3 1/8	220 3/4	218 1/4	13
Est vol 15,000; vol Tues 10,379; open int 5,423, +173.								
MAJOR MARKET INDEX (Prelim.)								
	219.82	224.56	219.82	224.18	+ 4.36	....	....	....
S&P 100 FUTURES INDEX (CME) 200 Times Index								
Aug	....	....	....	153.45	+ 2.45	152.90	148.00	14
Sept	151.90	154.40	151.90	153.95	+ 2.45	154.40	147.10	964
Oct	....	....	....	154.95	+ 2.45	153.00	151.90	13
Est vol 415; vol Tues 385; open int 991, +132.								
S&P 100 STOCK INDEX (Prelim)								
	151.45	153.61	150.18	153.51	+ 3.33			
NYSE COMPOSITE FUTURES (NYFE) 500 Times Index								
Sept	87.95	89.45	87.90	89.35	+ 1.70	103.10	85.45	5,189
Dec	89.35	90.80	89.35	90.70	+ 1.70	103.55	86.70	1,362
Mar85	90.85	91.95	90.85	92.00	+ 1.65	103.80	88.20	1,130
June	92.30	92.30	92.30	93.30	+ 1.65	105.00	90.00	155
Sept	....	....	....	94.60	+ 1.65	99.75	91.35	82
Est vol 15,141; vol Tues 12,485; open int 7,918, −393.								
NYSE COMPOSITE STOCK INDEX								
	86.70	88.58	86.70	88.58	+ 1.85			
KC VALUE LINE FUTURES (KC) 500 Times Index								
Sept	167.70	170.50	167.60	170.00	+ 3.20	213.50	161.80	3,492
Dec	170.00	173.15	170.00	172.70	+ 3.25	210.00	166.50	285
Mar85	173.40	175.50	173.40	175.25	+ 3.30	182.00	168.10	30
June	....	....	....	177.80	+ 3.35	173.90	172.30	4
Est vol 4,120; vol Tues 2,892; open int 3,811, +64.								
KC VALUE LINE COMPOSITE STOCK INDEX								
	164.68	167.79	164.68	167.78	+ 3.08			

Source: Reprinted by permission of *The Wall Street Journal,* © Dow Jones & Co., 1984.

in the index underlying the futures contract. Cash settlement is carried out by transferring funds into or out of the contract holders margin account in an amount based on the settlement price of the contract. Cash settlement is used because of the cost and logistical problems of buying the component stocks in the index in exactly the right amounts to carry out physical delivery.

Stock index futures have a specific termination time and date at which the final settlement price is set and the futures cease trading. For all stock futures contracts, the time is 4 P.M. (EST), of the last trading day of the contract. The final settlement price is therefore tied to the closing value of the index on the last trading day. All of the stock index futures except the MMI future terminate in the March, June, September, December cycle. There are some differences in the designation of the last trading day during the contract expiration months as shown in Exhibit 4–6.

Cash settlement can be carried out easily, because the losses

EXHIBIT 4-6
Contract Specifications for Stock Index Futures

	S&P 500 Futures	NYSE Futures	Value Line Future	Major Market Futures
Contract size	—	500 times value of index	—	100 times value of index
Delivery months	—	March, June, September, December	—	Next three months plus next month in March, June, September, December cycle
Delivery vehicle	—	Cash settlement based on closing index value on last day of trading		—
Trading hours	—	10 A.M.–4:15 P.M. (EST)	—	9:45 A.M.–4:15 P.M. (EST)
Minimum price change	—	.05 ($25)	—	.125 ($12.50)
Exchange	Chicago Mercantile Exchange	NY Futures Exchange	Kansas City Board of Trade	Chicago Board of Trade
Daily price change limit	None	None	None	None
Last trading day	Third Friday of month	Third Friday of month	Business day before last business day of month	Third Friday of month
Initial (maintenance) margin*				
Speculator	$6,000 (2,500)	$3,500 (1,500)	$6,500 (2,000)	$2,300
Hedger	2,500 (1,500)	1,500 (750)	3,250 (1,625)	500

* Subject to change.

or gains on the futures position have been marked-to-market daily in the variation margin account. This process ensures that funds exist at settlement in the variation margin account in an amount representing the difference between the price paid for the future and the settlement price. Thus, if the settlement price is above the price at which the futures contract was established, funds that have been marked-to-market by the futures sellers will be credited to those with long futures positions. If the settlement price is below the purchase price, funds in the marked-to-market account are credited to those who have sold futures contracts at prices in excess of the settlement price.

For example, assume a June 1985 S&P 500 futures contract was purchased on April 1, 1985 at a price of 183.35. Assume that on the last trading day, the price of the June future is 185.35. The profit of 2 points or $1,000 (500 × 2) would be the balance in the mark-to-market account. These funds would have been made available from debits to the variation margin accounts investors who have sold this contract at prices below 183.35 or investors who had bought at prices above 183.35. The process of marking-to-market is discussed in much greater detail in Chapter 8 of this book.

The four stock index futures contracts currently available cover four different broad market indexes and are each traded on different futures exchanges. Futures on the S&P 500 Index are the most actively traded equity futures contracts with daily volume in the range of 60,000–70,000 contracts (as of March 1985) representing roughly $5–6 billion in underlying market value. This can be compared to the $4.0 billion in value of a 100 million share day on the NYSE, assuming an average share price of $40. S&P 500 futures are traded on the floor of the Chicago Mercantile Exchange. Initial margin on this contract is $6,000 or 6.5 percent of contract value at a futures price of 185 and underlying contract value of $92,500.

The NYSE index futures contract calls for delivery of a market-weighted portfolio of all stocks listed on the NYSE. At the end of March 1985, the June NYSE futures were selling for around 106 points or a value of $53,000. Thus, one NYSE futures contract typically represents just under 60 percent of the value of an S&P 500 futures contract. The initial margin deposit is accordingly smaller than that of the S&P 500 futures—$3,500 versus $6,000. At a contract value of $53,000, this margin represents 6.6 percent of a contract value. The NYSE futures contract is traded at the New York Futures Exchange or NYFE and is the only stock futures contract traded in direct physical and organizational proximity to a stock exchange.

Value Line Index futures are traded at the Kansas City Board of Trade. These futures were the first equity futures contracts to trade, but their volume was quickly overshadowed by the S&P 500 and NYSE futures when they were introduced. At a price of 200 points, one contract represents $100,000 of underlying equity value. The initial margin is $6,500 or 6.5 percent of contract value. Also, the equal-weighting of stocks in the index makes the underlying index and the derivative futures contract more sensitive to the movement of small capitalization stocks.

The newest stock index futures contract, the Major Market Index, has only been trading since July of 1984. It trades at levels of volume and open interest roughly equal to the NYSE future. The MMI index future is smaller in size than the other index futures with a contract value of 100 times the level of the index, or approximately $25,500 as of the end of March 1985. It is also unique in that it commences trading at 9:45 New York time, 15 minutes prior to the opening of the equity market. This provides an early signal of the potential opening level of the Dow Jones Industrial Average.

The MMI futures also have different delivery dates and trading units than the other stock index futures. The contract months include in the next three consecutive months as well as the next month representing the end of a quarterly cycle. For example at the end of March 1985, the MMI future had April, May, June and September delivery contracts trading. This brings their delivery dates in line with the expiration dates of the option contracts on the Major Market Index. The units of trading are eighths of an index point, or $12.50, rather than the 0.05 of an index point, or $25, of the other stock index futures contracts. The initial margin is $2300 or roughly 9% of the underlying share value.

USES OF STOCK INDEX FUTURES MARKETS

A wide range of strategies is possible with stock index futures. The groups to whom the market offers the most attractive possibilities are investors and financial institutions with a broad capital base and with exposure to equity securities either as investors, dealers, or underwriters. In Part 2 of this book, chapters are devoted specifically to the ways in which financial futures can be used in investment strategies. Here, we provide an overview of current and potential applications of stock index futures.

Basically, stock index futures provide a means of adjusting, acquiring, or eliminating exposure to the fluctuations in value of overall stock market. These futures can be an extremely flexible risk management tool because of their liquidity and low transaction costs. Futures can also serve as short-term substitutes for positions in the stock index itself. Stock index futures strategies may be preferable to other means of adjusting equity exposure because of cheaper transaction costs, attractive prices available on the futures contract, ease of adjusting positions (liquidity), or the difficulty of moving funds quickly and on a large scale into and out of particular stocks. The different tax treatment of gains and losses on stock index futures versus stock portfolios may also be attractive to some investors. In some situations, investing in equities via stock index funds or index futures may be more cost-effective than purchasing the expertise to acquire particular "undervalued" stocks.

Adjusting Equity Exposure

Investors and institutions who wish to increase or decrease their position in stocks relative to bonds and cash can do so via stock index futures. For instance, if a portfolio manager wishes to increase the stock portion of a portfolio by 5 percent, this can be done quickly and cheaply by purchasing stock index futures contracts with a market value equal to 5 percent of their aggregate portfolio. The portfolio manager can subsequently acquire the stocks he or she wishes to hold in the portfolio without missing the profits of an increase in the general level of stock prices. As stocks are purchased, the futures position can be closed out to maintain the desired exposure to stock market moves.

An obvious example of such an application is the beginning of the most recent bull market in stocks in August 1982. An institution, attempting to increase its equity exposure (reduce cash), could have easily missed the 20 percent gain that occurred in the first month of the bull market. Purchases of stock index futures would have been an effective means of taking advantage of such a rapidly moving market. At times, one may want to increase or reduce exposure to equity market movements on a very temporary basis with the possibility of easy reversal. Stock index futures can be a much more efficient and cost-effective means of implementing short-term or tactical market-timing moves than moving into and out of actual stock issues.

Creating Synthetic Index Fund Portfolios

Futures can be used to create a portfolio that has cash flow characteristics similar to an index fund portfolio. Individual or institutional investors may wish to hold a portfolio that provides the returns very similar to those of a particular market index. These investors may find it expensive to acquire a portfolio as broadly diversified as the NYSE or S&P 500, but may wish to derive the diversification advantages of such a portfolio.

Managing index fund portfolios involves considerable oversight in terms of maintaining the correct weights as prices change and reinvesting any dividends that are received. Index futures can provide a means of cheaper access to such a portfolio. The commissions associated with stock index futures are only a fraction of those acquiring the stocks themselves.

This strategy involves purchasing stock index futures with a contract value equal to the desired value of the index fund. Funds not used for margin purposes are invested in very low-risk, liquid, short-term securities such as Treasury bills or Eurodollars. The index fund manager can be selective in choosing a time to purchase the stock index futures. When the futures are undervalued compared to the cash value of the index and dividends on the index, the manager can possibly lock in a return exceeding the index for the period to expiration of the future. This incremental return is based on the percentage that the contract is undervalued when it is purchased, the percentage (if any) it is overvalued when sold, and the commission savings on the futures relative to acquiring the index itself.

Hedging Stock Portfolios

The distinction between using stock futures to adjust equity exposure and hedging stock market risk with stock futures is not clear cut. Hedging has been used to describe a defensive strategy in which one wishes to insulate a portfolio (or position) from adverse market movements. An adjustment of equity exposure, alternatively, could be motivated by a desire to capitalize on a positive market movement, to insulate oneself from stock market declines, or to modify the beta or market risk of a portfolio.

The objective of hedging with stock index futures would be to reduce or eliminate the sensitivity of an equity portfolio to changes in the value of the underlying index. The sale of stock futures against a stock portfolio creates a hedged position with returns similar to what would be earned on short-term, fixed-income securities. Returns of a fully hedged position may differ from those of a short-term, risk-free security. The returns of the portfolio of stocks can differ from those of the index and the futures. If a stock index futures hedge is executed at futures prices above their theoretical value, the hedger might actually be able to earn a return in excess of what could be earned on a cash-equivalent security. With the sale of futures, the hedger will have to meet variation margin requirements during the time the short futures position is open.

Consider a portfolio manager who has an equity position with a beta of 1.2 (i.e., the portfolio is expected to increase or decrease in value by 1.2 percent for each 1 percent market move). This manager anticipates a near-term, flat or downward trend in the market. One possible strategy would be to reduce the beta by switching funds into cash-equivalent securities, such as Treasury bills, or into low beta stocks. Both of these options would constitute major reallocation decisions within the portfolio, would be costly in terms of transaction costs to implement, and would be cumbersome to reverse should the manager be wrong in his or her outlook.

A much more flexible option would be to sell stock futures contracts. Stock futures would be sold representing a market value equal to the market value of the portfolio times its beta. To the extent that the futures contracts move in tandem with the market index, the profits on the short position in futures should offset losses in the stocks in the portfolio associated with the overall market move.

Other important users of stock futures as hedging vehicles are brokers and dealers in equities. These institutions hold positions in stocks for short periods as a result of their trading operations. Depending on their customers' activities, they may be net-long or net-short stock issues at any given point in time. Their portfolios in fact look like the changes occurring in the portfolios of money management firms and individuals. When institutions are buying stocks in large quantities, brokers and dealers find themselves with net-short positions in equities.

Brokers and dealers can employ futures on stock indexes for hedging their positions when a major move is occurring in the market, and they are forced to have large amounts of their capital at risk in the process of meeting their customers orders. The ability of brokers and dealers to hedge their inventory with stock index futures should ultimately benefit investors. These institutions will be more inclined to carry inventories that they can easily hedge and be able to charge their customers a lower risk premium for their trading services. The stock futures market is a very handy tool for these trading firms, because the liquidity of the market is usually sufficient to absorb the very large trades necessary to hedge their positions.

The exchange specialists perform some of the same functions

as stock dealers and thus also have a use for stock index futures to hedge positions in the stocks in which they serve as market-makers. Specialists are usually given several stocks in which to make markets that are in different industries and of different risk levels. This enables the specialist to diversify away some of the risk of specific stocks. However, the specialist's inventory is much less diversified than the holdings of a portfolio manager who may hold as many as 50 or more different issues.

Like the portfolio manager or dealer firm, the specialist is exposed to the risk of market index movements based on the average beta of his or her inventory weighted by the market value of holdings. Stock index futures can be used by specialists to hedge the market risk of their inventory. Two examples of the calculations involved for determining the correct number of contracts for a specialist to sell are shown in Exhibit 4–7. In the first example, an equal number of shares is held in each of 10 stocks ranging in beta from 0.75 to 1.80. The specialist's market risk exposure is a beta of 1.22, assuming a beta of 1.00 for the NYSE Index future; 7.03 futures contracts with an underlying share value of $343,064 would provide the most effective hedge for the specialist's $581,250 stock inventory. If the index falls by 1 percent, the futures position should lose 1 percent of $343,064, or $3,430 in value. This is equivalent to 1.22 percent of $281,250 which is the decline in the portfolio that is expected to occur with a 1 percent market decline. It should be noted that the risk of such a hedge (i.e., the chance that the portfolio [specialist's inventory] performs differently than the index) remains for the specialist to bear.

In the second example, a hedge is constructed for a portfolio that has over 60 percent of its holdings in a low beta (0.85) stock and has a portfolio beta of 0.89. Here, the contracts used in the hedge represent only 89 percent of the market value of the portfolio. Also, there is considerably more risk remaining in the hedged position because of the concentration of the portfolio in only a few stocks (three stocks [15,28,30] represent 84.3 percent of the portfolio). This risk refers to the chance that the index associated with the future will have different returns from that of the stocks in the specialist's portfolio.

Capitalizing on Stock Selectivity

Certain investors may feel that they can profit most by purchasing stocks that are undervalued with respect to company-specific characteristics rather than making a judgement call on the overall stock market. These investors may not wish to subject to the risk of

EXHIBIT 4–7
Portfolio Hedging Strategy for a Specialist

1. Determine the stock positions held in inventory.
2. Calculate beta (volatility measure) for each stock. The Value Line for each stock, which is measured against the NYSE Index, was used in this example.
3. Record price per share.
4. Record number of shares (e.g., total shares outstanding or number of shares in inventory portfolio).
5. Calculate market value of stocks. Sum to get total market value of portfolio.
6. Calculate beta weight. This calculation weights each stock as to its impact on the portfolio.

$$\frac{\text{Market value}}{\text{Total market value}} = \text{Beta weight}$$

7. Calculate new weighted beta of each stock: beta × beta weight and sum to get new weighted beta of whole portfolio.
8. Calculate number of NYSE stock index futures contracts needed to hedge portfolio.

$$\frac{\text{Portfolio size} \times \text{beta}}{\text{Contract size}} = \text{Number of contracts needed to hedge}$$

Portfolio size = Total market value of portfolio
Beta = Weighted beta of whole portfolio (beta × beta weight)
Contract size = $500 × Value of NYSE stock index (settlement 11/29/83)
B = Beta = Volatility measure of stock
P/Shr = Price per share
$$BW = \text{Beta Weight} = \frac{\text{Market Value}}{\text{Total Value}}$$

Portfolio Hedging Strategy: Example 1

Number of Stock	Beta	($) P/Shr	Number of Shares	($) MV	BW	B × BW
6	.75	24.25	1,000	24,250	.0862	.0647
8	1.20	42.50	1,000	42,500	.1511	.1813
10	.95	7.25	1,000	7,250	.0258	.0245
12	.90	19.50	1,000	19,500	.0693	.0624
14	1.05	17.875	1,000	17,875	.0636	.0668
16	1.80	34.625	1,000	34,625	.1231	.2216
17	1.25	33.00	1,000	33,000	.1173	.1466
20	1.00	20.75	1,000	20,750	.0738	.0738
26	1.15	50.75	1,000	50,750	.1804	.2074
27	1.55	30.75	1,000	30,750	.1093	.1694

Weighted
beta of
portfolio
= 1.22

MV = Market Value
Total market value of portfolio = $281,250
Portfolio beta = 1.22

Contract size = 97.60 (11/29/83 settlement) × $500 = $48,800

$$\frac{\$281,250 \times 1.22}{\$48,800} = 7.03$$

Therefore, seven contracts needed to hedge.

Portfolio Hedging Strategy: Example 2

Number of Stocks	Beta	($) P/Shr	Number of Shares	($) MV	BW	B × BW
2	1.10	11.125	1,783	19,835.88	.0143	.0157
3	.65	62.00	50	3,100.00	.0022	.0014
7	1.05	22.25	2,742	61,009.50	.0440	.0462
13	.60	87.00	180	15,660.00	.0113	.0068
15	.95	48.00	3,001	144,048.00	.1040	.0988
20	1.00	20.75	1,574	32,660.50	.0236	.0236
28	1.00	32.375	5,433	175,893.37	.1270	.1270
30	.85	33.375	25,387	847,291.12	.6117	.5199
34	.65	16.625	4,000	66,500.00	.0480	.0312
39	1.15	22.625	850	19,231.25	.0139	.0160

Weighted
beta of
portfolio
= .89

Total market value of portfolio = $1,385,229.50
Portfolio beta = .89
Contract size = $48,000

$$\frac{\$1,385,229.50 \times .89}{\$48,800} = 25.26$$

Therefore, 25 contracts needed to hedge.

---

overall stock market movements. The strategy being employed has the objective of profiting from favorable movements in prices of these issues due to events uniquely favorable to these stocks.

As discussed above, short positions in stock futures added to a portfolio will reduce or eliminate the market-related component of that portfolio's return and risk, and leave the return and risk component associated with the company-specific features of the stocks in the portfolio. Thus with futures, an investor can more easily separate the market and nonmarket related returns and risk of a portfolio, thereby adjusting the portfolio's exposure to these different types of risk as appropriate. *Alpha* is a term used to describe returns above those consistent with the market risk (beta) exposure of a portfolio of stocks. A fully hedged portfolio would be managed to maximize the alpha return for a given level of nonmarket risk. Investment managers who wish to specialize in stock selection and sell this service can more easily do so with stock index futures.

Investment in U.S. Stocks with Reduced Currency Risk

Another application of stock index futures is uniquely suited to investors outside of the United States who are attracted to the U.S. stock market but who wish to insulate themselves from the risk of changes in the value of the dollar relative to their own currency. Consider the case of a Swiss investor who thinks that U.S. stocks are cheap but the dollar overvalued. If stocks appreciate but the dollar falls, capital gains from investment in U.S. equities may be reduced by currency losses.

This investor may wish to assume a position in the U.S. stock market with only a small dollar risk exposure by purchasing stock index futures contracts instead of U.S. stocks. Less than 10 percent of the value of the stock index futures would be required for margin purposes in the form of Treasury bills. The rest can be deposited in a Swiss bank account earning the Swiss short-term interest rate and be protected from exchange-rate shifts. In a sense, this strategy is a close substitute for an S&P 500 index fund denominated in Swiss francs. A variation of this strategy would be to purchase the U.S. stocks via S&P 500 or NYSE futures and then deposit the contract value not needed for margin in the currency that the investor thinks is most undervalued. This gives an international investor the opportunity to profit simultaneously on currency selection and market selection.

Speculating on Stock Market Moves

A large amount of stock index futures trading is done by investors on the floor (locals) and off the floor who are not necessarily using the futures market as a cheap and liquid alternative to the cash equity market. They are buying and selling futures as investment strategies in themselves, based on an opinion about the direction of stock prices and the relative value of futures. Some of these traders are called sentiment traders, and all are called speculators. Their presence in the market is critical to providing liquidity.

A separate chapter in this book is devoted to speculative futures strategies. Here we should mention that stock index futures provide a means to participate in the movements of the equity market as a whole using a high degree of leverage. Since a deposit of less than 10 percent is required to purchase or sell a stock futures contract, one can take on a considerable amount of market risk via index futures and reap the reward of being correct in a forecast of the stock market direction. For example, the S&P 500 provided a return of almost 60 percent between August 1982 and March 1983. A March 1983 S&P 500 futures contract could have been purchased with a $5,000 margin deposit in August 1982. This contract would have appreciated from 100 to 160 points and earned a $30,000 (60 × 500) profit on a $6,000 investment with a 500 percent return.

The risk, however, of the use of such extreme leverage is significant. A 60 percent drop in the market would have required the deposit of that same $30,000 in a mark-to-market account as the losses in the market occurred. Also, even with the 60 percent appreciation in contract value, a market correction of 15 percent during the period would have required a deposit of roughly $7,500 in variation margin at some time during the August–March period.

A wide range of speculative strategies are possible with stock index futures. In addition to an outright short or long position, one can create spreads between stock futures expiring in different contract months, between stock-and-bond or stock-and-bill futures, and between stock futures on different indexes. (Volume in stock index futures that are more than six months from delivery is generally too small to encourage spreads.) The basic notion associated with spread strategies is that the investor has an opinion about where the spread should be and either buys or sells the spread depending on whether he or she expects it to widen or narrow.

For example, since small capitalization stocks tend to be more volatile than large capitalization stocks, one might expect the NYSE contract to sell at a particular discount to the S&P 500 contract because of greater volatility associated with its broader coverage (after adjusting for differences in contract value). If the S&P 500–NYSE future spread is smaller than would be expected given risk differences, one would buy the S&P 500 futures and sell the NYSE future. If the spread widened, one would profit regardless of the direction of movement of each index.

Capitalizing on Different Tax Treatment of Futures and Equities

Given that it is possible to use stock index futures to construct a portfolio with returns very similar to that of an equity index or a short-term fixed-income security, the different tax treatments of those returns may make it advantageous for some investors to use equity futures. All profits and losses on stock index futures are effectively treated as long-term capital gains and losses (i.e., 60 percent are taxable and 40 percent are taxed as short-term gains or losses). This means that on an after-tax basis, an investor with a holding period of less than six months would be better off holding stock index futures in a period of market index appreciation and worse off (realizing a long-term loss) in a period of declining index values.

In an article in the *Journal of Futures Markets*, Herbst and Ordway (1984) point out that stock index futures contracts give investors the ability to separate the capital gains and ordinary income components of their returns. An investor purchasing stock index futures effectively receives a capital gain reflecting the foregone dividend payments. Cornell and French (1983) point out another important tax implication of stock index futures. Since positions are marked-to-market, all gains and losses on futures are realized at the end of the tax year. Futures are thus at a disadvantage to stocks. With stocks, one has the option to carry gains (or losses) over in the next tax year and the option of realizing short-term losses and postponing gains until they become long term.

Because of this tax option that is present in stocks but not in stock futures, Cornell and French argue that the relative value of stock futures should be lower than that of stock indexes (after incorporating other components of futures value). Although this option of delaying gains and taking losses should be considered by investors in choosing between equity futures and pure equity strategies, it is not clear that this option will in itself produce a downward bias in stock futures prices, because other strategies that also capitalize on different tax treatment may have biases of their own.

One of these other strategies is the use of stock index futures to create a hedged, low-risk position in stocks for investment of the working capital funds of corporations. The dividend stream of stocks held by corporations is currently 85 percent tax-free versus the fully taxable interest income that would be earned on low-risk fixed-income securities. Futures hedging makes it possible to greatly reduce the market risk of holding stocks that have this dividend treatment advantage. There is a further tax implication of this type of strategy in that after-tax gains and losses on the stock and stock futures position will not exactly offset one another, because the stock capital gains (losses) can be short term, and the futures gains (losses) are always long term.

It is difficult to generalize regarding the advantages and disadvantages of stock index futures from an after-tax perspective because of the differences in tax situations among investors, and because it is unclear how these aggregate advantages and disadvantages are translated in stock index futures prices. The major point in discussing these differential tax treatment strategies is that stock futures can be used as vehicles to structure after-tax returns for groups of investors in different tax situations. The appropriateness of stock futures depends on the taxation basis of the investor, individual, corporation, tax-example, and the price of the future at the time the strategy is analyzed.

SUMMARY

The success of fixed-income futures contracts has encouraged the creation of futures contracts on various stock indexes. Since their introduction in 1982, stock index futures have become an established means of adjusting the market risk of security inventories of the brokerage firms. They are also gaining more widespread use in portfolios of institutional and individual investors and as arbitrage trading vehicles. The liquidity and low trading cost of these markets make them suitable for hedging against short-term equity price declines and capitalizing on short-term volatility of indexes representing broad-based components of the equity markets. Many traders conduct arbitrage between stock index futures and the stocks themselves, adding liquidity to both markets. Stock index futures are dissimilar to many other futures contracts in that the equity futures call for cash delivery on the delivery instruments.

NOTES

[1] For a discussion of risk-adjusted performance measurement see Fama (1972) and Jensen (1969) or Jacob and Pettit (1984).

SELECTED REFERENCES

Cornell, Bradford, and Kenneth R. French. "The Pricing of Stock Index Futures." *Journal of Futures Markets* 3, no. 1 (Spring 1983), pp. 1–14.

————. "Taxes and the Pricing of Stock Index Futures." *Journal of Finance*, 1982.

Fama, Eugene. "Components of Investment Performance." *Journal of Finance* 23, no. 2 (June 1972), pp. 557–67.

Figlewski, Stephen. "Hedging Performance and Basis Risk in Stock Index Futures." *Journal of Finance* 39, no. 3 (July 1984), pp. 657–69.

————. "Hedging with Stock Index Futures: Theory and Application in a New Market." Columbia University Center for the Study of Futures Markets, no. 62, July 1983.

Figlewski, Stephen, and Stanley J. Kon. "Portfolio Management with Stock Index Futures." *Financial Analysts Journal*, January–February 1982, pp. 52–59.

Gastineau, Gary, and Albert Madansky. "S&P 500 Stock Index Futures Evaluation Tables." *Financial Analysts Journal*, November–December 1983, pp. 68–76.

Gressis, N.; G. Vlahos; and G. C. Phillipatos. "A CAPM-based Analysis of Stock Index Futures." *Journal of Portfolio Management,* Spring 1984, pp. 47–55.

Herbst, A., and N. Ordway. "Stock Index Futures Contracts and Separability of Returns." *Journal of Futures Markets* 4, no. 1 (Spring 1984), pp. 84–102.

Jacob, N. L., and R. Pettit. *Investments,* Homewood, Ill.: Richard D. Irwin, Inc., 1984.

Jensen, M. C. "Risk, the Pricing of Capital Assets, and the Evaluation of Investment Portfolios." *Journal of Business* 25, no. 3 (April 1969), pp. 167–247.

Jones, Frank J. "The Economics of Futures and Options Contracts Based on Cash Settlement." *Journal of Futures Markets,* Spring 1982, pp. 63–82.

Kipnis, G. M., and F. J. Fabozzi, eds. *Stock Index Futures,* Homewood, Ill.: Dow Jones-Irwin, 1984.

Modest, David, and Mahandevan Sundareson. "The Relationship Between Spot and Futures Prices in Stock Index Futures Markets: Some Preliminary Evidence." Columbia University Center for the Study of Futures Markets, no. 45, November 1982.

Nordhauser, Fred. "Using Stock-Index Futures to Reduce Market Risk." *Journal of Portfolio Management,* Spring 1984, pp. 56–62.

Tosini, Paula A., and Eugene J. Moriarty. "Potential Hedging Use of a Futures Contract Based on a Composite Stock Index." *Journal of Futures Markets,* Spring 1982, pp. 83–103.

Weiner, N. S. "The Hedging Rationale for a Stock Index Futures Contract," *Journal of Futures Markets* 1, no. 1 (Spring 1981), pp. 59–76.

Zeckhauser, Richard, and Victor Niederhoffer. "The Performance of Market Index Futures Contracts." *Financial Analysts Journal,* January–February 1983, pp. 59–64.

Valuation Fundamentals for Securities

Now that we have an understanding of the basic characteristics of financial futures contracts, the markets in which they trade, and the regulatory environment futures traders face, the next important step is to explore the sources of value for financial futures contracts. Financial futures prices are closely related to the cash market prices of the underlying securities. We will see in Chapter 6, exactly how cash and futures prices are related to one another. Before the specifics of the valuation of futures are discussed, it is first important to review the characteristics of fixed-income securities and equities. These characteristics interact to determine their cash price today or at any "future" point in time. In this chapter, principles of price determination for fixed-income securities and equities are reviewed. The focus is on those features that are important in setting relative cash and futures prices. These include the number of cash flows, their timing, and the discount rates used for converting these cash flows to a present value.

SECURITIES WITH A SINGLE, FIXED CASH FLOW

Certain types of fixed-income securities promise a single payment at a particular future point in time. Examples of such securities include a one-year U.S. Treasury bill, which pays the face value amount of $10,000 at maturity, and a "zero-coupon" 10-year bond with a face value of $1,000, which promises the holder a payment of $1,000 at the end of a 10-year period. The price you would be willing to pay for these securities depends on the return you would expect to receive on alternative equal risk investments, with either 1-year or 10-year maturities.

Assume that you require an 8 percent return for investment of your funds over the next year. To give up access to your funds for a total of 10 years, you would like a total return equivalent to 12 percent per year. An investment of $9,260 today earning 8 percent interest (compounded annually) would result in a $10,000 value in one year.

$$V_1 = V_0 (1 + r)^1$$
$$\$10,000 = \$9,260 (1 + .08)^1$$

(5–1)

where:

V_0 = Value today
V_1 = Value one period from now
r = The annual interest rate

Therefore, if you required an 8 percent annual return, you would be willing to pay no more than $9,260 today for the Treasury bill. The price or value today (V_0) of a single cash flow one period in the future can thus be determined by dividing the expected cash flow by one plus the total return (in decimal) over that period, or:

$$V_0 = V_1/(1+r)^1$$
$$\$9,260 = \$10,000/(1+.08)^1 \tag{5-2}$$

Similarly, an investment of \$322 today would cumulate to a total of \$1,000 at the end of 10 years if it increased in value at a rate of 12 percent each year. Note here that interest in years 2 through 10 is earned not only on the original \$322 but also on the increase in value in each of the previous years at a rate of 12 percent (i.e., it is compounded).

$$V_{10} = V_0(1+r)^{10}$$
$$\$1,000 = \$322 (1+.12)^{10} \tag{5-3}$$

Current or future values can be based on a single constant rate, say 12 percent as above, or on a series of different rates expected to prevail over the life of the security. For example, one may desire the return to increase 1 percent per year to 13 percent, 14 percent and 15 percent in years 8, 9, and 10 of the 10-year period. In this case, the most one would pay for a security promising a \$1,000 cash flow at the end of 10 years would be \$305.

$$V_{10} = V_0 (1+r)^7 (1+r_8) (1+r_9) (1+r_{10})$$
$$\$1,000 = \$305 (1+.12)^7 (1+.13) (1+.14) (1+.15) \tag{5-4}$$

where $r =$ the single period interest rate expected in years 1 through 7,

$r_8, r_9, r_{10} =$ the single period interest rates expected in years 8, 9, and 10.

It is now possible to express a general formula for the current price or value (V_0) of a single period cash flow in period n (V_n):
For a constant interest rate r,

$$V_0 = V_n/(1+r)^n \tag{5-5}$$

For a variable interest rate $(r_1 r_2 \ldots r_n)$,

$$V_0 = V_n/[(1+r_1) (1+r_2) \ldots (1+r_n)] \tag{5-6}$$

The number of compounding periods is represented by n and can be expressed in terms of days, months, years, and so on, or even continuously, depending on how frequently value increases are added to the base of funds growing at r_n. Financial instruments that can be valued in this way include Treasury bills, commercial paper, zero-coupon bonds, U.S. savings bonds, and equities that pay no dividends.

SECURITIES WITH MULTIPLE, FIXED CASH FLOWS

When multiple future cash flows are associated with investment in a financial instrument, application of the process outlined above is repeated to arrive at a price or value. Each future payment can be discounted to its present value by applying formulas (5–5) or (5–6), the choice depending on whether a single or multiple interest rate is appropriate. The current values of each cash flow can then be added to find the price or value of the instrument itself.

When cash flows that occur in several periods are of the same dollar amount, or are growing at a constant rate, some shortcuts are useful in simplifying current value calculations. These special cases in which simplified methods can be used include installment or mortgage loan agreements, coupon bonds, and stocks with dividends growing at a constant rate.

The simplest of these cases is a mortgage or other type of fixed-income security that involves equal dollar payments in each compounding period. Equal cash flows occurring in future periods are commonly referred to as annuities. If $100,000 were borrowed today at a 1 percent monthly interest rate (or 12 percent annual rate), this sum could be repaid in 20 years or (240 months) with equal payments of $1,100 per month. This relationship is shown in the formula below:

$$V_0 = \sum_{n=1}^{N} (A_n/(1+r)^n)$$

$$\$100,000 = \sum_{n=1}^{240} [\$1,100/(1+.01)^n] \tag{5-7}$$

where A = dollar amount of equal cash flows in each of N periods,
   N = total number of periods, and
   Σ = shorthand for summation of N terms

   (e.g., $\sum_{n=1}^{3} X_n = X_1 + X_2 + X_3$).

One can easily use an interest rate table or calculator to find the current or future values of annuity-type multiple cash flows. Only three pieces of information are needed: the amount of the annuity, the interest rate, and the number of periods. Futures contracts exist on certificates representing pools of mortgages (GNMA futures) that are priced according to this method. The deliverable security is a portfolio of installment loans that has payment features similar to those discussed above.

Other futures contracts exist on U.S. Treasury bonds and Treasury notes that call for delivery of securities that pay a principal amount at maturity and a fixed-dollar amount (annuity) of coupon payments at regular intervals, usually each six months until maturity. Pricing of coupon bonds involves a combination of discounting a single payment at maturity and an annuity of equal coupon payments. The single interest rate that discounts this series of payments to a specific price is referred to as the bond's *yield to maturity*.

For example, assume a 30-year Treasury bond with a coupon rate of 10⅜ percent (5³⁄₁₆ percent semiannually) is selling for a price of $905. At this price, the yield maturity is 5½ percent semiannually, which is slightly higher than the coupon rate. The relationship between the yield and cash flow is depicted below:

$$V_0 = \sum_{n=1}^{N} (C_n/(1+r)^n) + (V_N/(1+r)^N)$$

$$\$905 = \sum_{n=1}^{60} (\$51.85/(1+.055)^n) + (\$1,000/(1+.055)^{60}) \qquad (5\text{-}8)$$

where C_n = the coupon payment (annuity) received semiannually—5³⁄₁₆ percent of $1,000.

Because the cash flows are uneven over time, finding the yield for a bond with a given price requires cumbersome calculations. Bond tables, calculators, or computer software are usually employed to carry out this task. This formula (5–8) is only exactly correct when a bond is priced on a coupon payment date. To find the value of bonds on other dates reflecting accrued interest, see the Appendix B to this chapter.

Fixed-income securities that provide cash flows prior to maturity have a particular form of risk called "reinvestment" risk. This risk refers to the uncertainty associated with the level of interest income that will be earned on the cash flows between the time they are received and the maturity of the bond. Price formulas 5–7 and 5–8 implicitly assume coupon payments and mortgage installment payments can be reinvested at the rate of interest as measured by the bond yield to maturity. Since interest rates fluctuate over time, this constant reinvestment rate assumption is generally violated in practice. Obviously, securities that pay a high proportion of their cash flows prior to maturity have a high level of reinvestment risk. Also, this risk tends to be greater when the general level of interest rates is high (i.e., there is a relatively high probability that *future* rates at which cash flows can be invested will be *less* than those prevailing today).

EFFECTS OF CHANGING YIELDS ON FIXED-INCOME SECURITY PRICES

In order to understand how prices of futures move over time, one must be familiar with some basic principles that apply to price movements of fixed-income securities. These principles are rules derived from the mathematics of fixed-income security valuation. They relate to the way in which prices of bonds with different coupon rates and maturities react to the direction and size of changes in yields. These rules are listed below:

1. Prices of fixed-income securities move inversely with yields.
2. Prices of low coupon bonds react more (inversely) to a given change in yield than do prices of high coupon bonds that are equivalent in all features except coupon rate.
3. Prices of long maturity bonds react more (inversely) to a given change in yield than do prices of short maturity bonds equivalent in all features except maturity.
4. On a percentage price change basis, fixed-income securities selling at a discount from face value will react more (inversely) to a change in yields than those selling at a premium to their face value.
5. On a percentage price change basis, bond prices will fall less from a given increase in yields than they will rise from a given decrease in yields.

Given these principles of fixed-income security valuation, the risk and capital appreciation potential associated with changes in the general level of interest rates is demonstrated to be higher, the lower the coupon rate, the longer the maturity, and the greater the discount from face value represented by the current price.

These concepts are illustrated graphically and in table form in Exhibit 5–1 for two securities with very different characteristics—a Treasury bill maturing in six months and a 12 percent Treasury bond maturing in 30 years (both $1,000 face value). An increase in yields from 14 to 15 percent would result in a $57 drop in the long-term Treasury bond as compared to a $4 drop in Treasury bill prices. Similarly, a decrease in yields from 9 to 8 percent would result in an increase of $143 in the value of a

EXHIBIT 5–1

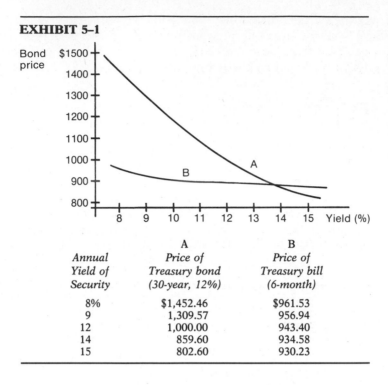

Annual Yield of Security	A Price of Treasury bond (30-year, 12%)	B Price of Treasury bill (6-month)
8%	$1,452.46	$961.53
9	1,309.57	956.94
12	1,000.00	943.40
14	859.60	934.58
15	802.60	930.23

Treasury bond, double the drop in value as opposed to a $4.60 gain for the Treasury bill.

FORWARD RATES AND THE TERM STRUCTURE

An important concept in the understanding of financial futures and interest rate hedging is to keep in mind that any interest rate can also be represented by a series of rates over *shorter* subperiods. Similarly, a given interest rate is itself also a part of a series of rates over a *longer* time period. Interest rates available on securities identical in all aspects except maturity are linked through what is called the *term structure of interest rates*. The sequence of bond yields at a given point in time for bonds maturing one period apart is referred to as the term structure.

To illustrate this concept, assume that investors have a horizon of *N* periods and are indifferent with respect to all security combinations that allow them to have their funds invested over these *N* periods. In other words, the following four alternatives would be equally favored for an investor with a three-year investment horizon:

1. Three one-year bonds.
2. A three-year bond.
3. A two-year bond followed by investment in a one-year bond.
4. A one-year bond followed by investment in a two-year bond.

If all investors accepted the assumption of indifference among these alternatives, the yields of bonds maturing one period apart would be entirely based on the rate on a single period security available today as well as the *forward* or expected rates that are anticipated to be available in the future. This is called the *unbiased expectations theory* of the term structure. Since forward rates and rates implied by financial futures prices are very closely connected, an understanding of forward rate determination is basic to the analysis of financial futures. In fact, most cash-futures arbitrage theories rely heavily on a comparison of the implied forward rate in a security available in the fixed-income market with the futures rate available in the financial futures market.

The role of forward rates in connecting the yields of securities of different maturities is best understood with an example. Assume a three-month Treasury bill is available at a price of 97.09 with a yield of 3 percent. (See Appendix A for methods of calculating yields of Treasury bills.) If 5 percent interest is available on a six-month security and 3 percent interest is available on a three-month security, traders of Treasury bills must expect to earn roughly 2 percent for investing their funds over the next 4 to 6 months. This 4- to 6-month rate is called a *forward rate*.

The prices of any two securities that differ only in time to maturity are linked by the forward rate expected to prevail between the maturity of the first security and the maturity of the second security. The basic formula relating spot and forward rates is given below:

$$r_{0,t} = [(1 + r_{0,1}) (1 + R_{1,2}) (1 + R_{2,3}). \ldots \ldots (1 + R_{t-1,t})] - 1.0 \quad (5\text{-}9)$$

The rate on a security maturing in period t $(r_{0,t})$ is related to the (spot) rate on a security maturing in one period $(r_{0,1})$ and forward rates (designated by R) prevailing between the end of period 1 and time t. In the example above, with six-month and three-month bills yielding 5 percent and 3 percent, respectively, we can find the 4- to 6-month forward rate $(R_{1,2})$ by simplifying equation (5-9) to the two-period case and solving it for $R_{1,2}$.

$$r_{0,2} = [(1 + r_{0,1}) (1 + R_{1,2})] - 1.0$$
$$R_{1,2} = [(1 + r_{0,2})/(1 + r_{0,1})] - 1.0 \quad (5\text{-}10)$$
$$2\% \cong 1.94\% = .0194 = [(1 + .05)/(1 + .03)] - 1.0$$

The price of a Treasury bill future calling for delivery in 90 days of Treasury bills with a three-month maturity will be based on the forward three-month rate contained in the price of a six-month Treasury bill. To see this, assume that the following prices are observed in the cash and futures Treasury bill markets. (These prices are expressed in terms of percentage of face value.)

98.04: Treasury bill with 90 days to maturity.
95.24: Treasury bill with 180 days to maturity.
97.14: Futures calling for delivery in 90 days of a Treasury
        bill with 90 days remaining to maturity.

The effective interest rate on a Treasury bill can be found using the formulas below:

$$r = [100.00/P] - 1.0$$
$$r_{0,90} = 100.00/98.04 - 1.0 = .02 \text{ or } 2\% \qquad (5\text{--}11)$$
$$r_{0,180} = 100.00/95.24 - 1.0 = .05 \text{ or } 5\%$$

Using (5–10), we can find the forward rate at time 0 for funds invested in Treasury bills from 90 to 180 days from now.

$$R_{90,180} = [(1 + .05)/(1 + .02)] - 1.0 = .0294 \text{ or } 2.94\%$$

The rate one would earn if Treasury bills were purchased via the future in 90 days at a price of 97.14 is equal to 2.94 percent as well.

$$r_{90,180} = 100.00/97.14 - 1.0 = .0294 = 2.94\%$$

Therefore, the forward rate structure in cash prices and the effective rate implied in futures at prices at a given point in time can be calculated and compared. If the differences between the forward rates and futures rates are more than would be expected given institutional factors, arbitrageurs may be inclined to enter the market with the highest forward rate (lowest price) seeking to take advantage of any discrepancies in relative prices. In fact, fixed-income futures market quotes are generally shown in the financial press in terms of both futures prices and the annualized effective rates that would be earned if the security was bought at the futures price and held to maturity.

Note also that if we knew the effective rate on a nine-month bill, we could find the forward rate $R_{2,3}$ for investment in the three-month period ending nine months from now. Assume a value of 9 percent for the rate on a nine-month bill bought today (price 91.74). The 7- to 9-month forward rate can be found using either the spot rate on the six-month bill or the three-month bill rate and the 4- to 6-month forward rate we just calculated:

$$R_{2,3} = [(1 + r_{0,3})/(1 + r_{0,1}) (1 + r_{1,2})] - 1.0$$
$$3.81\% = .0381 = [(1 + .09)/(1 + .03) (1.094)] - 1.0 \quad (5\text{--}12)$$

$$R_{1,2} = [(1 + r_{0,2})/(1 + R_{0,1})] - 1.0$$
$$3.81\% = .0381 = [(1 + .09)/(1 + .05)] - 1.0 \quad (5\text{--}13)$$

This "layer" of spot and forward rates is depicted in Exhibit 5–2. Forward rates can be thought of as the security market's current price for tying up funds over the future period to which the forward rate applies. The ability to buy a financial future calling for delivery of the future at a price set today allows one to avoid tying up funds by purchasing the security prior to the futures delivery date. Thus, financial futures prices are directly influenced by the forward rates that are implied in the yield of securities that are equivalent to those that can be purchased with future contracts.

Many argue that in addition to reflecting expectations of futures interest rates, forward rates contain a *liquidity premium*. This can be thought of as a bonus given on purchases of longer-term securities to compensate investors for the greater risk (interest rate sensitivity) associated with those securities. The phrase liquidity premium is based on the fact that prior to maturity, there is a greater risk with long-term securities that one will not be able to liquidate the security for the principal value (discounted by the promised yield at the time of purchase). This risk is associated with exposure to changing interest rates.

EXHIBIT 5–2
Forward and Spot Rates: Alternative perspectives

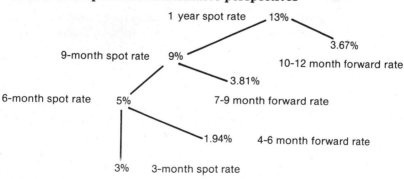

One-year rate 13 percent:

$.13 = [(1.09) (1.0367)] - 1.0$ (9-month spot rate)
$.13 = [(1.05) (1.0381) (1.0367)] - 1.0$ (6-month spot rate)
$.13 = [(1.03) (1.94) (1.0381) (1.0367)] - 1.0$ (3-month spot rate)

Proponents of the liquidity preference theory argue that investors would *not* be indifferent when given a choice between three, one-year bonds and a three-year bond as identified in the previous alternatives. Rather, they would prefer the three, one-year bonds, because they are less volatile in principal value over the three year horizon. With the shorter-term bonds, therefore, investors bear less risk of loss associated with sale prior to the end of the period. Because of the additional risk associated with longer maturities, investors may require as compensation a premium over the implied forward rate.

The differences in interest rate sensitivity of securities with different maturities is particularly important in determining the size of the futures position needed for hedging the risk of changing interest rates. The more sensitive a security is to interest rate changes, the larger the amount of futures that are needed to implement a hedge and the more useful futures are in reducing the overall risk of the position in the financial instrument. This can be easily seen from the fact that holders of long-term, low coupon securities face much greater risk of rising interest rates. They thus tend to benefit more than do holders of short-term securities from the use of futures instruments to reduce losses associated with rising interest rates.

One could restate formula 5–9 to incorporate a liquidity premium in addition to the forward rate:

$$r_{ot} = [(1 + r_{0,1}) (1 + R_{1,2} + L_{1,2}) (1 + R_{2,3} + L_{2,3}) \ldots ,$$
$$(1 + R_{t+1} + L_{t+1})] - 1.0 \qquad (5\text{--}13)$$

where $L_{t,t+1} \geq L_{2,3} \geq L_{1,2}$.

$L_{1,2}$ is the premium required for holding a two-period security instead of two, one-period securities. This expression assumes the liquidity premium is additive and increases in value with the number of periods. Exhibit 5–3 shows the incremental effect of the liquidity premium (solid line) on two yield curves based on different expected forward rates (dotted line).

Another theory of the term structure contrasts sharply with that based on forward rates and liquidity premiums. This *market segmentation theory* contends that rates are set by the relative supply and demand of institutions that tend to stay in one particular segment of the maturity spectrum when they issue and/or purchase securities. This theory is based on the idea that different institutions have a maturity composition in their liabilities or sources of funds that is more or less set by the industry in which they operate or by other institutional constraints. A common exam-

EXHIBIT 5–3
Yield Curve Based on Forward Rate Expectations and Liquidity Premium

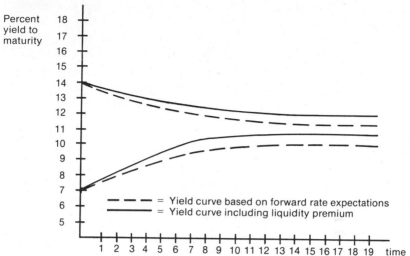

ple is that of commercial banks having short-term liabilities in the form of deposits.

Because of the desire to limit their exposure to changing interest rates, such institutions put their funds to work by acquiring assets that closely match the maturity of their liabilities. According to the market segmentation theory, short-term rates become high when institutions that concentrate on the short-end of the maturity spectrum reduce their demand for short-term investments or when the demand for short-term borrowing is above the level that can be supported by economic units that want to invest short-term. Similarly, for long-term rates to be stable according to this theory, institutions like insurance companies and pension funds need to be expanding their holdings of long-term bonds at a rate that matches the rate of growth of long-term bond issues. If for some reason long-term investors reduce their demand, rates in the long end of the maturity spectrum may rise.

The market segmentation theory is relevant to financial futures markets. The existence of futures on such securities as Treasury bills and bonds makes it easier for institutions to hedge or adjust maturities without limiting their assets and liabilities to a particular maturity class. Thus, market segmentation should be less important in setting rates to the extent that economic units use futures to adjust for mismatches between their assets and liabilities. For example, if a banker feels intermediate-term bonds are cheap compared to short-term bonds, he or she can buy the intermediate bonds and sell Treasury note futures to create a synthetic position in a short-term bond. Strategies like this will be discussed in greater depth later in the book. The importance here is that financial futures provide other means of adjusting the maturity of assets and liabilities and should therefore tend to erode support for the segmented markets explanation of the term structure.

SECURITIES WITH UNCERTAIN LIVES

Some fixed-income securities have maturity dates that are not fixed or have features that make the timing of their principal repayments unknown at the time of purchase. The present values of the cash flows for these types of securities is, therefore, an estimate based on assumptions made regarding the timing of the payments. Three types of long-term fixed-income securities that have an uncertain life are callable bonds, bonds backed by a sinking fund with a call provision, and securities collateralized by a pool of mortgages.

Callable Bonds

Many bonds, particularly corporate issues, are callable by the issuer at a premium to the bond's face value. Bonds tend to be called when yields are significantly below the coupon rate of the bond, such that the price exceeds the price the issuer must pay to retire the issue early. By calling the bond, the issuer can refinance at the lower prevailing interest rate. The yield of a callable bond should be based on the call price and number of periods to call whenever the bond is selling at a premium to par value of at least one year's coupon interest.

Sinking Fund Bonds

A bond issue with a sinking fund provision requires the issuer to make periodic and partial payments of the principal to a trustee. The trustee uses these funds to either buy back the bonds in the secondary market or to call them on a random basis at a small premium over par value. The latter procedure would only be followed if the bonds are trading above par and would tend to affect only a small proportion of existing bondholders. Typically, yield calculations are not adjusted for sinking fund provisions unless these provisions require a large amount of the outstanding bonds to be called early. In this case, the yield could be calculated as a weighted average of the yields to call with the proportion of total bond value called used as each weight.

Mortgage-Backed Securities

Certain securities, such as certificates issued by the Government National Mortgage Association (GNMA) and the Federal National Mortgage Association (FNMA), are backed by pools of mortgages on residential property. Cash flows from payments on these mortgages are passed on monthly to security holders. These securities have unique cash flows in two respects. First, the periodic payments are annuities composed of both interest and repayment of principal, instead of only consisting of coupon payments until maturity or call. Second, even though the mortgages have a maturity of 25 or 30 years, many of them are repaid early when properties are sold or loans are refinanced. Therefore, the maturity of GNMA or FNMA certificates is usually stated in terms of an expected average life rather than the actual maturities of the mortgages in the pool. Yields quoted in the financial press use a 30-year maturity with average prepayment of 12 years. In periods of low interest rates, prepayment of high interest rate mortgages tends to rise sharply, because borrowers are induced to refinance at the lower rates. This reduces the effective maturity of the GNMA or FNMA certificate. Therefore, any analysis of mortgage certificates should incorporate an adjustment to the estimated maturity that depends on the current level of rates as compared to the rate of the mortgages in the pool.

VALUATION OF EQUITY PORTFOLIOS

Futures have been introduced that call for delivery of the cash value of portfolios of equities at a particular delivery point. These portfolios may be broad indexes, such as the S&P 500, or they may be portfolios of stocks in a particular industry grouping such as the financial service or energy industry. Equity futures can be distinguished from most fixed-income security futures in three important ways:

1. The cash flows associated with the deliverable instrument are not fixed in time or dollar amount.
2. The deliverable instruments are portfolios of securities rather than individual issues.

3. The delivery process involves the exchange of the *cash value* of the stocks portfolio rather than the securities themselves.

These features of stock index futures have been discussed in detail in Chapter 4 and are considered in terms of the valuation of stock index futures in the next chapter. Prior to discussing stock index futures valuation, a good understanding of the pricing fundamentals of the underlying stock indexes must be developed. The first two of these features—uncertain cash flows and a portfolio of stocks as the deliverable vehicle—relate directly to the valuation process. They therefore are explored here.

Multiperiod Stock Valuation

The sources of value for shares of stock of a particular company are covered at length in any introductory finance course textbook. The usual valuation formula involved is very similar to that used above in valuing fixed-income securities with multiple cash flows (see formula 5–8). In stock valuation as compared to bond valuation, future cash flows are represented by *expected* dividend payments instead of by fixed coupon payments. The face value to be received at maturity (V_N) is replaced by the expected price received upon sale of the stock $\bar{P}_N$.

These substitutions are made below in what has come to be known as the *dividend discount model* of stock valuation:

$$P_o = \sum_{n=1}^{\infty} [\bar{D}_n/(1+r)^n] \qquad (5\text{--}14\text{a})$$

$$P_0 = \sum_{n=1}^{N} [\bar{D}_n/(1+r)^n] + [\bar{P}_N/(1+r)^N] \qquad (5\text{--}14\text{b})$$

The value of an equity security consists of the discounted value of future cash flows arising from ownership, including all dividends that may be paid $(\bar{D}_n)$ from now until infinity (∞). The capital gains form of the dividend discount model is shown in formula 5–14b. In this version, the dividend stream is terminated at N when the stock is sold at price $\bar{P}_N$.

The interest rate used to discount these cash flows would not be equivalent to the rate used on a bond that happens to pay coupon payments identical to the dividends and to have a face value equal to the expected stock price at N. A higher discount rate must be used for stock valuation to reflect the compensation investors require for the risk associated with the *uncertain* dividend payments and selling price. This additional risk of equities becomes obvious when one considers that stockholders do not receive any cash flows until after bondholders and other creditors have been paid all of the funds due to them.

Several approaches exist for determining the appropriate risk-adjusted discount rate to be used in equity valuation. One of the simplest and most subjective methods is to simply add 3 to 4 percent to the yield of long-term bonds issued by the company to reflect the greater risk of stocks. A more theoretically sound, but also more complicated, approach is to use the required return that is consistent with the current risk-free rate of interest, the risk premium in the equity market as a whole, and amount of risk in the stock itself that cannot be eliminated by diversification across stocks.

This approach to determining the required return on stocks is often referred to as the *capital asset pricing model*. This CAPM model rests on several restrictive assumptions, the most important of which are that all investors can borrow and lend at the same risk-free rate of interest and that they maintain similar expectations regarding the possible future returns on a particular stock. The CAPM specification of the required return on equity (r_s) is identified more concisely below:

$$r_s = r_f + (r_m - r_f) \quad \beta_s$$

$$r_s = \text{Risk-free} + \begin{bmatrix} \text{Required risk} & \times \text{Market-related} \\ \text{premium for} & \text{risk of stock} \\ \text{holding portfolio} \\ \text{of all risky assets} \end{bmatrix} \quad (5\text{--}15)$$

The market-related risk of the stock (β or beta) refers to the expected return behavior of the stock for each 1 percent return on portfolio m composed of all risky assets (market portfolio). For example, a stock that tends to move half (twice) as much as the broad market portfolio would have a beta of roughly 0.5 (2.0), indicating an expected return of 0.5 percent (2 percent) for every return of the market as a whole.

Valuation of Stock Portfolios

As mentioned above, most stock futures contracts specify delivery of the cash value of a particular portfolio or index of equity securities. The valuation of portfolios is more complicated than the valuation of the stock of any one company. The complexities arise from the fact that the risk of the future cash flows from the stocks in the portfolio depends not only on the uncertainty associated with individual dividend payments and future stock prices, but also on the extent to which cash flows from each of the stocks in the portfolio are correlated with one another.

This can be easily demonstrated by considering the differences in risk between two portfolios (I and II) each consisting of five equally-weighted stocks. Assume that each of the five stocks in portfolio I has expected dividend flows and selling prices identical to those of each stock in portfolio II. However, portfolio I consists solely of stocks in the oil industry, whereas portfolio II consists of stocks from five distinct industry groups. Clearly, portfolio II will be of lower risk, because its returns are not as tied to the fate of the oil industry as are the returns of portfolio I.

Broadly diversified portfolios have lower overall risk than is reflected in weighted average of the risk of their component stocks. This is true because diversification reduces a portfolio's exposure to factors affecting a particular company, industry group, or sector of the economy. The concept of portfolio risk was first developed by Markowitz [1952]. The advantage of holding portfolios consisting of the entire equity market (index funds) depends on whether one believes superior returns can be achieved by market timing of stock and fixed-income purchases and by superior selection of stocks. Most investors agree that some level of diversification is prudent to control total risk exposure.

The anticipated, single-period return (or required return) on a portfolio $\bar{r}_p$ can be expressed in terms of a weighted average of the expected returns $\bar{r}_i$ of the component securities:

$$\bar{r}_p = \sum_{i=1}^{N} w_i(\bar{r}_i) \qquad (5\text{--}16)$$

where w_i = the proportion of the portfolio invested in security i.
$\quad\quad N$ = the total number of securities in the portfolio.

When securities are held in portfolios that have all of the company-specific risk diversified away, the component returns $\bar{r}_i$ can be estimated using formula 5–15. This would be true for portfolios that are market indexes such as the S&P 500, Value Line Index, and NYSE Index on which futures are currently traded.

If portfolios are not diversified as much as possible, additional return, often called *alpha,* is required to compensate investors for any company-specific risk that exists in the portfolio

$$\bar{r}_p = \sum_{i=1}^{N} [w_i(\bar{r}_i + alpha_i)] \qquad (5\text{--}17)$$

where *alpha* = the additional return needed to compensate investors for the level of company i's diversifiable risk that remains in portfolio p.

The source of value for a portfolio in a multiperiod context can also be thought of as the sum of the dividends per share anticipated in each period and the proceeds of any sales of stocks in the portfolio. The present value of each dividend and cash flow further depends on their discounted values. The appropriate required portfolio return $(\bar{r}_p)$ is used as the discount rate. If the portfolio is changing in composition over time, the correct discount rate must be recalculated as these changes occur.

SECURITY DURATION AND VALUATION

The concept of a security's *duration* is important as a measure of the timing characteristics of the cash flows of that security and the sensitivity of its price to changes in the yield (bonds) or discount rate (stocks).[1] Earlier, we discussed the principles that govern the way in which bond prices react to changing yields. Several of these principles are related to the coupon rate and time to maturity of a bond. Duration is, in a sense, a measure that captures *both* the coupon rate and time to maturity influences on changes in bond prices. The comparable factors that would be reflected in a stock's duration are the dividend payments and the time to the receipt of the terminal value (selling price of the stock).

Duration is the weighted average time to maturity (or call) for fixed-income securities or to the terminal period in a stock valuation model. For bonds, the number of periods is based on features of the security itself. For a stock, the duration is uncertain and dependent on the number of periods chosen for use in the stock valuation model. The weights for each period w_i are based on the proportion of the security's total present value (or price) represented by the present value of that period's cash flow.

$$\text{Duration} = w_1 1 + w_2 2 + w_3 3 + \ldots + w_N N \qquad (5\text{--}18)$$

$$\text{where } w_i = \frac{C_i/(1+r)^i}{\text{Price}}$$

Exhibit 5–4 contains examples of duration calculation for four bonds that differ by maturity, coupon rate, and yield. Several general observations can be made regarding duration that are demonstrated in these examples.

1. A stock paying no dividends or a bond with no coupon payments (zero-coupon) would have a duration equal to its maturity or

EXHIBIT 5-4
Duration of Bonds with Different Maturities, Coupon Rates, and Yields

	Bond			
	A	*B*	*C*	*D*
Coupon	0%	10%	10%	10%
Yield	10%	10%	8%	10%
Price	74.62	100	105.24	100
Maturity	3 yr	3 yr	3 yr	2 yr

		Cash Flow Weight			
Periods		*A*	*B*	*C*	*D*
Year 1–1	1	0	.048	.046	.048
1–2	2	0	.045	.044	.048
2–1	3	0	.043	.042	.043
2–2	4	0	.041	.041	.864
3–1	5	0	.039	.039	
3–2	6	1.0	.784	.788	
		1.000	1.000	1.000	1.000
Duration (periods)		6	5.33	5.34	3.72
Duration (years)		3	2.66	2.67	1.86

to the number of periods until the terminal value is received. (Bond A)

2. For two securities of equal maturity, the higher the coupon rate or dividend yield, the lower the duration. (Bond A versus Bond B)

3. For two securities of equal coupon rate or dividend yield, the longer the maturity the longer the duration. (Bond B versus Bond D)

4. As yields or discount rates decrease, the duration of all securities (except zero-coupon bonds) increases. This occurs, because there is less reinvestment interest being earned on cash flows prior to maturity. This thereby decreases the proportion of cash flows that occur prior to maturity. (This effect is not large as seen in Bonds B versus C in the example.)

5. The duration number can be transformed to provide a measure of the percent of change in security price associated with a given change in yield. Duration is thus valuable as a proxy for the sensitivity of a bond's price to changing interest rates. Shorter (longer) duration bond prices are affected relatively less (more) by a change in interest rates.[2]

The implications of these results are also straightforward: by matching the time horizon and duration of an investment, a portfolio manager can almost completely neutralize the effects of rein-vestment rate risk.[3] This process is known as "immunization." Since the duration of a coupon-paying bond is normally less than its term to maturity, this means that if the investor wishes to mini-mize interest rate risk, it is generally preferable to hold bonds whose term to maturity exceeds rather than matches the invest-ment horizon.

The concept of duration is relevant to financial futures in two areas: hedging and the use of futures to alter bond or bond portfolio duration. With respect to hedging, we will see in Chapter 7 that the size of the futures position will depend on the duration of bond or portfolio being hedged. Also, one can view the process of hedging as effectively converting the duration of the securities being hedged to a value as close to zero as possible. This helps to protect the value of these securities from changes in yields (dis-count rates for stocks).

In addition, as futures approach delivery, the duration of the future will approach that of the deliverable security. Therefore, futures positions added to cash portfolios in either long or short positions can be tools for controlling duration and, therefore, inter-est rate risk exposure.

SUMMARY

Prices of financial futures are directly related to pricing fundamen-tals of the underlying cash security. Therefore an understanding of these pricing fundamentals of the spot security is basic to an understanding of financial futures. This chapter reviewed the pric-ing fundamentals of fixed income and equity securities and intro-duced the concepts of forward rates and the term structure of interest rates.

The prices of both fixed-income and equity securities were shown to be related to the future cash flow stream that is associated with holding a security. For Treasury securities this cash flow stream is fixed and certain. The cash flow of GNMA securities depends on the prepayment and default experience of loans in the mortgage pool. Stocks have future cash flows that are uncertain and must be forecasted to find an expected dividend level. The security's cash flows must be discounted to determine the price, using a discount rate that represents the return required for invest-ments of equivalent risk to the security.

Several principles were identified that indicate how a fixed income security price will be affected by changing interest rates. Essentially, the longer the maturity, the lower the coupon rate, and the greater the price discounted from face value, the more a bond will appreciate (depreciate) in value from a given decrease in bond yield.

Another fundamental aspect in the pricing of a fixed-income security is that the promised yield on a long-term asset cannot be less than the return of a combination of shorter-term securities encompassing the same time period. If one could obtain a greater return by rolling over shorter-term securities than by holding a long-term bond, the long-term security would be sold. This would cause the yield of this long-maturity security to become comparable to the combination of short-term rates. Higher yields on long-term securities can also be attributed to a preference for the greater liquidity of short-term securities.

Due to different cash flow expectations among securities, even assets of equal maturity may not be priced the same. Alternative measures such as duration have also been used to explain relative security pricing. From an understanding of the pricing fundamentals of securities, one can proceed to a better understanding of the relative price movements of the securities and the associated financial futures contracts.

APPENDIX A

The Mathematics of Yields

Most yields, especially long-term yields, are quoted in coupon-equivalent terms. Short-term yields, by contrast, are often stated in what is called the discount basis. The two yields are computed differently and can produce rather different numbers. Coupon-equivalent yields assume that interest payments take place semiannually and are based on 365-day year. Discount yields, in contrast, work with a 360-day year and assume that the interest is deducted at the outset. As a result, stated discount-basis yields are somewhat below the coupon-equivalent yield computed for the same security.

The formula for a one-year security's discount-basis yield is:

$$d = \frac{D}{F} \tag{5-19}$$

where: d = discount-basis yield,
F = face value, and
D = discount from face value.

Thus, a $1,000 face value one-year bond selling for $900 would be priced at a $100 discount and would offer a discount yield of 10 percent ($100/$1,000).

A slightly more complicated formula is required for maturities of less than one year:

$$d = \frac{D}{F}\left(\frac{360}{M}\right) \tag{5-20}$$

where: M = number of days to maturity

Accordingly, the discount yield for a Treasury bill with 250 days until maturity selling for $9,500 would be computed as follows:

$$\frac{\$500}{\$10,000} \times \frac{360}{250} = 7.20\% \tag{5-21}$$

We can compute the simple-interest yield from the discount basis yield with the following formula:

$$i = \frac{365\,d}{360 - d\,M} \tag{5-22}$$

where:

i = simple-interest yield

Applying formula (3) to our previous example produces:

$$i = \frac{365\,(.072)}{360 - (.072)(250)} = 7.68\% \qquad (5\text{--}23)$$

Thus, we see that the simple-interest yield (7.68 percent) appreciably exceeds the discount-basis yield (7.20 percent) for this security.

The simple-interest yield approximates but does not equal the coupon-equivalent yield. The two yields differ, because the simple-interest formula assumes that the interest payments are received at maturity while the coupon-equivalent yield takes account of semiannual interest payments. When a security has less than six months to run, the two rates are equivalent. For long-maturity instruments, however, the following formula is employed to compute the coupon-equivalent yield on a security that is priced on a discount basis.

$$r = \frac{\dfrac{2\,M}{365} + 2\left(\dfrac{M}{365}\right)^2 - \left(\dfrac{2\,M}{365} - 1\right)\left(1 - \dfrac{1}{p}\right)}{\dfrac{2\,M}{365} - 1} \qquad (5\text{--}24)$$

where: r = coupon-equivalent yield,
P = price as a percentage of face.

Thus, a six-month Treasury bill selling at \$9,506.53 with 190 days to run would be handled as follows:

$$9.95 = r = \frac{\dfrac{2(190)}{365} + 2\left(\dfrac{190}{365}\right) - \left(\dfrac{2(190)}{365} - 1\right)\left(1 - \dfrac{1}{.950635}\right)}{\dfrac{2(190)}{365} - 1}$$

APPENDIX B

Pricing Bonds on Dates between Interest Payments

If a bond is bought on a date that falls between coupon payments, the seller of the bond should receive the portion of the semiannual interest that was earned by the bond while the seller still held it. The buyer of the bond will be the holder on the next coupon date and will receive the full six month's interest even though the buyer owned the bond for less than six months.

To resolve this inequity, the buyer of the bond pays the seller the accrued interest earned between the last interest payment and the sale date. This payment should be included in the valuation of the bond on the trade date. The formula below reflects accrued interest payments (both the coupon payment and yield are measured semiannually):

$$V_0 = \sum_{n=1}^{N} \frac{\{[C_n/(1+r)^n] + [V_N/(1+r)^N] + C_N\}}{(1+r)^{d/182}} - \{C_N[1 - (d/182)]\}$$

The numerator of the first term in the formula contains the price of the bond as of the next coupon date and the interest payment received at that time. This is then discounted for the portion of the six-month period left to the interest payment date using $(1+r)^{(d/182)}$. Finally, the accrued interest for the portion of coupon payment period up to the trade date $[1 - (d/182)]$ is subtracted to find the value V_0.

NOTES

[1] Numerous articles have discussed the problems and uses of duration in security analysis. See McEnally (1980), and Reilly and Sidhu (1980), and Gultekin and Rogalski (1984) for background on these issues.

[2] A modification is necessary to use duration directly in predicting percent changes in bond prices. This transformation simply divides the duration in (5–18) by $(1+r)$. Thus we can say:

$$\text{Estimated percent changes in } P = -\frac{\text{Duration}}{(1+r)} \times \text{change in } r.$$

[3] An assumption made in deriving duration is that yield curve shifts are parallel (i.e., equal for all maturities). To the extent that this does not hold, (5–18) will be an approximation.

SELECTED REFERENCES

Fabozzi, F. J., and I. M. Pollach, eds. *The Handbook of Fixed-Income Securities.* Homewood, Ill.: Dow Jones-Irwin, 1983.

Feldstein, Martin, and Otto Eckstein. "The Fundamental Determinants of the Interest Rate." *Review of Economics and Statistics* 52, no. 4 (November 1970).

Fisher, Irving. "Appreciation and Interest." *Publication of the American Economic Association* XI.

Gultekin N. B. and R. J. Rogalski, "Alternative Duration Specifications and the Measurement of Basis Risk: Empirical Tests." *Journal of Business*, LVII, no. 2 (April 1984), pp 241–264.

Homer, Sidney, and Martin Liebowitz. *Inside the Yield Book.* Englewood Cliffs, N.J.: Prentice-Hall, 1971.

Lutz, F. A. "The Structure of Interest Rates." *Quarterly Journal of Economics* LV (November 1940).

Malkiel, Burton G. *The Term Structure of Interest Rates: Theory, Empirical Evidence, and Applications.* New York: McCaleb-Steeler Publishing Company, 1970.

Markowitz, Harry M. "Portfolio Selection." *Journal of Finance* 7, no. 1 (March 1952).

McEnally, Richard. "How to Neutralize Reinvestment Risk." *The Journal of Portfolio Management,* Spring, 1980, pp. 59–63.

Modigliani, Franco, and Gerald Pogue. "An Introduction to Risk and Return." *Financial Analysis Journal* 30, no. 2 (March–April 1974), and 30, no. 3 (May–June 1974).

Modigliani, Franco, and Richard Sutch. "Innovations in Interest Rate Policy." *American Economic Review* LVI (May 1966).

Reilly, Frank, and R. Sidhu. "The Many Uses of Bond Duration." *Financial Analyst Journal* (July–August 1980), pp. 58–72.

Sharpe, William F. "Capital Asset Prices: A Theory of Market Equilibrium under Conditions of Risk." *Journal of Finance* 19, no. 4 (September 1964).

————. "A Simplified Model for Portfolio Analysis." *Management Science* 10, no. 1 (January 1963).

Van Horne, James C. *Financial Market Rates and Flows,* 2nd ed. Englewood Cliffs, N.J.: Prentice-Hall, 1984.

CHAPTER 6

Valuation Fundamentals
for Financial Futures

In their simplest form, futures prices are prices set today to be paid in the future for goods or securities. The price of a futures contract thus depends in part on an assessment of the future price of the underlying instrument at delivery, based on information currently available in the market. Part of this market information is the fact that for some securities, one can arrange to own the underlying instrument on the delivery date by buying it *today* at the current market price and storing it until that time. If this opportunity is available, the cost associated with immediate purchase and storage until delivery will certainly be an important factor in the price one is willing to pay for a futures contract. Holding the futures contract enables one to avoid the investment of cash and the storage, or carrying costs, that would be incurred if the good or security is bought "early" and stored until delivery.

Other important factors may influence the market's assessment of the futures price of the underlying instrument. These include: (1) uncertainty in the supply or demand for the deliverable security between the date in which the futures price is set and the delivery date, (2) any cash flows, such as dividends or interest payments, that one would receive if the security rather than the futures contract were held, and (3) any risks or uncertainties that futures contract holders are exposed to that makes them willing to pay less for a futures contract than they would in the absence of such risks.

These risks include "basis risk" which must be borne by hedgers using financial futures. This risk arises from fluctuations in the spread between the cash and futures price. Some movement in the basis is expected over the life of a future. However, the underlying motivation for hedging is that the "basis" is much less volatile than the prices of the underlying security. Another risk associated with futures positions is the need to immediately make good for losses in the value of a futures contract (referred to as marking-to-market). Uncertainty with respect to the exact instrument that will be delivered and the prices at the point of each settlement also can play a role in price determination for futures. In this chapter we will be discussing each of these factors and risks in turn, as they relate to the valuation of financial futures. At each point, one example will be given of the financial future to which a particular form of the pricing model applies.

TAXONOMY OF FINANCIAL FUTURES

To understand the valuation of the different types of financial futures that are available today, it is useful to categorize financial futures in terms of the features that are important to the valuation process. Exhibit 6–1 highlights these distinctions among financial futures contracts. The first distinction that should be made is between futures involving *storable versus perishable* instruments for delivery.[1] For futures based on physical instruments, storable delivery items include grains, metals, and petroleum products. Perishable futures contracts are those based on items that are not necessarily deliverable in more than one particular futures contract month. Such physical commodities as cattle, hogs, and broilers are perishable in that they may only meet the contract specifications for delivery in one particular month.

Storable physical commodities are referred to as "carry commodities," because they can be carried from one contract month to another if a later delivery is advantageous. Hence, the basic model for valuation of futures contracts is called the *carry-cost model.* Relative prices for the commodity in the cash market and in the futures market depend on the cost of carrying or storing that commodity over the time to delivery.

With respect to financial futures, most contracts call for delivery of securities that can be carried for delivery in several alternative contract months. Thus, the carry-cost model is the starting point for financial futures valuation. The exceptions to "storable" security futures are Treasury bills, Eurodollars, and CD futures. Since these futures call for delivery of a 90-day security, the security delivered into a particular futures contract will have perished or matured before the delivery date of the next futures contract 90 days later.

Even for futures on these 90-day securities, there is always a security available that can be purchased and carried to contract delivery and that will have 90 days remaining to maturity on the

---

EXHIBIT 6–1
Categorization of Financial Futures Contracts

Storable and Income-Producing		*Perishable*
U.S. Treasury note futures		Treasury bill futures
U.S. Treasury bond futures	versus	Negotiable CD futures
GNMA CDR futures (I and II)		Eurodollar futures
Stock index futures		

Cash Delivery		*Security Delivery*
Stock index futures		Market-basket delivery option
Eurodollar futures	versus	U.S. Treasury bond note futures
Municipal bond futures		GNMA CDR futures (I and II)
(proposed)		CD futures
		Treasury bill futures

delivery date. Therefore, it is possible to estimate the cost of carrying a security that will be acceptable for delivery into any financial futures contract. For example, any Treasury security that has exactly three months remaining to maturity on the delivery date would be acceptable for delivery. This could include Treasury bills originally issued as one year or six month bills. As we pointed out in the preceding chapter, the price of a six-month Treasury bill reflects the current three-month interest rate and a forward rate for the subsequent three months. Therefore, even financial futures based on nonstorable securities can be valued in terms of the cost of carrying a deliverable security into the next futures contract.

Another important distinguishing characteristic among financial futures contracts is whether the deliverable security provides *income* in the form of interest and dividends. This income may be certain, as in the case of interest on fixed-income securities, or uncertain, as in the case of dividends on stock indexes. The income received on the security is a disincentive to purchasing the future as an alternative to the cash security. We shall see that the net of this income received and the carrying costs associated with the cash security determines the extent to which futures prices are above or below cash security prices.

The *timing* of income payments over the time to delivery can also affect the pricing of financial future contracts. For instance, dividend payments on stock indexes do not occur evenly over the time remaining to delivery. The pattern of dividend flows is thus important in stock index futures valuation. If income flows are uncertain, as are GNMA certificate payments and stock index dividends, riskless arbitrage between cash and futures is not possible.

Finally, the *form of delivery* is important in the valuation of financial futures. With cash delivery futures, such as stock index and Eurodollar futures, the delivery price is set at a particular time on the delivery date. The difficulty in arranging for a cash market transaction exactly at the precise time the delivery price is set, means that there will always be some basis risk for this type of financial futures. A trader with a short future and long cash position is unlikely to receive the exact dollar equivalent of the gains or losses reflected by the futures contract price at maturity, if an attempt is made to sell the securities in the cash market.

Other types of financial futures allow for alternative securities to be delivered. These are called market-basket delivery contracts. The delivery proceeds for each acceptable security are set by the exchanges. The seller has a "delivery option" and may choose to deliver the security that has the highest invoice price as compared to its purchase cost in the cash market. This security is called the *cheapest-to-deliver*. GNMA and Treasury bond and note futures are in this category. In addition, the futures seller can choose to execute delivery on any day in the contract month. In these types of financial futures, only the seller of futures can engage in riskless arbitrage, because the buyer cannot be certain as to what particular security will be received prior to delivery or what the exact date and time of delivery will be.

We develop the pricing fundamentals for financial futures by analyzing the valuation of each of these different types of contracts. Examples of financial futures that fit into each particular category will be given. Futures contracts that are introduced subsequent to publication of this book can be analyzed in terms of these particular features and valued accordingly.

THE PURE CARRY–COST MODEL OF FUTURES PRICES

Explanation and Examples of the Model

The simplest process for valuation of futures applies to those contracts that call for delivery of a security that has a liquid cash market, has a supply that is relatively fixed in quantity (or highly predictable), and that provides no intermittent cash flows such as interest or dividends. An example of a future that meets most of these criteria is the Treasury bill future. New bills are issued weekly, so the supply is not certain, but Treasury funding requirements are announced prior to issue. Unanticipated variations in the amount of new issues are a small portion of the total amount outstanding.

The carrying cost concept of futures pricing links current prices of futures to current cash prices and to the cost of "carrying" deliverable securities until the futures contract expires. This linkage is possible, because purchasers and sellers of Treasury bills (and CDs) view the cash and futures markets as a competing means of acquiring and selling these securities. When prices in either the cash or futures market are cheap relative to the other market after reflecting carrying costs, marginal purchasing will occur in the market with the lowest price, and selling will occur in the market with the highest price. The trader with the cheapest access to funds will dominate the price setting mechanism in the marketplace.

Assume that on December 20, 1984, investment managers A and B expect to be respectively buying and selling Treasury bills near the end of March 1985. Any cash available in the interim earns 0.8 percent interest per month or approximately 9.6 percent per annum. This is also the cost of borrowing funds. The buyer of the Treasury bills anticipates an increase in price (lower rates) prior to March and thus wishes to lock in an interest return by buying a 180-day Treasury bill today or by buying a 90-day Treasury bill on March 20 via the Treasury bill future, whichever is cheaper. Exhibit 6–2 contains an analysis of these alternatives. If he or she buys a 180-day bill on December 20 versus a 90-day March Treasury bill future, the total expenditure will be 95.20 plus 2.40 in interest expenses for financing costs the period of December 20–March 20 for total of 97.60 (prices are expressed in terms of percent of par value). The March Treasury bill future at 97.70 is thus more expensive. Investor A would attempt to buy the Treasury bill now in the cash market.

Investor B expects prices to fall (interest rates to rise) between now and the March 20 selling date for a 180-day Treasury bill he now owns. He thus would like to set a selling price based on either the cash or futures market price as of December 20. The March futures price of 97.70 is attractive to him relative to the 97.60 that he could receive if he sold the Treasury bill in the cash market today and invested the proceeds at 0.8 percent per month. He will therefore place an order in the futures market to sell the March contract.

Eventually, selling pressure in the futures market will force

---

EXHIBIT 6–2
Futures versus Cash Market Transactions and Carrying Costs

Assumptions: .8% Monthly Interest Rate (9.6% per annum)

December 20	December 20 to March 20	March 20
A: 1. Buy 180-day Treasury bill: annual discount rate 9.6%, price 95.20	3 months financing cost .8 × 3 = 2.40	Total cost of Treasury bill: 95.20 + 2.40 = 97.60
2. Buy March Treasury bill future: annual discount rate 9.2%, price 97.70	Interest cost = 0	Total cost of Treasury bill: 97.70

Savings from buying Treasury bill in cash market = 97.70 − 97.60 = .10 or $10/$10,000 Treasury bill

B: 1. Sell 180-day Treasury bill: annual discount rate 9.6%, price 95.20	3 months interest revenue from investing cash .8 × 3 = 2.40	Total cash from Treasury bill sale: 95.20 + 2.40 = 97.60
2. Sell March Treasury bill: annual discount rate 9.6%, price 97.70		Total cash from Treasury bill sale: 97.70

Savings from selling Treasury bill in futures market @ 97.60 = .10 or $10/10,000 Treasury bill the futures price to fall to a level where no clear advantage exists to buying in the cash market and selling in the futures market. If this does not occur, 10 basis points or $10/$10,000 Treasury bills can be earned risk-free for each Treasury bill purchased in the cash market on December 20 and sold via the March 20 futures contract.

The relationship expressed in the example above can be restated as:

$$FP_t = CP(1 + r)^t \qquad \text{(6-1a)}$$
or ignoring interest compounding
$$FP_t \approx CP + (CP \times r \times t) \qquad \text{(6-1b)}$$
Futures price = Cash price + Carrying costs

where FP_t = the current price of a futures contract calling for delivery in t months,

CP = the current price of a security deliverable into the future contract

r = the rate of interest per month, and

t = the number of months until delivery.

Note that we use a basic time period of a month in the formulas and examples. These could be easily restored in terms of a daily interest rate and days until delivery.

In the example above, the futures price should be no higher than 97.503 or:

$$97.503 = 95.20 \, (1 + .008)^3$$

The futures price (FP_t) will equal the price of the deliverable security CP plus the cost of financing the purchase of that security for t months until delivery at the monthly interest rate r. From another perspective, we can say that the futures price equals the amount that would be accumulated if one delayed purchase of the Treasury bill until the delivery of the futures and deposited the cash price (CP) in the bank to earn r interest for t months. (Both of these statements are true as long as the cost of financing equals the interest earned.)

It is useful to apply this relationship to the discussion of forward interest rates in the previous chapter. We showed there that the cash price of a six-month Treasury bill can be expressed as either:

$$CP = \text{Face value}/(1 + r_{0,2}) \qquad \text{(6-2a)}$$
$$CP = \text{Face value}/(1 + r_{0,1})(1 + R_{1,2}) \qquad \text{(6-2b)}$$

where $r_{0,1}$ and $r_{0,2}$ are the spot interest rates, and $R_{1,2}$ is the forward interest rate in terms of the three-month periods in the six-month period to maturity.

Since $r_{0,1}$ is also the carrying or financing cost over the first three months, (6–1a) can be restated in terms of the forward rates as:

$$FP_2 = [\text{Face value}/(1 + r_{0,1})(1 + R_{1,2})] \times (1 + r_{0,1}) \quad (6\text{–}3a)$$
$$FP_2 = \text{Face value}/(1 + R_{1,2}) \quad\quad\quad\quad\quad\quad (6\text{–}3b)$$

The futures price should equal the price of a forward contract based on the face value of the Treasury bill divided by the forward rate for the second 90-day period. This forward rate $(R_{1,2})$ is reflected in the cash price of the 180-day bill.

Other implications can be analyzed as well. The difference between the futures and cash price should approximate the carrying cost as a percentage of the securities' face value. This difference between the cash and futures price is often referred to as the *basis*. For financial futures, the basis is primarily a function of the financing costs of the cash security. Similarly, the difference between the rate implied by the futures price and the rate on a Treasury bill deliverable into the future (180-day) should equal the financing rate for the period prior to futures delivery. Finally, the sum of the rate on a 90-day bill $(r_{0,1})$ and a future calling for delivery in 90 days $(R_{1,2})$ should approximate the rate of a 180-day Treasury bill $(r_{0,2})$. This result is an approximation because it ignores the compounding of interest on a monthly basis.

Similar relationships should exist in the prices of Treasury bill futures for different delivery months. If the March Treasury bill future is "cheap" relative to the June future, a trader could buy Treasury bills with the March futures, sell the bills with the June future, and pay the three months of carrying charges. This will be profitable as long as the spread between the prices of the two futures contracts is higher than these carrying charges. This is illustrated below:

$$FP_{t_2} = FP_{t_1}(1 + r)^{(t_2 - t_1)} \quad\quad\quad (6\text{–}4)$$
$$97.93 = 97.70(1 + .008)^3$$

where: $t_1 = 3$ on the September future,
$t_2 = 6$ on the December future.

The price spread between the two futures prices, given monthly carrying charges of $r = 0.8\%$, should be equal to 0.24 percent of the \$1 million face value. $[0.24\% = (1.008^3 - 1) \cong (97.93 - 97.70)]$.

Thus, we would expect Treasury bill futures contracts of different delivery months to be priced in a pattern that reflects the market's assessment of the relevant carrying (financing) charges. If this is not true, those market participants with easy and cheap market access will quickly arbitrage away any significant deviations. Even more important, we would expect to see all Treasury bill futures prices respond to any change in carrying costs. That is, any information that changes the markets assessment of forward interest rates will result in changes in Treasury and CD futures prices as well as in cash market prices. The spread between futures and cash prices and futures prices in different contract months will widen as forward rates (carrying costs) rise and will narrow as rates fall.

Repurchase Agreement (Repo) Rates as Carrying Costs

The short-term interest rates that are usually associated with carrying costs in the cash and futures market are rates on repurchase agreements (repos) for Treasury securities. The "repo" market is commonly used to finance short-term government bond positions and for investing cash held by financial and nonfinancial institutions on a very short-term basis. It is a large dealer market in which most volume consists of overnight sales of government securities with an agreement to repurchase these securities a day later at a price reflecting overnight interest changes.

In a repurchase agreement the seller gets use of cash for one day (is in effect borrowing the cash using the securities as collateral). The buyer is investing (lending) cash overnight in government securities which are guaranteed by the legal agreement to be "repurchased" by the seller the next day. (This process is illustrated in Exhibit 6–3.) There is also a *term* repo market for periods longer than a day, but this is a much thinner market than the overnight repo market.

Most arbitrageurs in Treasury bill, note, and bond futures mar-

---

EXHIBIT 6–3
Structure of a Repurchase Agreement

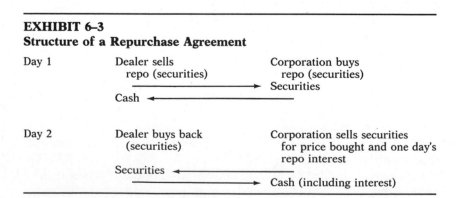

kets are government security dealers. These dealers are frequent traders in government securities who finance their inventories in the repo market. They regularly use the futures market to hedge their inventories and to engage in trades that attempt to profit from situations in which prices deviate from their values as implied by the carry-cost model.

An arbitrageur in the Treasury bond market may feel the carrying cost implied in futures prices is attractive versus rates available on repurchase agreements. He or she can borrow cash at the repo rate to finance a cash position in bonds, which can then be delivered into a short futures position. If the arbitrageur is right, the proceeds from the futures sale will be more than enough to repay the loan plus interest at repo rate, providing arbitrage profit.

What, if any, is the risk of such a transaction? Many experts argue that the term *arbitrage* can only be used when there is a clear no-risk profit to be made because of price discrepancies in different markets on identical instruments. For example, if a stock were selling for different prices on the NYSE and Pacific Coast Exchange, an arbitrage opportunity would be available by buying the stock in the cheaper market and selling it in the higher-priced market. In cash-futures price comparisons, there are very few instances of perfect arbitrage opportunities.[2] There are, however, many very low-risk situations in which those traders who have cheap access to both markets and who can finance their positions at repo rates can attempt to capitalize on perceived price discrepancies.

One source of risk is the fact that not all traders can lock in a carrying cost very cheaply for periods of more than a month. This means that whenever a future is more than one month from delivery, the trader cannot be exactly sure what the carrying costs will be. Assume, for example, a carrying cost (annualized) of 12 percent is reflected in the price of a future calling for delivery in two months. The overnight repo rate may currently be lower, say 11.5 percent. The trader does not know for certain what repo rates will be over the whole two-month period. Financing rates in the repo market could increase to 12.5 or 13 percent, in which case the financing charges could exceed the implied return in the futures market. Fortunately, as repo rates rise, the value of the futures contract will be falling, generating immediate profits for the seller that can be used to pay the increasing financing charges.

Another risk of cash-futures arbitrage is the need to immediately post cash equal to any losses on the futures position (marking-to-market). Consider the above example, but change the situation to one in which rates fall, resulting in losses to the futures seller as the futures price rises. There should be funds available from lower financing charges to make good on the losses on the futures position. A problem can arise, however, if futures prices do not change exactly in step with overnight repo rates. Savings from lower financing (repo) rates may not be sufficient to cover losses in the futures position. This problem also arises from the fact that it is difficult to lock in a financing arrangement exactly equal to the duration of the futures contract.

One can, therefore, think of the interest rate component of the carrying cost as reflected in futures prices as a multiperiod rate which can vary on a day-to-day basis until the futures delivery date. The repo rate implied in the futures contract is related to the current actual overnight rate and a series of daily forward rates for each day until futures delivery. Traders take long or short positions depending on their assessment of the forward daily repo rate structure as distinct from that implied by the "multiday" rate in the futures prices.

These illustrations of the carrying cost concept have all referred to Treasury bill futures. Because of their lack of default risk, financing for these securities can be secured very readily through the repo market. In contrast, the underlying instruments on other types of financial futures often have limitations on the amount that can be borrowed against positions. Therefore, only very large, financially sound traders engage in the arbitrage that relies on financing the cash side of the position. With respect to stock indexes, for example, most investors are subject to short sale margin regulations and can only borrow a maximum of 50 percent of the value of a stock portfolio. The proceeds of short sales of stocks in the cash market are not available for futures arbitrage and must be kept on deposit with the broker. Only brokerage firms have full use of funds from short positions in stocks. Thus, in many of the futures markets, the amount of cash-futures arbitrage based on carrying costs depends on the level of participation in positions in the cash market and the capacity to finance these positions.

PRICES OF FUTURES WITH CASH SETTLEMENT

Eurodollar and stock index futures are settled by an exchange clearinghouse with a simple transfer of the cash variation margin balances from any open long position to any open short positions remaining at the close of trading on the last trading day. Many proposed contracts, such as those on subindexes of stocks and on municipal bond and commodity price indexes, will be settled in cash if approved. The 1981 CFTC ruling approving a Eurodollar futures contract with cash settlement was critical to the introduction of the successful stock index futures contracts. It is possible that as many as half of the new futures contracts introduced in the next decade will involve cash settlement.

With cash settlement one cannot actually acquire or dispose of the deliverable instrument via the futures market. Ideally, one should receive (or pay) at settlement an amount of cash equal to what would be needed to execute a purchase or sale in the cash market at the exact time and date of settlement. The carry-cost model applied to cash settlement financial futures can be restated to include a random component which we will call lambda (λ).

$$\tilde{F}P_t = CP\,(1 + r)^t + \tilde{\lambda} \qquad (6\text{–}5)$$
$$\text{or}$$

Futures price $\cong$ Cash price + Carrying cost + Lambda

Lambda (λ) represents the difference between the cash received by the seller of futures at settlement and the proceeds that would be realized if those same securities were sold in the cash market. The *ex ante* value of λ (before termination of the futures contract) is equal to zero. For the investor with a long position in futures at settlement, λ represents the difference between the cash settlement value and the actual amount involved to acquire those securities in the cash market as close as possible to the exact settlement time and date. Because of the possibility of a time delay and transactions costs in implementing the transaction to buy or sell the securities (or goods) represented by the index, λ will take on values that vary from zero *ex post* (after contract settlements).

To see this more clearly, consider Bank S, the holder of a Eurodollar deposit. This bank wishes to hedge the risk of rising Eurodollar rates by selling Eurodollar futures. The bank holds the contract to the delivery point. At this time, rates have risen and a profit on the short futures position is credited to Bank S in cash. The rate on which cash settlement is based is the average of quotes selected from the sample banks at two points in time on the last trading day of the Eurodollar futures.

Since the bank cannot sell the Eurodollar deposit directly into the futures contract, an arrangement is made to sell the deposit to another bank, Bank B, at its quoted Eurodollar rate at the close of trading on the futures delivery dates. If Bank B's rate is above the rate on which cash settlement of the futures is based, Bank S with the short futures position will not have sufficient profits from the futures delivery to offset the lower price at which the future is sold. In all likelihood, Bank S will shop around to find a bank that will in fact purchase the Eurodollar deposits from Bank S at a price higher (rate lower) than that realized from cash settlement of the Eurodollar future.

Another example of this cash settlement effect is the case of stock index futures. Assume the manager of an index fund wishes to lock in the cost of a portfolio of S&P 500 securities by buying S&P 500 futures. The manager takes delivery of S&P 500 futures contracts and receives cash equal to the difference between the price of the futures position and the closing value of the S&P 500 on the day the contract closes. The fund manager can wait until the opening of the exchange the next business day to acquire the actual stocks and bear the risk of new overnight information. The manager could alternatively begin buying the stocks just prior to the close of trading on the last trading day of the future. In the latter case, however, the portfolio manager will have the risk of changes in the value of the index during the last trading hour.[3] There will also be transaction costs of executing the purchase of the stocks in the index.

Since the expected value of λ is zero, the carry-cost model does not need to be modified for use in futures valuation. However, it is important to recognize that pure riskless arbitrage with cash settlement options is usually not possible. Observed deviations between the futures price and cash price close to delivery can be partially explained by this uncertainty as represented by λ.

PRICES OF FUTURES ON INCOME–PRODUCING SECURITIES

A further modification of the futures valuation model is required to account for the fact that the holder of futures gives up any interest or dividend income that would be received if the cash security were held. The link between futures and cash prices depends on the relative cost or benefit of holding futures as opposed to cash market instruments. One must, therefore, consider all the relevant cash flows that would accrue to holders of a cash market position.

In other words, if futures prices depend on the costs of financing or carrying a security during the life of the future, they also depend on the income derived from holding this security. For deliverable securities that are expected to produce income (e.g., dividend payments or coupon interest between the time of price determination and delivery), this income amount must be netted against any financing or other carrying charges to determine the theoretical futures price.

Futures prices on Treasury bonds, GNMA securities, and stock indexes are influenced by the amount and timing of any coupon income or dividend receipts that would be received during the life of the future if one held the deliverable instruments. The greater the income return on the deliverable instrument, the lower the futures price, because purchase of the future as an alternative to the cash security means foregoing such income.

The timing of the income receipts is also important. The earlier income flows are received, the greater is the "reinvestment income" that can be earned on that income. The present value of such income discounted at the rate at which it can be invested becomes a component of the futures price. For futures on securities that have such intermittent cash flows, equation (6–5), representing the pure carrying cost model of futures prices, can be rewritten as

$$\tilde{F}P_t = CP\,(1+r)^t - \Sigma_t\,I_t/(1+r)^t + \tilde{\lambda} \qquad (6\text{–}6)$$

where $I_t =$ the cash flows accuring to holders of the deliverable security during month t.

We can further simplify (6–6) by letting *INC* represent the present value of income received on the cash security or

$$INC = \Sigma_t\,I_t/(1+r)^t$$
$$\tilde{F}P_t = CP\,(1+r)^t - INC + \tilde{\lambda} \qquad (6\text{–}7a)$$
$$\text{or}$$
$$\tilde{F}P_t \cong CP + (CP \times r \times t) - INC + \tilde{\lambda}. \qquad (6\text{–}7b)$$
$$\tilde{F}P_t - CP \cong (CP \times r \times t) - INC + \tilde{\lambda} \qquad (6\text{–}7c)$$

The coupon income of fixed-income securities is constant over time. The carrying cost r is not. Relative values of the futures and cash price change with the financing rate as detailed previously for Treasury bill futures. However, the difference between the futures and cash price will be smaller than it would be in the absence of coupon income. The income flows on stock indexes in the form of dividends are not fixed and vary over time as individual stocks pay dividends at different times during the year. The income component of stock futures prices is estimated with uncertainty. The dividend flows of the index depend on the earning levels and payout rates of the stocks included in the index. There is some seasonality in dividend and coupon payments that can be quite important in pricing stock index futures around seasonal payment peaks and drops. Also, differences in dividend flows among the various stock indexes on which futures are traded are a factor influencing their relative prices.

If the underlying security pays a stream of income that is evenly distributed over the time remaining to futures delivery at constant monthly rate i, the formula (6–7b) can be further simplified to:

$$FP_t = CP(1 + r - i)^t \qquad \text{(6–8a)}$$
$$FP_t \cong CP + (CP \times t \times r - i) \qquad \text{(6–8b)}$$

Consider the situation in which the hedger buys the securities one month before delivery at the cash price and sells (delivers) them the following month at the futures price to earn a rate of return $f = [(FP - CP)/CP] + i$. In this case, the futures price should be such that the rate of return on the hedge (f) should equal the one-month rate of interest or carrying cost.

$$f = \frac{FP - CP}{CP} + i$$

from equation 6-8b   (6–9a)

$$FP - CP = CP\,r - CP\,i$$
(dividing by CP)

$$\frac{FP - CP}{CP} + i = r \qquad \text{(6–9b)}$$

$$f = r$$

This is the expected result, because the fully-hedged (risk-free) position would be expected to return the risk-free rate of interest r.

Another way of looking at this same relationship is to see that the percentage difference between the future and the cash price will be equal to the difference between the carrying cost r and the income rate i, or

$$\frac{FP - CP}{CP} = r - i. \qquad \text{(6–10)}$$

Therefore, when the repo rate or carrying cost exceeds the income return, futures prices will be above cash prices. Cash prices will be higher than futures prices when the carrying cost is below the income rate. For futures on intermediate and long-term bonds, this means that when the yield curve is downward sloping, cash prices will be below futures prices, and futures prices of near-term futures will be below those of long-term delivery futures. When the yield curve is upward sloping, futures prices will be lower than the cash prices and will decrease as a function of the number of months to delivery.

These pricing relationships are illustrated in Exhibit 6–4, in which Treasury bond futures prices are shown for two dates, March 15 and December 15 of 1982. In March of 1982, the federal funds rate (which tends to be very close to the overnight repo rate) averaged 14.68 percent versus the yield on long-term bonds of 13.75 percent. In December, the short-term rate was 8.95 percent, and the long-term rate 10.62 percent. As shown in the table, the futures prices as of March reflect an increasing net cost of carry (after income) while the futures prices as of December reflect a decreasing net cost of carry.

Before moving to the topic of valuation of Treasury bond futures, we wish to discuss the valuation of stock index futures. These futures, like long-term fixed-income futures, have an income stream on the underlying security reflected in their prices. This income is in the form of dividends on the stocks in the index. If the total dividends occurring over the period to delivery were paid in equal amounts on each day of the period to delivery, the percent difference between the futures and cash prices would be equivalent to the difference between the annualized repurchase agreement rate r and the dividend yield i as shown in equation (6–10). As long as this short-term interest rate exceeds the dividend yield, which is usually the case, we would expect to see stock index futures prices exceeding cash prices:

$$\frac{FP - CP}{CP} = \text{Short-term interest rate} - \text{Dividend yield.}$$

In fact, because of the uneven nature of the timing of quarterly corporate dividend payments, the above relationship only holds

---

EXHIBIT 6–4
Treasury Bond Futures Prices—An Example of Relative Prices in Different Yield Curve Environments

Downward Sloping (Inverted) Yield Curve (March 15, 1982)		Upward Sloping (Normal) Yield Curve (December 15, 1982)	
March 1982	62–04	December 1982	76–15
June	62–14	March 1983	75–22
September	62–28	June	75–05
December	63–04	September	74–22
March 1983	63–15	December	74–13
June	63–25	March 1984	74–04

exactly three or six months prior to futures delivery. Even at this point in time, one should adjust for the difference in the *discounted* value of the dividends versus the carrying cost or interest. Even though the total amount of dividends received over the quarter is unrelated to their timing, the discounted value of these dividend payments would depend on payment timing. Over 80 percent of the total dividends are paid in the first two of the three months in the quarter.

The stock index futures valuation model can be specified in one of the two forms below:

Futures price:
$$SFP = SCP + r\,SCP - INC + \tilde{\lambda} + \tilde{u} \qquad (6\text{--}11)$$

Percent difference between futures and cash prices:
$$\frac{SFP - SCP}{SCP} = r - d + \tilde{\lambda} + \tilde{u} \qquad (6\text{--}12)$$

where r = the interest rate applicable to the period remaining to delivery,

INC = the dividend income (per unit of the index) that will be paid prior to delivery,

$d = INC/SCP$ or the effective dividend yield for the period remaining to delivery of the future, and

$\tilde{u}$ = the prediction error in the forecast of INC.

Exhibits 6–5 and 6–6 show the dividend distribution patterns for the NYSE Index for the fourth quarter of 1983. Almost 60 percent of the dividends received are paid in the fifth week of the quarter. Almost 90 percent are paid by midquarter. Thus, a buyer of NYSE futures on October 27, 1983, would be willing to pay much less for the futures than one buying the future 15 days later on November 12, even though the cash price of the NYSE may not have changed at all. In an article in the *Financial Analysts Journal*, Gastineau and Madansky [1983] provide tables for determining the theoretical futures value at different levels of interest rates, annual dividend yield, and days to contract delivery.

As an example of this income effect, the theoretical value of the NYSE futures can be determined at two points in time. Let us assume that we are valuing the NYSE future 60 days prior to the last trading day with 80 percent of the quarterly dividends still to be paid and 45 days prior to delivery with only 20 percent of the dividends yet to be paid. On both dates, we will assume the cash price of the index is 100, and the interest rate is 10 percent. We will use 4 percent as an annual dividend rate (1 percent per quarter).

EXHIBIT 6–5
Intraquarter Percentage Dividend Distribution, Quarter IV, 1983.

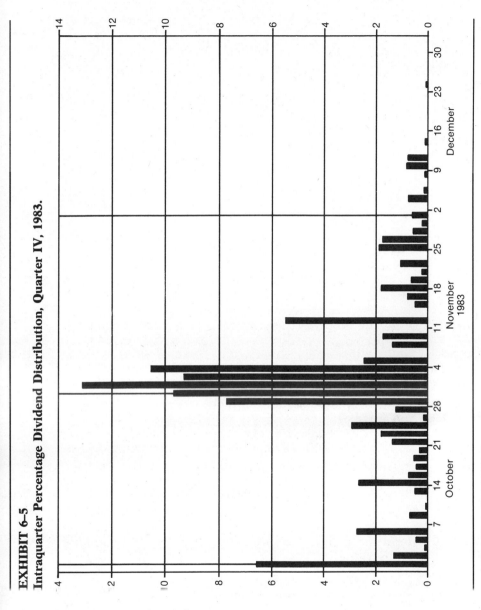

All stocks in the NYSE index.
Source: New York Stock Exchange (estimated as of 11/2/83).

EXHIBIT 6–6
Cumulative NYSE Dividends, Quarter IV, 1983.

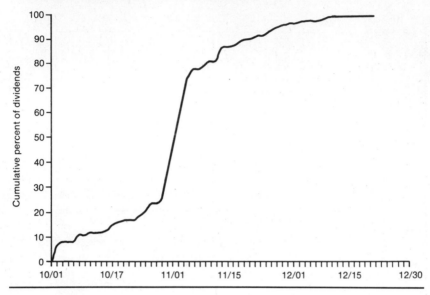

Step 1.   Find the interest (carrying cost) rate r for 60- and 45-day periods.

$$60 \text{ days: } 10\% \times 60/365 = 1.6\%$$
$$45 \text{ days: } 10\% \times 45/365 = 1.2\%$$

Step 2.   Find the amount of interest for 100 points of index value.

$$60 \text{ days: } 100 \times 1.6\% = 1.60$$
$$45 \text{ days: } 100 \times 1.2\% = 1.20$$

Step 3.   Find the dividend rate d applicable for each period.

60 days: 1% × 80% of dividend left to be paid = 0.8%
45 days: 1% × 20%   "   "   "   "   = 0.2%

Step 4.   Find the dollar amount of dividends for 100 points of index value.

$$60 \text{ days: } 100 \times 0.8\% = \$.80$$
$$45 \text{ days: } 100 \times 0.2\% = \$.20$$

Step 5.   Find the prices of futures.

$$SFP_{60} = 100 + 1.60 - .80 = 100.80$$
$$SFP_{45} = 100 + 1.20 - .20 + 101.00$$

Step 6.   Find percent difference between futures and cash price.

$$\frac{SFP_{60} - SCP}{SCP} = 1.6\% - .8\% = 0.8\%$$

$$\frac{SFP_{45} - SCP}{SCP} = 1.2\% - .2\% = 1.0\%$$

This example illustrates the effect of the cash security's income payments on futures prices. All else equal, the payment of income will increase the attractiveness of the stock index future vis-à-vis the stock index, thereby making the future more attractive for purchase. The net effect is an increase in the price of the future.

Stock index futures prices tend to differ from their theoretical values by much greater amounts than do prices of Treasury bond or Treasury bill futures.[4] The typical range of prices around the theoretical value had been roughly plus or minus 1.0 percent until the fall of 1984.[5] Since that time deviations from the theoretical value have been much larger, with prices at times as much as 4 or 5% above theoretical values. Arbitrageurs watch the market closely for these mispricings and will act very quickly to attempt to bring prices back into line.

Several reasons have been given for this apparent mispricing, most of which relate to features of the contract that cannot be easily incorporated into the valuation model. These include the risk of uncertain dividends, cash settlement, and the transaction costs associated with arbitrage. An additional explanation for this mispricing is that many traders in the stock index futures market are felt to be more motivated by overall market sentiment than by arbitrage considerations. Because of the leverage available in futures on equity indexes, speculators can trade based on a market opinion with limited amounts of capital. Also, the broad index base presents an opportunity to acquire or sell a single instrument representing a large portion of the stock market. When new information is released that affects assessments of equity value, this new information may be reflected in futures prices before it can be reflected in the value of an index composed of numerous stock issues that trade independently of one another.

When any of these factors drive the stock index futures prices out of line from their carry-cost values, cash-futures arbitrageurs should step in to exploit this opportunity. Because the futures are based on such a broadly-defined index, however, arbitrage can be quite expensive. Thus, we would only expect arbitrageurs to enter the market when prices deviate from their theoretical value by more than the cost of arbitrage. This is shown in Panel A of

Exhibit 6–7. Futures prices could fluctuate within a band defined by these arbitrage costs without encouraging intervention by arbitrageurs.

In fact, with such broad-based stock index futures as the NYSE, S&P 500, and Value Line, the cost of arbitraging the more than 500 stocks in the index over short time periods is simply too high to make such arbitrage feasible. Instead, a smaller index-proxy portfolio of approximately 50–100 stocks that tracks the movements in the index closely is typically used for cash-futures arbitrage. There is some basis risk in this type of trade, but the savings

---

EXHIBIT 6–7
Deviations of Futures Prices from Theoretical Value

A.

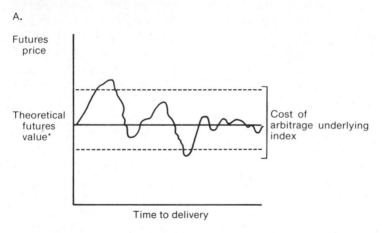

B.

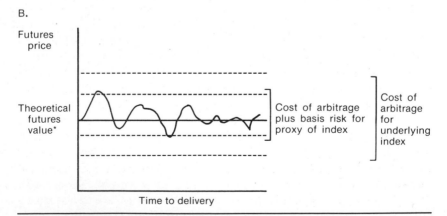

* The theoretical value will of course change over time, but is held constant here for illustrative purposes.

in trading costs tend to more than offset the additional basis risk taken on by the arbitrageur. As shown in Panel B, we can then expect to see stock index futures prices fluctuate within a band defined by the cost of arbitraging this index-proxy and the desired amount of compensation the arbitrageur wishes to receive for assuming the basis risk associated with the proxy. The Major Market index future consisting of only 20 stocks is much easier and less costly to arbitrage. We would expect MMI futures to have fewer instances of mispricing and would expect their underlying stocks to be actively traded by these arbitrageurs.

The deviations of stock index futures prices from their theoretical value provide opportunities for buyers and sellers to time the opening and closing of their positions. In particular, those using stock index futures contracts as hedging instruments should look for situations in which the futures prices are at the upper end of this arbitrage band as an opportunity to sell futures and situations in which futures are at the bottom of this band when they are attempting to buy futures.

These futures could possibly stay on one side of the theoretical value for the entire life of the contract. This means that if one sold stock index futures when they were overvalued, they may remain slightly overvalued or even get more overvalued within this band all the way up to the last trading day. In this case, one would have to actually accept delivery in order to profit from the extent to which the futures were overvalued when opening the short position.

PRICES OF FUTURES WITH MARKET–BASKET DELIVERY

Delivery Criteria

Futures on GNMA pass-throughs and Treasury bonds are designed to permit the seller to deliver alternative securities that fit delivery criteria specified in the contract. The delivery criteria for Treasury bond futures is a maturity or call date at least 15 years from the first futures delivery date. Treasury note futures require delivery of notes with 6½ to 10 years remaining to maturity from the first day of the delivery month.

The GNMA CDR contract calls for delivery of a collateralized depository receipt for a specific principal amount of GNMAs. Any GNMA security can be used for collateral for the CDR. The principal balance required is adjusted to make alternative GNMAs equivalent to $100,000 of the principal of 8 percent GNMA certificates.

The new GNMA futures contract, GNMA II, accepts for delivery any GNMAs with a coupon rate at or below the coupon rate on GNMAs issued within roughly six months of the delivery date. The GNMA's must also have at least 20 years remaining to maturity at the end of the delivery month.

At the time any futures contract is trading, only one futures price will be quoted. This will be the futures price based on the standard-grade 8 percent coupon bond with 20 years to call or maturity. However, all or most of the bonds available for delivery are nonstandard, each with a different coupon rate and call or maturity date.

This market-basket delivery is made possible through the use of *conversion factors*. These conversion factors are used to determine the principal or face value amount of a particular Treasury or GNMA security that should be delivered. At delivery, the buyer must pay an invoice price per contract. *(IP)* that is equal to the futures prices times the conversion factor *(CF)*.

$$IP = FP \times CF \qquad (6\text{–}13)$$

The total invoice amount in dollars will equal the invoice price (expressed as a percent) multiplied by the size of the contract ($100,000) and the number of contracts involved, plus any accrued interest on the bonds being delivered.

Total invoice amount $= [(IP \times$ Contract size$) +$ Accrued interest per contract$] \times$ Number of contracts   (6–14)

Conversion Factors

The conversion factor *(CF)* is the bond price (expressed in decimals) of a standard issue that is acceptable for delivery and that will provide an effective yield of 8 percent. For calculation, the time to call or maturity is rounded to the nearest quarter starting from the first day in the delivery month.[6] For those bonds with an even number of semiannual periods to maturity, the conversion factor formula becomes:

$$CF = \left(\sum_{t=1}^{n} \frac{C_t/2}{(1.04)^t} + \frac{1,000}{(1.04)^n} \right) \div 1,000$$

$$= \left(C_t/2 \frac{\dfrac{1}{1 - (1.04)^n}}{.04} + \frac{1,000}{(1.04)^n} \right) \div 1,000 \qquad (6\text{–}15)$$

where $n =$ number of semiannual periods to call or maturity and $C_t/2 =$ semiannual coupon payment.

If the number of semiannual periods to maturity includes an extra quarterly period, this formula must be modified:

$$CF = \left\{ \left[\frac{\left(\sum_{t=1}^{n} \frac{C_t/2}{(1.04)^t} + \frac{1,000}{(1.04)^n} \right) + C_t/2}{(1.04)^{3/6}} \right] - C_t/2(1 - 3/6) \right\} \div 1,000$$

As an example of calculating a conversion factor, consider the 12¾ percent Treasury bond of November 15, 2010, callable in the year 2005. The last contract that this bond could be deliverable against is the September 1990 contract. If this bond had been delivered on December 10, 1980, against the December 1980 Treasury bond futures contract, there were 24 years, 11 months, and 5 days to first call. This period would be rounded down to 24 years and 9 months, or 49 semiannual periods plus a quarter. The conversion-factor calculation would then be derived:

$$CF = \left\{ \left[\frac{\left(\sum_{t=1}^{49} \frac{127.5/2}{(1.04)^t} + \frac{1000}{(1.04)^{49}} \right) + 127.5/2}{(1.04)^{3/6}} \right] \right.$$
$$\left. - 127.5/2(1 - 3/6) \right\} \div 1,000 = 1.5082$$

Given that there exists a different futures price for every deliverable bond, the seller of futures will want to deliver that Treasury bond which has the highest invoice price (delivery-equivalent price + accrued coupon interest) relative to the price of the underlying cash instrument (quoted bond ask price + accrued interest to date of purchase). This bond is known as the *cheapest-to-deliver,* and all futures contracts should be priced in relation to this bond. The reason this relationship should hold is that arbitrageurs can make money on cash-futures price discrepancies by simultaneously buying the Treasury bond in the cash market and selling a corresponding Treasury bond contract in the futures market.

Many of the arbitrageurs in the futures markets are government securities dealers who will finance their purchase of Treasury bonds in the overnight market for repurchase agreements (repo market). If the financing costs of the arbitrageur are less than the gross return on the cash-futures position, the arbitrageur will earn a "risk-free" profit. Since any bond satisfying the futures contract specifications can be delivered, the arbitrageur will deliver that bond that maximizes his or her net profit. The arbitrage will be continued until the futures price declines or the cash price rises such that profits can no longer be made from the transaction. This equilibrium pricing relationship is examined more closely in the next section.

Futures Valuation for Market-Basket Delivery Contracts

As with stock index futures, these fixed-income futures are priced based on the price of a cash security that provides income to the holder. The relevant income for all bonds and notes acceptable for delivery into Treasury futures is the coupon interest remaining to be paid until delivery. In addition, the cash price of the bond or note must be adjusted upward from quoted prices to include any accrued interest between the last coupon date and the pricing date.

The amount of accrued interest A can be found by multiplying the annual coupon payment by the portion of the year since the last coupon payment.

A = Annual coupon payment $\times$
(Number of days from last coupon payment/365 days)   (6–16)

The income *(INC)* received by holding the bond or note (or GNMA certificate) to delivery of the future is also based on the coupon rate.[7] This is found most easily by multiplying the annual coupon payment by the portion of the year left until futures delivery:

INC = Annual coupon payment $\times$
(Number of days until delivery/365)   (6–17)

The theoretical invoice price *(IP$_t$)* can be determined using a carry-cost approach:

$$IP_t = (CP + A)(1 + r)^t + INC \qquad (6\text{–}18a)$$
or
$$IP_t = (CP + A) + (CP + A)rt - INC \qquad (6\text{–}18b)$$

The theoretical futures price can then be derived from this invoice price by dividing IP_t by the relevant conversion factor:

$$FP_t = IP_t/CF \qquad (6\text{–}19)$$

As with stock index futures, this formula can be restated in terms of the difference between the coupon rate and short-term interest rate applicable to the period remaining to delivery.

$$\frac{(FP_t \times CF) - (CP + A)}{(CP + A)} = r_t - c_t \qquad (6\text{–}20)$$

where r_t = the interest rate applicable to the period
remaining to futures delivery.
c_t = the annual coupon rate times the portion of
year remaining to delivery.

For example, consider a Treasury bond future with exactly 90 days remaining to delivery. Assume that a cheapest-to-deliver bond has a conversion factor of 1.5, is priced at par, and has a coupon rate of 12¾ percent. The coupon rate for 90 days (c_t) would be equal to 12¾ percent divided by four or 3.19 percent. If the annual repo rate is 10 percent, r_t would equal 2.5 percent. Assuming there have been 60 days since the last coupon payment, the accrued interest would be 2.09 or $(60/365 \times 12.75)$.

$$FP_t = \frac{(100 + 2.09) + (102.09)(.025) - (.0319)(100)}{1.5} = \frac{IP_t}{CF}$$

$FP_t = 67.63$, $IP = 101.45$ or (67.63×1.5)

Similarly, the difference between the repo rate and coupon rate $(.025 - .0320 = -.0063$, or $-.63\%)$ is equal to the percent difference between the invoice price and the cash price plus accrued interest, or $[(101.45 - 102.09)/102.09]$.

Once one determines the cheapest-to-deliver security, the futures value or invoice value would be found using the formula above. These can be compared to the quoted futures price to see if the future is selling at a fair value relative to the cheapest-to-deliver. The futures price can always be multiplied by the conversion factor to be compared directly with the invoice value of the cheapest-to-deliver security.

To reiterate, this seemingly complex valuation process is actually very similar to that for stock index futures, with two exceptions:

1. The cash (quoted) price must always have any accrued interest added to it since that is the price one would pay to acquire the bond.
2. The futures price (quoted) must be multiplied by the appropriate conversion factor.

After making these two adjustments to the cash and futures price, one can proceed to find the relevant carrying costs and income on the cash security. With bonds, the income on the cash security is actually simpler to calculate than income for stock indexes, because it occurs evenly throughout the period remaining to delivery.

A valuation analysis of any of these market-basket delivery futures must begin with a comparison between the invoice prices and market prices (including accrued interest) of all bonds acceptable for delivery. The bond for which this difference is the largest will be the "cheapest" to purchase and deliver and should serve as the basis for the valuation calculations. Futures market participants will be focusing on the cheapest-to-deliver bond in setting their bid-and-ask prices. Since bond prices are changing constantly in the cash market, anyone using market-basket delivery futures for hedging or speculation should frequently update his or her analysis of which security is cheapest-to-deliver for a particular futures contract.

INSTITUTIONAL AND MARKET STRUCTURE INFLUENCES ON FUTURES PRICES

We now explore some other issues that are important in the pricing of futures. These influences on the one hand justify the existence of the futures market as a separate market and on the other hand result in futures prices that can differ from those suggested by the valuation models detailed above. The reasons for differences between the prices of futures and forward contracts will be discussed.

Futures prices can at times reflect expectations about future price levels of the underlying instrument and carrying costs that are not incorporated in current cash prices. The magnitude of the effect of expectations on futures prices varies among futures contracts depending on the ease and cheapness with which cash-futures arbitrage can be carried out and on the breadth and efficiency of the cash market. For example, as we discussed above, the U.S. Treasury bond futures market is felt by many traders to be a "carrying cost" market. Stock index futures markets are said to be significantly influenced by expectations or trader sentiment due to the difficulty of arbitraging broadly-based stock indexes.

Institutional factors often intervene in the process linking cash, futures, and forward prices. These institutional factors include unique characteristics of the futures market, some of which we have already discussed in the context of valuation: differences in market structure, marking-to-market of gains and losses, liquidity, uncertainty regarding actual security that will be delivered, initial margin requirements, transaction costs, different methods of taxing gains and losses, and performance guarantees.

Separation between Cash and Futures Markets

The separation between cash and futures markets can be attributed in part to market structure. It is useful to identify some of the most important reasons for this separation at this point in our discussion. First, futures markets are accessible to many individuals and institutions for whom the cash market is either closed or has high entry costs. In many security markets, transaction costs are very high for small transactions, and the minimum transaction size limits direct entry into the market. In some markets, acquiring and managing the underlying instrument would involve substantial expertise, time, and money. Such is the case with stock index funds. Also, except for brokers and dealers, investors cannot implement a short position in a security without giving up access to the proceeds of the short sale until the position is closed out with a stock purchase. This limits the extent to which asset holdings can be hedged and restricts available strategies to those involving long positions in securities.

Second, futures markets may be more liquid and efficient than cash markets, particularly when those cash markets are dealer markets dominated by a few large dealer firms. The futures exchange provides a central marketplace in which price quotations are public and widely disseminated. The presence of floor traders who trade actively keeps commission costs per trade low. In actively traded futures, such as the Treasury bond and stock index futures, a large position can often be acquired with a smaller impact on bid-ask spreads in the futures market than if the trade were executed in the cash market. Third, many economic units that wish to hedge anticipated positions on a security may not have access to the financing that would be necessary to carry out such a hedge in the cash market.

Marking-to-Market

Profits and losses on futures positions must be posted in cash on a daily basis for the duration of the futures position. The overall impact of this requirement is discussed at length in Chapter 8. This posting of variation margin (marking-to-market) deserves considerable attention in a discussion of financial futures, because it is a unique feature of futures as compared to other financial instruments. Black [1976] and Cox, et al. [1981], provide a theoretical treatment of the difference in futures and forward prices due to the initial and variation margin requirement of futures. At this point in our discussion, it is important to understand the effect of marking-to-market on the relative prices of forward and futures contracts.

Assume an individual has the opportunity to buy either a forward or futures contract on a Treasury bill at the same price. This price is considered "cheap" by the individual, given his or her expectations regarding future Treasury bill rates. The Treasury bill future would offer definite advantages should the investor be correct, because profits on the future would be marked-to-market (i.e., available for immediate withdrawal and investment elsewhere). If a forward contract were purchased, the investor would not realize profits until expiration of the contract. Similarly, other market participants might consider the same price "high" (on forward and futures) and choose to sell the future in an attempt to earn quicker profits.

This marking-to-market requirement can also be perceived as a distinct disadvantage. The investor could be wrong regarding his or her assessment of the direction of prices. Losses on the futures position would need to be made good immediately, imposing an opportunity cost disadvantage on futures relative to forward contracts. In either case, it should be clear that this institutional feature may result in price disparities between futures and forward contracts. Investors will choose between the two instruments depending on their risk preferences, confidence in their forecasts, and the opportunity costs associated with posting variation margin. Relative prices in the future and forward markets will therefore depend on the relative distribution of these characteristics among investors.

Liquidity Factors

Liquidity factors can be a potential source of price differences between futures and forward contracts. Forward contracts have the advantage of being structured to meet the exact denomination and maturity requirements of the investor. Futures, on the other hand, are standardized in terms of delivery date and the type of securities to be delivered. There is a tradeoff involved in that futures are more liquid because of their standard terms. However, these same standard terms may introduce risks to an investor who does not wish to trade in exactly the security units and delivery date called for in the futures contract.

Liquidity is useful, because the expectations of the investor may change prior to the delivery date, or the investor may wish to close out the position earlier than initially planned. A futures position may be easily closed out by an offsetting trade in the futures market at any time. A forward contract is usually held until delivery and, it can be effectively terminated by engaging in another offsetting forward contract for the same amount.

Delivery Risks

As discussed above, the buyer of futures contracts does not always know the characteristics of securities that will be delivered into the future. The contract rules provide for some discretion on the part of the futures seller as to the actual securities delivered. Even though a certain security may be theoretically the best to deliver examining quoted prices, there may be a shortage in the amount of that security that is actually available for sale.

Cash settlement may serve as the delivery mechanism in the futures and not in the forward market. Therefore, buying securities via futures versus forward contract arrangements has a disadvantage for the purchaser who does not have total control over the type of securities that are delivered or who cannot bear the timing risk associated with cash settlement. Treasury bond and note futures have several elements of timing risk in the delivery process that should be noted as potential influences on futures prices. The futures seller may choose any day in the delivery month to deliver including after the futures contract ceases trading. Delivery may also occur up to 6 P.M. (EDT) in the trading day at settlement prices set at 2 P.M.. These provisions are options to the Treasury bond (note) futures seller that are likely to be reflected in prices of the futures (See Gay and Manaster [1984] for further discussion.)

Taxes, Transaction Costs, and Initial Margin Requirements

Initial margin requirements exist with futures and not with forward contracts. This margin is usually only a small percentage (less than 10 percent) of total contract value and can be posted in the form of cash or Treasury bills on which the investor continues to earn interest. It is not, therefore, a burden for those who already hold government securities in the normal course of their business. Since no margin requirements exist *per se* for forward contracts, some market participants might be willing to pay a higher price for a forward position to avoid posting the initial margin.

Specific tax rules apply to futures contracts in that 40 percent of such profits are treated as short-term gains and 60 percent as long-term gains. The relative tax effects between futures and forward contracts are very specific to the particular situation of the market participant. It is important here to realize that such differences do exist and can also result in price differences.

Costs of trading in futures markets are based on whether one is or is not a member of a futures exchange. A round-trip trade of one contract typically costs around $30 to $60 for nonmembers and $2 for members. Costs of forward market transactions are not easily measured. No commissions are charged, but large financial institutions participating in the markets bear the costs of maintaining the staff, trading network, and bookkeeping. This may therefore be implicitly factored into price quotes of market-makers in the forward market. Here again, the differences in market structure would be expected to influence relative prices.

Performance Guarantees

Lastly, differences in prices between futures and forward contracts can occur due to different performance guarantees between the two markets. In futures markets, the clearing corporation insures that all contracts are upheld should one of the parties default. In effect, the cost of this insurance is paid in the form of fees to the clearing corporation by futures market participants. No such formal performance guarantee exists in forward markets. However, entry into a forward contract is restricted to these firms or traders who meet the financial criteria of the market-makers. Also, informal penalties can be applied in the case of contract default (i.e., other business with the defaulter can be terminated, further entry into the market can be restricted by communications of the default among market-makers, etc.). There is sufficient cause for one to include these different types of default control in the list of institutional causes of futures and forward price disparities.

SUMMARY

This chapter dealt with the valuation of different types of financial futures contracts. The simplest type of financial future is valued by adding the price of the underlying security to the cost of carrying that security until it can be delivered into the futures contract. Treasury bill futures were used as an example of futures whose prices follow the pure carry-cost model.

Other types of financial futures have special characteristics that must be considered in the valuation process. Cash settlement futures such as Eurodollars and stock index futures cannot be exactly valued or perfectly arbitraged because the futures buyer making delivery or futures seller taking delivery must execute a transaction in the cash (security) market to actually buy or sell the "deliverable" instrument.

Any income payments associated with the deliverable security serve to offset the carrying cost component of the futures price. Therefore, for stock indexes, bonds, notes, and GNMA futures it is necessary to forecast the income stream and timing of that stream through the delivery date to obtain an accurate assessment of the value of the future. This was shown to be especially important for stock index futures because the timing of dividend payments is uneven during each quarter.

Treasury bond, Treasury note, and GNMA CDR futures have a market-basket delivery process in which several securities are acceptable for delivery. The valuation process for these futures must therefore be preceded by a determination of which outstanding security is cheapest-to-deliver at any point in time. For this security a conversion factor is needed to adjust the futures value to a level that can be compared to the exchange price to determine if the futures for Treasury bond and GNMA futures is undervalued or overvalued. Valuation of the market-basket delivery futures is also complicated by the fact that one does not know with certainty prior to delivery the bond that will be cheapest-to-deliver in the delivery period.

Institutional and market structure factors that can potentially impact the futures valuation process were also identified. These factors included the separation between cash security and futures markets due to different access privileges, differences in liquidity, and market structure. The marking-to-market requirement of futures, contract liquidity, the delivery process, taxes, transaction costs, and performance guarantees were also discussed in terms of differentiating between the value of futures and forward contracts.

NOTES

[1] Frank J. Jones provided an interesting explanation of this distinction and its importance in an article in the 1982 *Journal of Futures Markets* (1981).

[2] See Kolb, Gay and Jordan (1982) for a discussion of riskless arbitrage opportunities in Treasury bond futures.

[3] There have been several instances of large changes in the value of stock indexes in the hours preceding futures contract expiration. See Hill (1985) for a more detailed discussion of this topic.

[4] For empirical studies of the efficiency of prices in the Treasury bill futures, Treasury bond futures, see Rendelman and Carabini (1979), Kolb et al. (1982), Resnick and Hennigar (1983).

[5] In the early months of the S&P 500 futures contract, there was a systematic undervaluation of the futures prices of as much as 5 or 6% of index value.

[6] Conversion factors are available from the Chicago Board of Trade Marketing Department or from the Financial Publishing Co., Boston, MA 02215.

[7] Accrued interest for GNMA CDRs is paid monthly at a rate of $635 per month or 7.62 percent per year. The holder of a CDR would be entitled to 635 times the portion of the month up to the delivery day.

SELECTED REFERENCES

Anderson, R. "The Determinants of the Volatility of Futures Prices." *Center for Study of Futures Markets,* no. 33 (June 1982).

Arak, M., and C. McCurdy. "Interest Rate Futures." *Quarterly Review of the Federal Reserve Bank of New York,* Winter 1980, pp. 44–46.

Black, F. "The Pricing of Commodity Contracts." *Journal of Financial Economics* 3 (1976), pp. 167–79.

Cornell, Bradford. "The Relationship Between Volume and Price Variability in Futures Market." *Journal of Futures Markets,* Fall, 1981, pp. 303–16.

—— and K. R. French. "The Pricing of Stock Index Futures." *Journal of Futures Markets* 3, no. 1 (1983), pp. 1–14.

Cox, J. C., J. E. Ingersoll, Jr., and S. A. Ross. "The Relation Between Forward and Futures Prices." *Journal of Financial Economics* 9 (1981), pp. 321–46.

——, and Stephen Ross. "The Relation Between Forward Prices and Futures Prices." *Center for Study of Futures Markets,* no. 9 (May 1981).

Draper, D. W., and J. W. Hoag. "Portfolio Strategies Using Treasury Bond Options and Futures." *Review of Research in Futures Markets* 2, 1 (1983), pp. 82–98.

French, Kenneth. "A Comparison of Futures and Forward Price." *Center for Study of Futures Markets,* no. 42 (November 1982).

Friedman, Daniel, Chenn Harrison, and Jon W. Salmon. "The International Role of Futures Markets." *Center for Study of Futures Markets,* no. 50 (December 1982).

Gastineau, G., and A. Madansky. "S&P 500 Stock Index Futures Evaluation Tables." *Financial Analysts Journal,* November–December 1983, pp. 68–76.

Gay, G. D., and S. Manaster. "Implicit Delivery Option and Optimal Delivery Strategies for Financial Futures Contracts." *Center for the Study of Futures Markets,* no. 95 (October 1984).

Hill, J. M., and T. Schneeweis. "An Analysis of the Impact of Variation Margin in Hedging Fixed-Income Securities." *Review of Research in Futures Markets,* 2, no. 1 1983, pp. 136–59.

Hill, J. M. "Price Swings and Arbitrage Strategies." *Intermarket,* Vol. 2, no. 4 (April 1985), pp 36–39.

Jarrow, R. A., and G. S. Oldfield. "Forward Contracts and Futures Contracts." *Journal of Financial Economics* 9 (1981), pp. 373–82.

Jones, F. J., "Spreads: Tails, Turtles, and All That." *Journal of Futures Markets* 1, no. 4 (1981), pp. 565–96.

——. "The Integration of Cash and Futures Markets for Treasury Securities." *Journal of Futures Markets* 1, no. 1 (1981), pp. 33–57.

Kamara, A. "Issues in Futures Markets: A Survey." *Journal of Futures Markets,* Fall 1982, pp. 261–94.

Kane, Edward. "Arbitrage Pressure and Divergence Between Forward and Future Interest Rates." *Center for Study of Futures Markets,* no. 21 (May 1980).

Kolb, R. W., G. D. Gay, and J. V. Jordan. "Are There Arbitrage Opportunities in the Treasury Bond Futures Market?" *Journal of Futures Markets,* Fall 1982, pp. 217–29.

——, J. V. Jordan, and G. D. Gay. "Futures and Expected Future Spot Prices." *Review of Research in Futures Markets* 2, no. 1 (1982), pp. 110–23.

Lang, R., and R. Rasche. "A Comparison of Yields on Futures Contracts and Implied Forward Rates." *Federal Reserve Bank of St. Louis*, December 1978, pp. 21–30.

Liebowitz, M. "The Analysis of Value and Volatility in Financial Futures." Monograph 1981–83, Salomon Brothers Center for the Study of Financial Institutions, New York University.

———. "Yield Basis for Financial Futures." *Financial Analysts Journal*, January–February, 1981, pp. 43–51.

Modest, D., and M. Sundaresan. "The Relationship Between Spot and Futures Prices in Stock Index Futures Markets: Some Preliminary Evidence." *Journal of Futures Markets* 3, no. 1 (1983), pp. 15–42.

Rendleman, R., and C. Carabini. "The Efficiency of the Treasury Bill Futures Market." *Journal of Finance* 34, no. 4 (September 1979), pp. 895–914.

Resnick, B. G. "The Relationship Between Futures Prices for U.S. Treasury Bonds." *Review of Research in Futures Markets* (forthcoming), 1984.

Resnick B. G., and E. Hennigar. "The Relationship Between Futures and Cash Prices for U.S. Treasury Bonds." *Review of Research in Futures Markets* 2, no. 3 (1983), pp. 282–99.

Schneeweis, T. R., J. M. Hill, and M. G. Philipp. "Hedge Ratio Determination Based on Bond Yield Forecasts." *Review of Research in Futures Markets* 2, no. 3 (1983), pp. 338–49.

Telser, L. G., and H. N. Heginbotham. "Organized Futures Markets: Costs and Benefits." *Journal of Political Economy* 5 (1977), pp. 969–99.

Working, Holbrook. "Futures Trading and Hedging." *American Economic Review* 43 (June 1953), pp. 314–43.

———. "New Concepts Concerning Futures Markets and Prices." *American Economics Review* 52 (June 1962), pp. 431–59.

Hedging Strategies

Financial futures markets offer a means to hedge the risk of unexpected price changes because they permit the future purchase or sale of an asset at a price set today.[1] Corporations, security dealers, investment companies, insurance companies, pension funds, and banks are all exposed to price volatility risk associated with stock and bond holdings, anticipated stock and bond purchases, and the sale of stock and bond issues.

A hedge is simply the purchase (sale) of a futures market position as a temporary substitute for the sale (purchase) of the security in the cash market. A hedge is usually carried out by buying (selling) a futures contract to initiate the hedge and closing out the position when the cash market transaction occurs by selling (buying) the contract in the futures market rather than taking (making) delivery. A hedge can generally be classified as a *cash hedge* or an *anticipatory hedge*. The cash hedge involves the hedge of an existing position in the cash market. In contrast the anticipatory hedge entails the hedge of a cash position that has not been taken but is expected to be taken in the future. When a futures contract is available in the financial instrument owned, a *direct hedge* may be conducted. When a futures contract is not available for the financial instrument to be hedged, a cross-hedge may be constructed with a futures contract calling for delivery of another security.

In a hedge, risk is reduced to the extent that the gain (loss) in the futures position offsets the loss (gain) on the cash position. Thus, hedging has the effect of exchanging the risk of possible price changes in the cash market for the risk of a change in the relationship between the cash and futures prices. As shown in Exhibit 7–1, while hedging with futures reduces the risk of loss, it also reduces the chance of gain compared to the unhedged asset. The hedge position has a smaller chance of a low return but also a lower chance of a high return. Hedging is normally conducted only when the hedger is uncertain of future price movements.

THE BASIS

Since hedging in the financial futures market involves establishing a position in the futures market to offset an existing or planned security position, hedgers must consider the relationship between value of the security being hedged and the price at which the corresponding futures contract trades. The benefits of financial futures depend on how well the security's cash price follows the futures price. The difference between the cash and futures price is called the *basis*.

EXHIBIT 7–1
Return Distribution for Assets Hedged by Selling Futures

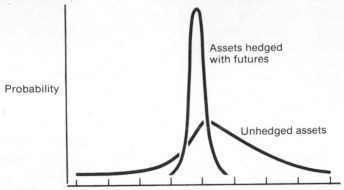

The basis can be positive or negative. As pointed out in Chapter 6 the price of a futures contract should equal the price of today's deliverable cash security less any difference between the income from the deliverable cash security and the cost of borrowing the deliverable security. An example of basis is given in Exhibit 7–2. In measuring the basis for Treasury bonds, Treasury notes, and GNMAs, the futures price is multiplied by the conversion factor of the cash security. This permits the cash price and futures price to be compared directly (see Exhibit 7–3).[2]

As shown in Exhibit 7–3, the basis is not constant during a hedge period. In fact, with a direct hedge the cash and futures prices should converge at delivery as cost of carry approaches zero and arbitrage keeps prices of like financial assets in line.

EXHIBIT 7–2
Financial Futures—Basis

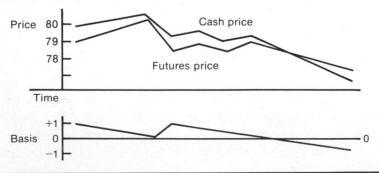

Prior to delivery, the basis can change due to unexpected changes in the cost of carry as well as unexpected changes in the price relationship between the cash security and the futures contract. The chance of changes in the direction or magnitude of the basis is called basis risk.[3] For a hedge to reduce risk, the price variation of the hedged position should be less than the price variation of the cash instrument. A hedge should reduce risk by substituting the smaller variability in the basis for the security's larger price variation. Thus, for a hedge to be successful, the characteristics of the cash and futures contract should be sufficiently similar to

EXHIBIT 7–3

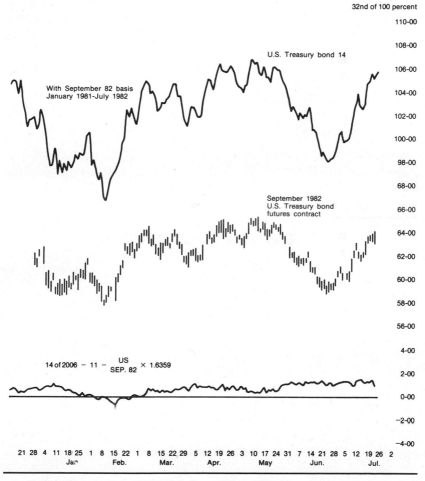

Source: Chart courtesy of Data Lab Corp., Chicago, Illinois.

result in a high degree of positive correlation in their respective price changes during the hedge period.

HEDGING AND THE BASIS

The goal of hedging is the construction of an offsetting futures position to a cash market position such that the dollar price change will be identical but opposite in direction on each side of the hedge. Understanding the basis (the difference between the cash price and futures price) is central, therefore, to establishing a proper hedge.[4]

A proper hedge attempts to match a change in the cash price to the change in the futures price. If a hedger sells the future short to protect against an unexpected decrease in cash prices, the hedge is referred to as a *short hedge*. It is important to remember that in a short hedge, hedgers wish to sell the cash security later and offset their short futures position by buying back their futures contract. In a short hedge, a hedger has a net gain if the cash price rises more rapidly relative to the futures price or if the futures price falls more rapidly relative to the cash price (e.g., the basis increases in value or strengthens).

If a hedger buys the future to protect against an unexpected increase in price, the hedge is referred to as a *long* hedge. In long hedges, a hedger wishes to later purchase a cash security and offset his or her long futures position by selling the futures contract. Thus, in a long hedge, the hedger has a net gain if the cash price falls faster relative to the futures price or if the futures price rises more rapidly relative to the cash price (e.g., the basis decreases in value or weakens).

The effect of basis changes on profitability can be better seen when we view the basis as either increasing in value (i.e., "strengthening") or decreasing in value (i.e., "weakening"). Thus, as illustrated in Exhibit 7–4, a *short hedger* who buys the basis will have a net gain if the basis strengthens (e.g., becomes increasingly more positive or less negative). As illustrated in Exhibit 7–5, a long hedge will have a net gain if the basis has weakened (e.g., become increasingly more negative or less positive).

In Exhibit 7–4, the short hedge that results in a net gain is the one in which the basis increases in value (example 2). The short hedge that results in a net loss is the one in which the basis decreases in value (example 3). In Exhibit 7–5, the long hedge results in a net gain when the basis decreases in value (example 2). The long hedge results in a net loss when the basis increases in value (example 3). Even when the hedge results in a net loss,

EXHIBIT 7–4
Short Hedge

		Cash		Futures		Basis
(1)	Buy:	100	Sell:	97		+3
	Sell:	93	Buy:	90		+3
		−7		+7	change:	0

Net: 0. No change in basis.

		Cash		Futures		Basis
(2)	Buy:	100	Sell:	103		−3
	Sell:	98	Buy:	97		+1
		−2		+6	change:	+4

Net: +4. Basis increases in value.

		Cash		Futures		Basis
(3)	Buy:	100	Sell:	97		+3
	Sell:	93	Buy:	92		+1
		−7		+5	change:	−2

Net: −2. Basis decreases in value.

EXHIBIT 7–5
Long Hedge

				Futures		Basis
(1)	Market price:	100	Buy:	97		+3
	Buy:	105	Sell:	102		+3
		−5		+5	change:	0

Net: 2. No change in basis.

				Futures		Basis
(2)	Market price:	100	Buy:	97		+3
	Buy:	105	Sell:	103		+2
		−5		+6	change:	+1

Net: +1. Basis decreases in value.

				Futures		Basis
(3)	Market price:	100	Buy:	105		−5
	Buy:	110	Sell:	108		+2
		−10		+3	change:	−7

Net: −7. Basis increases in value.

the gain in the future's position does offset a portion of the loss in the cash position. Over time the net change in value of a hedged position will generally be less than the change in an unhedged cash position. This is true since the variability of a hedged position is dependent only on changes in the basis, whereas the variability of an unhedged position is dependent on changes in the level of the cash security's price.

Good hedge management, therefore, necessitates a decision-making process that explores the possible gains and losses due to basis fluctuation. The hedge decision also involves a determination of hedging alternatives and a program to initiate and execute the hedge. It is important again to note that hedging will not insure an investor or trader against losses or assure gains. Anticipated price changes are built into the structure of futures prices. Therefore, only unanticipated price changes may be hedged. However, a hedged position should, over time, have a lower variability in value than an unhedged position.

HEDGE RATIO DETERMINATION

Since price changes of the cash security and the futures contract are often not of the same magnitude, the success of a hedging strategy depends on determining the proper hedge ratio. The hedge ratio represents the principal (face value) of the futures contracts held relative to the principal (face value) of the cash security position. Since the face value of the cash position is not always equal to the face value of the futures contract, the number of futures contracts to be purchased or sold can be determined as follows:

Number of futures contracts
$$= \frac{\$ \text{ Face value of cash security or portfolio}}{\$ \text{ Face value of futures contract}} \times \text{Hedge ratio}$$

The important point to remember is that the goal of a hedge is to exchange the variability of the unhedged cash position for the variability of the hedged position. The hedge ratio that results in the maximum possible reduction in variability of the value of the hedged position is called the *minimum risk hedge ratio*. There are various methods for determining the hedge ratio used to find the number of futures contracts necessary to minimize the variability of a particular hedged position. In this chapter we review several basic hedge ratio models; (1) naive, (2) conversion factor, (3) regression, (4) basis point, (5) duration, and (6) yield forecast.

The Naive Hedging Model

In the naive model, the principal value of the futures contracts is set equal to the principal value of the cash position. The hedge ratio therefore is equal to 1. For instance, as shown in Exhibit 7–6, on October 1, 1984, a portfolio manager holds $1 million of

20-year, 8 percent Treasury bonds priced at 86.00 (yielding 9.58 percent). To protect the current holdings from a rise in interest rates and a decline in value, the portfolio manager executes a short hedge by selling 10 December Treasury bond futures contracts at 86.875. Each Treasury bond contract has a principal value of $100,000 such that the 10 futures contracts have a principal value equal to the $1 million cash position. On October 31, interest rates have risen while futures prices and bond prices have dropped. The position is offset by purchasing 10 U.S. Treasury bond futures contracts at 85.075 for a gain of $18,000 on the 10 contracts. Bond prices have fallen to 84.00 (yielding 9.84 percent), producing a loss on inventory of $20,000. This loss is partially offset, however, by the $18,000 gain in the futures market.

In this case, the hedge reduced the loss in the cash position. The naive model assumes that for equal principal value cash and futures positions that the price changes in the cash position will be offset by an equal price change in the futures market. The naive model ignores possible differences in the cash security and futures deliverable which may cause relatively unequal price movements of the cash security and futures contract.

Conversion Factor Model

The security being hedged often differs from the security acceptable for delivery of the contract. For instance, the Chicago Board of Trade Treasury bond contract is based on an 8 percent coupon. Matching $1 million in futures contracts (10 contracts at $100,000 each) against $1 million of higher coupon bonds may not provide the best protection against unexpected yield changes. The price movements of the two instruments can move differently and a simple matching of principal values is not adequate. For a given change in yield, the dollar value of lower coupon bonds changes by a larger dollar amount than the dollar value of higher coupon

---

EXHIBIT 7–6

	Cash Market	Futures Market*
October 1	Holds $1 million, 20-year, 8% Treasury bonds priced at 86.00 (yield 9.58%)	Sells 10 December Treasury bond futures contracts at 86.875 (yield 9.4735%)
October 31	Prices for bonds fall to 84.00 (yield 9.84%)	Buys 10 U.S. Treasury bond futures at 85.075
	Loss: $20,000	Gain: $18,000

* Yield equivalents are based on 8% 20-year bonds.

issues. To compensate for the differences in the price movement, the futures position can be adjusted by the conversion factor of the deliverable security. For Treasury bonds, the conversion factor is the price (assuming a par value of $1) at which the delivered bond will yield 8 percent at its current time to maturity or, if callable, at its current time to call. Thus, bonds with coupon rates higher (lower) than 8 percent will have a conversion factor greater than (less than) one. For instance the conversion factor for a 10⅜ percent Treasury bond maturing November 15, 2004–2009 is approximately 1.24. The conversion factor of 1.24 implies that for equal yield changes the 10⅜ percent bond is 1.24 times as volatile as the 8 percent bond.

As shown in Exhibit 7–7, to compensate for the greater volatility in dollar value of the 10⅜ percent Treasury bond versus the Treasury bond futures price, one could weight the hedge by selling 12 futures contracts rather than the 10 contracts the naive model would suggest. The 12 futures contracts are derived by multiplying the conversion factor by the principal value of the cash security divided by the principal value of the futures contract (e.g. ($1 million ÷ $100,000) × 1.2).

The conversion factor hedging model is designed for hedging Treasury bonds and Treasury notes. An alternative conversion factor model is used for GNMA CDRs and is presented in Chapter 12.[5] The conversion factor model assumes, however, that the cash security and the adjusted futures position are affected equally by changes in yields despite any differences in coupons or maturity. Alternative methods include techniques which attempt to more closely equalize the dollar change between the futures contract and the security being hedged for a given change in yield (e.g., basis point model, regression model, duration model, and yield forecast model).

EXHIBIT 7–7

	Cash Market	*Futures Market**
May 30	Holds $1 million 10⅜ Treasury bonds at 100.3125. Market value: $1,003,125	Sells 12 December Treasury bond contracts at 79.718. Market value: $956,625
September 30	Sells $1 million 10⅜ Treasury bonds at 87.50. Market value: $875,000	Buys 12 December Treasury bond contracts at 68.90. Market value: $826,875
	Loss: $128,125	Gain: $129,750
	Net Gain: $1,625	

* Based on 8 percent, 20 year bonds.

Basis Point Model

For cross-hedges, or when the cash and deliverable securities differ in maturity or coupon, the basis point model adjusts for relative price movements of the instrument to be hedged and futures contract. The hedge objective is to match the change in the dollar value of the security to be hedged with the change in the dollar value of the futures contract. For Treasury bond and Treasury note futures, the change in the price of the futures contract can be measured by the change in the dollar value of the cheapest-to-deliver security divided by its conversion factor. Moreover, the relative price change of a cash security to the cheapest-to-deliver security can be estimated by their relative basis point values. A basis point value represents the dollar change in the value of a $100,000 face value security in response to a .01 percent change in yield.

The cash security to be hedged and the cheapest-to-deliver security may however, have different yield volatilities in terms of how they respond to changes in economic conditions. Therefore the ratio of the basis point value of the cash security to the basis point value of the cheapest-to-deliver security (adjusted by its conversion factor) should be multiplied by an estimate of the yield volatility of the cash security to the cheapest-to-deliver security. The basis point model hedge ratio is given as:

$$HR = \left(BVC_s \div \frac{BVC_{cd}}{CF_{cd}} \right) \times B \qquad (7\text{--}1)$$

where HR = hedge ratio,
$\quad BVC_s$ = dollar value change per basis point of the cash security to be hedged,
$\quad BVC_{cd}$ = dollar value change per basis point of the cheapest to deliver security,
$\quad CF_{cd}$ = conversion factor for cheapest-to-deliver,
$\quad B$ = relative yield change volatility of cash to cheapest-to-deliver security.

B can be derived by regressing the historical changes in the yield of the cash security against historical changes in the yield of the cheapest-to-deliver security.

For example, assume that the cheapest-to-deliver cash security against a Treasury note futures contract is a 10⅛ percent note of May 1993 with a basis point value of $61.35 and a conversion factor of 1.14. The security position to be hedged is $1 million in 8¾ percent notes of May 1988 with a basis point value of $40.85. The relative yield volatility is 1.2. The hedge ratio is given by:

$$HR = \left(40.85 \div \frac{61.35}{1.14}\right) \times 1.2 = .91 \qquad (7\text{--}2)$$

The number of futures contracts to be purchased would be obtained by multiplying the hedge ratio by the relative principal values of the cash position and the futures contract (e.g., ($10 million ÷ $100,000) × .91 ≈ 9).

Since basis point values change over time in response to changing yield levels the hedge ratio must be continuously monitored. To the degree that proper estimates of basis point sensitivity and yield sensitivity are made, the hedge ratio should provide an estimate of the change in the value of the cash for a change in the value of the future.

The Regression Model

The regression model originates from the body of academic literature commonly referred to as *modern portfolio theory.* In modern portfolio theory, decisions are made on the basis of achieving the minimum level of risk at each possible return level. In constructing a hedge position, the primary goal is viewed as risk minimization, that is, the finding of the value of the futures position that reduces the variability of price changes of the hedged position to the lowest possible level. The hedge ratio that will minimize the risk of price changes in the hedged portfolio has been shown to be equal to:

$$HR = \frac{\sigma_{cf}}{\sigma_f^2} \qquad (7\text{--}3)$$

where σ_f^2 is the variance of the price changes of the futures during the period hedged, and σ_{cf} is the covariance between the cash and futures price changes. The slope of a regression of historical price changes of the cash instrument to be hedged (ΔCP) against the price changes of the futures contract (ΔFP) has been shown to provide an estimate of HR in equation 7–3 (see Ederington (1979)).[6]

$$(\Delta CP)_t = a + HR\,(\Delta FP)_t \qquad (7\text{--}4)$$

If HR = .90, a $1 change in the value of the futures position is estimated to result in a $.90 change in the cash position. If a manager holds a $1 million principal value position in the AAA bonds, he or she would take a $900,000 value position in the futures market (0.9 × \$1 million). This translates into 9 Treasury bond contracts, since each contract has \$100,000 par value. If the manager holds a \$1 million position in a stock index, a \$900,000 principal position (0.9 × \$1 million) should also be taken in the futures market. For stock index futures the number of contracts depends on the level of the index. For example, if the S&P 500 index futures price is \$167.80, the face value of the contract is \$83,400 (\$500 × 166.80). For a *HR* = .90 this would translate into 11 S&P 500 index futures contracts since each contract has an \$83,400 value (e.g., (\$900,000 ÷ 83,400) ≈ 11). For the regression-based hedge ratio model, the historical relationships between price changes of the cash security and the futures contract are assumed stable.[7] For fixed income securities, price changes are a function of the security's duration. A security's duration, however, changes through time. The duration-based hedge ratio model attempts to account for a security's changing duration.

The Duration Model

As in the previous models, the basic strategy of this model revolves around choosing the number of futures contracts such that over the life of the hedge the changes in the value of the futures position will offset the changes in the value of the cash position. The hedge ratio may be derived as follows:

$$\Delta CP + \Delta FP HR = 0 \qquad (7\text{--}5)$$
$$HR = \Delta CP / \Delta FP \qquad (7\text{--}6)$$

where ΔCP and ΔFP are, respectively, the change in value of the bond to be hedged and the futures contract. For a given interest rate change, the size of ΔCP and ΔFP depends on the sensitivity of the bond and the futures contract to the change in yields. Duration, provides a measure of the expected change in the price of a security given a change in yields such that:

$$\Delta CP = -D_C \times CP \times R_C \qquad (7\text{--}7)$$
$$\Delta FP = -D_F \times FP \times R_F \qquad (7\text{--}8)$$

Substituting equations (7–7) and (7–8) in equation (7–6) the hedge ratio is:

$$HR = \frac{R_C \times CP \times D_C}{R_F \times FP \times D_F} \qquad (7\text{--}9)$$

where: R_F = the expected change in yield to be obtained on the instrument underlying futures contract,

R_C = the expected change in yield on bond,
FP = the price agreed in futures contract to be paid upon maturity of the futures contract for title to the instrument underlying the contract,
CP = the price of bond i expected to prevail on *(a)* the planned termination date of the hedge for an anticipatory hedge and *(b)* today's date for a cash hedge,[8]
D_C = the duration of the bond expected to prevail on *(a)* planned termination date of the hedge for an anticipatory hedge, and *(b)* today's date for a cash hedge,
D_F = the duration of the instrument underlying futures contract expected to prevail at the delivery date.

For example, assume the duration of a 10 percent coupon, 26-year corporate bond yielding 12.64 percent (Price = $82.00) is 8.24 years. The duration of the cheapest-to-deliver 8 percent coupon, 20-year Treasury bond with a yield of 8.5 percent is 10.14 years. The price of the futures contract is $96.87. Both the cash security and the cheapest-to-deliver bond have equal yield volatilities (e.g., $R_F = R_C$). Solving equation 7–9 for HR using the information provided gives:

$$HR = \frac{(\$82.00)\,(8.24)}{(96.87)\,(10.14)} = .70 \qquad (7\text{–}11)$$

If a manager holds $1 million bonds, he or she should buy approximately 7 Treasury bond futures contracts (e.g. ($1 million ÷ $100,000) × .70 ≈ 7).

The duration model like the previous models, involves some implicit assumptions.[9] First, there are many alternative definitions of duration. Second, regardless of the duration definition used, the model requires an estimate of the relative change in yields of the cash and futures contract to shifts in the yield curve. The model is therefore dependent on the duration measure used and the forecast accuracy of the relative yield volatility estimates.

Yield Forecast Model

As an alternative to analytical models for delivering a *single* minimum risk hedge ratio, a model may be constructed to calculate hedge ratios for *an array* of possible yield levels. In Exhibit 7–8 the Southern Bell Telephone 12⅞ of 2020 is used as the hedged bond. As noted earlier, the price of a Treasury bond futures contract is a function of two principle variables: *(a)* the price of the

EXHIBIT 7–8
Hedging Analysis of the Southern Bell Telephone 12.875% of October 5, 2020

A1	A2	A3	A4	A5	A6	A7	A8
Price of Hedged Issue	Yield	Price of 12.75% of 2005	Yield	Current Price Spread	Current Yield Spread	March 1981 Future Price	Implied Financing Rate
97.94	13.14	108.67	11.67	−10.72	1.47	72.50	14.76

	B1	B2	C1	C2	D	E	F1	F2	F3
	Hedged Price	Issue Yield	12.75% of Price	2005 Yield	Yield Spread	Change from Today	Future Price	Change from Today	Optimal Hedge Ratio
(a)	10.72	12.65	112.42	11.25	1.40	3.77	75.06	2.56	1.48
(b)	100.14	12.85	111.05	11.40	1.45	2.20	74.14	1.64	1.34
(c)	54.99	13.55	105.45	12.05	1.50	−2.95	70.37	−2.13	1.36
(d)	93.62	13.75	104.23	12.20	1.55	−4.33	69.54	−2.96	1.47
(e)	93.62	13.75	105.04	12.10	1.65	−4.33	70.09	−2.41	1.80

Source: T. Schreeweis, J. Hill, and N. Philipp, "Hedge Ratio Determination Based on Bond Yield Forecasts," *Review of Research in Futures Markets* 2, no. 3 (1983), p. 347.

cheapest deliverable long-term Treasury bond and *(b)* assumptions as to the carrying cost (i.e., the financing cost versus the current income on the deliverable Treasury bond) between now and the time the futures contract terminates.[10]

In order to obtain minimum risk hedge ratios, the maturity or call date and coupon for the issue to be hedged must be specified. In addition, the yield to maturity or call relationship between the hedged issue and the 12¾ bellweather Treasury bond issue (cheapest-to-deliver) must be specified for all yield pairs (*B2* and *C2*). These yield pairs reflect the projections of the yield of the hedged issue relative to the 12¾ bellweather bond. For example, in order to set the parameters for a risk/reward analysis, one may choose to define yield pairs within a trading range, bounded by the best and worst case assumptions on market movements. The dollar price of the bonds at each yield level, as well as the yield spread between the current coupon bellweather Treasury bond issue and the hedged issue, are given in Exhibit 7–8 (*B1, C1,* and *D*).

The future will sell for close to the price of the cheapest-to-deliver long Treasury bond in the delivery month. Due to carry gains or losses, however, futures may sell above cash before contract expiration. The closer in time to delivery and the closer the financing cost is to the current yield on the cheapest-to-deliver Treasury issue, the closer the future will sell to cash.

In order to include the effect of the financing cost, the cost of carry, and the convergence of the futures to the cash market, hedgers may wish to indicate various dates on which they might choose to remove the hedge. Each of these dates can be viewed with the same projected financing costs. Alternatively, one date can be selected with three different financing costs to be applied to that point in time.

Using the model in Chapter 6 to estimate the futures price, the change in the price of the hedged issue *(E)* may be compared with the change in the price of the future *(F2)*. The hedge ratio is then a matter of simple division *(F3)*. Thus, if yields have fallen to 11.25% on the bellweather bond then looking at line *a*, there has been a change in the price of the hedged issue from an original price of 97.94 *(A1)* to 101.72 *(B1)*—a change of 3.77 points *(E)*. Based upon the yield spread in *(D)*, the 12¾ has gone from 108.67 *(A3)* to 112.42 *(C1)*. At that yield spread, given the assumption that the hedge will be reversed on our assumed date and at an 18.5 financing rate, the price of the future would be expected to equal the prices computed. For example, at an 18.5 percent financing rate, the optimum hedge ratio for line *a* would be 1.48 *(F3)* since the future would be selling at 75.06 *(F1)* compared to 72.50 now *(A7)*—a change of 2.56 *(F2)*. A matrix of hedge ratios can be developed across the spectrum of yield spreads, financing costs, and time horizons.

Delivery Months and Hedge Ratio Determination

One of the principal decisions a hedger must make is in determining the contract month in which to place his hedge. For most financial futures, contract months extend out two years. For hedgers who wish to hedge a position for greater than two years, no contract months exist. One possible solution is purchasing the most distant liquid contract and then rolling over the futures contract before the delivery month occurs (see Baesel and Grant (1982), and McCabe and Franckle, (1983)). The next chapter contains a section on selection of delivery months in hedging strategies.

The delivery month also affects hedge ratio determination in that the basis relationship for a direct hedge is not constant and approaches zero at delivery. In addition, the price variability of the futures contract is often affected by the time to maturity. As maturity approaches, the variability of price changes of the futures contract often increases. This increase in variability may be due to the greater volume of trades as contract maturity approaches or to the effect of an increasing amount of new information on the deliverable security.[11]

For simplicity's sake, the examples were explained without making adjustments for contract month or maturity. The hedger may wish to make necessary adjustments to hedge ratio estimates to account for this problem. For instance, if variability of price change increases as maturity approaches, the hedge ratio (number of futures contracts) may be reduced to reflect the greater anticipated movement in the price of the futures contract.

MEASUREMENT OF HEDGING PERFORMANCE

A principle objective of hedging with financial futures is to reduce risk. The primary measure, therefore, of hedging effectiveness is the proportional reduction in the variance of the unhedged security price changes that comes from maintaining a hedged rather than an unhedged position. As alternative models exist for determination of hedge ratios, alternative models exist for the measurement of hedging performance. The traditional method of evaluating hedging potential is to focus on the variability of the basis $(Var\ B_t) = Var\ (CP_t - FP_t)$ relative to the variability of the spot price $(Var\ CP_t)$. A long (short) hedger is essentially investing in (selling short) the basis rather than the cash contract, and risk exposure is reduced to the extent that $Var\ (B_t)$ is less than $Var\ (CP_t)$.

The appropriate measure of hedging effectiveness would then be the proportional reduction in variance due to hedging or:

$$E_f = \frac{Var(CP_t) - Var(B_t)}{Var(CP_t)} = 1 - \frac{Var(B_t)}{Var(CP_t)} \qquad (7\text{--}12)$$

This measure assumes, however, that the hedge ratio (HR) is equal to 1 (an equal position in the futures contract and spot contract). It is often the case, however, that the hedge ratio is not equal to 1.0, given the variability of futures prices and association between cash and future price changes. Therefore, E_f, derived using equation (7–12), is the appropriate measure of hedging effectiveness only for the special case that the minimum risk hedge ratio is equal to 1. Equation (7–12) may be adjusted by the actual hedge ratio (HR).

$$E_f = \frac{1 - HR\ Var(B_t)}{Var(CP_t)} \qquad (7\text{--}13)$$

Since the hedger is primarily concerned with the change in value of his combined cash and futures positions relative to the change in value for an unhedged cash position, equations (7–12) and (7–13) can also be presented in change-in-value form:

$$E_f = \frac{1 - Var(\Delta B_t)}{Var(\Delta CP_t)} \qquad (7\text{--}14)$$

$$E_f = \frac{1 - HR\ Var(\Delta B_t)}{Var(\Delta CP_t)} \qquad (7\text{--}15)$$

For the regression-based hedge ratio model, the coefficient of determination, or r^2, is an estimate of the percentage reduction in the variability of changes in the value of the cash position from holding the hedged position.

Some caveats regarding the measurement of hedging performance are necessary. First, the price changes and standard deviations do not reflect the variation margin that must be posted during the hedge.[12] Variation margin is a unique characteristic of futures that is based on the fact that changes in contract values must be settled daily in cash. This means that profits resulting from a drop in futures contract value may be realized immediately and reinvested, and any losses incurred as contract values rise must be posted in cash to a variation margin account. The cost of this variation margin requirement is an uncertainty that must be borne by the hedger, and the availability of cash for meeting this requirement is a prerequisite for hedging activity. Second, in measuring hedging performance, the hedger must remember that the basis is not necessarily stationary. For instance, the basis movement (and hence the hedge ratio) at any point in time (1) results from current and future anticipated supply and demand, (2) may be highly seasonal, and (3) always converges to zero in the delivery month at the delivery point for the deliverable item. Third, while the measure of ex ante hedging effectiveness, the coefficient of determination of the regression in equation (7–4), is useful for gauging the expected performance of a minimum risk hedge; if one is choosing among alternative ratios, it may be of little major interest. The coefficient of determination is concerned only with the minimum variance hedge versus no hedge at all. It does not consider levels of hedging that differ from the minimum cash hedge ratio.[13]

MEASUREMENT AND METHODOLOGY IN HEDGE RATIO ANALYSIS

Any hedging plan must be concerned with the process of determining the hedge ratio.[14] Practical problems do exist in hedge ratio determination and may be divided into (a) data measurement, (b) return measurement, and (c) methodological problems. The problems in hedge measurement should not restrict a hedger from using financial futures. Through an understanding of the problems in deriving a proper hedge ratio, a more successful hedging system may be established.

Data Measurement

One of the first problems in deriving hedge ratio estimates is determining the correct data source. The Chicago Mercantile Exchange (CME), the Chicago Board of Trade (CBT), and other services provide historical end-of-the-day, opening-of-the-day, and high-and-low futures prices. Private firms offer on-line computer access to current futures prices. In addition, most daily newspapers, like *The Wall Street Journal*, report the previous day's futures prices.

Biases in hedge ratios may result from the use of historical quotations as of the end of the day, the opening, or the high or low.

Cash market prices for fixed-income securities and infrequently traded stocks are even more difficult to obtain. Most of the cash market for debt securities is not an exchange market. The supply of tradable corporate bonds is very thin, and many of the prices are obtained from computer-based pricing services. Even if the cash price obtained is transaction price and not merely a quoted computer price, there are always some random reporting errors. The hedger must ensure the accuracy of bond prices used to determine the hedge ratios.

In an effort to get around the problem of incorrect cash prices, some traders have used price indexes. Price movement in an index, however, may not correspond with price movement of an individual issue. Also, indexes have a lower total variability than really exists if one is trading a single-spot instrument. In addition, the hedge ratio may change as one moves from weekly to monthly to quarterly data. Traders must obtain prices for the interval that they wish to hedge.

Return/Risk Measurement

Even if accurate futures and spot prices are available, one must decide on how to measure change of value of the futures and cash position.[15] The hedger may wish to use return measurement (change in price over original investment value). For futures, however, there is no initial investment cost. The initial margin is only a security deposit. As a result, simple price changes rather than returns are most often been used to measure change in value. Even if one assumes that a correct change in value can be measured, the question remains on how risk is defined. Risk reduction may be viewed as lower variance. Other hedgers look at risk reduction as removing the chance of losing a certain value. Lastly, risk may be viewed either in a single-trade framework or in multiple trades over a particular time period.

Methodology

Even after one has decided on return and risk measures to be used, several methodological problems still exist in all the hedge ratio techniques. First, the hedge ratios are often given in odd-lot form such that adjustments to full contracts are necessary. Second, the hedge ratios and measure of effectiveness assume that the derived hedge ratio will remain stable and that the trading pattern matches the interval used to derive your hedge ratio. Lastly, past performance over a previous time period is only indicative of future performance over a similar time period length. Actual hedge performance over any one period may vary considerably from predicted performance.

SUMMARY

One of the principal uses of financial futures contracts is to hedge the unexpected price changes of cash market securities. The hedge is simply the purchase (sale) of a futures market position as a temporary substitute for the sale (purchase) of the security in the cash market. The hedge is initiated by buying (selling) a futures contract and is closed out by selling (buying) the contract in the futures market rather than taking delivery. Risk is reduced to the extent that the gain (loss) in the futures position offsets the loss (gain) on the spot position.

The success of the hedge, therefore, depends on how closely the futures price follows movements in the cash price. The difference between the cash price and the futures price is called the basis. While the' basis is not perfectly constant during a hedge period, a high degree of positive correlation will generally exist between changes in cash prices and changes in futures contract prices.

In order to hedge a spot position with a futures contract, a decision must be made of the number of futures contracts to hold relative to the value of a spot position. Alternative techniques are available to determine how many futures contracts should be held such that the expected value change of the futures contracts equals the expected value change of the cash position.

These alternative methodologies include (1) naive approach (hedge ratio equals 1), (2) conversion factor, (3) basis point, (4) regression approach (hedge ratio equals slope of the regression of the change in value of the cash security on the change value of the futures contract), (5) duration method, and (6) yield forecast. In order to test the effectiveness of a hedge ratio technique the performance of the hedged position in contrast to an unhedged position must be evaluated. One such measure of performance may be the percent reduction in the variance of the hedged position relative to the unhedged spot position.

The practical use of hedge ratios must be undertaken with care. Problems exist in the measurement and methodology of the various techniques. These problems range from simple data collection to instability in historical relationships used to forecast basis movement. Thus the financial futures trader is counseled to develop a sound implementation strategy before becoming involved in the use of financial futures.

APPENDIX

Immunization

Various methods may be used to immunize an asset from future price risk. These include (1) zero coupon bonds, (2) duration, and (3) futures. Purchasing zero-coupon bonds equal to the planning-horizon is by far the easiest. Thus a large pension fund with easily forecastable payment-obligations could purchase a series of zero-coupon securities that mature at times and in amounts that correspond to the projected net cash outflows. Such a strategy encounters two basic difficulties, however. First, cash outflows can rarely be forecasted precisely. Second, zero-coupon bonds may not be available in the exact maturities needed. Moreover, since the assembled zero-coupons are priced to produce profits for their sellers, their yields tend to be somewhat below otherwise equivalent coupon issues. Accordingly, most immunization strategies involve some degree of managing (with or without some zero-coupons in the portfolio).

A second method involves assembling and managing a bond portfolio so that its average duration equals the owner's planning-horizon. For instance, a bond is immunized from interest rate fluctuations if its holding period is equal to its duration. When the reinvestment rate exceeds the initial yield to maturity, the additional coupon reinvestment offsets the capital loss due to higher rates. If the reinvestment rate is below the initial yield to maturity the capital gain due to decreasing yields is offset by the decreased coupon reinvestment.

The third approach to immunization combines a portfolio of debt securities with interest rate futures positions to achieve the desired duration level. Futures offer two potential advantages over ordinary immunization strategies. A portfolio of bonds can be chosen without regard to the durations of the component bonds. The portfolio can be constructed to emphasize current income, deferred capital gains, or other characteristics that may be of interest to an investor. For example, a portfolio designed for income purposes would be heavily weighted with high coupon bonds. This would tend to cause the duration to be short, thereby limiting the opportunity to immunize long holding periods. An opposite argument can be made for a portfolio oriented toward capital gains. By using futures contracts, the portfolio manager can construct an immunized portfolio without regard to the durations of the component bonds. Furthermore, since duration is inversely related to yields, during periods of very high interest rates it may be difficult to locate bonds with long durations. Hence, investors with long holding periods can often not achieve immunization with cash securities but can use futures to obtain this result.

NOTES

[1] Cash markets offer means of reducing price risk (e.g., duration, interest rate swaps) that serve as alternatives to hedging with futures.

[2] In estimating the basis for Treasury notes, Treasury bonds and GNMAs, the futures price should be adjusted by the conversion factor of the cash security.

[3] For a discussion of the source of basis risk for stock index futures see Figlewski (1984) and for fixed income futures see Toevs and Jacobs (1984) Since both the cash price and the futures contract price and expected to change a better definition of basis risk may be unexpected changes in price magnitude or direction.

[4] In some studies (e.g., Figlewski, 1984) the basis is defined as the futures price less the cash price. Readers should be careful to note the basis measure used.

[5] GNMA CDR futures do not use a conversion-factor-based settlement procedure. The invoicing system, however, does attempt to adjust for the value of GNMA certificates with an equivalent principal balance (EPB) factor. To find the amount of futures to hedge an established cash position one only needs to take the reciprocal of the EPB. This is similar to the conversion factor for Treasury bonds and notes. Hedge ratio determination for GNMAs is discussed in Chapter 12.

[6] The higher the correlation between price changes on bonds and futures, the higher the expected effect of the futures hedge for reducing the risk of a particular corporate bond position. Instead of using price changes in equation (7–4), price levels may be used with Cochrane–Orcutt adjustments for possible serial correlation in residuals (see Pitts, 1982).

[7] This model fails to strictly account for coupon and maturity differences. Franckle (1980) shows how to properly account for maturity differences between pure discount instruments, but he provides no solution for the handling of instruments with coupon payments.

[8] See Toevs and Jacobs (1984) for the differences of the duration model in anticipatory and cash hedges.

[9] Chance (1982) has presented an alternative duration-based hedge ratio formula. In addition, Little (1984) has discussed problems with the use of duration-based hedge ratios when income standards have negative cash flows. For a background in the use of OLS regression and duration hedge ratio determination, see L. Ederington "The Hedging Performance of the New Futures Markets," *Journal of Finance*, March 1979, pp. 157–70; J. Hill and T. Schneeweis, "On the Estimation of Hedge Ratios for Corporate Bonds Positions," *Advances in Financial Planning and Forecasting*, ed. C. F. Lee. Greenwich, Conn: JAI Press, 1985; R. Kolb and R. Chiang, "Improving Hedging Performance Using Interest Rate Futures," *Financial Management*, Autumn 1981, pp. 72–79.

[10] This model is developed further in T. Schneeweis, J. Hill, and M. Phillip, "Hedging Ratio Determination Based on Bond Yield Forecasts," *Review of Research in Futures Markets* 2, no. 3 (1983), pp. 338–49.

[11] For a discussion of the effect of delivery date on the price variability of futures contracts see R. Anderson and J. Danthine, "The Time Patter of Hedging

and Volatility of Futures Prices," *Center for the Study of Futures Markets,* no. 7 (April 1981).

[12] Hedge ratios may also be affected by taxes. The hedge ratios models derived in this chapter ignore taxation effects. For a discussion of taxation effects see R. L. McDonald, "Taxes and the Hedging of Forward Commitments," *Center for the Study of Futures Markets,* no. 86 (May, 1984).

[13] For a discussion of hedge ratio determination for other than the minimum risk hedge see Howard and D'Antonio (1984).

[14] An extended version of this section was published in T. Schneeweis "Comment" *Review of Research in Futures Markets.* Vol. 1, no. 2 (1982), 127–29.

[15] The use of returns or price changes in empirically determining optimal hedge ratios may seriously affect hedge ratio estimates. See J. Hill and T. Schneeweis, "Hedging Effectiveness for Financial Futures," *Measurement and Methodology,* working paper, University of Massachusetts, 1983, and F. Grauer and J. Rentzler, "Are Futures Contracts Risky?", *Center for the Study of Futures Markets,* no. 12 (1980).

SELECTED REFERENCES

Anderson, Ronald W., and J. Danthine. "The Time Pattern of Hedging and the Volatility of Futures Prices." *Center for the Study of Futures Markets,* no. 7 (April 1981).

Baesel, J. and D. Grant. "Optimal Sequential Futures Trading." *Journal of Financial and Quantitative Analysis,* December 1982, pp. 683–95.

Chance, D. "An Immunized-Hedge Procedure for Bond Futures." *Journal of Futures Markets,* Fall 1982, pp. 231–42.

Chance, D. "Futures Contracts and Immunization." Working paper, VPI, December 1983.

Chiang, Raymond C., and R. Graig Tapley. "Day of the Week Effects and the Futures Markets." *Review of Research in Futures Markets* 2, no. 3 (1983), pp. 356–410.

Cornell, Bradford. "The Relationship Between Volume and Price Variability in Futures Markets." *Journal of Futures Markets,* Fall 1981, pp. 303–16.

Cox, J., J. Ingersoll, and S. Ross. "The Relationship between Forward and Futures Prices." Unpublished working paper, University of Chicago, 1980.

Ederington, Louis. "The Hedging Performance of the New Futures Market." *Journal of Finance,* March 1979, pp. 157–70.

Franckle, Charles T. "The Hedging Performance of the New Futures Market: Comment." *Journal of Finance,* December 1980, pp. 1272–79.

Gay, G. D., and R. W. Kolb. "The Management of Interest Rate Risk." *Journal of Portfolio Management,* Winter 1983, pp. 65–70.

Hill, Joanne, and Thomas Schneeweis. "On the Estimation of Hedge Ratio for Corporate Bond Positions." In *Advances Financial Planning and Forecasting,* ed. C. F. Lee, Greenwich, Conn.: JAI Press, forthcoming.

_____. "Risk Reduction Potential of Financial Futures for Corporate Bond Positions." In *Interest Rate Futures Concepts and Issues,* eds. G. D. Gay and R. W. Kolb. Richmond: Robert F. Dame, June 1982, pp. 307–23.

Johnson, L. L. "The Theory of Hedging and Speculation in Commodity Futures." *Review of Economic Studies,* 1959–60, pp. 559–66.

Kolb, Robert W., and Gerald D. Gay. "Immunizing Bond Portfolios with Interest Rate Futures." *Financial Management,* Summer 1982, pp. 81–89.

Kolb, Robert W., and Raymond Chiang. "Improving Hedging Performance Using Interest Rate Futures," *Financial Management,* Autumn 1981, pp. 72–79.

Kuberek, Robert C., and Norman G. Pefley. "Hedging Corporate Debt with U.S. Treasury Bond Futures." *Journal of Futures Markets,* Winter 1983, pp. 345–54.

Lanstein, R., and W. Sharpe. "Duration and Security Risk." *Journal of Financial and Quantitative Analysis,* November 1978, pp. 653–68.

Leibowitz, Martin L. "A Yield Basis for Financial Futures." *Financial Analysts Journal,* January–February 1981, pp. 42–47.

Little, Patricia K. "Negative Cash Flows, Duration, and Immunization: A Note." *Journal of Finance,* March 1981, pp. 283–88.

McCabe, G. M., and C. T. Franckle. "Effectiveness of Rolling the Hedge Forward in the Treasury Bill Futures Market." *Financial Management,* Summer, 1983, pp. 21–29.

McEnally, Richard W., and Michael L. Rice. "Hedging Possibilities in the Flotation of Debt Securities." *Financial Management,* Winter 1979, pp. 12–18.

Markowitz, H. "Portfolio Selection." *Journal of Finance,* March 1952, pp. 77–91.

Neftci, Salih N. "Some Econometric Problems in Using Daily Futures Price Data." *Center for the Study of Futures Markets,* no. 55 (March 1983).

Pitts, Mark. "Cross-Hedging, Autocorrelated Errors, and the Trade-Off between Risk and Return." New York: Eastern Finance Association, 1983.

Pitts, Mark, and R. Kopprasch. "Hedging Short-Term Liabilities with Interest Rate Futures." Presented at the Financial Management Association Meetings, San Francisco, October 1982.

Stein, J. L. "The Simultaneous Determination of Spot and Futures Prices." *American Economic Review* LI, no. 5 (1961), pp. 1012–25.

Trainer, Francis H. "The Uses of Treasury Bond Futures in Fixed-Income Portfolio Management." *Financial Analysts Journal,* January–February 1983, pp. 27–34.

Toevs, A., and D. Jacobs. "Interest Rate Futures: A Comparison of Alternative Hedge Ratio Methodologies." Morgan Stanley, June, 1984.

Wardrep, Bruce, and James F. Buck. "The Efficacy of Hedging with Financial Futures: A Historical Prospective." *Journal of Futures Markets,* Fall 1982, pp. 243–54.

Working, H. "Futures Trading and Hedging." *American Economic Review,* June 1953, pp. 314–43.

Strategies and Applications

Part 2 of this book deals with strategies and applications involving financial futures. In Chapter 8 procedures for implementing and managing financial futures are covered. In Chapters 9–13 applications of futures in banking, investment banking and trading, pension and insurance portfolio management, mortgage finance, and corporate and municipal management are presented. In Chapter 14 speculation and arbitrage opportunities in futures markets are discussed.

CHAPTER 8

Implementation and Management of Futures Strategies

SETTING THE OBJECTIVE

In Part 1, several strategies involving financial futures were introduced. The next several chapters of the book are devoted to specific applications involving financial futures that are consistent with the management objectives of different types of institutions, such as banks, pension funds, and nonfinancial corporations. Before these particular applications are addressed, certain aspects of implementing futures strategies that are common to most users of the markets are covered. These include the selection of a particular futures contract to use in the strategy, the allocation of a cash reserve for marking-to-market, the control and accounting procedures necessary to monitor the performance of the futures strategies, and the dynamic management of futures as risk management tools.

The first consideration in implementing an investment strategy with (or without) financial futures is the need to delineate a clear objective and rationale for the strategy. Futures can be used in so many diverse applications—speculation, hedging, short-term substitutes for cash market transactions—that it is critical to first set out the goals and guidelines that will be followed in each situation. This is particularly important in an institutional setting in which several parties may be involved in the decision-making and review process. In many instances, an outside money manager may be hired to handle the futures trading. The rules of operation for this manager must be specified prior to execution of any futures trades.

Exhibit 8–1 is a sample of a goal statement for a financial futures strategy involving the use of stock index futures as a surrogate for purchase of the index core of an equity portfolio that is part of a pension fund. Since financial futures are but one of many investment alternatives available for meeting a given objective, it is important to state both the objective as well as the reason why financial futures have been chosen as the best means of achieving this goal.

In developing the objective, one should be specific regarding the time frame as well as the expected return and risk advantage that is to be achieved with the use of futures. In some instances, the return advantage may simply consist of lower transaction costs and greater liquidity. In other instances, it may be more complicated, such as in the case of combining a municipal bond portfolio with a short position in Treasury bond futures. Here the objective would be to shorten the portfolio's maturity and interest rate risk exposure. The portfolio manager may specify an objective of higher

---

EXHIBIT 8–1
ZYDEX, INC.: Use of Stock Index Futures as the Index Core of an Equity Portfolio

Objective. To provide returns in excess of 1.5 percent above that of the S&P 500 (after transactions costs) over the next year for 80 percent of the pension fund portfolio of Zydex, Inc. This portion of the pension portfolio is targeted to be similar in composition and risk to that of the S&P 500 market index.

Means. This will be accomplished by purchasing S&P 500 stock index futures at times when they are "undervalued," given the cash price of the S&P 500 and expected dividend stream and financing costs associated with buying the index outright. When S&P 500 futures are overvalued relative to the index, the funds will be shifted to an index fund managed by DEX Investment Management Company. When futures are held, the funds in the index core normally will be allocated as follows:

92 percent in Eurodollar time deposits at Chase Brooklyn Bank (London branch).
8 percent in overnight, repurchase agreements with Chase Brooklyn Bank.

The repurchase agreements will be used for raising cash to post as variation margin, should there occur any losses on futures positions.

Monitoring. The value of the stock futures position will be calculated weekly on a Friday. At this time, Eurodollars and repos will be bought or sold to readjust the weights to 92 percent and 8 percent. If futures contracts are considered to be overpriced, contracts should be sold as expeditiously as possible, and the contract value should be allocated to the index fund. Weekly reports of futures, Eurodollars, repurchase agreement, and index fund positions and returns will be compiled and sent to all interested parties.

Rationale. S&P 500 futures have, from time to time, been "under-" and "overvalued" from the perspective of equity portfolio managers. This provides an opportunity to earn a return which is above that of the S&P 500. If the futures position can be closed out at a time when S&P 500 futures are overvalued, the excess return above that of the index can be increased further. The liquidity of the futures market and low transaction costs as compared to that of purchasing the index fund make this strategy particularly attractive.

Risk and Concerns. Stock index futures tend to be more volatile than the underlying stock indexes. Also, losses on the position are realized immediately in terms of cash moved from other pension fund investments into the variation margin accounts. Should the futures position need to be terminated unexpectedly prior to contract expiration when the contracts are still "undervalued," performance could be lower than that of the S&P 500 stock index. There is also an opportunity cost of foregoing interest on the cash that needs to be deposited in the variation margin account until such time that the futures can be sold for a profit. Stock index futures prices may be such that no opportunity exists for earning returns in excess of the S&P 500 after transaction costs. In this situation, the funds will continue to be held in the index fund and earn a return very close to that of the S&P 500.

---

after-tax coupon income of long-term municipal bonds while remaining subject to the basis risk between municipal and Treasury securities.

Once the objective is set, the success or failure of the futures strategy will depend on performance relative to this objective.

Progress reports should address this comparison and suggest any changes in the objective that are warranted by changes in the investment environment.

SELECTING THE FUTURES CONTRACTS

Types of Futures

Once the objective of the futures strategy has been established, one can proceed to select the particular financial futures contracts that will be bought or sold. The types of futures selected depend primarily on the characteristics of the security for which the future is being used as a substitute or hedging vehicle. This is also true when one is using futures for speculative purposes. In the example shown in Exhibit 8–1, the choice of the futures is fairly obvious. Since the futures will be used as a substitute for an S&P 500 index core portfolio, the S&P 500 index futures would be used. When futures will be used as short-term substitutes for other securities or as hedging instruments for an existing portfolio, the future selected should be the one whose price changes are most highly correlated with the securities in the alternative portfolio or portfolio being hedged. The future with the greatest correlation is often referred to as the one that best *tracks* the cash market security(ies) or that has the lowest *tracking error*.

Unfortunately, tracking performance can only be examined historically and can shift significantly as changes occur in cash markets. Historical correlation can also vary greatly depending on the time period and trading interval (days, weeks, months) over which it is measured. For example, evidence exists that the correlation between GNMA pass-through securities and GNMA futures changed significantly after October 1979 when the Federal Reserve shifted its policy to allow short-term rates to fluctuate more broadly.[1] More recently, the tendency of the GNMA future to track the cheapest-to-deliver GNMA CDR has resulted in poor tracking performance with respect to newly issued GNMA securities.

Increases in the daily trading volume of a futures contract can improve its tracking ability over time. When negotiable CD futures were first introduced, the volume was such that Treasury bill futures were better vehicles for hedging CD issues or positions in CDs. Over time, the improving liquidity of the CD futures and shifting spreads between CD and Treasury bill rates changed market conditions. Now the CD futures are typically preferred to Treasury bill futures when a negotiable CD position is being hedged.

This points to another important factor in the selection of a futures contract—*liquidity*. Since a very small portion of futures traders actually make or take delivery, a futures contract should be selected that is liquid enough to absorb the trades that need to be made to open and close out a position without influencing the futures price. Consider the choice between using the NYSE index future versus the Value Line index future to hedge a portfolio consisting of many stocks in small capitalization companies. The Value Line index may be the best choice in terms of tracking performance. However, the trading volume on the NYSE index future is many times greater than that on the Value Line future. Thus, one must make a trade-off between the potential tracking error of the NYSE future and the liquidity risk of the Value Line future.

In some situations, there may be a choice of futures to use. For example, assume an insurance company has a high-rated corporate bond portfolio. An increase in long rates relative to intermediate rates is anticipated and the insurer would like to reduce the portfolio duration from 8 years to 5 years to reduce its sensitivity to an increase in interest rates. There are many ways to implement this via the futures market.

1. Sell a sufficient number of Treasury bond futures to reduce the duration to 5.
2. Sell Treasury bond futures to reduce the duration as close to zero as possible, and buy Treasury note futures to reach a duration of 5 years.
3. Sell some corporate bonds and buy Treasury bill futures as a surrogate for increasing the allocation of funds in short-term securities.

The choice among these strategies is not clear-cut. The prices at which each future can be bought or sold are important. It is helpful to consider all the alternatives in order to take maximum advantage of any pricing discrepancies in the financial futures market and to avoid any potential liquidity problems.

Selection of Contract Delivery Month and Rollover Strategies

For each delivery instrument on which futures are traded, there are a series of futures contracts available that specify different delivery dates for the underlying instrument. Most financial futures contracts have a quarterly delivery cycle—March, June, September, December—with additional contracts available for eight quarters into the future. In practice, however, the volume and open interest varies sharply among contracts with different delivery dates. In some financial futures markets, such as the equity index futures, trading in contracts beyond the next two quarterly deliveries is extremely thin. In others, such as Treasury bond futures, there is usually open interest of a few hundred contracts in contracts as far out as eight quarters.

The selection of a delivery month for futures strategies and the timing of a rollover into another delivery month depends on several factors:

1. The horizon on which the futures strategy is based as specified in the objective statement.
2. Liquidity of the delivery month contract at the time the position is opened.
3. Liquidity of the delivery month contract at the time the position is closed.
4. The desire to avoid or accept delivery.
5. Relative prices of contracts across delivery months.
6. Tax considerations.

Each of these factors will be discussed in terms of how each may impact the choice of a contract.

Horizon. Futures contracts, in contrast to forward market contracts, have standardized delivery dates. In many cases, the delivery months available will not coincide exactly with the end of the investment horizon. At times this horizon may exceed the periods in which there are liquid contracts. In certain instances, the futures trading horizon may be uncertain at the time the position is opened. In these situations, one may need to "roll over" contracts, closing out one position while opening another in a contract with a later delivery date.

As a general rule, one should select the delivery month for the futures contract that closely follows the end of the investment horizon. This rule can be followed as long as there is an active market in this contract at the time the position is opened and as long as the contract price is not significantly out of line with its theoretical value (i.e., undervalued if the contract will be sold, overvalued if the contract will be purchased). Liquidity at the time the contract will be closed out should not be a problem since it will be the one closest to delivery at that time. The contract closest to delivery is usually the most actively traded.

Matching the horizon with the delivery month enables one to keep basis risk to a minimum. As shown in Chapter 6, the price of a future will approach the cash price of the underlying security as a contract approaches delivery.[2] This occurs because the carry-cost component of the futures prices decreases with time (assuming stable short-term interest rates). The futures trader can then close out the position at a price close to the price of the security in the cash market. With futures contracts farther from the delivery at the time the futures position is closed, there is a greater chance that the basis—futures price relative to the cash price of the security—will change to the disadvantage of the trader, increasing the risk of the futures position.

Selection of a delivery month beyond but closest to the futures strategy horizon is particularly important in hedging strategies. For example, for a firm hedging the risk of increased costs of a debt issue, the future with a delivery month closest to the month of the debt issue will be selling at a price closest to the debt costs in the cash market at the time of the issue. Therefore, gains on the futures trade will provide the closest offset to increased interest costs in the cash market.

Futures calling for delivery closest to the end of the period over which a hedge is to be implemented, generally provide gains and losses that most closely match gains and losses on the financial assets being hedged. This is because futures calling for delivery at a later date will reflect anticipated market conditions or carrying costs over a period longer than the anticipated hedging period. The use of a series of shorter delivery futures rolled over as each approaches delivery can incur additional transactions costs for the hedger as well as exposing him or her to basis risk at the time the one contract must be closed out and another purchased.

The future closest to delivery is most suitable when futures are used as a temporary substitute for an investment in the cash market security. The prices of these near-term futures will generally track the cash security the closest. Arbitrageurs will be most active in futures trading in the near-term contract because of the greater ease and lower risk of obtaining financing over short periods. In equity index futures, for example, the near-term futures are by far the most active and are used by those portfolio managers using stock index futures to create surrogate index funds. With cash settlement, one can take delivery and then buy the next delivery date contract.

Delivery Period. When using fixed-income financial futures for cross-hedging or when futures delivery is undesirable, it is best to close out the futures position before the delivery period begins. If the futures strategy is to be continued, one can roll out into the futures contract with the next delivery date.[3] This strategy involves some basis risk, because the price at which the futures position is closed out may not be as desirable as that available at delivery or at a later point in time. Incurring such basis risk is often preferred by those with long futures positions to being forced to accept delivery of the securities.

Institutions with short futures positions may not be holding the securities that qualify for delivery or that are most desirable (cheapest) to deliver into the contract. Rather than swapping the securities held for those acceptable or cheapest-to-deliver and incurring the transaction costs, the futures position can be closed out by buying back the same futures contract before it expires. The futures price can, however, differ from the cash price at delivery.

In the days prior to the delivery (expiration) month there is often an increase in trading activity as those with open positions seek to avoid delivery and roll out to the next contract.[4] At times the futures contract can become significantly overvalued or undervalued during these periods depending on the net position (long or short) of those seeking to roll out their positions. It is wise to begin looking for opportunities to roll out a position several weeks before the beginning of the delivery period.

Another reason for closing out positions several weeks prior to the delivery period is that open interest declines and liquidity decreases as the end of each delivery period approaches. For Treasury bonds, Treasury notes, and GNMA futures, delivery can occur anytime during the delivery month at the option of the short. Thus, traders with long positions in these futures contracts who wish to avoid delivery should look for an opportunity to roll out their futures position during the month prior to delivery. Those with short positions who want to close out their position prior to delivery can do so anytime prior to the end of the delivery period. However, they should recognize that a decline in contract liquidity occurs during the delivery months. Exhibit 8–2 shows the average daily sales volume for the September 1983 and December 1983 and March 1984 futures contracts in the last six months of 1983. Average daily trading volume during the delivery month for the contracts shown is significantly below the daily volume of the previous month.

EXHIBIT 8–2
Average Daily Sales Volume, September 1983, December 1983, and March 1984 Treasury Bond Futures

	September 1983 Contract	December 1983 Contract	March 1984 Contract
July 1983	70,867	5,087	708
August	76,768	20,952	1,309
September	3,940	70,059	2,327
October	—	79,645	5,060
November	—	55,978	17,091
December	—	9,091	58,025

Source: *1983 Statistical Annual, Interest Rates and Metal Futures,* Chicago Board of Trade, 1983.

Liquidity. An important concern in the selection of a contract is the liquidity available to open and close the futures position. Liquidity for futures is measured in terms of trading volume and open interest—the number of contracts outstanding at any point in time. Different types of financial futures contracts vary considerably in terms of the liquidity of the contracts available "in the back months." This is the term used for contracts whose expiration dates are more than six months in the future.

Exhibit 8–3 shows the open interest at month end for Treasury bond contracts in different delivery months in July through December 1983. As seen in Exhibit 8–2 and Exhibit 8–3, Treasury bond futures have some volume in contract and open interest months beyond the two near-term contracts. A pattern of declining liquidity is apparent, however. The liquidity available in back-month Treasury bond (and GNMA) futures is primarily related to trading

EXHIBIT 8–3
Open Interest—September 1983, December 1983, March 1984 Treasury Bond Futures (end of month)

	September 1983 Contract	December 1983 Contract	March 1984 Contract
July 1983	89,052	28,504	12,372
August	22,685	70,783	16,824
September	—	97,658	20,542
October	—	98,167	31,970
November	—	50,119	80,548
December	—	—	108,966

Source: *1983 Statistical Annual, Interest Rates and Metal Futures,* Chicago Board of Trade, 1983.

strategies involving spreads across contracts with different expiration dates and to long-term hedging strategies.

The liquidity across contracts also reflects spreading activity in the futures market. In a spread trade, interest rates implied by futures prices in two different delivery months are compared to those implied by prices in the cash market. Any arbitrage opportunities or discrepancies between implied rates and investor expectations are exploited. One would buy the "cheap" delivery month contract and sell the "rich" delivery month contract. These types of transactions contribute to open interest and volume in the back delivery months of the Treasury bond futures contracts.

Stock index futures are an example of contracts that have very thin markets in contracts beyond the two closest to delivery. The primary reason for this is the difficulty in engaging in cash-futures arbitrage and the problem of forecasting the (dividend) cash flows associated with holding the index over periods beyond the next five to six months. Stock index futures prices are influenced in part by investor sentiment with respect to the near-term prospects for the equity markets. This "sentiment trading" also serves to concentrate most trading volume in the near-term delivery month contracts.

In selecting a delivery month, the liquidity of the futures contract is a primary concern. In addition to differences in liquidity across contract months, overall sales volume changes on a daily basis as interest in a particular type of investment surges and wanes. A futures broker should be able to assist in timing futures transactions to take advantage of liquidity differences across contracts and over time. If a large position is being taken, it may be advisable to spread the purchases or sales over several delivery months of futures contracts. This diversifies the basis risk and reduces the likelihood that one will be forced to accept an unfavorable price because of the impact of a large transaction on the price. Another tactic used in dealing with thin markets is to accumulate contracts in the position over several trading days rather than in one trading session.

When liquidity is poor in contracts calling for delivery at the end of the investment horizon or when contracts do not exist for the period covering the horizon, one can *roll a hedge forward.* This is accomplished by taking a position in the contract farthest from delivery that has a sufficient trading volume to absorb the trade efficiently. When a new contract with a later delivery date reaches adequate trading volume, the old position is closed out, and a position in the new contract is opened. McCabe and Franckle

(1983) have shown that such a strategy can be effective for banks using Treasury bill futures to hedge fixed-rate term loan commitments that extend beyond the available delivery months trading when the loan is granted.[5]

Relative Prices of Futures Deliverable in Different Months. Another consideration in the selection of a delivery month is the price available in the markets as compared to the assessment of the fair price, given the fundamentals or technical factors associated with the particular future. If a range of liquid contracts are available that meet the needs of the trading or hedging horizon, one should buy the "cheapest" contract for the long position and sell the most overvalued contract for the short position. The under- and overvaluation will be based on a model or technique of establishing a theoretical futures price for the contract such as those shown in Chapter 6. This approach allows one to profit from the move of the price to the expected level as well as to achieve the hedging or speculation goals of the particular strategy being employed.

There may be circumstances in which the futures trade should not be initiated, because the contract price is significantly out of line with the price that is reasonable for such a contract. For example, one may wish to sell S&P 500 index futures to reduce exposure to a declining stock market over the next three months. Based on a valuation model for a stock futures contract, this contract appears to be selling for a much lower price than warranted by the valuation model. This could arise because others like you have a negative opinion of the short run prospects for the market and have bid the price down. In this case, the best course of action may be to sell some of the equity portfolio directly.

PROVISION OF FUNDS FOR MARKING-TO-MARKET

To those familiar with the management of investment positions in stocks and bonds, futures are often perceived as unique and very risky investment vehicles because of the requirement that daily changes in the value of futures position be reconciled in cash. The requirement to *mark-to-market* means, in effect, that there are no unrealized gains or losses in futures. The rationale for the daily marking-to-market is the fact that the futures trader posts only a small security deposit called *initial margin* at the time the position is opened. By requiring daily marking-to-market, the exchanges and clearinghouse can be certain that all parties to contracts have sufficient funds on hand to close out their futures position. Funds carried in connection with daily marking-to-market are referred to as *variation margin.*

One of the most critical factors in the success of futures trading is to plan the strategy carefully, ensuring that cash or capital will be readily available to absorb interim losses on the futures positions. The allocation of a cash reserve to absorb futures losses may not be as critical for certain hedgers, such as banks, that have easy and cheap access to liquid funds, as for other hedgers that would not typically have liquid assets on hand to cover futures losses.

Consider, for example, a corporation that has sold futures in anticipation of a debt issue that will raise badly needed cash. The futures hedge helps to protect this firm from an increase in rates that would make the interest costs on the debt issue more expensive. If rates fall prior to the issue, the futures position will realize losses that must be made good immediately in cash. The savings in interest costs from the lower rates on the debt issue will not be realized until far into the future. In the worst situation, the firm may be forced to close out the futures position early because of insufficient funds to meet further losses associated with rate decline, only to see rates turn back up to higher levels at the time of the debt issue. Losses would have been incurred in both the futures and cash position because of the failure to correctly plan for the cash needs over the duration of the hedge.

An added dimension to the marking-to-market requirement is the fact that futures positions are deceptively cheap to initiate. Transactions costs are low, initial margin requirements are usually 10 percent or less of market value, and this initial margin can be satisfied with interest-bearing government securities. The marking-to-market process, however, applies to changes in the full value of the contract, such that a 10 percent change in price could easily require one to post an amount of cash equal to or greater than your initial margin. An example is shown in Exhibit 8–4 comparing the purchase of $300,000 of IBM stock at $100 a share versus a purchase of four S&P 500 index futures requiring $24,000 in initial margin.

Determination of Size of Reserve for Marking-to-Market

Speculators in futures contracts need to have a sufficient capital base and liquid funds to absorb typical changes in contract value that may easily be two or three times as great as the initial margin amount. Futures hedgers need to consider the following points:

EXHIBIT 8–4
Analysis of Marking-to-Market S&P 500 Futures Versus IBM Stock

			Funds Invested		
			IBM $300,000** $100/share	S&P 500 Futures $24,000*	
Value of IBM	S&P 500 Future	Percent Change	Unrealized Gain (loss) on IBM	Realized Gain (loss) on Future	Percent of Initial Margin ($24,000)
120	180	20%	60,000	60,000	250
110	165	10%	$ 30,000	$ 30,000	125%
90	135	−10%	(30,000)	(30,000)	(125)
80	120	−20%	(60,000)	(60,000)	(250)

* Assume price of S&P 500 futures @ 150 with contract value of $75,000 (150 × 500).
Four contracts represent underlying share value of $300,000.
** Assume price of IBM of $100 (share × 3,000 shares = $300,000).

1. Basis risk can result in futures losses that are not equal in value to the gains on the cash position. This can occur due to poor correlation between the security being hedged and that deliverable into the future, arising from differences in the characteristics of the two securities or the separation of the futures and cash market.

2. Losses on the futures may need to be posted in cash prior to the realization of gains on the cash security. The liquidity of the cash security or the accounting impact of its premature purchase or sale may make realization of gains on the cash position difficult.

Hedgers are concerned with fluctuations in a futures position during the duration of the hedge only under certain conditions. There is no cost or risk of marking-to-market as long as the value of the spot position they are hedging is moving daily in lock step (in a perfect negative correlation) with the futures position, and as long as portions of the spot position are easily and cheaply convertible into cash that can be quickly transferred into variation margin account. Under these circumstances, realized profits on the spot position would be sufficient to cover declines in the futures' position at each daily interval within the hedge. This perfect offset rarely occurs from the beginning to end point of the hedging period and is extremely unusual to observe on a daily basis. The greater the dissimilarity between the deliverable instrument of the future and the spot portfolio being hedged (i.e., the weaker the price-change correlation), the greater the likelihood of disparities between daily profits and losses on the spot and futures position.

There may also be market imperfections or tax considerations that impose a cost on the hedge or that limit the opportunity to transfer unrealized gains on the security into cash that can be used for variation margin purposes. Realization of gains may incur a tax liability that could be avoided if no variation margin requirement existed. Certain types of assets being hedged (e.g., mortgage securities, corporate bonds, municipal bonds) may have illiquid secondary markets or high transactions costs for small unit orders that makes it costly to frequently convert increases in the value of the cash position into cash. In such situations, hedgers may wish to maintain a portion of the portfolio in liquid, low-risk securities that can be used for margin purposes. This "hedging reserve" has an opportunity cost in terms of higher returns that would be available if those funds were otherwise invested.

The best way to determine the amount of funds that needs to be available either in the form of a liquid cash reserve or line of credit is to analyze the daily price fluctuations of the futures contract being used.[6] It is important to plan ahead when using futures trading or hedging strategies. Decision rules should be present, identifying the conditions under which the futures position will be closed. Funds need to be readily available to absorb average fluctuations in futures prices, and provisions should be made for access to additional cash reserves should sizable losses be incurred. The provisions may involve sale of securities that are being hedged, borrowing cash against the proceeds of planned bond issues, or the closing out of a portion of the futures position.

Size of "Hedging Reserve" and Cost of Marking-to-Market

The determination of the size of this hedging reserve should be based on the range and frequency of possible daily futures losses that might occur during the hedging period, on the liquidity of the cash market position, and on the expected correlation between the future and the position being hedged. For example, the hedge of a six-month Treasury bill that is deliverable into a short futures position would need little cash reserve. Neither would the hedge of a Treasury bond that is the cheapest-to-deliver into the Treasury bond futures contract. It also should be clear that the "reserve" needed for the hedger tends to be less than that of the speculator, because it is assumed that the hedger has a cash market position that would be generating some profits as the futures position is realizing losses.

The conditions under which marking-to-market risk is most significant to hedgers can be restated. If gains on the cash position are costly to liquidate or will be realized in the future, as in the case with an anticipatory hedge, or if the value of the position being hedged is not highly correlated with the future, funds must be available for marking-to-market. These funds serve as a "hedging reserve" for covering losses on the futures position that may or may not be accompanied by realized gains on the cash portfolio or asset. The size of this hedging reserve depends on the size of the futures position, on the volatility of daily futures prices, and on the amount of liquid assets available to the hedgers as part of their normal operations.

Interest earned on the investment of interim profits in the variation margin account and interest expenses from the financing of interim losses are usually less than 5 percent of total futures profits and losses. There can be, however, large fluctuations in mark-to-market account levels over the hedging period. A short hedge in fixed-income futures tends to be profitable during periods dominated by rising interest rates. Thus, the inclusion of interest on variation margin balances increases this profit as interest is accrued at increasing interest rate levels.

It can be said, therefore, that the *ex ante* returns and risks of short (long) positions in fixed-income futures are usually higher when variation margin investment and financing results are taken into account. This would be true to the extent that futures prices are negatively related to increases in short-term interest rates. For the case of equity futures, the amplifications of gains and losses by the marking-to-market would also be true when a decline in the equity index is associated with rising interest rates.

CONTROL AND INTERNAL
REPORTING PROCEDURES

Institutions initiating a financial futures program should establish internal control and reporting procedures at a very early stage in the process. This step is critical, because the futures position will impact cash flow on a daily basis. Prices in fixed-income and equity markets can change very quickly and by large amounts. The accounting standards require documentation for audit purposes and for futures trades to qualify for special "hedging" treatment. Procedures should be in place to monitor positions continuously. Contingency plans should be set for actions to be taken under various market scenarios.

Because of the leverage and sharp price fluctuations that can occur in futures markets, it is very important to have adequate control procedures to guard against unauthorized trading. Since positions must be marked-to-market daily through a broker, any unauthorized transactions will be quickly detected as long as brokers' reports are reviewed by several parties. It is still critical to establish trading limits and to have a central function that is responsible for monitoring the combined positions of all authorized traders with all brokers through whom trades are executed.

The level of sophistication of the reporting and control system depends on the amount of risk exposure and degree of centralization of the futures trading within the firm. At a minimum, there should be three separate administrative units involved that will provide checks and balances to one another:

1. The futures trading and strategy unit.
2. An administrative section that
   a. records trades,
   b. tabulates daily balances for all positions and for firms as a whole.
   c. records and pays commissions,
   d. provides regular reports to the trading unit and management.
3. A manager to monitor and evaluate all futures positions for the firm and to examine the relationship of these positions to other corporate activities and controls.

Procedures need to be established for recording individual trades, for setting trading limits, and for production of reports. As new trades occur, a new entry should be made in the accounting file. The futures position statement should include:

— Trade date
— Buy or sell
— Type of contract
        Deliverable instrument
        Delivery date
— Number of contracts
— Price of future
— Number of units in contract
— Associated security position (if hedging)

- Price of associated security
- Account in which the associated security is held
- Type of security
- Market value
- Book value
- Name of person initiating trade
- Name of person authorizing trade
- Broker

On a daily basis, the futures broker will provide a report of the required or available variation margin in the traders' futures account. These brokers' reports should be reconciled punctually by the trader and accounting or audit unit. At a minimum, a weekly report of open positions, positions closed that week, and cumulative profits and losses should be sent to all interested parties. If possible, the value of associated cash market positions should also be included on these reports.

If the firm is managing a futures strategy for a client, the client should be included in those receiving the brokers' statement and weekly reports prepared for management. If a futures trader is managing futures positions for several clients, separate reports should be prepared by the broker. A good method of organization is to report positions by type of futures and delivery month and, within these categories, chronologically by position opening dates. Trading limits should be noted also to compare to the size of current open positions in futures. When futures positions are closed, either partially or fully, the closing trade information should be reported under the open position information in the report produced immediately following the closing of the position. In the weekly reports, cumulative profits (losses) over the preceding period should be reported on all open positions as well as those closed during the year.

In addition to the steps outlined above, policy decisions need to be made in several areas. These policies might include some or all of the following:

1. Procedures for submitting objectives for futures strategies against which performance will be judged.
2. Identification of authorized brokers and persons who can authorize trades in the firm.
3. Trading rules for opening positions (e.g., if losses are greater than $X per contract) close out position.
4. Trading limits for client, account, trader, and firm as a whole.

5. Reporting of required information to regulatory authorities (CFTC).
6. Regular audits of accuracy of futures recordkeeping and report activities.

Obviously, the actual procedures followed will depend upon the administrative structure of the institution undertaking the futures program. Careful control and recordkeeping enable management to evaluate the success of futures trading or hedging and to monitor closely the risk and cash flow implications. Arthur Anderson & Co. has prepared a very useful booklet, *Accounting for Interest Rate Futures (1985),* that suggests internal control procedures for firms using financial futures.

ACCOUNTING TREATMENT OF FINANCIAL FUTURES

Accepted industry accounting procedures as defined by The American Institute of Certified Public Accountant's (AICPA) issue papers have had a significant impact on the use of financial futures contracts. When financial futures were introduced to the public in 1975, regulators employed stringent accounting interpretations which inhibited the use of these futures contracts. The concept of marking-to-market on accounting reports became associated with all transactions. The futures positions required a daily mark-to-market while the cost or value of associated cash positions could not be recognized until they were sold or matured. Therefore, the use of futures by financial institutions was self-penalizing. Quickly, many senior financial officers discarded financial futures applications, since their quarterly profit and loss statement became temporarily distorted.

During 1980, it became evident to the financial industry and their regulators that the proper use of financial futures could reduce financial and currency risk exposure. Accountants were asked to review the procedures associated with such transactions. Specifically, a request was made to permit the profits or losses generated by anticipatory hedging and hedging of existing assets and liabilities to be recognized in a manner other than marking-to-market. During the past five years, significant progress has been made in accommodating this request.

In August 1984, generally accepted accounting principles for exchange-traded futures contracts were at last established by the Financial Accounting Standards Board (FASB). At that time the

FASB issued *Statement of Financial Accounting Standards (SFAS) No. 80* after receiving comments on an exposure draft of this statement released in July of 1983. With this important step, most of the accounting issues concerning the handling of profits and losses from financial futures trading activity have been resolved.

SFAS No. 80 calls for futures contracts to be carried on a market value basis and for gains and losses to be recognized in the period in which they occur, unless the futures activity meets specific criteria that qualify this activity as undertaken for hedging purposes. If the futures transaction meets the conditions for hedge accounting, the treatment of the futures gains and losses depends on the accounting treatment for the item being hedged. Accounting symmetry is followed in accounting for each side of the hedged position.

For hedged items that are carried on a market value basis, the futures contract is also carried at market value with gains and losses recognized in the period in which the cash flows occur. However, if a hedged financial asset or liability is carried at lower-of-cost-or-market or on a historical cost basis as is the case with the most long-term securities, the futures gain or loss is deferred as an adjustment to the carrying amount of the financial asset or liability. For example, if futures are sold in connection with the issuance of long-term debt, the profits (losses) on the futures trade would be allocated over the life of the debt issue as a reduction (increase) in the interest expense reported each period. This treatment is basically in line with what was requested by the futures industry and by institutions using futures as risk management vehicles.

The most important and controversial part of *SFAS No. 80* deals with the standards that must be met before a futures transaction can be classified as qualifying for the hedge accounting treatment described above. In establishing these standards or criteria, the FASB has attempted to define hedging activity for an enterprise as distinct from speculative activity. Because of the significance of accounting treatment to a firm's willingness to engage in futures trades, we should expect to see most organizations structure their hedging programs to insure these criteria are met.

The conditions that must be satisfied in order for a financial futures transaction to qualify for hedge accounting are as follows:

1. The item to be hedged exposes the firm or enterprise to interest rate, equity, or currency risk.
2. The futures contract used for hedging reduces this risk. (There

is evidence of correlation between the price of the item being hedged and the future.)

3. For hedges of anticipated transactions, the transactions must have a high probability of actually being carried out. The significant characteristics and terms of the anticipated transaction must be identified prior to implementing the hedge.

These criteria impose two standards on the hedging institution. It must be able to measure and evaluate the risk exposure of the firm as a whole as well as the extent to which each asset and liability that may potentially be hedged contributes to that risk. The accounting statement does allow for an exception for firms that pursue risk management on a decentralized basis. These firms can apply the first criteria at the business unit level. The question of how a business unit will be defined is open at this point and will hopefully be resolved as these new standards are applied in practice.

Taxation of financial futures transactions depends on whether the trades are classified as being for speculative or hedging purposes. The most recent legislation that specified tax treatment for "regulated futures contracts" was the Tax Reform Act of 1984, implemented in July of that year. Speculative profits and losses must be marked-to-market at year end and are taxed as 60% long-term and 40% short-term capital gains or losses.

Hedging transactions are not subject to the end of year mark-to-market rule. These types of trades produce ordinary income or losses that are recognized at the time the futures position is closed. To be classified as a hedging trade for tax purposes, several conditions must be met. The trade must be identified as a hedging trade upon initiation of the transaction. The futures trade must reduce the risk of assets or liabilities held (or going to be held) by the taxpayer. Futures trades of banks and other financial institutions can be treated as hedges for tax purposes as long as they are undertaken in the normal course of business of the financial entity.

DYNAMIC MANAGEMENT OF FUTURES STRATEGIES

In this chapter, we have discussed most of the operational aspects of implementing a futures strategy. In the final section of this chapter, we present some guidelines for the management and control of futures positions over time.

The best way to illustrate the task of dynamic management of futures strategies is in the context of particular commercial applications, such as continuous hedging, selective hedging, and the use of futures as temporary substitutes for cash market positions strategy. This highlights the key role of the strategy objective in the futures management process. The objective should serve as the benchmark against which the success of the futures program will be judged.

The first and most basic requirement of dynamic futures management is a good measurement or performance system for evaluating the progress of the futures program. In terms of evaluation of the futures position, profits (losses) must be measured against those identified in the objective. Consider, for example, the case of a bank that makes a fixed-rate loan to a commercial customer for one year and sells a series of CD futures to fix its financing cost over the same time period. After three months have passed, rates have increased sharply and all the CD futures can be repurchased at a considerable profit. Closing out the futures position will leave the bank unhedged against further rate increases and violate the objective of "fixing" the funds cost for the loan. However, the likelihood of further rate increases may be small in the opinion of the bank. Clearly, the objective must be reconsidered, given the change in the interest rate environment. Is controlling the funds cost as important now as it was three months ago? If the answer is yes, the futures strategy is on target and should not be changed. If locking in the costs is no longer necessary, the futures position can be closed, leaving the bank in a position to gain from a decline in interest rates.

The three futures strategies mentioned above—continuous hedging, selective hedging, and short-term substitutes for cash positions—all require a careful monitoring of the value and risk exposure of the securities being hedged (or replaced) with futures. In a situation in which one is hedging a long-term, high-quality, corporate bond portfolio with futures, careful management depends on the ability to identify, price, and track the weighted average duration or maturity of the bonds being hedged. This requires close coordination between the units managing the cash and futures market activities.

Any change in the size of the bond portfolio due to interest rate changes or bond transactions may also warrant an adjustment in the futures position. One can easily see how problems could develop if significant amounts of 20-year corporate bonds were replaced with 6-year notes. The interest rate risk of the bond portfolio has been reduced. If no adjustment is made to the futures position, losses (or profits) on the futures that are geared to a longer maturity portfolio can be far in excess of subsequent gains (or losses) in the bond portfolio.

Continuous Hedging

This strategy would be used by institutions that wish to totally eliminate the price risk of a security position or portfolio. The assets may be held strictly for the coupon return, or the securities (stocks or bonds) may be held on a temporary basis during which the owner wants to protect their value to the greatest extent possible. In this situation, dynamic hedge management can be based on the size and risk of the position being hedged. Given this information, the amount of futures bought or sold can be established and adjusted as market conditions warrant. Expiring futures would be "rolled out" to other contracts. Changes in security duration might warrant futures trading, as may changes in the market value of the securities not matched by changes in the futures (basis risk).

Selective Hedging

This practice refers to the construction of futures strategies based on an assessment of the under- or overvaluation of security and futures prices. The characteristics of the securities being hedged must also be analyzed. Selective short hedgers would sell futures when a price drop is expected beyond that which is already reflected in futures prices. Selective long hedgers would buy futures in anticipation of future purchases of stocks or of fixed-income securities; however, they would only do so when they expect prices to rise beyond the level of the futures price.

Dynamic management of selective hedging is much more complex, because one must be aware of changes in the security positions that arise from transactions or market conditions. One must also be continually involved in an analysis of price movements of both the cash security and the futures. Selective hedgers are always weighing the alternatives for current or prospective futures positions. Selling of futures is appropriate as a selective hedge if the outlook for bond or stock prices is bearish and the cost of selling the stocks or bonds and repurchasing them is high relative to the cost of executing a similar strategy via financial futures.

Market conditions must be carefully watched to identify opportune times to close out futures positions. Depending on market conditions, one may choose to be unhedged or to control risk with an alternative strategy that does not involve futures. Successful selective hedging requires a thorough knowledge of both cash and futures markets. One of the best ways to acquire these skills is to begin a selective hedging program on a small scale and expand as expertise is acquired. Brokers and security dealers have the most interest in selective hedging because of their great exposure to short-term security price changes. They also have an advantage because their basic business involves a familiarity with financial markets and security price movements.

Financial Futures as Temporary Substitutes for Security Positions

As we have seen in previous chapters, financial futures sometimes have advantages as short-term substitutes for holding financial assets. This is true, because futures positions can be initiated cheaply and easily in markets that are often lower in transaction cost and greater in liquidity than the actual security market. If the security(ies) underlying the futures are very similar to those being bought or sold, the number of futures contracts traded should have the same underlying market value as the amount of securities. When some basis risk is present, one can reduce or increase the number of futures contracts depending on the degree of expected price change correlation or on any differences in duration or market risk.

Once the futures position is established, the task becomes the timing of the conversion of all or part of the futures into the cash market securities. Ideally, one would like to sell long futures positions at a profit that exceeds the increased price that must be paid for the actual stocks or bonds. The reverse is of course true for the situation in which one has sold futures in anticipation of a bond or stock issue. Therefore, futures and cash prices must be analyzed continuously to find the best time to carry out the conversion from futures to cash market instruments.

If this type of tactical market timing is the objective of the futures strategy, one should plan the scenarios under which one would reverse the futures trade by closing out the position. The conditions under which the tactical futures position would be closed out and replaced with a cash market purchase or sale should be predetermined.

Cross-Hedging

A final comment on dynamic futures management in *cross-hedging* situations is warranted. It is very important for the hedger to monitor the price spread or relative values between the securities being hedged and those underlying the futures positions. When futures are sold against a stock or bond portfolio, situations in which the underlying security is likely to gain in value relative to the portfolio can involve considerable risk of losses.

Consider a situation in which a short Treasury bond futures hedge was initiated on a municipal bond portfolio when the spread between municipal bond yields and Treasury bond yields was narrow compared to its long-term average value. Long-term interest rates rise, and the spread widens to a level in excess of typical historical levels. This means that the municipal bond portfolio has declined in value less than the profits earned on the futures, giving the hedger a net profit as well as interest rate risk protection. Initiating or continuing to the short Treasury bond futures position when the spread is wide carries the risk that the futures may actually produce losses in excess of the gains on the bond as the spread returns to the normal range.

Thus, cross-hedgers should keep a careful watch over the basis risk in their portfolio by looking out for major changes in price or yield spreads and for shifts in the correlation between price changes in the futures and cross-hedged securities. Either of these conditions would call for a reevaluation of the size of the futures position or commitment to futures in general. Situations may also arise in which hedging is made even more attractive by the relative values perceived in the securities being hedged and the securities on which the futures are based. An example here would be the case in which the holder of a portfolio of large capitalization (blue-chip) stocks hedges with NYSE futures. The portfolio manager has a bearish outlook for equities and thinks the NYSE index will be declining more or rising less than the stocks held in the portfolio.

SUMMARY

The application of financial futures to corporate and investment management requires more than an understanding of the futures market and pricing fundamentals of futures contracts. Successful futures strategies also require a plan for implementation and management of futures positions. First the objective of the futures strategy must be determined and understood by all parties directly involved in and indirectly responsible for trades. Since futures contracts can be used in such a wide range of strategies, it is necessary to specify the goals and guidelines that will be followed by each institution.

After the goals and guidelines have been established, the type and amount of futures contracts must be determined. The liquidity of the contracts, the time horizon of the futures strategy, and many other considerations (e.g., delivery, taxes) must also be analyzed.

After determining the appropriate objectives of the futures strategy, management procedures for monitoring the futures position must be established. Provisions must be made for marking-to-market, as well as for control and internal reporting procedures. In addition to internal monitoring an understanding of accounting principles and accounting treatment for external reporting is also required. The various FASB accounting standards are continually being updated and readers are cautioned to consult professionals.

Futures strategies require constant review. Decisions must be made to continue or discontinue a hedge position as market conditions change. A changing financial environment for the firm may call for changes in goals and strategies of futures programs. In the following chapters we review the use of financial futures in the context of the goals and strategies of different types of institutions.

NOTES

[1] See Liro et al. (1983) for further discussion.

[2] An important caveat must be made here for futures strategies designed to hedge debt securities. The security's maturity is changing over the hedging horizon. Thus, in the case of a hedge implemented over an extended period, the correlation between the price changes of the security being hedged and the futures may actually decline as delivery approaches. This can occur because the security underlying the future has, in effect, a constant maturity while the security being hedged is varying in maturity over the period the hedge is being implemented. In this type of situation, the size of the futures position can be adjusted periodically to take into account the changing characteristics of the security relative to the deliverable instrument of the futures contract.

[3] See McCabe and Franckle (1983), and Baesel and Grant (1982) for further discussion of rolling futures positions forward.

[4] There is conflicting theory and evidence as to whether the variability of futures prices increases as delivery approaches. Samuelson's work (1965, 1976) supports the case of higher volatility levels for price changes of futures contracts closer to delivery. Anderson and Danthine (1981) maintain that there is no inherent tendency for futures prices to become more volatile as delivery approaches. Rather, they conclude that a more accurate statement is that the volatility of futures prices depends on the rate at which uncertainty is being resolved. Examining the implied stock index futures volatility as reflected in prices of options on S&P 500 futures, Park and Sears (1985) find that volatility declines as the delivery date approaches. For an empirical analysis of delivery month effects see Milonas (1984) and Melonas and Vora (1985). They point out that any empirical analysis of delivery effects must also take into account nonstationarity across different delivery periods.

[5] George McCabe and Charles Franckle, (1983) consider an example in which

the hedge is rolled only once. Baesel and Grant (1982) derive a more general multi-period rolling rule.

⁶ See Hill et. al. (1983) and Kolb et. al. (1984) for a more in-depth treatment of this topic. Hill et. al.'s analysis examines the question of the size of a hedging reserve for Treasury bond futures. For the more general case, Kolb et. al. provide a model that provides an estimate of the probability that a pool of funds set aside for daily marking-to-market will have a zero balance.

SELECTED REFERENCES

Accounting for Interest Rate Futures, Arthur Anderson & Co., 1985.

Anderson, R., and J. P. Danthine. "The Time Pattern of Hedging and the Volatility of Futures Prices." *Center for Study of Futures Markets (CSFM)* no. 7 (April 1981).

Baesel, J. and D. Grant. "Optimal Sequential Futures Trading." *Journal of Financial and Quantitative Analysis,* December 1982, pp. 683–95.

Beaver, William. "Accounting for Interest Rate Futures Contracts." *Center for the Study of Futures Markets (CSFM),* no. 11 (March 1981).

Goodman, Laurie S., and Martha J. Langer. "Accounting for Interest Rate Futures in Bank Asset-Liability Management." *The Journal of Futures Markets,* Winter 1983, pp. 415–29.

Grant, D. "Rolling the Hedge Forward: an Extension." *Financial Management,* Winter 1984, pp. 26–28.

Hill, J.; T. Schneeweis; and B. Mayerson. "An Analysis of the Impact of Marking-to-Market in Hedging with Treasury Bond Futures," *Review of Research in Futures Markets* 2, no. 1 (1983), pp. 139–59.

Kolb, R. W., G. D. Gay, and W. C. Hunter, "Liquidity and Capital Requirements for Futures Market Hedges." *Review of Research in Futures Markets,* 1984.

Liro, J.; J. Hill; and T. Schneeweis, "Hedging Performance of GNMA Futures under Rising and Falling Interest Rates." *Journal of Futures Markets,* Winter 1983, pp. 403–14.

McCabe, G., and C. Franckle. "The Effectiveness of Rolling the Hedge Forward in the Treasury Bill Futures Market." *Financial Management* 12, no. 2 (Summer 1983) pp. 21–29.

Milonas, N. "Liquidity, Price Variability, and Storage Asymmetry: A Study of the Behavior of Prices in Futures Markets." Ph.D. dissertation. City University of New York, 1984.

Milonas, N., and A. Vora. "Sources of Nonstationarity in Cash and Futures Prices." Paper presented at Eastern Finance Association, February 1985.

Park, H. Y., and R. S. Sears, "Estimating Stock Index Futures Volatility through the Prices of Their Options," *Journal of Futures Markets,* Summer 1985, pp. 223–37.

Samuelson, P. "Proof That Properly Anticipated Prices Fluctuate Randomly." *Industrial Management Review,* Spring 1965, pp. 41–59.

Samuelson, P. "Is Real World Price a Tale Told by the Idiot of Chance?" *Review of Economics and Statistics,* February 1976, pp. 120–123.

CHAPTER 9

Applications of Futures for Banking Institutions

Commercial banks and savings and loan institutions represent the primary U.S. depository institutions. With a few exceptions they are the only financial institutions permitted to hold demand deposits. Banks are also among the most important financial intermediaries participating in the financial markets.[1] They act both as depositories of savings and as a source of loanable funds. Despite banks' unique financial role, bank goals and objectives are in many ways quite similar to those of other financial and nonfinancial firms. Bank management desires to maximize investors' return and minimize investors' risk. The central concern of bank management is therefore how to meet the conflicting demands of depositors and creditors while maximizing bank profitability.

Bank profitability management has become increasingly difficult. The growth of alternative investment vehicles, such as money market funds and nonbank financial service companies, has led to greater competition for sources of bank funds as well as for traditional earning assets. In this new financial environment, financial futures provide banks with an additional tool for managing assets and liabilities. Initially, banks were slow to use financial futures. As shown in Exhibit 9–1, banks have recently indicated an increasing interest in financial futures.[2] Financial futures offer new applications and strategies in a bank's trading and dealer activities, trust and investment departments, debt and loan management, and financial services.

For banks, financial futures' greatest potential may lie in their ability to provide banks with an additional means to manage their financial assets and liabilities. Banks wish to maintain a positive net interest margin (differential between interest earned on assets and interest paid on liabilities as a percentage of earning assets).[3] For banks with greater interest-sensitive liabilities than interest-sensitive assets, a rise in short-term rates can reduce bank profits. An asset or liability is generally regarded as interest-sensitive if its cash flows are affected in the short run by changes in interest rates. In efforts to reduce interest rate exposure, banks attempt to match interest-sensitive assets with interest-sensitive liabilities and fixed-rate assets with fixed-rate liabilities. Variability in loan demand and deposits often prevents a bank from achieving a close match between the interest rate sensitivity of assets and liabilities. As a result, a bank may fund fixed-rate assets with interest sensitive liabilities and interest-sensitive assets with fixed-rate sources of funds. When the interest rate sensitivity of assets and liabilities does not match, financial futures contracts enable banks to hedge the net interest rate exposure.

EXHIBIT 9–1
Banks Hedging with Financial Futures

Type of Institution	Used Futures in 1983	Use Futures Now	Expect To Use More	Will Start Using	Would Not Use
Money center banks	5%	21%	11%	42%	0%
Large regional banks	8	8	6	33	6
Medium banks	4	5	2	29	12
Small banks	2	4	3	30	14

Source: *Securities Week*, May 2, 1983.

Fluctuations in loan demand and in the level of bank deposits, however, may restrict the ability of financial futures to hedge the net exposure of a bank. The purchase or sale of a futures contract to reduce a financial institution's expected net interest rate exposure may result in an increase in actual net interest rate exposure within a few days. Instead of hedging net interest rate exposure, a bank may choose to use financial futures to hedge only those projects with high perceived risk. For instance, futures can be used to hedge unexpected changes in interest costs on sources of bank funds. If a financial futures contract is sold short and interest costs rise, the gain on the repurchase of the futures contract at a lower price can be used as an adjustment to the increased interest cost. Futures can therefore permit a bank to offer fixed-rate loans even during periods of interest rate uncertainty.

While banks are regarded principally as a source of loans and investment, they are also engaged in a number of related financial activities. Financial futures permit banks to better manage their own investment portfolios and trust department investments. For those banking institutions that act as government dealers and security traders, the futures market provides a means to hedge anticipated purchases as well as existing inventory and to profit from arbitrage and trading activities. Many financial institutions have even established subsidiaries to offer trading advice and execution to customers involved in the management of financial futures.

As competition between banks and nonbank financial institutions grows, financial futures provide an additional means of forming competitive strategies in all areas of bank profitability management. The major components of bank profitability can be broken down into (1) asset and liability management, (2) investment portfolio and trust fund management, (3) trading and dealer activities, and (4) fee-based services (Exhibit 9–2). In the following sections

---

EXHIBIT 9–2
Commercial Bank Profitability

Bank asset and liability management $\longrightarrow$ Net interest
$\qquad\qquad\qquad\qquad\qquad\qquad\qquad\qquad\quad$ margin
Portfolio and funds management $\quad\longrightarrow$ Investment income

Trading and dealer activity $\qquad\quad\longrightarrow$ Trading profits

Finanical $\qquad\qquad\qquad\qquad\qquad\qquad$ Fee
services $\qquad\qquad\qquad\qquad\qquad\longrightarrow$ income

---

we review various applications of financial futures to bank profitability management.

ASSET AND LIABILITY MANAGEMENT

Banks act primarily as intermediaries between those who wish to lend capital and those who wish to borrow funds. In order to provide loan and investment capital, banks must first acquire funds. These funds are liabilities to the bank. As shown in Exhibit 9–3 a bank's principle sources of funds are demand, savings, and time deposits. The residual item in Exhibit 9–3 is the capital account consisting primarily of equity capital and subordinated long-

---

EXHIBIT 9–3
Assets and Liabilities of Domestically Chartered Commercial Banks (December 1983)

	$ Billion	Percent of Total
Assets		
1. Commercial and industrial loans	380.8	19.33
2. Other loans	714.4	36.27
3. U.S. Treasury securities	181.4	9.10
4. Other securities	248.7	12.62
5. Cash	190.5	9.67
6. Other assets	253.8	12.86
Total assets	1,969.5	100.00
Liabilities and Capital		
7. Demand deposits	871.0	18.84
8. Savings deposits	460.7	23.39
9. Time deposits	650.8	33.04
10. Borrowings	216.3	10.98
11. Other liabilities	117.9	5.98
12. Residual (assets/liabilities)	152.8	7.75
Total less	1,969.5	100.00

Source: Federal Reserve Bulletin, August 1984.

term debt. Each liability has a unique cost. Demand, savings, and time deposits are generally obtained at a lower cost than long-term debt and equity.

Bank assets provide the revenue necessary to cover the cost of bank liabilities. As shown in Exhibit 9–3 and Exhibit 9–4, banks' primary sources of earning assets are loans. Bank loans are usually classified as (1) commercial and industrial, (2) real estate, (3) consumer, (4) agricultural, (5) loans for purchasing or carrying securities, and (6) loans to other financial institutions. The importance of each classification varies, of course, from bank to bank. Commercial industrial, and consumer loans make up the major portion of commercial and retail loan portfolios. For savings and loan institutions mortgage loans play the dominant role. For banks in farm states, agricultural loans dominate.[4]

Recently, higher interest rate levels (Exhibit 9–5) have resulted in a shift in customer demand to higher cost time and savings deposits relative to lower cost demand deposit accounts (Exhibit 9–6). New funding alternatives available to corporations (e.g., commercial paper) have increased the level of uncertainty in corporate

EXHIBIT 9–4
Principal Classes of Loans and Investments (all commercial banks)

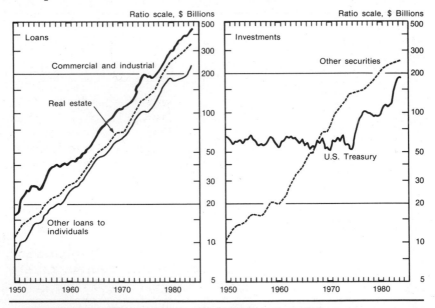

Source: 1984 Historical Chart Book, Federal Reserve Board of Governors.
Note: Semiannual call report dates, 1950–73; seasonally adjusted quarterly averages, 1973–.

bank loan demand. The sensitivity of a bank's fund flows to interest rate changes has focused attention on asset and liability management. For instance, the lower cost of short-term debt may be offset by the necessity to refund it at frequent intervals. In matching assets and liabilities a bank's major concern is to maintain a positive spread between the rate received on loans and the rate paid for funds. If, for example, variable rate short-term funds are used to finance fixed-rate long-term loans, increases in short-term rates may effectively lower a bank's net interest income. This is in fact what happened to savings and loan institutions during the 1970s. Long-term, fixed-rate mortgage loans were funded with higher cost short-term funds.

Hedging Interest Rate Risk at the Macro Level

In bank asset and liability management, banks are increasingly focusing their attention on the concept of gap management. Gap management obtains its name from the management of the difference (gap) between the dollar amount of rate-sensitive assets and rate-sensitive liabilities (net interest income). In most of the gap

EXHIBIT 9–5
Long- and Short-Term Interest Rates

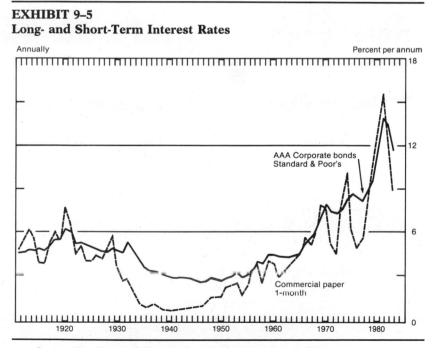

Source: 1984 Historical Chart Book, Federal Reserve Board of Governors.

EXHIBIT 9–6
Balance-Sheet Ratios (all commercial banks)

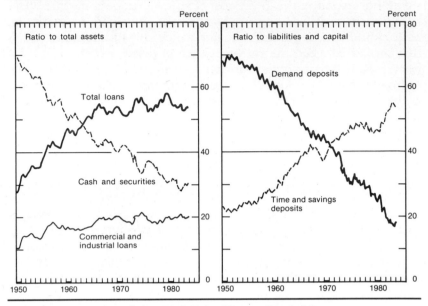

Source: 1984 Historical Chart Book, Federal Reserve Board of Governors.
Note: Semiannual call report dates, 1950–73; end of quarter, 1973–.

management literature, net interest margin is analyzed instead of net interest income. Net interest margin is obtained by dividing the book value of earning assets into net interest income. To implement a gap management model, the bank must first select the time period over which the interest income is to be managed. In Exhibit 9–7, a bank's assets and liabilities are broken down into two time periods; greater and less than 90 days to maturity. The

EXHIBIT 9–7
Asset/Liability Balance (in $ millions)

Maturity	Assets	Liability	Net Exposed Balance
Interest rate sensitive, 0–90 days	$ 4	$10	(6)
Noninterest sensitive	$25	$19	
	$29	$29	

bank must then determine the amount of interest-sensitive assets and interest-sensitive liabilities.[5] An asset or liability is regarded as interest *sensitive* if its cash flows vary with changes in rates over the time period the interest income is to be managed. An asset or liability is identified as interest *insensitive* if its cash flows are not affected by changes in rates over that time period.

In periods of interest rate volatility a mismatch of interest-sensitive assets and liabilities may result in a decline in profits. A positive asset gap (interest-sensitive assets exceed interest-sensitive liabilities) in a period of falling rates requires that maturing assets be invested at lower rates. A negative asset gap (interest-sensitive liabilities exceed interest-sensitive assets) in periods of rising rates requires that new funds be obtained at higher costs. Banks that desire to minimize interest rate sensitivity would match interest-sensitive assets and liabilities as closely as possible.

There are different approaches to interest rate risk management. A loan could be tied to a bank's cost of funds. With floating loans the yields on the loans vary over the life of assets.[6] However, several problems exist with floating rate notes. First, there is often a lag between rate changes in sources of bank funds and the rate to which the loan is tied. Second, many corporate bank customers are reluctant to borrow at floating rates. Most corporate customers regard interest rate risk management as the proper concern of the bank rather than the corporation. As an alternative to floating rate loans, banks may use interest rate swaps (debt exchanges between institutions) to obtain proper balance between interest-sensitive assets and interest-sensitive liabilities.[7] Banks may also layer (e.g., match) the amount of interest-sensitive assets and liabilities by maturity sector. In analyzing the maturity sectors in Exhibit 9–7, managers are able to focus on the differences in assets and liabilities between the predefined periods. These period gaps may be liability gaps where liabilities to be repriced exceed assets or asset gaps where assets to be repriced exceed liabilities. For example in Exhibit 9–7 a bank is exposed to a liability gap of $6 million or 20% of its $29 million in earning assets.

Despite their widespread use, interest rate swaps and layering have their limitations. Swap transactions are difficult to reverse and tend to be in large amounts (e.g., $25 million or greater). In addition, swap payments are not guaranteed. Layering also has its disadvantages. Layering is only an approximation of individual asset and liability matching. Instead of matching individual loans, a bank attempts to match maturity sectors. However, bank loans are made to suit customers needs, so it is often difficult to keep a perfectly matched maturity sector policy.

Financial futures offer an alternative to interest rate swaps and permit a more complete layering strategy. Financial futures can be used to balance both positive gaps and negative gaps. In Exhibit 9–7 the interest rate spread on $4 million of the 0–90 day interest-sensitive liabilities is not affected by refunding the liabilities. If interest rates rise, $4 million of the 0–90 day assets have also matured and can be reinvested at a higher rate to maintain the spread. The bank has a near term net exposed balance of $6 million. By selling financial futures the bank can reduce the risk of interest rate increases on funding the new debt. The bank would simply have to sell the necessary number of financial futures contracts. Since $6 million must be funded (purchased) at 91 days the bank could sell an appropriate futures contract with a face value of $6 million (e.g., 6 Treasury bill futures with contract delivery at time of the liability's refunding). If rates rise, the increased cost of financing the debt will be offset by gains from the repurchase of the futures contract at a lower price.

It is important to point out that some difficulties exist in the measurement of net interest rate exposure.[8] A bank must determine the maturity groupings for interest rate sensitivity analysis. The defined maturity grouping used may contain assets and liabilities of widely varying maturities. An asset's duration may serve as a better measure of an asset's interest rate sensitivity.[9] Even if a bank's interest income is insensitive to interest rate changes, the market value of its noninterest-sensitive assets and liabilities may be greatly affected by rate changes.

Gap differences are a means for banks to profit from superior interest rate forecasting. A bank may plan for a deliberate gap mismatch to benefit from a particular interest rate outlook. With rising short-term rates, a positive gap (interest-sensitive assets greater than interest-sensitive liabilities) would increase net interest margin as funds from retired assets are reinvested at higher rates. Likewise, with declining short-term rates a negative gap would increase the spread (interest income versus interest expense) as new liabilities would be obtained at lower rates. Lastly, present accounting rules require that gains and losses for futures contracts that cannot be tied to a particular cash position must be marked to market.[10] Reporting financial futures positions as they are marked to market, while defering the cash market gains and losses until realized, may result in an increase in reported earnings volatility. For bank management concerned with reported accounting earnings rather than true economic cash flows, financial futures may not be considered.

Hedging Interest Rate Risk at the Micro Level

As an alternative to using financial futures to hedge overall bank interest rate sensitivity (macro hedge), a bank may wish to hedge specific asset or liability positions (micro hedge). Assume a bank has issued six-month money market certificates (MMCs). The bank manager fears that interest rates will be higher at the maturity date of these MMCs. The manager may decide to hedge this exposure by selling a Treasury bill futures contract for delivery near the time of the MMCs renewal. The Treasury bill futures position should be twice the value of the MMC. This is so because the maturity of the Treasury bill contract is half that for a six-month MMC; therefore, the effect on a Treasury bill future of a 1 percent rate change is half that for the MMC. The additional interest cost due to a rise in MMC interest rates would be at least partially offset by gains in the Treasury bill futures position. Unexpected increases in interest rates for commercial paper, Federal funds, certificates of deposits, and bankers acceptances may also be similarly hedged with interest rate futures. If interest rates rise, the gain in repurchasing a short futures contract can be included as an adjustment to the cost of the liability issued.

Another application of financial futures would permit a bank to offer fixed-rate loans while hedging increasing interest rate costs during the life of the loan. For example, assume a loan officer approves the issue of a one-year $10 million loan at a fixed rate. The loan is to be financed by rolling over 90-day CDs for the one-year life of the loan. During this period, the bank is concerned that interest rates will rise. The loan officer can reduce the risk of a rise in borrowing costs by selling 90-day Treasury bill futures that expire close to the three 90-day periods that the 90-day CDs will need to be rolled over to provide financing for the loan. An example of such a hedge was illustrated in Chapter 3 (Exhibit 3–5).

In the same way that financial futures can be used to hedge unexpected changes in costs and returns of short-term domestic assets, Eurodollar futures may be used to hedge changes in deposit rates in Eurodollar markets. Trading volume in Eurodollar futures has recently even surpassed that of Treasury bill futures. Treasury bonds and Treasury notes can also be used to manage the risk of the changing cost of a bank's long-term sources of funds.

A bank's use of financial futures markets to hedge the cost of funds is not without risk.[11] Crises in the banking industry can affect overall rates as reflected in CD and Treasury bill futures prices, but leave interest costs unchanged for a particular bank.

Likewise, for a bank experiencing significant loan losses, CD rates may rise while the overall level of interest rates fall.

Basis risk is not the only problem in hedging costs of funds. For fixed-rate loans, a bank can sell futures to protect itself against rising short-term costs of funds. If the loan contains prepayment options, however, the effectiveness of the hedge depends on possible prepayment. If the loan prepayment option is exercised, the bank will suffer an immediate loss in assumed revenue. Moreover, if the cost of funds had been fixed in the futures market, the bank's futures contract position is left exposed. The cost of loan prepayment must be high enough to cover risk of futures contract exposure.

Reducing the gap between interest-sensitive assets and interest-sensitive liabilities is not the only source of bank concern. Banks are also concerned with the value of long-term asset positions. For instance, many banks are actively involved in the mortgage market and the origination and packaging of mortgage pools to investors and government agencies. The market value of mortgages held in inventory would decline as mortgage interest rates rise. GNMA futures can be sold short to offset the possible decline in the value of the mortgages (the use of GNMA futures for real estate financing is explored in detail in Chapter 12). In the next section we discuss further the use of financial futures to hedge the risk of value change of specific bank assets (e.g., corporate and government securities).

BANK INVESTMENT AND TRUST FUND MANAGEMENT

Security investment provides an important residual use of bank funds after customer loan demand has been met. A bank's investment portfolio must meet government requirements for pledged assets in connection with bank operations. A bank's trust department services a wide variety of customer needs. Assets under trust management include real estate, bond, and equity investments. The trust department's goals are similar to the goals of a bank's investment portfolio; that is, protection of asset value and return maximization.

Bank investment and trust divisions primarily use financial futures in two ways: (1) as a long hedge to lock in prices on futures investments and (2) as a short hedge to protect the asset value by offsetting the effects of falling prices on the value of the portfolio. In Exhibit 9–8 the investment or trust manager wishes to lock

EXHIBIT 9–8

	Cash Market	*Futures Market* *
September 1:	Plans to purchase a $1,000,000 of 20-year 8% Treasury bonds with a present price of 69.00 ($690,000) (yield 12.16%)	Bank purchases 10 December Treasury bond futures contracts at 59.40 ($594,062.50) (yield 14.13%)
November 1:	Bank purchased $1,000,000 worth of 20-year 8% Treasury bonds at a price of 70.00 ($700,000) (yield 11.98%)	Bank sells 10 December Treasury bond futures contracts at 63.0625 ($630,625) (yield 13.326%)
	Loss: $10,000	Gain: $36,562.50

* These yield equivalents are based on 8 percent 20-year bonds.

in the 12.16 percent rate on a planned Treasury bond investment of $690,000. To hedge a fall in interest rates the bank purchases Treasury bond futures at 59.40. By the time cash becomes available, interest rates have decreased to 11.98 percent and the price of the Treasury bonds in the cash market has increased to $700,000. The opportunity cost of delaying the security purchase was $10,000. At the same time as the purchase of Treasury bonds in the cash market, the Treasury bond futures positions is selling for $63.06. The sale of the Treasury bond futures position for $630,625 results in a gain of $36,562. The $10,000 opportunity loss in the spot market was offset by the $36,000 gain in the futures market.

Bank investment portfolios must also balance liquidity needs with income earned on investment holdings. Long-term securities generally provide higher yields than short-term securities; however, the prices of the longer term securities are more sensitive to interest rate movement. The lower yields on short-term securities can be viewed as a cost to a bank of protecting itself from decreases in asset value due to possible increases in market interest rates. Based on interest rate movement expectations, a bank may change the maturity structure of its investment portfolio by shortening the maturity structure in periods of expected rising rates and by lengthening it in periods of expected falling rates.

As an alternative to lengthening or shortening its portfolio maturity, the financial futures market provides a bank with a means to manage the maturity structure of its investment portfolio. In periods of expected interest rate increases, rather than shortening the maturity structure of the investment portfolio and thereby reducing yields, a bank may sell financial futures. If rates rise, the gain on the close of the short futures position should help to offset any losses in the investment portfolio.

EXHIBIT 9–9

	Cash Market	Futures Market*
September 1:	Bank holds $5 million of 20-year 8% Treasury bonds at a price of $63.00 ($3,150,000) (yield 13.33%)	Bank sells 50 December Treasury bond futures at 59.406 ($2,970,300) (yield 14.13%)
November 1:	Bank holds $5 million of 20 year 8% Treasury bonds at a price of 60.00 ($3,000,000) (yield 14.001%)	Bank purchases 50 December Treasury bond futures at 55.81 ($2,790,500) (yield 15.02%)
	Loss: $150,000	Gain: $179,800

* These yield equivalents are based on 8% 20-year bonds.

For example, in Exhibit 9–9 the portfolio manager has $5 million Treasury bonds selling at 63.00 for a total value of $3,150,000. To hedge the inventory position the investment manager sells 50 near term Treasury bond futures at 59.40. Rates rise, and the market values of bonds falls to $3,000,000. The price of the Treasury bond futures have also fallen to 55.81 for a gain of $179,800. The decline in the portfolio value of $150,000 was more than offset by the gain of $179,800 in the futures contract.

It should be noted that if prices rise unexpectedly, the gain on the portfolio's cash position would be reduced by the loss on the futures contract. Through an interest rate cycle, however, the objective of lowering the risk of capital loss should be realized.

TRADING AND DEALER ACTIVITY

Bank loans and security investments provide the principle source of profits for financial institutions. A bank's trading account and dealer activities, also supply a substantial amount of additional income. The principal purpose of a bank's trading department is to maintain a secondary market in government, corporate, and municipal bonds necessary to meet bank and customer needs. Securities in a trading account are normally not held to maturity but are sold based on market demand. The size and variety of issues traded depends on the bank's operational goals. Selected financial institutions also act as primary dealers for U.S. government securities. Banks designated as primary dealers must maintain an active market in government bills, notes, and bonds. Dealer activities are normally centered at a bank's money market desk and are described more fully in Chapter 10.

The trading account and dealer responsibilities require a bank to hold inventories of government, corporate, and municipal bonds. In their efforts to meet customer needs, traders often take positions contrary to the market demand. When customers are selling, banks may be purchasing. Likewise, when customers are buying securities, banks are selling to meet their orders. Financial futures enable banks to manage the uneven purchasing and selling patterns of their investment customers.

The hedge decision, however, is not an easy one. A futures position that improves performance under certain market conditions depresses profit in others. The trader's predictions of rising interest rates may be wrong. The trader could realize gains on his cash position but losses on his futures position. In addition, other factors (e.g., transaction costs, the tax implications of the bond sale, and the value of interest payments made to the bank on holding the bond) must be considered before final decision to hedge is made. However, if the bank is successful in its efforts to hedge interest rate risk, the bank may be able to position a larger inventory and reduce customers' bid-ask spreads.

Because futures contracts are limited in contract size, specific delivery dates, and deliverable securities, traders are often required to conduct cross-hedges. For cross-hedges, equal price movements in the cash and futures positions are not likely. As a result, a hedge can typically be employed only to reduce the risk of interest rate movements on identified trading account positions, not to eliminate risk.

In addition to the maintenance of trading account inventory value, the trading department may also use futures to maximize income for its own account. In accordance with the bank's income objective, a bank may choose to use futures as a trading instrument or to arbitrage against other trading account positions. Arbitrage involves the simultaneous purchase and sale of similar securities. Pure arbitrage is defined as a riskless position that requires zero net investment and generates positive profits. Arbitrage should ensure that similar assets in competing markets should produce similar returns. A trader must be aware that, like a perfect hedge, pure arbitrage opportunities are very rare. In pure arbitrage, prices must be simultaneously available in the two markets. In practice, arbitrage often represents a reduced risk trade rather than a riskless position. A more extended discussion of speculative and arbitrage trading is given in Chapter 14.

BANK SERVICES AND FCMs

In banks' attempts to maximize profits while limiting risks, banks have sought new markets and supplied new services. Indicative of this growth has been the establishment of bank holding companies. Bank holding companies enable banks to expand their services in a broad range of financial products. Banks may establish businesses (subsidiaries), which provide services closely related to finance and banking. Bank's entry into additional finance areas is especially important in light of the move of many traditional nonbank financial firms to provide financial services.

For instance, banks have become increasingly involved as futures commissioner merchants (FCMs). Exhibit 9–1 shows that only a limited number of banks use futures today. In a 1982 study, the shortage of trained personnel was cited most often as the principle obstacle to using financial futures.[12] Educating boards of directors was mentioned as another common problem. Bank managers must be educated in the working knowledge of financial futures. For instance, a bank's FCM may advise bank personnel on the use of futures in planning bank strategy. FCMs may also provide help in establishing special interest control procedures that should be initiated prior to engaging in the futures contract transactions. The mechanics of the futures market require periodic cash settlements, open positions, and margin deposits. Controls must be properly integrated with the bank's system of internal control and management reporting. Documented policies and procedures defining segregation of duties and establishing trader limits are essential. Further, these activities should be subject to internal audit review to determine that the bank has complied with its stated and approved policies and procedures.

SUMMARY

Financial futures have applicability in many areas of bank management. Financial futures are used by banks in trust departments, trading activities, portfolio investments, debt issuance, and asset and liability management. In their trading activities bankers use futures to hedge the value of their positions against market price changes caused by interest rate fluctuations. In the area of investment and trust management, banks have used futures (1) to protect against a market decline in their investment portfolio, (2) to maintain liquidity by offering a substitute to immediate security sales, and (3) to lock in prices on anticipated asset purchases. Futures offer banks a means to fix the rates on loans and debt issuance. Futures also provide an additional tool in a bank's strategy of asset and liability management. Finally, financial futures have become an additional area in which banks can offer financial expertise. These services increase fee-based income as well as provide a source for the education and training of bank personnel.

NOTES

[1] The term *banks* as used here includes both commercial banks and savings and loans. Differences in asset structure and regulation result in different hedging policies among various financial institutions. For instance, savings and loans are generally restricted to short futures positions (see Koch (1982)).

[2] Recent surveys of financial institutions (Koch et. al., (1982), and Viet and Wallace, (1983)) have shown an increasing use of financial futures. Problems in instituting financial futures programs include educating a board of directors, start-up costs, administration, and performance evaluation.

[3] Earning assets include loans and security investments of the bank. Nonearning assets include such items as cash due from banks, fixed assets, other real estate owned (ORE) and income receivables.

[4] For a discussion of the use of futures in agricultural banks, see M. Drabenstott and Anne O'Mara McDonley, "The Impact of Financial Futures in Agricultural Banks," Federal Reserve Bank of Kansas City, *Economic Review*, May 1982, pp. 19–30.

[5] See Binder and Linquist (1982) for an example of a daily gap model.

[6] As an alternative to hedging the fixed rate, a bank may enter a loan agreement with a customer for a specified duration at a floating rate (e.g., a loan whose rate is not fixed but instead tied to some index like the prime rate). The corporation may then hedge the risk of an interest rate rise by shorting futures contracts. If interest rates rise, the corporation pays a higher rate (e.g., prime rate plus 1 percent in borrowing costs). The corporation's higher interest costs may be offset by a profit received on the repurchase of a short futures position. The customer has reduced interest rate risk while the bank receives the higher loan rate. Corporations, however, are reluctant to obtain floating rate loans. Most corporations regard interest rate risk management as a bank's concern. For competitive purposes, banks are therefore often required to issue fixed-rate corporate loans even in periods of volatile interest rates. Financial futures, however, permit the bank to offer the corporate manager a fixed-rate loan by using futures to hedge the risk of changes in cost of funds. Corporations' use of financial futures is detailed in Chapter 13.

[7] See Arnold (1983) for a discussion of interest rate swaps.

[8] For a discussion of problems in determining overall balance sheet risk, see E. M. Caulfield, "Asset and Liability Management in Financial Institutions," in *Handbook of Modern Finance*, ed. D. Logue (New York: Warren, Gorman and Lamont, 1984).

[9] For an example of gap management using duration matching, see M. T. Belongia and G. J. Santoni, "Hedging Interest Rate Risk with Financial Futures: Some Basic Principles," *Federal Reserve Bank of St. Louis, Review*, October 1984 pp. 15–25.

[10] For a discussion of new Accounting Standards Board statements on hedge accounting for banks see D. Fisher, "Accounting Standards Board Finalizes Position on Futures," *CME Market Perspectives* (November, 1984).

[11] For instance, *The Wall Street Journal* recently reported that a bank lost over $2.2 million in an attempted hedge against rate fluctuations on its money market accounts. The futures instrument did not correlate closely enough with

its money market accounts. ("Some Thrifts and Other Concerns Find Hedging against Rate Changes Costly," *The Wall Street Journal,* November 5, 1984.)

[12] See Koch et. al. (1982).

SELECTED REFERENCES

Asay, Michael R., Gisela A. Gonzalez, and Benjamin Wolkowitz. Financial Futures, Bank Portfolio Risk, and Accounting." *Journal of Futures Markets,* Winter 1981, pp. 607–18.

Arnold, T. A. "How to Do Interest Rate Swaps" *Harvard Business Review,* September–October, 1984, pp. 96–101.

Batlin, C. A. "Interest Rate Risk, Prepayment Risk, and the Futures Market Hedging Strategies of Financial Intermediaries." *Journal of Futures Markets,* Summer 1983, pp. 177–84.

Binder, B., and T. Lindquist. *Asset/Liability and Funds Management at U.S. Commercial Banks.* Bank Administration Institute, 1982.

Daane, Kenneth E., and Albert J. Fredman. "How Banks Can Use Interest Rate Futures." *Bankers Monthly Magazine* 15, April 1979.

Dew, James Kurt, and Terrence F. Martell. "Treasury Bill Futures, Commercial Lending, and the Synthetic Fixed Rate Loan." *The Journal of Commercial Banking Lending,* June 1981, pp. 27–38.

Goodman, L., and M. Langer, "Accounting for Interest Rate Futures in Bank Asset Liability Management." *Journal of Futures Markets,* Winter 1983, pp. 415–28.

Hill, Mark. "How a Commercial Bank Trader Uses the Treasury Bond Market for Various Hedging Applications." *Review of Research in Futures Markets* 1, no. 3, 1982, pp. 204–9.

McCabe, George M., and James M. Blackwell. "The Hedging Strategy: A New Approach to Spread Management Banking and Commercial Lending." *Journal of Bank Research,* Summer 1981.

McCabe, George, and Robert W. McLeod. "The Use of Financial Futures in Banking." *The Journal at Commerical Bank Lending,* August 1982, pp. 6–21.

Parker, Jack W., and Robert T. Daigler. "Hedging Money Market CDs with Treasury Bill Futures." *Journal of Futures Markets,* Winter 1981, pp. 597–606.

Koch, D., O. Steinhauser, and P. Whigham. "Financial Futures as a Risk Management Tool for Banks and S&Ls." *Federal Reserve Bank of Atlanta Economic Review,* September 1982, pp. 4–14.

Kolb, R. W., S. G. Timme, and G. D. Gay. "Macroversus Micro Future Hedges at Commercial Banks." *Journal of Futures Markets,* Spring 1984, pp. 47–54.

Koppenhaver, G. D. "Bank Funding Risks, Risk Aversion, and the Choice of Futures Hedging Instrument." *Journal of Finance,* March 1984, pp. 241–56.

Koppenhaver, G. D. "Trimming The Hedges: Regulators, Banks, and Financial Futures." *Federal Reserve Bank of Chicago Economic Perspectives,* November–December 1984, pp. 3–12.

Simonson, D., Carl W. Allendoefer, and George H. Hempel. "Improving GAP Management for Controlling Interest Rate Risk." *Journal of Bank Research,* Summer 1982, pp. 109–15.

Toevs, Alden L., and William C. Haney. "Measuring and Managing Interest Rate Risk: A Guide to Asset/Liability Models Used in Banks and Thrifts." Morgan Stanley, October 1984.

Toevs, Alden L. "Gap Management: Managing Interest Rate Risk in Banks and Thrifts." *Federal Reserve Bank of San Francisco Economic Review,* Spring 1983, pp. 20–35.

Veit, E. T., and Wallace W. Reiff. "Commercial Banks and Interest Rate Futures: A Hedging Survey." *Journal of Futures Markets,* Fall 1983, pp. 283–94.

CHAPTER 10

Applications of Futures for Investment Banking and Trading

The capital markets in the United States offer a means for lenders of capital to provide funds in exchange for financial assets offered by borrowers. In addition, investors can exchange financial assets as well as sell financial claims in order to meet current consumption needs. Investment bankers, security dealers, and security traders (e.g., market makers and block traders) are among the principle nonbank financial intermediaries in the capital markets.[1]

Investment banks have been established to help provide financial capital to both private industry and Federal, state, and local governments.[2] In the primary market for new corporate and state and local issues, investment bankers often purchase (underwrite) the securities from a corporation or governmental unit and assume the risk of security placement. As underwriters, investment bankers can use financial futures to hedge the risk of price changes on the value of these newly purchased issues. The classic demonstration of financial futures in hedging the risk of underwriting new security issues is Salomon Brothers' hedge of an IBM debt issue in 1979. After the Federal Reserve Board announced in October 1979 that it was going to allow more freedom for the marketplace to establish interest rates, bond prices plunged. Salomon Brothers was acting as lead underwriter on a $1 billion IBM debt issue. They had sold interest rate futures short and thus recovered in the futures markets much of the losses they realized in the cash market.

Many investment bankers also act as security dealers and traders. They offer and manage money market funds, mutual funds, and pension plans. Some investment bankers also provide personal loans, insurance, and brokerage services. The futures markets permit investment bankers to hedge the price risk of securities held and of future security purchases.

Security dealers participate mainly in the primary and secondary market for U.S. government security issues. Security dealers bid for new government issues (e.g., Treasury bill, note, bond, and U.S. agency issues) and resell them to investors. Security dealers also maintain inventories of various issues of government securities and buy and sell securities for themselves and their clients. Security traders make markets in listed and unlisted corporate and state and local government securities. As both block traders and market makers, security traders often hold large, although temporary, inventory positions necessary to provide liquidity in the purchase and sale of existing corporate and municipal securities. Security dealers and security traders are therefore highly exposed to unexpected changes in security prices. Financial futures not only help security dealers and traders to manage a security's price risk, but also provide a means to hedge quantity risk. Quantity risk refers to the risk that even very small changes in price may affect the aggregate value of an inventory position by a large dollar amount. This quantity risk may prevent security dealers and traders from taking large asset positions even in stable price environments. Financial futures enable security dealers and traders to hold large asset positions while greatly reducing the risk of losses in total inventory value from even small unexpected price movements.

Given the degree of price and quantity risk in the capital market, it is not surprising that investment bankers, security traders, and security dealers are currently the largest users of financial futures. However, they do face potential costs in their use of financial futures. First, a futures position designed to protect against unexpected and unfavorable interest rates or stock market moves also prevents gains on the cash position from unexpected yet favorable price changes. Second, due to basis risk, changes in futures prices may not correspond exactly with changes in the price of the security to be held or purchased. Third, security dealers, security traders, and investment bankers provide a number of auxiliary services. They face the problem of deciding between the hedging of a net position across all their financial service areas versus the hedging of individual asset positions. If the net exposure of the firm is not considered, a hedge may reduce the risk on an individual security position while increasing the total risk of the firm. In the following sections we review the use of futures markets for security dealers and security traders as well as investment bankers' underwriting activities.

UNDERWRITERS

The capital markets provide an important means for corporations and state and local governments to obtain funds from investors. Exhibits 10–1 and 10–2 show the annual total of the gross proceeds of state and local government and corporate security issues. New state and local government bond issues as well as corporate stock and bond issues are often purchased (underwritten) and offered for resale through investment banking houses. Commercial banks, are also permitted to underwrite and sell general obligation bonds of state and local governments.[3]

An underwriter commits to purchase the original issue from the corporation or municipality at a fixed price. This price may be determined through private negotiation or public bid. Normally, an issue will be purchased at a discount. This ensures that, even if the issue has to be retailed at par, the underwriter will obtain

EXHIBIT 10–1
Corporate Security Issues Gross Proceeds (annual totals)

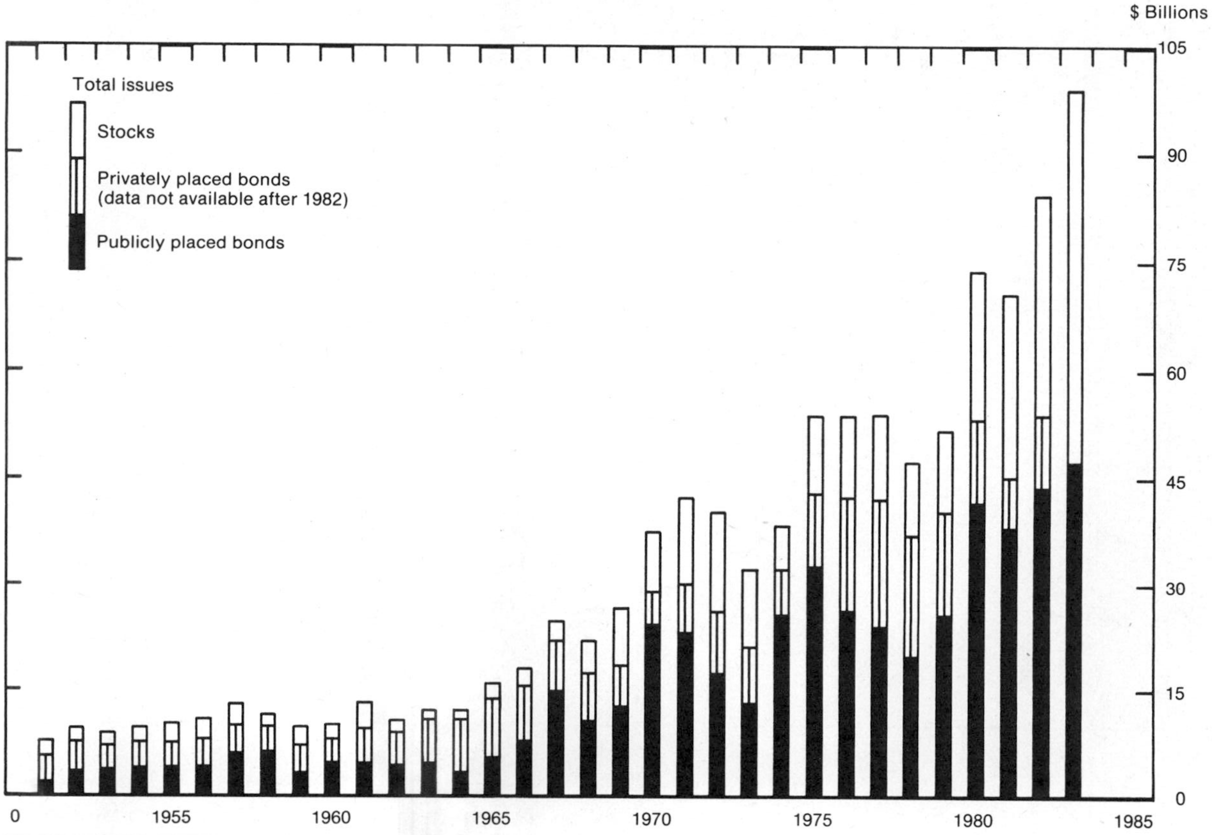

$ Billions
105
90
75
60
45
30
15
0
Total issues
Stocks
Privately placed bonds
(data not available after 1982)
Publicly placed bonds
0
1955
1960
1965
1970
1975
1980
1985

Source: 1984 Historical Chart Book, Federal Reserve Board of Governors.

EXHIBIT 10-2

State and Local Government Security Issues, Gross Proceeds (annual totals)

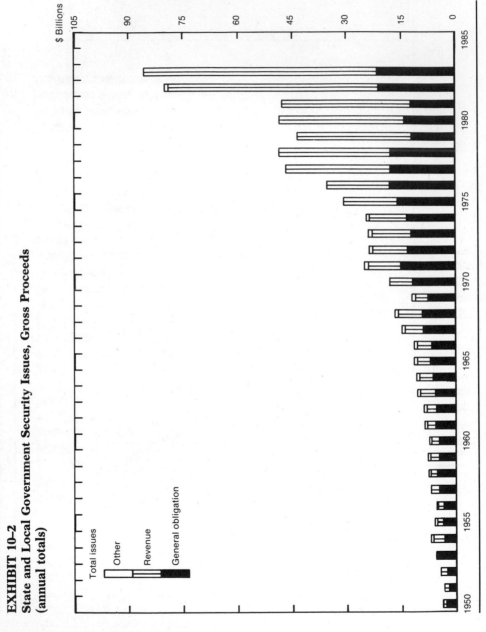

Source: 1984 Historical Chart Book, Federal Reserve Board of Governors.

revenue for his or her efforts. For large issues, a group of underwriters combine and form a syndicate to purchase an issue. Each syndicate member agrees to purchase a portion of the original issue.

For newly purchased bond issues, the underwriters face the risk that interest rates will rise (prices will fall) before the issue can be retailed to the public. For new equity offerings, the underwriters face the risk that stock market prices will fall before the issue can be sold. Exhibits 10–3 and 10–4 show the wide variability in historical stock and bond prices. Faced with the risk that stock or bond prices may fall significantly before the securities can be retailed, underwriters may simply not bid or may lower their bid price (raise the cost to the issuer). Interest rate and equity futures reduce underwriter risk by permitting the underwriter to hedge their purchases by selling futures until the bonds or stocks are marketed.

Financial futures are especially important since new government rules have increased flexibility on sale of corporate securities, but also have increased underwriters risk. Recently, shelf registration adopted by the SEC in November 1983 permits eligible firms to register all securities it plans to issue over the next two years

---

EXHIBIT 10–3
Stock Market, Standard & Poor's Price Index (quarterly averages)

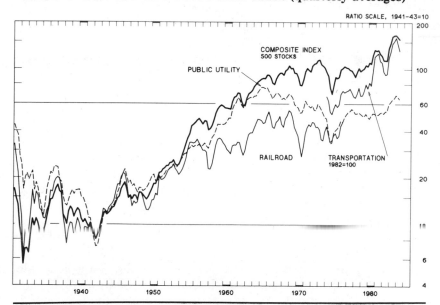

Source: 1984 Historical Chart Book, Federal Reserve Board of Governors.

EXHIBIT 10–4
Long-Term Bond Yields (quarterly averages)

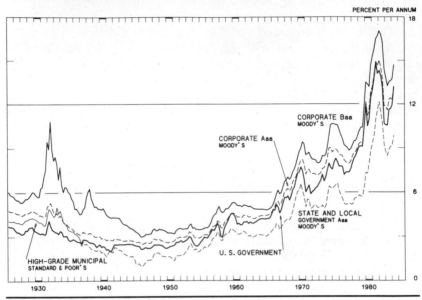

Source: *1984 Historical Chart Book*, Federal Reserve Board of Governors.

and then to sell some or all of the securities whenever it desires. Due to the reduced lead time in offering these new issues, the pricing of primary issues has become more risky. Corporations can act almost as if they are immediate block traders. Old benchmarks of market supply and demand are gone. Market rallies can be cut off as large issuers move immediately to obtain favorable rates.

Consider a situation in which a sudden decline in interest rates causes a corporate treasurer to contact an underwriter for an immediate sale of a corporate bond. The corporation has earlier submitted necessary shelf registration material to the SEC and is prepared to go to the market in two days. The underwriter, however, knows that a large number of issues are likely to enter the market and is concerned about the effect of this supply on corporate bond rates over the next few days. Given the importance of the client relationships, however, the underwriter does not wish to miss the sale. In order to secure the bid rate to the firm and reduce the uncertainty associated with the proceeds of the issue at resale, the underwriter sells an appropriate number of futures. If rates rise before the issue is marketed, the decrease in the proceeds of the bond issue to the underwriter is partially offset by a profit

EXHIBIT 10–5

Cash Market	Futures Market*
March 1:	
Owns $1 million of 20-year 8% corporate bonds at 59.00 (yield 14.23%)	Sells 10 Treasury bond futures contracts at 65.00 (yield 13.35%)
March 3:	
Sells $1 million of 25-year 8% corporate bonds at 58.00 (yield 14.475%)	Buys 10 Treasury bond futures contracts at 62.00 (yield 13.55%)
Loss: $10,000	Gain: $30,000

* Yield equivalents are based on 8% 20-year bonds.

in the futures position (see Exhibit 10–5). Since no futures contract exists for corporate bonds, a cross-hedge is required. The actual number of futures contracts to be purchased depends on the anticipated relative price movements in the corporate bond and Treasury bond futures market (see Chapter 7 on hedge ratio determination).

It is important to point out that for new issues of corporate and municipal bonds, only cross-hedges are presently available. For long-term corporate and municipal bond issues, cross-hedges are best conducted through the sale of Treasury bond futures contracts. For medium-term corporate and municipal bond issues, cross-hedges may be constructed with Treasury note futures. For short-term corporate and municipal issues, Treasury bill and Eurodollar futures offer alternative hedging vehicles. For an issue whose maturity does not match the maturity of the security underlying the futures contract, multiple hedge positions (e.g., combinations of Treasury bill and Treasury bond or Treasury note futures contracts) can be made to create a portfolio of futures with expected price volatility equal to the issue underwritten. Even for securities that have futures markets offering direct hedges, liquidity, open interest, and other institutional constraints may result in a cross-hedge being the preferred hedge vehicle.

In addition to underwriting corporate and state and local government bonds, investment banks are active in underwriting new common stock issues. A stock underwriter's profits come primarily from the difference between the buying and selling price of the issue. The underwriter may choose to reduce the risk of overall stock market price declines over the underwriting period by selling stock index futures. The stock index future used depends on the security being hedged. Some stocks are highly correlated with the S&P 500 Index. Other firms may find their stocks are more highly correlated with the NYSE Index or the Major Market Index. Regardless of the index used, the hedging process is similar.

Assume an investment banker must underwrite an issue of

$10 million in CDE Corporation's common stock. The underwriter has estimated the selling price to be $100 per share. On the day the underwriter agrees to the price, the S&P 500 Index future is priced at 160 points or $80,000 (160 × 500). The underwriter wishes to protect the unsold stock portion by selling 125 contracts (125 × $80,000 = $10 million). In the following four days, the entire issue has been sold at an average price of $90 for a loss of $1 million. The S&P 500 futures index has also fallen to 150 points or $75,000 (150 × 500). He buys back his 125 contracts at $9,275,500 (125 × $75,000) for a $625,000 gain. As shown in Exhibit 10–6 the gain in the futures market reduced the underwriting loss to $375,000 from $1,000,000.

Price risk management, however, does not insure price risk elimination. In Exhibits 10–5 and 10–6, the underwriter purchased an equal principal amount of bond or stock index futures as the issue being sold. In order to determine a proper hedge ratio, a firm must analyze the historical relationship between price movement of the security and the futures contract being sold or use other hedge ratio determination techniques as discussed in Chapter 7. Historical information on price movements of bonds and stocks with bond and stock index futures does not necessarily provide the proper hedge ratio for protection against unexpected price moves of new issues. First, new security issues may briefly depress a firm's security price. During the resale of primary issues, historically derived hedge ratios may therefore offer little information on the relative price movement of the security and the index. In addition, for many securities cross-hedges are necessary. A low correlation between the price movements of the security and the relevant stock index future is evidence of basis risk.

Despite possible basis risk, empirical studies have shown that usually more than half the variance in price changes on corporate and state and local government bond issues as well as individual stock issues can be eliminated with interest rate and stock index

---

EXHIBIT 10–6

Cash Market	*Futures Market*
September 1	
Underwriter purchases 100,000 shares of CDE Corporation at $100 per share ($10 million)	Underwriter sells 125 contracts of the S&P 500 Index at 160 ($10 million)
September 4	
Underwriter has sold 100,000 shares at an average price of $90 ($9 million)	Underwriter purchases 125 contracts of the S&P 500 Index at 150 ($9,375,000)
Loss: $1,000,000	Gain: $625,000

futures.[4] For corporate bonds, the futures markets have been most effective in reducing the variance in price changes for high-quality bonds with coupons close to the cheapest-to-deliver security. For stocks, the stock index futures market has been most effective in reducing the variance in price change for well-diversified firms with limited unsystematic risk. For small undiversified firms, a more effective hedge may be achieved with individual stock options. Despite these limitations, financial futures markets do provide the investment banker a means of reducing price risk. Financial futures thereby permit investment bankers to bid aggressively on new issues as well as reduce the necessary spreads in resale.[5]

SECURITY DEALERS

In recent years the net federal debt has risen to over $1,200 billion (Exhibit 10–7). Each year the maturing portion of this debt must be refunded. In addition each year the government must issue securities to fund the federal deficit. In 1984 the deficit was near $200 billion (Exhibit 10–8). New issues and refundings of govern-

EXHIBIT 10–7
Net Federal Debt

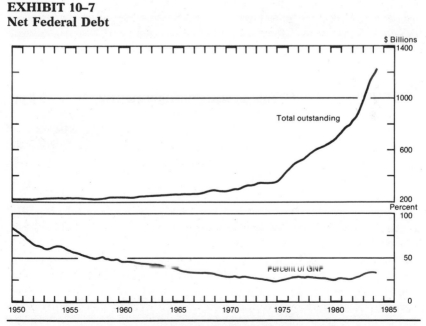

Note: Amount outstanding; End of Year, 1950–51; seasonally adjusted, end of·quarter, 1952–

Source: 1984 Historical Chart Book, Federal Reserve Board of Governors.

EXHIBIT 10–8
Federal Budget Fiscal Year Totals (unified budget)

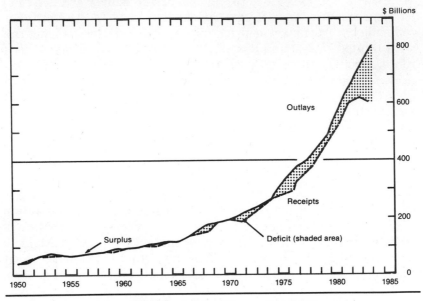

Source: 1984 Historical Chart Book, Federal Reserve Board of Governors.

ment securities are sold through the government security dealer market.

New long-term issues are announced by the Treasury through the Federal Reserve banks who act as fiscal agents for the government. For these issues, there exist about 36 fairly important dealers (see Exhibit 10–9) who subscribe to the major portion of new issues and resell them to the public or hold them in inventory. The government dealer faces the risk that the government issue will be sold in a bear market and that prices will fall significantly before the securities can be retailed. A commitment can be hedged by selling futures until the bonds are obtained and marketed.

For example, a government dealer is concerned that prices will fall between the time the bid is made (the dealer becomes committed to a purchase price) and the issue is sold to other dealers or retail customers. As shown in Exhibit 10–10, to reduce the risk of a price decline, the dealer initiates a short hedge. If bond prices decline, the hedge will allow the dealer to at least partially offset the loss on the cash position. If the primary dealer believes that rates have settled or are about to fall, he or she may also lift the hedge at any time. The success of this strategy of lifting or "managing" a hedge is obviously dependent on the dealer's ability to judge

EXHIBIT 10-9
Primary U.S. Government Securities Dealers

Bank of America NT & SA
Bankers Trust Co.
Bear, Stearns & Co.
Briggs, Schaedle & Co. Inc.
Carroll McEntee and McGinley Inc.
Chase Manhattan Government Securities, Inc.
Chemical Bank
Citibank, N.A.
Continental Illinois National Bank
　and Trust Co. of Chicago
Crocker National Bank
Discount Corp. of New York
Donaldson, Lufkin & Jenrette Securities Corp.

Drexel Burnham Lambert Government
　Securities
First Boston Corp.
First Interstate Bank of California
First National Bank of Chicago
Goldman, Sachs & Co.
Greenwich Capital Markets Inc.
Harris Trust and Savings Bank
E.F. Hutton & Co. Inc.
Kidder, Peabody & Co. Inc.
Kleinwort Benson Government Securities Inc.
Aubrey G. Lanston & Co. Inc.
Lehman Government Securities Inc.

Manufacturers Hanover Trust Co.
Merrill Lynch Government Securities Inc.
Morgan Guaranty Trust Co. of New York
Morgan Stanley and Co. Inc.
The Northern Trust Co.
Paine Webber Inc.
William E. Pollock Government Securities Inc.
Prudential-Bache Securities Inc.
Refco Partners
Salomon Brothers Inc.
Smith Barney Government Securities Inc.
Dean Witter Reynolds Inc.

Source: Federal Reserve Bank of New York (as of September 1984).

EXHIBIT 10–10

Cash Market	Futures Market*
April 1:	
A bid of 12.00% on $10 million of seven-year 12% notes is accepted	Sell 100 June Treasury note futures contracts at 73.02 ($7,302,000) (yield 12.86%)
April 10:	
Sell $10 million notes at 96.37 ($9,637,000) (yield 12.80%)	Buy 100 June contracts at 72.10 ($7,210,000) (yield 13.03%)
Loss: $363,000	Gain: $92,000

---

* Yield equivalents are based on 8% 10-year Treasury notes.

the basis movement between the futures contract and the spot asset being hedged.

In addition to marketing new issues of government debt, a distinguishing feature of the government security dealers is that they provide an active secondary market in outstanding government issues. Government security dealers absorb demand by selling from their own inventories when demand is increasing and buying for their inventories when investors are selling. Dealers must be prepared to hold large amounts of inventory ready for sale. To purchase the required large amounts of inventory, government dealers must borrow. For most government dealers, 90 to 95 percent of their inventory position is financed. Due to this highly leveraged position, even small changes in inventory value are extremely risky. To protect the inventory value in times of interest rate uncertainty, the government dealer could sell futures contracts. An unexpected fall in bond prices would result in a decline in the value of the inventory but an increase in the value of the futures position.

In the absence of financial futures market, government dealers would vary the level of their inventories with the perceived uncertainty in interest rates. Widely fluctuating interest rates would encourage government security dealers to hold low bond inventories. Financial futures permit government dealers to hold higher levels of inventory, to improve market liquidity, and to lower the bid-ask spreads.[6]

SECURITY TRADING: MARKET MAKERS AND BLOCK TRADERS

Block trading operations and market makers provide active secondary markets in certain listed and unlisted corporate and state and local government securities. Block trades are large round-lot trades made directly between two institutions. Block trades are conducted off the floor of bond and stock exchanges. They permit transactions to take place quickly and with less cost then auction market trades. Block trades are generally arranged by brokers who specialize in finding institutions that desire to purchase a security block or that wish to sell a similar block of securities. Block trading has grown rapidly in recent years. For instance, in the mid-1960s there were on average nine equity block trades per day, or about 3 percent of the NYSE volume. In 1982 there were 1,000 block trades per day, or about 41 percent of the NYSE volume.

In contrast to block traders, a market maker is a specialist in a particular security or group of securities. For instance, the secondary market activity in corporate and municipal bonds is much smaller in magnitude than that of stocks because many bond owners tend to hold their bonds to maturity. Most trading therefore occurs in the over-the-counter market. More than 80 percent of corporate and municipal bond resales take place on the "off board" rather than on the organized exchanges. For securities with little "floor" trading, market makers bridge time gaps between arriving public purchases and sales. Their actions buffer fluctuations in public demand and reduce possible volatility in asset prices. They act mainly as principals for their own accounts, "making markets" for customers and other dealers by quoting prices or spreads at which they are willing to buy and sell.

Although futures contracts cannot eliminate all the risk of holding asset positions, block traders and market makers can use futures to hedge unexpected changes in the value of their security holdings. For instance, block traders may find themselves short a security if they have sold stock to complete a block sale to an institution. Until the stock can be purchased, a stock index future could be bought to protect against rising prices due to a general stock market move. Likewise, a market maker may be forced to hold a large open position overnight. By selling an index contract the market maker may hedge against an unexpected drop in the value of his book.

Risk in hedging market makers' and block traders' positions does exist, however. In determining the number of futures to buy or sell, a common approach is to adjust for the relative price movement of the security and the future. In order to determine the weights, historical data on relative price changes is often used. For block traders the sale of a large block may depress an issue price, while the purchase may raise its value. As a result, a security's relative price movement on days of block trading may differ from that commonly occurring on other days.

Moreover block traders and market makers often trade in one or more securities. The trader may decide to individually hedge the risk of each security (micro hedge). By hedging an individual asset, the total risk exposure of the trader's inventory position may be increased rather than decreased. As an alternative the trader may desire to hedge his net or total asset position (a macro hedge). Finally, while the principal source of profit from acting as a trader is from commission or bid-ask spreads, value enhancement of the inventory is also a source of gain. A continuous hedging program of inventory to reduce the possibility of loss also removes a chance of gain in inventory value. As an alternative a hedge may be placed when uncertainty about future inventory value increases the risk of loss beyond an acceptable level.

SUMMARY

Underwriters, security dealers, and security traders all use financial futures in their market activities. As underwriters, investment bankers have used financial futures to protect the prices on primary market security purchases. For security dealers, futures can protect the value of government securities held in inventory. Block traders and market makers use futures markets to cover open positions from unexpected price changes.

Financial futures can reduce the risk of a rise in prices on planned investments as well as the risk of a fall in prices on planned sales. Certain costs and risks associated with the use of financial futures in this context should also be considered. A futures position initiated to protect against unexpected and unfavorable price moves also reduces the benefit of unexpected but favorable price moves. In addition, when cross-hedges are conducted, the basis may change in such a way to produce losses on both the cash and future position. Finally, the investment banker, security dealer, or security trader who is involved in a number of related services may find that a futures position that reduces the risk of a single cash asset increases their overall risk position.

NOTES

[1] There is often little distinction between security dealers and traders—security dealers are security traders who carry inventory and act for their own account. Thus specialists and market makers can be called dealers. In the "trade", however,

the term security dealer is often restricted to government security dealers. Market makers and block traders are often referred to solely as security traders. In this chapter security dealers refers only to government security dealers.

[2] Investment banks grew in response to the Glass-Stegall Act of 1933 in which commercial banks were prevented from dealing in private debt and equity securities.

[3] It is important to note that the Glass-Stegall Act does not restrict commercial banks from underwriting and selling U.S. government or general obligation state and local government bonds. Thus in the area of public securities, commercial banks can often compete as underwriters and security dealers.

[4] See J. Hill and T. Schneeweis, "Risk Reduction Potential of Financial Futures for Corporate Bond Positions," in *Interest Rate Futures*, G. Gay and R. Kolb, eds. (Richmond, Va.: Dame, 1982); and S. Figlewski, "Hedging Performance and Bases Risk in Stock Index Futures," *Journal of Finance*, July 1984, pp. 657–69.

[5] In addition to offering opportunities for underwriting and security trading, the introduction of financial futures has permitted investment banks to offer additional services to their trading and investment customers. For instance, many investment banks have established FCMs. FCMs are intermediaries between the brokers in the pit and the customers. They serve customers in a number of ways. FCMs handle margin funds, provide basic accounting services, and offer research capabilities.

[6] For the importance of futures markets in reducing the bid-ask spread on traded securities, see A. Bearman, "Treasury Bill Futures and the Determinants of the Bid–Ask Spread," *Quarterly Review of Economics and Business*, Summer 1982, pp. 84–100.

SELECTED REFERENCES

Arak, Marcelle, and Christopher McCurdy. "Interest Rate Futures." New York Federal Reserve Bank *Quarterly Review*, Winter 1979, pp. 33–46.

Boquist, John A., and John M. Finkelstein. "The Uses of Interest Rate Futures Contracts." In *Financial Markets: Concepts and Issues*, ed. J. Brick. Reston, Va.: Reston Publishing, 1984.

Garbade, Kenneth. *Securities Markets*. New York: McGraw-Hill, 1982.

McCurdy, Christopher J. "The Dealer Market for U.S. Government Securities." New York Federal Reserve *Quarterly Review*, Winter 1977, pp. 35–47.

Rosenbloom, Richard H. "A Review of the Municipal Bond Market." Federal Reserve Bank of New Richmond *Economic Review*, March/April 1976, pp. 10–19.

Zwick, Burton. "The Market for Corporate Bonds." New York Federal Reserve *Quarterly Review*, Autumn 1977, pp. 27–36.

CHAPTER 11

Applications of Futures for Pension Funds and Insurance Companies

THE LONG–TERM INVESTMENT MANAGEMENT PROCESS: PENSION FUNDS AND INSURANCE COMPANIES

Nature of Pension Fund and Insurance Management

Pension funds and insurance companies make long-term commitments to pay benefits under certain conditions. These benefits are predictable with a reasonable degree of accuracy by actuaries who use statistical tools and historical data to forecast the long-term cash flow payments that have been contracted by these institutions. Forecasting pension benefits involves assumptions regarding such factors as worker attrition, retirement age, life expectancy of actual and potential beneficiaries, and future salary levels (inflation and productivity growth). Forecasting life insurance payments is very similar to forecasting pension benefits, involving many of the same factors. The forecasting process has a greater degree of uncertainty in the property, casualty, and disability insurance areas.

Because pension funds and insurance companies have contractual, long-term commitments, they must set aside funds to enable them to pay the promised benefits when they are due. Insurance premium payments and pension fund contributions are made by beneficiaries or by the firms who employ them to provide for a pool of funds that will grow over time. These payments are supplemented by investment income until they reach a level sufficient to pay the promised benefits. High investment returns on assets enable these institutions to keep premiums and contributions at low levels. The management of pension fund or insurance company assets is thus geared to meet two related objectives:

1. Sufficient funds must be on hand to meet contractual commitments in all future periods.
2. The amount of periodic additions to the pool of assets in the form of either premiums or pension contributions should be minimized (i.e., assets should be managed such that the maximum amount of funds for benefits should come from *investment income* rather than new cash inflows).

The second objective is clearly subordinate to the first. It may be possible to maximize investment income by taking on extreme levels of risk in the investment pool or by keeping the pool small in size. This policy, however, would significantly increase the chance that investment losses would be incurred that would jeopardize the funds' ability to pay benefits when due. State and federal regulations require that most private pension funds make at least a minimum contribution each year. This contribution is a function of benefits accrued over the period and of unfunded benefits earned in prior periods. Insurance companies must establish reserve accounts for existing and expected obligations contingent on the occurrence of events that would require payment.

Typical Allocation of Investment Funds

Life insurance companies in particular tend to emphasize the safety of the principal value of their assets. The inability to pay commitments has much more serious consequences than the loss of the higher investment income that could be earned by taking on greater amounts of investment risk. The major asset holdings of life insurers consist of corporate bonds, loans, mortgages, loans to policy holders, and equities. The increase in the general level of long-term interest rates that occurred over the last decade seriously eroded the value of the fixed-income securities, causing these insurers to reassess their investment approaches with the goal of finding better means of protecting principal.

Property and casualty insurers can also be hurt by the increased underwriting costs associated with high levels of inflation. These costs are not always matched by rising returns on their investment portfolio. The portfolios of these insurers are invested primarily in municipal and corporate bonds. When they are profitable, property insurers prefer the tax-free coupon income of municipals to the taxable income of government and corporate bonds.

Pension funds, on the other hand, are exempt from taxes on their investment income and can take on greater risks in the pursuit of higher return, because their claims are more predictable and less volatile in nature. Pension funds tend to concentrate their holdings in stocks, bonds, real estate, and mortgage securities, switching among these groups and also into short-term securities as the investment environment changes. Pension *"sponsors,"* as the owners of the funds are called, usually hire money management firms to handle their investments for an annual fee related to the market value of the assets managed. A large component of the pension sponsor's time spent is involved with the selection and evaluation of these money managers.

General Applications of Financial Futures

How do financial futures fit into the long-term investment management process of pension funds and insurance companies? Some general observations are appropriate before this question is answered in detail. First, because of the long-term nature of the obligations of these financial institutions, investments are structured to meet long-term investment goals and have a much lower level of turnover than assets of other financial institutions, such as banks, security dealers, and the like. Unless short-term market trends are very predictable, switching among different types of securities over very short periods can be quite costly in terms of transaction costs and risk. On the other hand, it makes sense to adjust positions to accommodate major trends in the securities market.

Financial futures can be used as short-term management tools to hedge the risk of declining asset values or to increase the allocation of funds to asset classes that are expected to increase in value. Financial futures serve as vehicles for restructuring the asset allocation of the pension fund or insurance assets in an efficient and cost-effective manner. The advantage of using futures for short-term trading strategies as compared to trading in the underlying securities arises from the high degree of liquidity and low transactions cost of futures markets. This cost-efficiency makes it feasible to adjust portfolios to take aggressive and defensive postures over short periods and thereby reduce the volatility of the portfolio value.

A second general area in which futures can be useful is in preparing for large cash inflows or outflows and in implementing switches across asset categories or among different money managers. The amount of funds involved in large asset or cash transfers at these institutions is often quite large. Payments to pension funds tend to be uneven throughout the year. There is often a difficulty in investing cash or in converting investment assets to cash without affecting prices of the securities or making others aware of your intent to buy or sell. Many pension sponsors hire investment banks to help them switch large amounts of money from one money manager to another or to liquidate a large amount of their assets.

Financial futures markets can be helpful in this process because of their low cost and ability to efficiently absorb very large trades. Positions can be added or liquidated in financial futures until the actual stocks or bonds can be bought or sold in an orderly fashion. The futures position can be closed out as the actual investment assets are acquired or sold. In this way, pension funds and insurance companies can minimize the opportunity losses associated with unintended cash holdings.

A third general area in which financial futures are of value to these institutions has yet to be realized fully. Futures allow long-term investors to separate the broad asset allocation decision (stocks versus bonds versus cash) from the choice among assets in each of these categories. This separation facilitates specialization in investment management and thereby encourages the development of new money management products.

This separation of investment tasks was not possible before the introduction of the stock index and Treasury bond futures. For example, the only way one could earn exactly the returns of a stock index was to buy each stock in that index with the exact weights—a costly proposition. In addition, one could not easily diversify away the risk of the asset category to isolate the potential profit associated with the underpricing of an asset in that category. For example, a particular stock might appear attractive, but stocks in general might be expected to decline in value. Prior to stock index and Treasury bond futures, there was almost no way for institutional investors to short the stock or bond market in order to profit from the net overperformance of a particular stock or bond relative to that market.

Stock index and Treasury bond futures can, therefore, add a whole new dimension to investment management by allowing one manager to concentrate on stock or bond selection and another to focus on market timing. Not all money managers need to be skilled at both. The power of financial futures to allow this separation, and the opportunity to capitalize on specialized investment management skills has yet to be utilized in the long-term money management business. This may, however, be an important development associated with financial futures over the next decade.

APPLICATIONS OF FINANCIAL FUTURES IN PORTFOLIO MANAGEMENT

There are two levels of investment decision-making in the management of pension funds—that of the pension sponsor and that of the portfolio manager.[1] The sponsor is an employee of the public or private institution that owns the pension fund investments and that has made the contractual commitments to beneficiaries or policyholders. The sponsor determines the objectives, selects the managers of the securities, and evaluates their performance relative to these objectives. In selecting the managers and providing them with direction, the sponsor exerts considerable influence over the allocation of funds among asset categories, such as stocks, bonds, real estate, and international securities.

The portfolio manager is directly involved in the day-to-day operations of the portfolio, selecting securities, reinvesting dividends and maturing securities, and deciding which securities to sell to provide needed cash. The portfolio manager may be employed "in-house" by the sponsor or may be employed by a money management firm that is receiving management fees from the sponsor. When pension funds are managed externally, there are usually several managers. Very frequently, there is a group of managers that handles the fund's fixed-income assets, another group that manages the equities, as well as specialized managers for such asset classes that may require special expertise and market knowledge such as real estate, international securities, and options.

Futures can be of significant value at the levels of both the portfolio manager and pension sponsor. We first consider the applications of interest to the portfolio manager and then the uses by the pension sponsor or the manager of the insurance company assets.

Before we begin, a word should be said regarding the position of regulators on the use of financial futures by pension funds. Private funds are regulated by the Employee Retirement Insurance Security Act of 1974 (ERISA). This act has been interpreted to accept the use of financial futures as prudent investments provided they are used in conjunction with the overall diversification strategy of the fund and are not used to increase the risk of the fund to levels that would not be prudent or reasonable considering the other types of investments held. In other words, pension funds that use the leverage potential of financial futures would very likely be found in violation of ERISA. In fact, the use of financial futures by the pension funds of such widely-respected institutions as IBM, Exxon, Westinghouse, and Harvard University has helped to increase the acceptance of futures as investment management tools.[2]

Investment Manager Applications of Financial Futures

Changing Asset Allocation. One of the most important decisions made by the portfolio manager is the allocation among broad classes of investment assets: stocks, bonds, and cash-equivalents. This decision is so important that it is often dictated by the sponsor or done only with the consultation of the sponsor. Usually, a large component of the performance in any given period is associated with this asset allocation decision. Asset allocation is also an important decison because it is costly to change in terms of transaction costs. Because of the expense involved, changes in the asset mix are usually done infrequently and tend to be small in magnitude, usually representing 20% or less of the portfolio.

Financial futures are helpful in changing asset allocation in two ways. First, the liquidity and low commission costs of financial

futures make them desirable vehicles for adjusting the asset allocation without incurring the cost of buying or selling the actual securities in the portfolio. Second, when a decision is made to change
the asset mix by switching from one security class to another,
the move can be implemented quickly and expeditiously with financial futures. Once the futures position is in place and the new
asset mix is set, the individual securities can be bought (sold) gradually at prices that are attractive to the portfolio manager and
in amounts that are cost-effective from a trading perspective. The
futures position can be gradually closed out as the individual security sale or purchase is implemented.

Because of the liquidity and low commissions of financial futures markets, changing the asset mix in the short-run with financial futures has significant benefits. The cost of increasing the
weights of stocks, bonds, or cash, and reversing that decision if
market conditions change can be an impediment to short-term
market timing adjustments in the portfolio. With the reduced cost
of financial futures, the mix can be altered easily and cheaply.
Moreover, if the outlook changes quickly, the position can be adjusted accordingly without a large disruption to the assets in the
portfolio. Most of the securities on which financial futures are
based—stock indexes, Treasury bonds, notes and bills—are representative of the performance of broad asset classes and can serve
as good short-term substitutes, increasing or decreasing the holdings in equity, long-term, intermediate-term, or short-term segments of the fixed-income markets.

Exhibit 11–1 contains a comparison of typical commissions
for institutional trades in stock index futures versus the stocks
themselves. Futures trading costs are often 10–20% of that of the
trading costs of an equivalent amount of stocks or bonds. The
example illustrates such comparison based on a $.10 per share
stock commission and $20 per contract futures commission (one-
way). (Actual commissions per share can vary greatly depending
on the size of the trade, the price of the stock, and the institutions'
arrangement with the broker. A range of $.05 to $.15 a share is
fairly typical for most institutional trades.) The spread between
the bid and ask price for stock index futures is considerably smaller
than that in the equity market for equivalent amounts of share
value. Therefore, simply based on transaction costs savings, a return advantage of as much as .5 percent (or 1 percent round trip)
can be realized with stock index futures.

The existence of financial futures provides several means of
adjusting the asset mix. These choices can be evaluated based on
the relative values provided in the various markets. For example,
if one wished to increase the weight in equities, three actively

---

EXHIBIT 11–1
Comparison of Trading Costs Associated with Stocks versus Stock Futures

	Stocks	Stock Index Futures (S&P 500)
Price per share/contract	$40	$170
Number of shares/units	2125	500
Market value	$85,000.00	$85,000.00
Commission per share/contract	$.10	$20
Total commission	$212.50	$20
Typical bid/ask spread	.125 points/share or $266	.10 points/contract: or 50.00
Commission plus spread	$478.50	$70.00

$$
\begin{aligned}
\text{Trade size} &= \$85{,}000 \\
\text{Savings in commission: } (\$212.50 - \$20) &= 192.50 \\
\text{Savings in spread: } (\$266 - \$50) &= \underline{216.00} \\
\text{Total savings:} &\quad \$408.50 \\
&\quad \underline{\times 2} \\
\text{Round trip savings:} &= \$817.00 \\
\text{Savings as a percent of trade: } \$817/85{,}000 &= .0096 \\
&= .96\%
\end{aligned}
$$

---

traded contracts, the S&P 500, Major Market Index, and NYSE Composite futures, are available. Reducing equity exposure can be accomplished by selling any of these futures. The opportunities for adjusting the maturity or duration of a fixed-income portfolio are even more diverse. The interest rate sensitivity of a portfolio invested in long-term bonds can be reduced in any one of three ways: (1) selling Treasury bond futures, (2) buying Treasury bill futures as a substitute for cash-equivalents, or (3) selling Treasury note futures. A brief case study of the use of stock index futures for changing the equity allocation of a portfolio is given below.

A $50 million equity portfolio is allocated 90 percent to equities and 10 percent to cash equivalents in June 1983. The equity market (as measured by the S&P 500) has appreciated 60 percent over the last year, and the portfolio manager feels that a moderate price decline is likely over the next three or four months. The manager decides to use stock index futures to reduce the equity weight to 80 percent through the September futures expiration date. On June 24, she sells $5.14 million (approximately 10 percent

---

EXHIBIT 11–2
Example of Adjusting Equity Exposure with Stock Index Futures

Portfolio of $50 million allocated 90 percent equities, 10 percent to cash-equivalents earning 9 percent annual rate of interest.

June 24, 1983
Sell 60 S&P 500 September futures at	171.45
Value of S&P 500*	169.13

Theoretical value of futures
169.13 − 90-day dividend yield + 90-day interest
169.13 − 1.125% (169.13) + 2.25% (169.13)
16.913 − 1.903 + 3.80   171.03

August 26, 1983
Buy 60 S&P 600 September futures at	163.45
Value of S&P 500	163.35

S&P 500	S&P 500 Futures
June 24 169.13	June 24 171.45
August 26 163.35	August 26 163.45
5.78	8.00
percentage change: −3.41	percentage change: −4.66

Gain on futures = 8.00 × 500 × 60 contracts = $240,000
Loss on $5.14 million of equities (3.41%) =   175,137
Net profit of hedge   = $ 64,863

Contribution to Overall Portfolio Return:

Return Unhedged			Return 10% Hedged	
Capital return	(3.41)	× .9	Total return	−1.83%
Dividend return	1.125	× .9	Return on futures	.48%
Interest return	2.25	× .1	$240,000/$50 million	−1.35%
Total return	−1.83%			

* Timing of dividend payments is not considered in this example.

---

of the portfolio) of September S&P 500 futures (60 contracts) at a price of 171.45 points. (Contract value = $500 × 171.45 or $857.25 per contract.) The portfolio manager will watch the market closely so that she can close out the position if a rally should occur.

On August 26, an evaluation of both the stock and stock index futures position shows that the S&P 500 has fallen by 3.41 percent, while the stock index futures have fallen even more, by 4.66 percent. Based on this favorable spread, the manager decides to close out the futures position at a price of 163.45. If the stock index futures had not been used to capitalize on a short-term opinion on the market, the $5.14 million would have fallen in value by

$175, 137 over the two-month period. The futures trade provided a gross profit of $240,000 and a net profit on the hedged 10% of the portfolio of $64,863. In terms of the entire $50 million portfolio, the impact of hedging 10 percent of its market value with futures increased its total return by 0.48 percent.

Maximizing Returns on Index Funds or the Index Core of a Pension Portfolio. Many pension funds have some of their assets allocated to a fund that has the goal of tracking the returns of a market index or benchmark portfolio as closely as possible. These so-called index funds or index surrogates are often equity funds targeted to the S&P 500 Index. They may also be fixed-income funds designed to track some bond market index. The basis for investing in index funds has been discussed in Chapter 4.

Many pension funds and other institutional investors attempt to purchase a portfolio of stocks that resembles the overall equity market in hopes of participating fully in the appreciation that occurs in equities in general. The management of these index funds is quite different from traditional portfolio management. It involves: (1) monitoring the weight of different securities in the market index and adjusting positions to maintain appropriate weights, (2) reinvesting dividends or coupon payments as quickly as possible so as to achieve weights that approximate those of the index, and (3) trading off the commission cost of frequent and small adjustments to track the index versus the risk of investing in a portfolio that differs from the index and may underperform it.

For broadly-based equity indexes like the S&P 500, many portfolio managers do not hold all stocks in the index because of the cost of managing so many different positions. Instead, they use mathematical programming techniques to find smaller portfolios of stocks that have had returns very close to the S&P 500 over some prior period. This "index-surrogate" portfolio is adjusted over time to different stocks and stock weightings that minimize the tracking error between the surrogate portfolio and the index.

Stock index futures are of interest to managers of these index funds. Carefully designed strategies can allow index fund managers to purchase the equivalent of the index in the futures market and realize return performance close to that of the index. This is possible, because the equivalent of an index can be purchased via stock index futures by buying contracts with a market value equal to that of the index fund and investing any funds not used as margin in a highly-liquid low-risk security such as a Treasury bill.

As discussed in Chapter 6, stock index futures sell from time to time at prices that are above or below the theoretical value of those futures. In such situations, arbitrageurs enter the market when these pricing inefficiencies between the index and the index futures are large enough to cover the costs and basis risk of switching funds between an index proxy portfolio and the futures. The band around the theoretical futures value within which prices have fluctuated before returning to the theoretical value has been large enough to allow futures purchasers to lock in returns several percent above the S&P 500. The largest undervaluation of stock index futures occurred in the summer of 1982 when the stock index futures markets were only a few months old and a very bearish outlook prevailed on Wall Street. The opportunity to earn a return 5–6% in excess of the index returns was quick to encourage arbitrageurs to enter the market. Their activity has helped to make futures prices stay much closer to their theoretical value, usually within 1–3 percent. Thus, money managers using the index futures market as a short-term substitute for investment in the index can expect to earn 1 to 3 percent above or below the index returns depending on whether the cost basis of the futures is above or below its theoretical value, the skill with which the futures position is managed, and the trading costs of the futures.

There are further advantages in futures that encourage their use. First, one can find opportunities to buy when the futures are selling below their theoretical value. These situations still occur in futures prices for short periods when sentiment is very bearish for the future value of the underlying index. Second, intermittant cash flows, such as dividends and small cash contributions by the sponsor, can be held in index futures until they have accumulated to an amount that can be invested directly in index stocks at a reasonable commission. A risk exists that the portfolio will perform worse than the index if dividends are not reinvested quickly in the correct stocks and proportions to maintain correspondence with the index. Finally, when large additions or withdrawals are made from an index fund, index futures can be helpful.

Prior to the availability of these futures, one would have to invest funds in a large number of stocks very quickly if a large amount of funds were added to an index fund. These simultaneous purchases and the knowledge that a large buyer is in the market could adversely affect the price paid for the stocks. The liquidity of the index futures contracts, especially the S&P 500 and NYSE, is sufficient to absorb large orders without materially affecting market prices. The futures positions can be closed out gradually as stocks are purchased to maintain appropriate weights in the index fund.

For the case of forthcoming cash withdrawals from a portfolio, one can sell an index futures contracts calling for delivery at the time of the withdrawal. It is not possible to actually deliver the stocks into the futures contract, but one can be assured of receiving the cash value of the stock index at the price at which the future is sold. The risk associated with a large drop in the market just prior to the withdrawal is thus reduced. A portfolio manager who anticipates a withdrawal may wish to look for an opportunity of overvaluation in futures to execute the sale in the futures market.

Substitute for Cash-Equivalents. Most portfolios have at least some of their assets invested in short-term, low-risk securities such as Treasury bills, project notes, commercial paper, and the like. These types of securities are often called *cash-equivalents*. We have seen in Chapter 5 that the prices of financial futures are a function of the interest rate available in cash-equivalents, in particular the rate available on securities such as a term repurchase agreement or a Treasury bill. As shown in Chapter 6, a fully hedged portfolio, invested in the securities deliverable into the futures contract and hedged by the sale of the futures contracts is expected to return the cash-equivalent interest rate applicable to the period of the hedge.

What does this have to do with the cash-equivalent position of pension funds? A pension fund may hold assets very similar to the index or security deliverable into a futures contract, such as a stock index, or Treasury bond, and may desire to exchange these assets for low-risk assets that earn a fixed short-term rate. Instead of selling the securities and incurring the trading costs, these assets can be hedged by the sale of futures to create a "synthetic" cash-equivalent position. The risk of a fully hedged position is slightly greater than that of cash-equivalents, because the basis risk remains. However, the basis risk can be small if the securities creating the cash-equivalent position are very similar to those deliverable in the futures contract.

The advantages of considering a fully hedged financial futures strategy as a cash-equivalent substitute are several. First, futures can frequently be sold for prices in excess of their theoretical value which would enable the hedger to earn a higher effective short-term interest rate. In late 1984 and early 1985, there were several opportunities to earn 4–5% above the annual Treasury bill yields by selling S&P 500 index futures against a portfolio of stocks constructed to track the returns of the index. Secondly, the costs of switching into cash-equivalent securities and back again when the market outlook changes are above those of executing a similar strategy in the futures market. Finally, the portfolio manager may like the securities he or she is holding long-term but may simply wish to be less fully invested in the short-run. By selling futures, the manager reduces the risk of missing a large gain in these securities if the switch had been made into cash-equivalents. The short futures position can be closed out quickly to limit opportunity losses on the securities held.

Market-Timing. Both stock index and fixed-income futures can be used to increase or decrease a portfolio's sensitivity to movements in the equity market or in the general level of interest rates. Investment theory posits that the expected return of a particular class of assets such as stocks or long-term taxable bonds is a function of the rate available on risk-free securities (r_F) and the return premium associated with other risk factors $(r_{Ri}, i = 1,2, . . , N)$ present in the class of securities.

This relationship is shown below:

$$E(r_C) = r_F + \sum_{i=1}^{N} W_i \, E(r_{Ri}) \tag{11-2}$$

where: $E(r_C)$ = the expected return of a class of securities,
$\quad\quad r_F$ = the risk-free rate of interest
$\quad\quad E(r_{ci})$ = the expected return premium associated with each factor present in class C.
$\quad\quad W_i$ = the weight of each factor present in class C.

If C is a portfolio of equities that has as its only common factor the market factor m, equation [11–2] reduces to the Capital Asset Pricing Model (CAPM) and W_i equals the beta (β_i of that portfolio).

$$E(r_C) = r_F + \beta_c \, E(r_m) \tag{11-3}$$

For the case of a portfolio of Treasury bonds that have duration as their only risk factor, equation (11–3) can be expressed as:[3]

$$E(r_C) = r_F + D_c/D_m \, E(r_m) \tag{11-4}$$

where D_c = the duration of portfolio C, and
$\quad\quad D_m$ = the market value-weighted duration of the Treasury bonds outstanding.

In both of these cases, if the return of the market factor or duration factor is anticipated to be above its long-term expected value, the appropriate policy would be to increase the weight associated with that factor (i.e., increase beta or duration). This is another way of saying very simply that portfolio managers typically increase their risk (market exposure or duration) when they are bullish on investment returns and reduce their risk when they are bearish.

Financial futures can serve as alternative vehicles for adjusting the market risk or maturity of pension portfolios. Since buying a stock index future is roughly equivalent to acquiring an index fund, these futures can be purchased and sold to adjust the beta of a portfolio. A *beta* for a portfolio measures the sensitivity of the value of the portfolio to changes in the general level of stock prices. For example, portfolios with betas greater than 1.0 are expected to increase or decrease in value by more than one percent for each one percent change in overall stock prices.

As an example, let us assume that the beta or β of the near-term futures contract is β_F.[4] Let W_F be the proportion of the portfolio represented by the market value of the futures contracts.

$$W_F = \frac{\text{Market value of futures} \begin{matrix} (+ \text{ if long}) \\ (- \text{ if short}) \end{matrix}}{\text{Market value of portfolio}}$$

The portfolio beta with futures (β_{PF}) will equal:

$$\beta_{PF} = \beta_P + W_F \beta_F \qquad (11\text{--}5)$$

where β_P = the beta of the portfolio.

Therefore, the beta can be increased by increasing the market value of futures held long or decreased by increasing the market value of futures sold. This market risk adjustment can all be done without changing the stocks held.

This ability to adjust market risk exposure with futures is very significant, because it is the key to the power of financial futures to separate stock selection from market timing. The market risk of selected stocks, can always be adjusted via stock index futures to the level desired by the pension sponsor. In fact, cases may arise in which the pension sponsor may prefer to manage the market risk using stock index futures or index funds and let the money manager simply pick stocks.

A similar application for Treasury bond futures can be used by fixed-income portfolio managers. Given the duration of the portfolio D_P and the duration of the cheapest-to-deliver Treasury bond futures D_F, a long or short position in these futures can be introduced to adjust the portfolio duration to the target level.

In this situation, the duration of the portfolio with futures (D_{PF}) will be determined as below:

$$D_{PF} = D_P + W_F D_F \qquad (11\text{--}6)$$

The weight of the futures is the same as above except that one would use the market value of the futures adjusted by the factor appropriate for the cheapest-to-deliver Treasury bond and the duration of this bond.

Specialization in Stock or Bond Selection. A new investment management specialty is possible with financial futures because of the ability to use these futures to reduce to a minimum the overall equity or interest rate risk of stock and bond portfolios. By selling stock index or fixed-income futures to fully hedge the market risk of a portfolio, one is left with a portfolio whose returns will be based on the return the securities achieve independent of overall market returns.

In portfolio theory, the difference between the return of a particular security from the average earned on a class of assets (stocks or bonds) of which the security is a part is called by several alternative names. These names include: alpha, excess return, residual return, abnormal return, stock-specific return, and nonmarket return. The risk remaining in a portfolio after the beta or market risk of a portfolio is eliminated is called residual risk, stock specific risk, or nonmarket risk. For our purposes, we will call this risk and return *security-specific* to differentiate it from market-related risk and return and to include other asset types in addition to equities.

Prior to the ability to hedge changes in levels of interest rates or stock indexes, specialists in stock selection were left to work with only the portion of portfolio return that was not associated with these broad market changes. This portion varies from portfolio to portfolio but is rarely more than 30–40 percent. By using financial futures at either the money manager or pension sponsor level, the manager can make investment decisions independent of the overall market or interest rate outlook. Rather, his or her function becomes the selection of securities that will outperform the market as defined by a set of securities deliverable into a futures contract.

Market performance has served as a cushion for poorly performing managers in years of good markets and a nemesis for good managers in years when security selection was good but market performance poor. With the introduction of financial futures, we expect to see more managers specialize in either stock selection or market timing. Pension sponsors would need to have different performance expectations for each.

Total portfolio risk and return (variance of return) can be segmented as below:

$$\left(\begin{matrix}\text{Portfolio} \\ \text{risk}\end{matrix}\right) = \beta_p \left(\begin{matrix}\text{Market} \\ \text{risk}\end{matrix}\right) + \sum_{i=1}^{N}(W_i)^2 \left(\begin{matrix}\text{Security-} \\ \text{specific risk } i\end{matrix}\right) \qquad (11\text{--}7)$$

where W_i =   the weight of security in the portfolio;

$$\left(\begin{matrix}\text{Portfolio} \\ \text{return } p\end{matrix}\right) = \beta_p \left(\begin{matrix}\text{Market} \\ \text{return}\end{matrix}\right) + \sum_{i=1}^{N} W_i \left(\begin{matrix}\text{Security-} \\ \text{specific return } i\end{matrix}\right) \qquad (11\text{--}8)$$

The ability to specialize in stock selection means that the portfolio management problem can be split into two. Managers who are market timers maximize the market component of portfolio returns, adjusting the portfolio beta by switching among cash-equivalents, index-surrogate portfolios, and index futures. Managers who wish to be measured in terms of stock selection attempt to maximize the security-specific return of the portfolio and are concerned with minimizing the security-specific risk. This security-specific risk is reduced by diversification.

The process of managing investments to maximize security-specific returns of a portfolio of stocks (bonds) involves selecting the undervalued securities, finding their beta or duration, and selling a sufficient quantity of financial futures to reduce the beta or duration as close to zero as possible.

Reducing the Currency Risk of U.S. Investments for Foreign Investors. Non-U.S. residents who wish to invest in U.S. securities, need to first exchange their local currency into dollars. The investment returns they earn are therefore related to the appreciation of the U.S. security in dollars as well as the appreciation or depreciation of the dollar. If foreign investors do not wish to be exposed to this currency risk, there are several hedging techniques available to reduce it. The usual procedure is to either borrow the dollars or sell them (purchase the local currency) for future delivery in the forward or futures market. All of the hedging techniques involve a cost of eliminating this currency risk: the net of the dollar interest rate versus the local currency rate, or the net of the forward (future) rate versus the spot rate.

The availability of stock index and fixed-income futures suggests another strategy for reducing currency risk. By purchasing stock index or fixed-income futures, one can participate in the returns of the underlying U.S. securities. Only the margin requirements and the profits (losses) need be converted into dollars. The rest of the market value of the futures (denominated in dollars) can be held in the currency of the foreign investor's choice. Therefore, only a small portion of the funds invested (usually less than 10 percent) is subject to currency risk.

Stock index futures also give the foreign investor access to an instrument resembling the entire U.S. equity market in its risk and return. They thus can capture the diversification benefit of investing in a broadly-based index without selecting a portfolio of different U.S. stock issues. This can be helpful to non-U.S. investors who are bullish on the U.S. economy and U.S. equity values but who do not feel familiar enough with particular firms to assess their value. These foreign investors may also be unable to sufficiently diversify across individual U.S. stocks with the funds available to them for U.S. investment.

Management of Capital Additions and Reductions to the Portfolio. Frequently, firms make large contributions to their pension fund or insurers add to their asset pool at particular points of time. These contributions or withdrawals are often based on financial considerations within the entity rather than on conditions in the security market. Often these additions (or withdrawals) come close to the end or beginning of the fiscal years. Pension funds need to add to their pension assets based on minimum funding requirements. They may also choose to withdraw the funds needed for benefit payments over some subsequent period. Insurance companies may need to increase their cash reserves or pay large claims. When a new money manager is hired, funds allocated to the manager are often converted to cash before they are transferred.

At times of cash additions, a portfolio manager typically carries cash-equivalents at levels in excess of those normally held until particular securities are chosen to purchase in the quantities desired at favorable prices. The risk of carrying this excess cash is that the stock or bond market will rally before the funds can be invested. Most money managers prefer assuming this risk rather than buying securities haphazardly or randomly just to get the funds invested.

Stock and bond futures present a mechanism to accelerate the investment of cash in broad asset categories. Because commissions are so low and the markets are able to absorb very large positions without significantly affecting price levels, financial futures are very helpful in such situations. The portfolio manager can minimize the time that the portfolio differs from his or her desired stock, bond, cash, or maturity allocation. As particular securities are selected, portions of the futures position can be closed out in the amounts equal to the market value of the securities purchased. The asset manager still has the basis risk of futures.

This is the risk that the futures will over- or underperform the securities that the manager would have purchased had the funds been placed immediately in the stock or bond market.

In order to prepare for withdrawals from the portfolio, the manager can sell financial futures that are deliverable around the date of the withdrawals. This reduces the risk of a market decline between the time the withdrawal is announced and the time it is implemented.

Pension Sponsor Applications of Financial Futures

The second level at which financial futures strategies can be beneficial to the management of portfolios of long-term securities is at the level of the pension sponsor or owner of the investment assets being managed. Up to now, we have been discussing applications for the portfolio manager, the individual designated to directly oversee the management of securities. The applications we will now discuss relate to the problems and decisions faced by these with ultimate control or fiduciary responsibility for the investment portfolio. These would include the pension officer of the corporation with the pension fund, the chief financial officer in the insurance company, or the manager of an endowment or trust fund.

This individual sets overall policy guidelines and objectives for the portfolio, decides how the funds will be managed (in-house or externally, by one or several money managers), oversees the management and performance of the fund by the portfolio managers selected, and handles the additions and withdrawals by the corporation to the pool of funds under management. For our purposes, we will refer to this function as that of the fund *sponsor*, the term used in the pension industry. These applications are also applicable to the senior investment officers of an insurance company, foundation, or endowment fund that sets policy and management guidelines for assets under their control.

When investment assets are managed in-house, there may be an overlap between the functions of the portfolio manager and the sponsor. For the in-house management situation, many of the uses of financial futures described in the previous section are applicable as well. We will cover here the investment management problems unique to the sponsor and discuss how futures can help in solving these problems.

Controlling the Overall Asset Mix. Sponsors decide on the broad allocation between stocks, bonds, and cash and may even delineate breakdowns within those categories, such as large capitalization versus small capitalization stocks, actively versus passively managed stock portfolios, and corporate versus municipal bonds. This allocation will be a function of the nature of business of the sponsor, the cash flows needed regularly by the sponsor, the sponsor's tax situation, and the general economic outlook for the different investment alternatives.

Once overall allocation is set, portfolio managers are hired either externally or internally based on their special skills in managing particular categories of assets. These managers are judged individually on their own performance and pursue diversification strategies in their portfolios within the category of investments in which they specialize. This diversification on the part of portfolio managers may not always be in the sponsor's best interest. The sponsor has already set allocation policy in selecting and directing managers and has diversified by choosing multiple versus single managers. By using financial futures, the sponsor can offset asset allocation decisions made by portfolio managers to bring the overall fund in line with policy. The sponsor can also better control the beta of the stock portfolio to keep it in line with the objective for the fund's market risk.

For example, a sponsor may have recommended a long-term allocation of 50 percent stocks, 40 percent bonds, and 10 percent cash, giving money managers some flexibility to vary from this allocation as they see fit. The maximum weight permitted for cash-equivalents is 20 percent. Assume many of the stock and bond managers foresee a period of poor returns for long-term securities. To maximize their own performance, they are carrying a total of 30% of their funds in cash-equivalents. At this point, the sponsor can tell the stock and bond managers to reinvest the cash to get the weight down to 20 percent. The managers may argue that it is not in their interest to do so, since their performance is being compared to other managers and they bear the risk of being fired. They argue that they have been hired to exercise their best judgment and would like to be evaluated based on their own results.

The sponsor can give portfolio managers this discretion over allocation by using stock index and bond futures to fine-tune the allocation to the targets set at the sponsor level. This requires a mechanism for monitoring the asset allocation of portfolio managers at any point in time so that a futures strategy can be set based on the differences between the policy targets and the aggregate weighting of the portfolio managers. In this situation, the pension sponsor could purchase stock index and Treasury bond futures with a delivery value equal to 10% of the total funds under management. This would effectively reduce the cash-equivalent weight to roughly 20%.

Sponsors of very large pension funds with many different managers may find financial futures to be particularly helpful in controlling the overall asset mix. The use of stock index and bond futures in this fashion is another level of separation between broad asset allocation (which can effectively be handled by the sponsor) and the selection of the portfolio to maximize return and minimize risk by diversification within a particular segment of the investment market.

The implementation of a financial futures strategy by the sponsor to control the asset mix would be the same as that discussed above with respect to the use of futures for asset allocation by the portfolio manager. There are currently money managers who are now offering special services to sponsors to help them use stock index and bond futures to adjust their asset allocations.[5] These managers receive from the sponsor a list of the holdings in cash and securities and then determine the appropriate number of futures to buy or sell to bring the fund in line with the desired allocation.

Controlling Market Risk and Weights in Market Sectors. The sponsor may also wish to override the weightings in market sectors, the betas, or the bond duration in the portfolios of their stock managers. In many cases, the sponsor will direct the manager to change policy as soon as he or she notices the market risk or allocation is off-target. It may take the manager time to change policy, or the sponsor may not wish to interfere with the manager's "style."

Stock index futures can be purchased or sold by the sponsor to increase or decrease the beta of the portfolio temporarily. When and if futures become available on market sectors, such as energy stocks, utilities, and large capitalization stocks, they can also be used to give the sponsor the flexibility of adjusting sector weights to target levels.

It should be clear that the availability of financial futures gives the fund sponsor much more control and opportunity to exercise discretion. This makes the sponsor's job more interesting and more difficult. Sponsors using financial futures for asset or sector allocation now will also have to bear more responsibility for the risks and rewards of any investment strategy moves that are implemented at the sponsor level.

Performance Analysis. The ability to manage the asset allocation with financial futures has implications for performance measurement and attribution of portfolio managers. Since broad asset allocation, market timing, and selection are now separable, the objectives set for each of these investment management processes should be distinct. If managers are able to specialize more, their performance analyses must be more sophisticated than a simple comparison of performance to the S&P 500 or to other managers with different specialties. Also, there exists a new type of management skill, that of the financial futures strategy manager. This manager would have the responsibility of determining the number of futures contracts necessary to restore portfolios to policy targets, the particular contracts (delivery months) to buy or sell, the timing of futures purchases and sales to take advantage of pricing opportunities and to minimize basis risk, and other tasks associated with implementing financial futures strategies. New performance criteria need to be used for this financial futures manager as well.

Portfolio Cash Management. The sponsor is also a cash manager of the funds designated to be added or withdrawn to assets under management. These funds may temporarily be in accounts directly under the sponsor's control until they can be assigned to particular portfolio managers or until benefits or claims are paid. These funds always need to be available for payment of corporate obligations that arise from time to time. The sponsor may also be aware of a large injection of cash to the funds managed that will have to be absorbed quickly into the investment management process.

If funds are available that will be added to equity or bond portfolios, financial futures equal in contract value to the market value of these funds can be purchased in anticipation of such a move. This was discussed above as a means for the portfolio manager to get funds quickly in line with the desired asset allocation of the portfolio. A similar strategy can be used by sponsors while they await decisions from their superiors as to who will be selected to manage the funds or how they will be used within the firm.

A sponsor may also be aware of a forthcoming withdrawal of funds from the long-term security portfolios and wish to sell some futures to reduce the risk of a drop in the market at the time the withdrawal is actually made. The futures hedge effectively converts the holdings to those of cash-equivalents immediately (ignoring the basis risk). This gives the sponsor time to inform the manager of the bonds or stocks of the withdrawal and permits the manager to execute it in an orderly fashion.

Portfolio Restructuring. Financial futures also have applicability in assisting in the switching of funds from one external manager to another or from in-house to outside management and vice versa. Situations also arise in which a new manager is hired with new funds added to the asset base. Often in such circumstances, the old portfolio (if there is one) is liquidated to give the new manager a clean slate. This type of portfolio restructuring has several risks. First, while the funds are temporarily in cash, the value of securities sold could appreciate sharply. Second, the sale of a large number of stocks or bonds and the subsequent repurchase can itself affect price levels in the market to the disadvantage of the sponsors.

Financial futures can be used to ease the transition. If a sponsor is shifting from one stock manager to another, he or she can direct the selling manager to sell off the stocks in an orderly fashion, purchasing stock index futures contracts in the name of the sponsor as portions of the portfolio are liquidated. The new manager can then be given discretion over these index futures contracts or be permitted to close out the futures positions as issues selected by this manager can be purchased at attractive prices.

The only incremental costs of using financial futures in this transitional, restructuring situation are the round-trip commissions on the futures contracts and the funds tied up by futures margin requirements. This is quite small considering the alternative risks and potential costs. The availability of financial futures makes it less cumbersome and costly to switch asset managers and may, therefore, indirectly benefit sponsors by allowing them additional flexibility here as well. If it is indeed possible to identify superior and inferior money managers, the efficiency of the money management business should be improved as a result.

APPLICATIONS OF FINANCIAL FUTURES FOR INSURANCE COMPANIES

Pension funds, life insurance, and property and casualty insurance companies all have assets consisting of stocks, government bonds, corporate bonds, mortgage securities, and cash-equivalent securities. The allocation of funds across these types of securities varies from firm to firm and over time. This allocation depends on the nature of their business, on commitments to beneficiaries and policy-holders, on their tax status, and on financial market conditions. The strategies and uses of financial futures outlined above are applicable to all three of these institutions in the management of their investment securities. In this section, we discuss uses of financial futures that would be of value to insurance companies in particular. Because these strategies relate to the different types of products and investment policies characteristic of life versus property and casualty insurance companies, we divide our discussion along these lines.

Insurance companies general account activities are regulated at the state level. This decentralized regulatory structure has impeded the growth in financial futures applications in the insurance industry. Many state regulators do not feel comfortable with these markets because they can be used in very speculative ways. Their primary concern is the protection of the claims of policyholders in their state. Often the perception of these instruments as risk-increasing rather than risk-reducing vehicles prevails.

Most states have followed the leadership of New York which recently permitted hedging against foreign currency and interest rate risk on up to 2% of the admitted assets of the insurer as of the end of the previous year. The most liberal state regulation is that of California which permits hedging as long as there is evidence of correlation between the future and the item being hedged. California is the exception rather than the rule, however, and most state guidelines either limit hedging to a small percentage (under 10%) of assets or prohibit the use of financial futures in general. The November 1984 issue of *Intermarket* contains a summary of the insurance regulations on the use of financial futures for each state.[6]

These regulatory limitations do not apply to investment management activities that insurers do on a fee-basis for clients. These assets are segregated from those in the general account. Financial futures strategies can be and are used here depending on the regulations applying to the owner of the funds being managed.

Financial Futures Strategies for Life Insurance Companies

The primary products of life insurers are term and whole-life insurance policies and individual and group annuity contracts. Whole-life policies are a form of contractual savings whereby policyholders pay a level premium which accumulates as assets of the insurance company until the terms of the contract are fulfilled by either death or maturity of the policy. From the insurer's point of view, fixed-rate annuities, including insured pension plans, are similar to whole-life except that they pay a fixed sum of maturity monthly for the life of the annuitant subsequent to retirement. Both whole-life and annuity contracts effectively shift the management of savings to the insurer in exchange for the promise of a fixed rate of return or payment.

Term insurance has no savings component and provides a smaller pool of cash that must be invested to provide funds for fulfillment of the policy when the policy holder dies. New types of policies have been recently introduced that provide more separation between the insurance and saving components and that have higher investment returns than previously available. Many of these new insurance products have variable investment returns. Funds generated by all these product lines are pooled in the general asset account of the insurance company which is closely regulated by state insurance commissions. In addition, life insurers can serve as money managers for uninsured pension funds. They can also sell group annuity contracts at higher rates than offered to individual policy holders.

Most life insurance companies concentrate their general account investments in long-term securities that pay a fixed return, such as government and corporate bonds, private placement loans to businesses, and mortgage securities. The emphasis is on high-quality securities because of their role as fidiciaries of policy holders' funds and also because of the close oversight by state regulators. These securities provide cash flows that are predictable and therefore usually sufficient to cover the long-term fixed commitments of the life insurers. The predictability of the cash flows to policyholders allows life insurers to keep short-term security holdings at a minimum. In this financial management process, there is an attempt to reduce interest rate risk exposure by the matching of current and future liabilities with expected investment income. In fact, there are cyclical risks in the life insurance business. As interest rates change, the market value of the long-term, fixed-income securities fluctuates. This means that even though these assets are carried at book value, an increase in interest rates can reduce the economic or market value of the assets of the firm. We shall see that financial futures, in particular futures on long-term government and mortgage securities, can be of value in dealing with the interest rate risk faced by life insurers.

Management of Incremental Cash Inflows and Outflows. In any given period, new funds become available for investment from premium payments on existing policies that are in excess of benefits paid on these policies and from new policies sold. The net cash inflow can be independent of the investment conditions for long-term, fixed-income securities. When rates are expected to rise, insurers may be reluctant to place these funds into long-term bonds. As an alternative to holding them in short-term securities, Treasury bond futures can be used to hedge purchases of long-term government and corporate bonds in a rising interest rate environment. This enables the insurer to acquire the bonds and include them in financial statements. By hedging the insurer can effectively earn the short-term, cash-equivalent rate on these newly purchased securities and reduce the risk of a quick drop in market value from further increases in rates. When long-term rates begin to decline, the insurer has the flexibility to remove the Treasury bond futures hedge.

An anticipated sale of bonds from the long-term assets can also be hedged against rising rates by selling Treasury bond futures. The futures will fall in value if rates rise, providing a profit to offset the losses of the lower selling price of the bond. Such hedging does involve the risk of changes in the spread between yields on Treasury bonds and the particular bonds being hedged.

Hedging Policy Loans. Many whole-life policies give holders the opportunity to borrow the cash value of their policies at a fixed rate specified in the insurance contract. This is a call option owned by the policy-holder and sold by the insurer. The chance that these options will be exercised increases as rates rise above the policy loan rate. When the option is exercised, the insurer is often supplying funds to policy holders at a lower rate than the cost of raising funds in the marketplace.

The risk of interest rate levels rising above policy loan rates and thereby increasing the cost of outstanding policy loans can be hedged with a short position in Treasury bill futures. As rates rise, a short futures position generates profits that will help offset the rising cost faced by the insurer of extending credit at low policy loan rates. The futures position would be closed out as rates begin to fall or when loans are repaid.

Hedging the option component of a policy loan commitment is best handled by purchasing an offsetting put option to sell some fixed income assets at a set price. (See Chapter 17 for a more in-depth discussion of options as compared to futures strategies.) This would increase in value as rates rise and prices fall and could be exercised to provide funds for policy loans. In situations where the insurer has made a commitment or sold an option, the risk of loss is best hedged with an offsetting option position. The use of financial futures would produce gains or losses even if the commitment or option were never exercised. With an option hedge, the insurer can exercise the hedged position when the insurer receives notice of exercise on the part of the policy or contract holder.

Hedging Forward Commitments. Many insurance companies are actively engaged in making forward commitments or firm contracts to buy debt securities. The commitments are made at a stated interest rate or security price and are in effect for a fixed period of time. These commitments are common in corporate lending via private placement and in the acquisition of mortgage securities. The rate agreed to in the commitment reflects the insurance company's expectations of the direction of changes in interest rates over the commitment period and the default risk or other special features associated with the particular debt offering. If rates increase beyond the expectations reflected in the commitment rate, the potential return is lost, and the borrower pays a lower rate on the funds than would have been received without the commitment.

Futures on Treasury securities can be helpful in two ways to assist in the forward commitment process of lending. First, the futures market itself provides a guide to the insurance company for setting the forward commitment rate. The price of a future that is deliverable close to the time that the commitment expires reflects the market's expectations of the course of rates over the period prior to delivery. After adjusting for differences in risk, coupon, maturity, and the cheapest-to-deliver bond in the futures contract, the forward commitment rates can be set relative to the available futures contract rate.

The insurer can also use the futures market to hedge the risk of increases in rates beyond those reflected in the futures prices at the time the commitment was made. By selling futures and repurchasing them at the time the commitment is fulfilled, the hedging insurer can offset some of the opportunity losses associated with rising rates at the expense of sacrificing the benefits of declining rates over the commitment period. Despite the fact that the forward commitment is hedged, the insurer still bears the risk of changes in the spread between the forward commitment rate and the rate of the security deliverable into the futures contract.

Hedging the Interest Rate Risk of Guaranteed Investment Contracts during the Offering Period. Many insurers sell a product called a GIC or guaranteed interest contract. These instruments pay a guaranteed rate of interest for all or at least part of the life of the contract. Upon receipt the insurer intends to invest the funds in fixed-income securities that will provide the cash flows promised in the GIC and earn a premium to the insurer for guaranteeing the interest rate risk over the life of the contract. The GIC offering rate is set based on current and expected interest rate levels and the competitive environment for GIC offering.

Usually, there is a period of time while the GIC offering is outstanding during which the insurer becomes committed to the interest rate that will be paid. During that period, the insurer bears the risk that interest rates will decline. This could result in a long-term negative rather than positive cash flow for the insurer. By purchasing Treasury bill, note, or bond futures in proportions based on the duration of the GIC, the insurer can reduce this risk. If rates decline, the futures will rise in value and produce a profit. This profit can be invested to provide additional income to add to the income of the bonds that will now be purchased at a lower price with the GIC investment funds.

Another advantage of fixed-income futures for GICs is that the futures yield can be used directly as the basis of the GIC offering rate. In this way, the return to the GIC seller is virtually fixed at the point the first offering is made, provided the hedge can be implemented at that futures yield. The basis risk and cost of variation margin do remain even if the GIC offering is fully hedged.

Financial Futures Strategies for Property and Casualty Insurers

Property and casualty (P&C) insurers provide a different intermediation function than do life insurers. They sell policies that pay claims in the event of damage to property or in the case of personal injury. The risk of such events occurring does not change dramatically over the life of the contract as does the risk of death benefit payments over the duration of a life insurance contract. P&C insurance companies manage their investments differently than do life insurers, because their claim payments are less predictable, more sensitive to inflation, and more volatile in level.

There is usually a shorter time between premium receipts and claim payments for P&C policies than for life insurance claims. This results in a lower rate of asset accumulation and in less participation in capital markets as compared to life insurers. P&C insurers do, however, play a very important role in the municipal security market and have substantial holdings of corporate bonds and equities. Because P&C insurers are taxed at the corporate tax rate, they tend to hold tax-exempt municipal bonds.

The assets of P&C insurers are managed more independently

of the insurance operations than those of life insurers. The income from investments is intended to provide a cushion for years in which underwriting losses occur. P&C policies are priced with the expectation of providing an underwriting profit. If the expected level of claims are paid, the receipts should be sufficient to cover those claims in addition to providing a profit to the insurer.

Because claim payments are difficult to predict and highly volatile, there are periods when underwriting losses occur. Competitive pricing can also serve to reduce the underwriting income of P&C insurers sharply. Investment income serves as a source of cash flow to reduce the impact of underwriting losses and as a source of incremental income when underwriting profits are higher than expected.

Financial futures can be beneficial to P&C insurers primarily in the management of their investment assets. Many of the applications are equivalent to those for pension funds because of the similarity of the securities they hold (i.e., government and corporate bonds and equities). Such futures strategies as changing the asset mix, accelerating the rate at which cash can be absorbed or withdrawn from long-term security positions, and stock index fund arbitrage would be applicable.

The fact that P&C insurers hold municipal securities sets them apart from pension funds. To reduce the maturity risk of the portfolio while preserving the tax-exempt income stream, a cross-hedge can be constructed for these long-term municipal bonds with Treasury bond futures. The sale of Treasury bond futures against the total market value of a municipal portfolio effectively converts the portfolio into a shorter-term portfolio with tax-exempt coupon income. The hedged returns also reflect any shifts in the relative prices of Treasury bonds versus municipal bonds. When futures on municipal indexes become available, the opportunity will exist to hedge shifts in the market value of the municipal market. The prospective returns of a fully hedged long-term municipal portfolio should be compared to a portfolio of a short-term municipal issue.

It should be noted that the price of the Treasury bond or other financial futures that are sold incorporates the current slope of the yield curve. In other words, Treasury bond futures are usually selling at prices below the cash market prices of Treasury bonds in an upward sloping yield curve environment. Even though long-term municipals will be earning higher coupons than short-term municipals, one cannot necessarily earn a higher rate of tax-free income simply by hedging the long-term municipal position. If there is no change in interest rates over the life of the future, the futures position will be closed out by a purchase at a higher price to produce a loss. This future loss will reduce and perhaps offset the incremental coupon income earned on the long-term security. (The higher price reflects the theoretical value of the future at a time closer to delivery when a smaller amount of coupon interest is being foregone by the futures' purchasers.)

In hedging municipal bonds with Treasury bond futures, there is a high degree of basis risk. The secondary market for municipal bonds is not very liquid, and spreads between municipal and Treasury bond yields can vary sharply from bond to bond and from period to period; for example, over the one-year period of July 1982–July 1983 by between 80 and 200 basis points. The basis risk for short hedgers using Treasury bond futures is the risk that the Treasury bond–municipal yield spread will narrow as the general level of rates rises. In these circumstances, the losses in the value of the municipal bonds will be greater than the gains on the futures, reducing the effectiveness of the hedge.

Another negative scenario would be the case in which spreads narrowed while the general level of interest rates fell. While the municipal bonds rise in value, the short Treasury bond futures could produce losses that exceed these gains in value. The P&C insurer could find that the hedged municipal bond portfolio actually declines in market value (considering Treasury bond futures losses) over a period of falling interest rates.

The basis risk of the municipal–Treasury bond hedge suggests that spread analysis is very important prior to opening and closing futures positions because of the frequency of shifts in spreads and the impact of these shifts on hedging effectiveness. Also, the prospective municipal index futures are an attractive alternative for investors in municipals who wish to hedge their portfolio more fully from both the risk of change in the general level of long-term rates and the relative yield changes of municipal versus Treasury bonds.

SUMMARY

Pension funds and insurance companies have many potential applications for financial futures. Most of these applications relate to the management of their investment assets in the short run. The liquidity and low transactions cost of financial futures allows long-term investment managers to take advantage of short-term market trends without costly rebalancing of their portfolios. Futures can reduce the cost of investment turnover and provide the flexibility for large institutions to move large amounts of funds quickly and cheaply with a flexibility they never had.

In addition, stock index futures representing broad segments of the market facilitate specialization of investment management functions. Individual security selection skills can be differentiated from those associated with market (or segment) timing. This should provide for more efficient allocation of resources in the investment management business. Financial futures also provide the opportunity to hedge forward price commitments for selling and purchasing securities. These commitments have been critical to the initiation of projects requiring large amounts of financing. With the ability to hedge such commitments, the flow of funds to such projects should be improved.

Ultimately, the savings in operational costs and lower risks that are possible with financial futures can be passed along to shareholders and beneficiaries of pension funds and insurers. This will only occur after a time sufficient to familiarize investment managers with the nature of the futures markets and the strategies available to them. Also, there must be enough experience with these strategies to establish, measure, and confirm the costs or benefits involved. Within the next 10 years, it is not inconceivable that long-term investment managers who are *not* using financial futures will need to explain their rationale rather than those who are.

NOTES

[1] There is also the fund consultant who helps in the setting of fund objective, the evaluation process, and fund manager selection. The role of the consultant is not central to the use of financial futures and will not be discussed here.

[2] See *Pension and Investment Age*, Chicago, Ill: Crain Communications, issues of October 28 and December 6, 1982, November 28, 1983, and January 9, 1984.

[3] The concept of duration is explained in Chapter 5. Equation (11–4) is based on the work of Boquist et. al. (1975) and holds strictly only under the assumption that the covariance between portfolio C and the market value-weighted portfolio of Treasury bonds is equal to the variance of the Treasury bond portfolio. This would be true if the return correlation between the two portfolios was close to one and if they had equal return variances.

[4] Beta estimates of stock index futures have actually been in the range of 1.1 to 1.2 unless the contract is held to delivery. See Figlewski (1984) and Hill and Schneeweis (1984). Movements in the futures tend to be somewhat greater than movements in the broad index for a day-to-day basis. In practice a beta of 1.0 is typically assumed for S&P 500 and NYSE stock index futures.

[5] See Blanton [1983] for a discussion of managers and sponsors using this approach.

[6] "Taking It Slow," *Intermarket* Vol 1 No. 6 (November 1984), pp 18–23.

[7] A municipal bond index futures contract designed by the Chicago Board of Trade has been given CFTC approval and began trading in June 1985.

SELECTED REFERENCES

Bishop, George, and Thomas R. Robinson. "Insurance Type Intermediaries." In *Financial Markets and Institutions*, ed. M. E. Polakoff and T. A. Durken, 3d edition. Boston: Houghton Mifflin, 1981.

Black, Fischer. "The Investment Policy Spectrum: Individuals, Endowments, and Pension Funds." *Financial Analysts Journal*, January–February 1976, pp. 23–31.

Blanton, Kimberly. "Tool for Sponsors Overrides Advisor, Asset Allocations." *Pensions and Investment Age*, (November 28, 1983), pp. 23–24.

Boquist, J. et al "Duration and Risk Assessment for Bonds and Common Stocks," *Journal of Finance*, December 1975, 1360–1365.

Chiang, R., and R. W. Kolb. "Improving Hedging Performance Using Interest Rate Futures." *Financial Management*, (Autumn 1981), pp. 72–79.

Elton, Edwin J., and Martin J. Gruber. *Modern Portfolio Theory and Investment Analysis*. New York: John Wiley & Sons, 1981.

Figlewski, Steven, and Stanley J. Kon. "Portfolio Management with Stock Index Futures." *Financial Analysts Journal*, (January–February 1982), pp. 52–59.

Figlewski, Steven, "Hedging Performance and Basis Risk in Stock Index Futures." *Journal of Finance* 39, No. 3 (July 1984) pp. 657–69.

Gay, G. D., R. W. Kolb, and R. Chiang. "Interest Rate Hedging: An Empirical Test of Alternative Strategies." *Journal of Financial Research*, (Fall 1983), pp. 181–98.

Hill, J., and T. Schneeweis. "Risk Reduction Potential of Financial Futures for Corporate Bond Positions." In *Interest Rate Futures: Concepts and Issues*, ed. G. D. Gay and R. W. Kolb. Richmond, Va.: R. F. Dame, Inc., 1982.

McEnally, R. W. and M. L. Rice. "Hedging Possibilities in the Flotation of Debt Securities," *Financial Management* 8:12–18 (1979).

Owens, Patricia. "How a Pension Fund Manager Uses Financial Futures to Hedge a Portfolio." *Review of Research in Futures Markets* 3, pp. 218–26.

Trainer, Francis H. "The Uses of Treasury Bond Futures in Fixed Income Analysis. *Financial Analysts Journal*, (January–February 1983), pp. 27–34.

CHAPTER *12*

Applications of Futures for Mortgage Finance

Selling what you do not own is frowned upon in business circles and can lead directly to jail. In mortgage banking, it is a necessary marketing procedure employed to protect a mortgage originator against violent and unexpected interest rate movement. These gyrations can occur between the time a loan is committed for permanent financing and the time it is closed. This interval can be one week or more than three months. During recent years, mortgage rates have deviated by more than 100 basis points during short periods of time. A change of that magnitude can generate an exposure of $50,000 or more for every million dollars of unsold loans.

EXHIBIT 12–1
Dollar Value, Per Million Dollar Face Value, of a GNMA Mortgage-Backed Security

Yield Level (%)	*Coupon*			
	8	*12*	*14*	*16*
10	$863,750	1,131,406	1,269,100	1,407,800
11	806,250	1,060,156	1,190,800	1,322,700
12	754,062	995,000	1,119,300	1,244,900
13	706,562	935,781	1,054,000	1,173,700
14	663,437	881,406	994,000	1,102,700

To reduce the risks resulting from price volatility, the mortgage industry has employed FNMA and Freddie Mac auctions, GNMA and FNMA forward markets, standby commitments, and the sale of whole loans. During periods of disintermediation, several of these alternatives become nonoperative as thrift institutions experience negative cash flows. The consistent availability of GNMA and bond futures contracts should be welcomed by mortgage investors and originators. The following review is illustrative of how and when interest rate futures should be used by mortgage originators, thrift institutions, and builders.

THE PROBLEM: HEDGING RESIDENTIAL ORIGINATIONS

When a branch office of a thrift institution or mortgage banking organization issues a 60-day point letter to a realtor or builder, the institution has bought a forward mortgage commitment. In effect, the letter has assured the realtor that the banker will purchase a mortgage at a future date, at an interest rate and price that was agreed upon prior to the closing. The realtor has agreed to deliver a mortgage to the originator within 60 days at the stated terms. To accomplish this responsibility, the realtor must bring the buyer and seller to a timely closing and deliver a perfected mortgage to the originator. In the terminology of the futures industry, the mortgage originator would now be considered to have a long position and the realtor a short position until the mortgage commitment was delivered.

If the mortgage originator selects to sell GNMA futures to hedge this outstanding commitment, the originator must be certain that the loans will close. If rates improve, the originator will experience a loss from the hedging transaction. If the permanent loans are not sold at a profit this loss can not be recovered.

Let us assume that on December 3, 1983, a First Federal loan officer issues a 60-day point letter to the North Avenue branch of the Unbelievable Reality Company for $1 million of 12 percent FHA/VA straight life loans at six points. It is the intention of the institutions to package these loans into a GNMA security which will be delivered in March 1984. On the commitment day, the cash bid quote for a GNMA 11½ percent security to be delivered in March 1984 was 93–16. This is a 12.44 percent yield to maturity (YTM). A whole loan buyer made an offer of 94–00 for 12 percent FHA/VA loans for March 1984 delivery. This is a 12.30 percent YTM when servicing income is included in the calculation. At that moment, the March 1984 GNMA CDR contract was trading at 69–12, or 69.375. This price is the equivalent of a YTM of 13.3 percent and reflects the value of 16 percent GNMA coupons which were still readily available for purchase in the cash markets.

The marketing manager of the First Federal S&L has three choices:

1. Do nothing.
2. Sell a $1 million March 1984 11½ percent GNMA into the cash forward market.
3. Sell the loans as whole loans with servicing at ⅜ percent of a point.
4. Sell a sufficient amount of futures contracts to hedge a $1 million 11½ percent GNMA until it is sold into the forward market at a later date.

The first alternative was quickly discarded. The third alternative was also eliminated, since servicing contracts have been frequently cancelled or renegotiated under duress. Therefore, the second and fourth solutions must be reviewed.

Based on the available supply of cash securities, it is estimated on December 3, 1983, that the 16 percent GNMA will be the cheapest available security for delivery in March 1984. To complete this analysis, it must be determined whether the futures price is rich or cheap compared to the cash market. If it is rich, futures contracts are suitable for selling.

The equivalent factor for a 16 percent GNMA provided by the CBOT is 0.622. When the factor is divided into 1 and the quotient of 1.6 is multiplied by the March 1984 GNMA CDR futures price of 69.375, the result is a price of 111. It is now apparent that on December 3, 1983, futures are trading above their fair value compared to 16 percent GNMA cash which was selling for 109.5 for immediate delivery.

Based on these facts, the thrift institution decides to delay selling an 11½ percent GNMA security until March 1984 and immediately short a sufficient number of GNMA CDR contracts. The equivalent factor for 11½ percent GNMAs is 0.739. When the factor is divided into 1, the quotient is 1.25. Therefore, the marketing manager must sell 12 or 13 March 1984 GNMA CDR contracts to hedge the outstanding obligation of the Unbelievable Reality Company.

During February 1984, when the loans are closed and packaged into a GNMA pool, the short futures positions will be offset by purchasing an equal number of March 1984 GNMA contracts. Simultaneously, the 11½ percent GNMA pool is sold into the cash market for immediate delivery. Although this procedure requires two "sell" transactions, it is often more efficient than a sale into the cash forward market months before delivery is to take place. It also eliminates the need to associate a sale with a specific coupon as is required in the cash market.

EXHIBIT 12–2

Cash Mortgage Market	*Futures Market*
December 3, 1983	
Issue point letter to realtor for $1 million straight life 12% FHA mortgages at 4 points for 60 days.	Sell 13 GNMA CDR March 1984 futures contracts at 69–12.
The 11½ GNMA March 1984 bid price available in forward cash market was 93–16. This sale is delayed until February 1984.	
February 14, 1984	
Close $1 million 12% FHA loans at 4 points. The 11½ GNMA cash market for March 1984 was now 94–08. It had improved $^{24}\!/_{32}$s.	
Sell $1 million 11½% GNMAs for March 1984 delivery at 94–08.	Buy 13 GNMA CDR March 1984 futures contracts for 69–28.
Gain: $^{24}\!/_{32}$s per million, or $7,500.	Loss: $^{16}\!/_{32}$ per contract, or (16 × 31.25) $6,500.

EXHIBIT 12–3
GNMA 11.5% Basis Comparison: GNMA II versus GNMA CDR

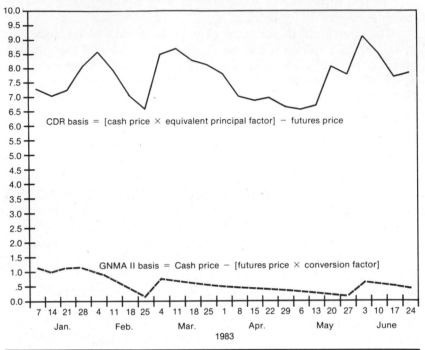

CDR basis = [cash price × equivalent principal factor] − futures price

GNMA II basis = Cash price − [futures price × conversion factor]

Source: CBOT Economic Analysis & Planning.

Summary of Hedging Strategy

On December 3, 1983, the March 1984 futures contract was over valued compared to the cash market. This made GNMA CDR futures ideal for selling. Since GNMA CDR futures traded like premium priced 16 percent GNMAs, they improve more slowly in a bull market than a discount bond. This accounted for the hedging profit of $1,000. During bear markets, this hedge could have generated a loss. GNMA CDR hedging results are seldom perfect but more precise when the cheapest deliverable bond is a discount bond. Exhibit 12–3 is a plot of cash versus GNMA CDR prices from January 1982 to August 1983.

STANDBY HEDGING

Permanent mortgage investors issue standby commitments to generate fee income now and to assure themselves of mortgage investments at current rates at a future date. A standby commitment is a willingness to fund mortgages at a future time at today's rates for a nonrecoverable fee. This investment policy is common during bull markets when the cash flow exceeds investment opportunities. Since 1975, this practice has been discontinued by most thrift institutions. It is again becoming visible for second mortgage securities and adjustable rate mortgages. If permanent mortgage rates continue to fall and investor deposits exceed withdrawals, their availability may once more become common. The costs for such commitments should be high, reflecting recent price volatility.

Simultaneously, builders can no longer obtain construction loans without first having negotiated a permanent take-out commitment. The rates for these take-out commitments can be fixed when construction begins or at the market rate in existence when the property is sold. Since the saleability of a project may often be associated with available financing as reflected in Exhibit 12–4, the cost of a take out must be included in calculating the cost of housing.

Only three things can happen after a standby is bought or sold. Yields can remain the same, go down, or increase. In the event of an unfavorable yield change, both the buyer and the seller

---

EXHIBIT 12–4
Annual Household Income Needed to Satisfy Bank Requirements to Secure a 30-Year $80,000 Mortgage at Fixed Rate—Assuming Homebuyer Devotes 32 Percent of Gross Monthly Income to Housing Expenses*

Mortgage Rate	Total Monthly Payments*	Annual Household Income Required for Mortgage
8%	$832.28	$23,710
9%	874.77	25,304
10%	718.54	26,945
11%	763.39	28,627
12%	809.17	30,344
13%	855.72	32,089
14%	902.92	33,880
15%	950.67	35,650
16%	978.85	37,457
17%	1,047.41	39,278

* Includes monthly principal and interest payments as well as $192 the median national monthly charge paid by new homeowners last year for real estate taxes, utilities and home insurance.
Source: United States League of Savings Association.

should consider the use of interest rate futures to protect themselves.

Standby commitments are issued for conventional, FNMA, and FHA/VA mortgage loans. Several studies have shown a positive correlation between conventional loans and GNMA CDR futures contracts. The proper use of futures enables a thrift institution that has written a standby to prevent opportunity losses which can result from a strike price becoming noncompetitive. This occurs when the strike price which was negotiated at the time of commitment, less any nonrecoverable fees earned, is higher in price, or lower in yield, than the prevailing market price at the time of closing.

Builders face a similar dilemma if the standby commitment they negotiated carried a market mortgage rate and mortgage rates escalate to levels where the average buyers can no longer qualify for a mortgage. When yields fall, or become lower, the builder might attempt to renegotiate the standby commitment or simply not deliver the loans against the contract. To reduce the exposure from such rapid changes in yield levels, a business plan must be developed by management which determines when a hedge should be instituted and offset, what contracts should be used, and how many contracts should be sold. The plan must be developed and approved before a standby is purchased or sold. It is impossible to recover losses that have already occurred before a hedge is implemented.

HEDGING CONSTRUCTION LOANS

Financing expenses associated with construction lending are estimated to be between 2.5 to 8 percent of direct construction costs. Unlike material costs, they are difficult to fix at the beginning of a project and may fluctuate a great deal during construction. The interest expense is normally a function of a variable like prime or 90-day certificates-of-deposit (CD) rates. During 1984 many commercial construction loans were tied to a variable index other than prime.

In order to minimize interest rate exposures associated with variable rates, builders can hedge construction loans with interest rate futures contracts. The technique is still an art and not a science, but its use should result in the recovery of at least 70 percent of the additional costs associated with increasing base rates. The ability to recover these expenses depends on when the base rate increased during the life of the loan, for how long rates remain at one level, and the accuracy of the initial draw schedule. Exhibit

12–5 illustrates the effect of random prime rate changes per $1 million outstanding for a 12-month period. A hedging program should be designed to recover only the additional costs above those associated with a fixed-rate construction loan.

Depending on the volatility experienced and the direction of yield level changes, a builder without a hedge program was exposed to no loss in program A and a loss of $50,000 per million dollars in program D. In order to implement a prudent and effective hedg-

---

EXHIBIT 12–5
Interest Expense, per Year, per Million Dollars Outstanding

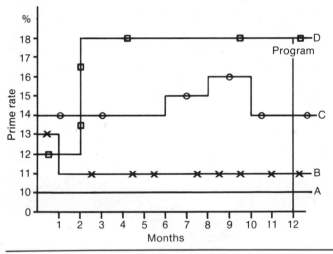

Program	Monthly Interest Expense	Number of Months	Total Annual Interest Expense	Annual Interest Expense without Change in Prime	Difference to be Recovered
A	$ 8,333	12	$100,000	$100,000	0
B	$10,833	1	$ 10,883		
	9,166	11	100,883		
			$111,766	$130,000	($18,234)
C	$11,666	6	$ 70,000		
	12,500	2	25,000		
	13,333	2	26,666		
	11,666	2	23,332		
			$144,998	$140,000	$ 4,998
D	$10,000	2	$ 20,000		
	15,000	10	150,000	$120,000	$50,000
			$170,000		

ing strategy, the following questions must be answered before any hedge action is instituted.

1. What contract should be used to hedge the construction financing exposure?
2. When must this action occur?
3. Under what conditions should some or all futures contracts be offset?
4. How many contracts should be sold?
5. What is the maximum cash flow exposure?

Selection of an Appropriate Contract

Most base rates used by construction lenders are variable rates tied to the prime rate, Treasury bills, or 90-day CD's. The available futures contracts that have the best correlations and the smallest standard deviations to these base rates are the 90-day Treasury bill, the 90-day CD, and occasionally the 90-day Eurodollar contracts. At various times, all of these contracts have a high level of basis risk. Such moments occurred primarily when weak money fled to the U.S. dollar or the government raised new cash by increasing the size of its weekly auctions.

The CD contract has generally been the best hedging vehicle as measured by statistical norms, but it may also experience short-term distortions when the demand for loans at money center banks is temporarily depressed. Additionally, the open interest of the contract must be watched closely if sizable hedging is contemplated. During 1985 the open interest for the CD contract was small.

Eurodollar contracts have seldom been used for the purpose of hedging domestic construction loans but can be selected for this task. At specific moments, they could be priced more advantageously for this application than other short term contracts. During 1985 these contracts had large open positions and were easy to trade.

In all situations, current basis relationships must be understood between contracts and their cash counterparts.

When Should a Hedge Be Initiated?

The answer is a function of a business plan that should dictate under what economic conditions a loan is fully or partially hedged. These variables may be altered periodically by management. It may not always be advisable or necessary to initiate a hedge position when a loan is closed or the first draw is taken down. If management embraces that concept, they must include a section in their plan identifying those conditions that may cause a hedge to be initiated and offset. The reestablishment of a hedge must also be addressed. The latter is most important since changes in the prime rate are seldom smooth or consistent in direction. The triggers that are used to initiate these actions must be carefully designed, keeping cash flow of the construction project in mind. If positions are entered and offset rapidly, churning is likely to occur, resulting in an unsatisfactory program due to the high commission costs generated from numerous buy and sell transactions.

How Many Contracts Should Be Sold?

A 100 basis points change for one year will change the annual interest rate expense associated with $1 million construction loan by $10,000. A similar change in a futures contract, whose maturity is 90 days, will result in a profit or loss of $2,500. Therefore, hedging construction loans on a dollar-for-dollar basis would be unsatisfactory if the loan has a remaining horizon of more than 90 days. Identifying the appropriate number of contracts that should be used and selecting their expiration months is the most difficult task in designing a hedge for a construction loan. Each time a hedge position is initiated, the average dollar amount outstanding for the remaining term of a loan must be recomputed. The construction loan draw schedule must be current before this calculation is made. As an example, assume that the remaining draw schedule for the Bur Oak Subdivision is:

$10 million	Now
5 million	Now + 2 months
5 million	Now + 6 months
4 million	Now + 8 months
Payoff	Now + 12 months

The mean dollar amount outstanding over the 12-month period is:

Millions		Months		
10	×	12	=	$120 million
5	×	10	=	50
5	×	6	=	30
4	×	4	=	16
				$216 million
216	÷	12	=	$ 18 million

If the average rate for an $18 million loan is increased by 1 percent for a 12-month period, the builder would be exposed to an increased cost of $180,000. If 18 Treasury bill contracts were sold to hedge this exposure and yield levels increased by 1 percent, the positions would generate a $45,000 profit. The difference between the two amounts is due to the horizon, or time frame, of each transaction. The mean construction loan balance was outstanding for one year. The Treasury bill contract reflects the price change of a 90-day maturity. Therefore, it would be necessary to sell 72 (4 × 18) Treasury bill contracts if the full $180,000 was to be recovered. This strategy is risky and expensive.

Treasury bill rates could improve (decline) without a similar decrease in the prime rate. This would generate an immediate loss in the hedge position without an offset in the actual interest rate expense. This deficit could be temporary or permanent, if the prime rate was not reduced during the first 90 days. If the prime rate remained constant for the first 90 days and began its increase thereafter, no offsetting gain would be generated from the futures positions, since the protection they offered expired with the contracts.

If the developer had decided to hedge only the first 90-day exposure, 18 contracts would have been sold to guard against a rate change of 100 basis points, or 1 percent. This strategy, too, has inherent risks. If interest rates increase rapidly during this time and never return to the beginning rate level during the reamining nine months, a major portion of the increased expense would not be recovered. Selling a combination of expiration months may also be used to ease this problem.

If the business plan required a hedge protection for 200 basis points, twice the number of Treasury bill contracts would have to be sold. The number of contracts selected are generally trade-offs between the length of the horizon and the estimated change in interest rate levels.

Expenses and cash flow requirements are also affected by these decisions. Open positions require an initial margin deposit in addition to a commission charge when offset. The developer must also be prepared to meet daily maintenance margin calls with cash.

When Should Hedge Positions Be Altered?

Circumstances that will dictate a change from a partial to a fully hedged position or the removal of all positions are governed by intrinsic and extrinsic factors. Clearly, if the discount rate has been lowered for the second time in a quarter and prime has been reduced several times in the same period, the need for hedging appears slight. Conversely, if 90-day Treasury bill rates have increased by 25 basis points in each of the last three weekly government auctions, there should be a need to examine the wisdom of initiating, or increasing, a hedge position. The following basis relationships should be observed closely. A meaningful change in one number may not be sufficient to trigger action, but a simultaneous distortion in several of these ratios may activate a hedge program.

— 90-day CD rate versus prime rate.
— 90-day Treasury bill rate versus prime rate.
— 90-day CD rate versus overnight fed funds rate.
— 90-day nearby Treasury bill contract versus 90-day cash Treasury bill rate.
— 90-day nearby CD contract versus 90-day cash CD rate.
— Changes in weekly government auctions.
— Volatility of daily futures contract price changes.
— Movement in yield curve.

Summary

In summary, designing a construction loan hedge is a task requiring professional skills, economic knowledge, and the discipline to follow a plan. All areas of management, including your banker and auditors, should be aware of your program. It may be desirable to separate the hedge-planning function from your broker's responsibility since there are periods of time when no trading action may be required.

COMPOSITION OF A HEDGE BUSINESS PLAN

1. Statement of purpose.
2. Justification of a cross-hedge. Is the selected futures contract a sound hedging vehicle for the type of mortgage exposure?
3. How many contracts should be sold at current yield levels?
4. What expiration months should be sold?
5. When should these contracts be offset?
6. Is there sufficient cash available to meet margin requirements?
7. Is a partial hedge satisfactory?
8. If appropriate, are Federal Home Loan Bank Board or Comptroller regulations being met?
9. Are accounting procedures understood?
10. Is senior management informed?

EXHIBIT 12–6
GNMA 16% versus CBT GNMA December 1982 Contract

Date	GNMA 16	GNMA CDR December 82	Difference
6/1/82	100/28	60–07	40–21
7/1/82	99/19	58–18	40–01
8/1/82	104/11	62–15	41–28
9/1/82	107/16	65–08	42–08
10/1/82	110/03	67–24	42–11
11/1/82	109/06	69–27	39–11
11/22/82	107/31	69–18	38–13

IDENTIFICATION OF FUTURES CONTRACTS SUITABLE FOR HEDGING MORTGAGE COMMITMENTS

A great deal of analysis and discussion has taken place on how best to hedge the many different mortgage instruments currently issued by the industry. Traders have used both Treasury bond, notes, and GNMA CDR futures to hedge mortgage obligations. Over occasional periods, the bond contract may produce superior results. This is usually valid when yield levels have been improving rapidly and are beginning to increase again. During these periods Treasury bond futures prices tend to fall more quickly than GNMA CDR prices. On a sustained basis, the GNMA CDR contract has provided the best answer. The price behavior of this contract is based on the estimated value of the cheapest readily available GNMA mortgage-backed security. The cheapest GNMA security is usually the one with the highest coupon.

Depending on the contracts used, the extreme price volatility experienced during the second half of 1982 provides examples of satisfactory and unsatisfactory hedging results. During the first 45 days of the last quarter of 1982, Treasury bond and GNMA yields hit all time highs. In November and December of 1982, a flight from money market funds into longer maturities occurred as inflation subsided and commercial loan demand weakened. Short-term rates began to fall. Between November and December 1982, the long bond improved by nearly six points. Mortgage rate improvements lagged bonds and Treasury bills during this price correction but finally plunged, making the 16 percent GNMA an undesirable premium bond. Exhibit 12–6 and Exhibit 12–7 are vivid examples of properly and improperly designed hedge results.

During the second half of 1982, the cheapest GNMA instrument was the 16 percent GNMA mortgaged-backed security. At the same

EXHIBIT 12–7
GNMA 16% versus CBT Treasury Bond December 1982 Contract

Date	GNMA 16	Treasury Bond Futures December 1982	Difference
6/1/82	100/28	60–07	40–21
7/1/82	99/19	59–18	40–01
8/2/82	104/11	62–15	41–28
9/1/82	107/16	67–02	40–14
10/1/82	110/03	72–02	38–01
11/1/82	109/06	77–25	31–13
11/22/82	107/31	77–18	30–13

time, the cheapest Treasury bond available for delivery vacillated between the 8⅜ of 2008 and the 14 percent of 2011.

By analyzing the data in Exhibit 12–6 and Exhibit 12–7, it is apparent that a mortgage originator who sold a GNMA December 1982 contract instead of a December 1982 Treasury bond contract to hedge his production on June 1, 1982, would have obtained far better results.

The cash GNMA 16s improved 7–03 in value during the June to November period. Simultaneously, the GNMA futures contract experienced a 9–11 point improvement, and the Treasury bond futures contract increased by 17–11. Bond prices improved much more rapidly, because short-term funds began flowing into longer maturities as inflation fears subsided. This improvement lagged in mortgage-related investments due to the existence of unusually high premium-priced bonds and a lack of demand by thrist institutions. A mortgage originator who had selected the 5.0. Treasury bond contract for hedging his GNMA production would have been disappointed in the hedging results. The user of the GNMA contract would have generated a net loss of 2–08 points. Although not perfect, this magnitude of loss could have been improved by the prudent uses of stop-loss techniques and weighting the hedge. This scenario repeated itself in the spring of 1985.

COMPARISON OF FUTURES VERSUS FORWARD CONTRACTS

There are numerous similarities between forward markets found in the mortgage industry and the commodities futures markets.

The following highlights are the major contrasts between a forward contract for GNMAs or whole loans and a GNMA CDR futures contract.

1. Terms and conditions of contract.

Forward: Can be negotiated. Subject to interpretation. Can lead to "failure to perform problems." Minimum size: $1 million for competitive price.

Future: Standard provisions. No exceptions are made. Delays in performance are penalized. Minimum size: $100,000.

2. Margins.

Forward: No initial margin required unless a nonrefundable fee has been negotiated. Thereafter, no daily mark-to-market is computed in the whole loan market until delivery takes place. GNMA pass-through transactions may require a periodic mark-to-market, based on individual dealer policies.

Future: Initial margins are always required. They may be posted in cash or Treasury bills. The minimum amount per contract is designated by the clearing corporation. In addition, maintenance calls are made to reflect market price movements. These daily calls must be paid in cash. If margin balance is a credit, the surplus may be withdrawn.

3. Liquidity.

Forward: GNMA and private mortgage securities sold in forward markets can be offset by a purchase transaction or delivery of a pool with a specific coupon at any time. Offsets must be transacted with the same dealer. Some dealers will issue difference checks to satisfy an offset transaction.

Whole loan commitments cannot be reassigned. They cannot be offset during the life of the commitment.

Futures: Can be offset at any time by buying or selling a contract with the same expiration date. Cash balances in commodity accounts are then returned after deducting commissions and exchange fees.

4. Pricing.

Forward: Negotiated with a GNMA dealer or thrift institution. Quotations have two to $\frac{8}{32}$ second spreads.

Futures: Prices are displayed nationally on a real-time basis. The bid offer is normally $\frac{1}{32}$-second spread.

5. Accounting.

Forward: Mark-to-market at expiration.

Futures: Mark-to-market daily. Thrift institutions and commercial banks amortize profits and losses of those trades that are used to hedge bond and mortgage portfolios.

6. Credit.
Forward: Only as good as either party to the agreement.
Futures: Trades are guaranteed by a clearing broker and a clearing corporation.

In summary, GNMA interest rate futures transactions will not replace cash or forward trades but complement them. Their use should be triggered by relative price levels, liquidity, and timeliness. They are a temporary hedge and normally not used for delivery. These factors will be discussed in this chapter.

PRICING FUNDAMENTALS

The value of a bond in the debt market is based on the following criteria:

— **Maturity.** Remaining life of bond.
— **Credit.** The balance sheet of the issuer and/or additional guarantees.
— **Coupon.** The interest rate at par.
— **Liquidity.** Is there an active secondary market?

Once these factors have been analyzed, a security is classified by private rating agencies as an A, AA, or AAA bond. Bonds sold by the U.S. government are classified as Treasury bonds or agency bonds. GNMAs fall into the latter category. FHLMC mortgage-backed securities, often called participation certificates, are rated slightly below an agency bond since their guarantee is limited to the assets of the Federal Home Loan Mortgage Corporation. Conventional whole loans and conventional mortgage-backed bonds are more difficult to rate. Generally, their rating reflects the credit of the issuer, the quality of the loans, and the private mortgage insurance associated with a package.

Yields

There are numerous ways of expressing a yield in the mortgage industry. In this chapter, only yield to maturity (YTM) will be employed. For fixed-rate FHA/VA loans, yields are generally computed for a 30-year life and prepaid at the end of 12 years. This prepayment term is associated with a historical 100 percent FHA

EXHIBIT 12–8

GNMA Coupon (%)	Nov 25, 1983	Aug 21, 1984
8	11.65	13.25
9	11.83	13.70
11	12.13	13.66
14	13.41	13.99
16	14.53	14.57

Source: WSS.

experience factor. To increase the value of a specific GNMA pool which has experienced a rapid payoff rate during its early years, some dealers compute the price of a pool on a shorter prepayment term. This practice should be reviewed carefully by a buyer, since it increases the value of a mortgage security without any assurance that a fast payoff experience will continue. Fixed-rate conventional loans may have a shorter prepayment history since their underwriting criteria differs from insured loans. The yield to maturity on variable rate loans must be computed individually.

Currently, there are more than one dozen actively traded GNMA coupons in circulation. Based on bond mathematics, their acceptance in the marketplace is not uniform. This is reflected by their yields, as in Exhibit 12–8 on two arbitrary dates, November 25, 1983, and August 21, 1984. This is also discussed in Chap. 5. On both dates, the 16 percent coupon was priced to generate the highest yield. This yield difference is reflective of the risk associated with a premium-priced bond and the expected prepayment rate, should mortgage rates decline rapidly. In addition, it may be difficult to reinvest monthly interest payments at a rate of 16 percent for the remaining life of the pool. The following example illustrates the concept of selecting the cheapest coupon for delivery.

During November 1983, an 8 percent GNMA could be purchased in the cash market at 68–02 and a 16 percent GNMA at 105–15. Simultaneously, the December 1983 GNMA CDR contract closed at 65–05. Assuming that all transactions involved principal balances of $100,000 and that accrued interest was not computed, the following computations depict the cash flow involved in a hypothetical transaction of delivering a CDR futures contract and using 16 percent GNMAs as collateral at the depository bank.

Invoice price available at CBOT:

$$\begin{array}{c} \text{Principal} \\ \text{balance} \end{array} \times \begin{array}{c} \text{Closing} \\ \text{CDR price} \end{array}$$
$$\$100,000 \times 65.16 = \$65,160$$

Cost to purchase cheapest eligible collateral:

$$\underset{\text{balance}}{\text{Principal}} \times \underset{\text{for 16\% GNMA}}{\text{Cash price}} \times \underset{\text{factor}}{\text{CDR principal}}$$

$$\$100,000 \times \quad 105.47 \quad \times .622 = \$65,602$$

Cost to purchase eight percent GNMAs

$$\$100,000 \times 68.0625 \times 1.0 = \$68,062$$

It appears that on November 24, 1983, the futures market was not properly priced to make a CDR delivery attractive. On that day, the price of the December 1983 GNMA contract was cheap compared to cash. In conclusion, the short will generally deliver the cheapest allowable commodity only if profitable. When a contract expires, its price will most likely reflect the yield of the cheapest GNMA coupon and not the yield level of the 8 percent coupon.

BASIS BETWEEN CASH AND GNMA CDR FUTURES CONTRACTS

Critical to designing an appropriate hedge is an understanding of the term *basis*. It is used to describe the dollar difference between a price for a security in the cash market and futures contract. A basis can also be the price difference between two futures contracts with different delivery dates. If a March GNMA contract trades at 65–15 and a June GNMA at 65–10, then the price basis is a plus five. Basis can be measured in dollars or yield.

If the basis relationship between cash and a futures contract remains constant over a period of time, it has strong correlation. This is a mathematical term that measures the probability that both the cash security being hedged and the futures contract move in the same direction with similar amplitudes. Practical experience dictates that a minimum correlation measurement of 0.85 over a three-month period is desirable for successful hedging. A high coefficient of correlation is normal if the cash security being hedged is identical to the one being delivered in the futures market. Therefore, straight-life insured FHA/VA production is easier to hedge than conventional production. However, if the coefficient of correlation of any mortgage instrument and the GNMA futures contract is above 0.85 over a recent three-month period, the originator would be better advised to cross-hedge unsold production rather than closing naked loans. A shifting of the yield curve or a change in the psychology of the market can cause material changes in basis relationships between cash and futures and between future expiration months.

COMPUTATION OF HEDGING RATIOS

It has been repeatedly stated that all interest rate futures contracts trade like the cheapest readily available cash security eligible for delivery. This makes it necessary to analyze the effects of yield changes on the price of bonds with other than 8 percent coupons. In addition, it must be recognized that a 100 basis points move represents a variable percentage of increase or decrease in yield depending on the base yield level.

Exhibit 12–9 illustrates that a constant yield change produces a larger percentage of change at lower yield levels. In addition, a 100 BP yield reduction generates a greater percentage of change than an equivalent 100 BP yield increase. (See Chap. 5) This is the result of the denominator being decreased while the numerator remains constant. Since the amount of a yield change varies with yield levels and direction, it becomes evident that price changes must also be variable. Exhibit 12–10 reflects GNMA mortgage-backed security prices in 32s at various yield levels for different GNMA Coupons.

As is seen in Exhibit 12–10 the higher the coupon of a GNMA security, the greater is its exposure to a yield change in terms of dollar value. Therefore, the owner of $1 million face value 16 percent GNMAs must sell more than 10 contracts to protect the value of a portfolio in a rising interest rate market environment. The proper ratio is computed by dividing the equivalent factor for a 16 percent GNMA security into 1. The remainder will indicate

---

EXHIBIT 12–9

100 Basis Points Yield Increase	Yield Change (%)
8 to 9%	12.5
9 to 10%	11.11
10 to 11%	10.00
11 to 12%	9.09

100 Basis Points Yield Decrease	Yield Change (%)
12 to 11%	8.33
11 to 10%	9.09
10 to 9%	10.00
9 to 8%	11.11

EXHIBIT 12–10
GNMA Prices in 32s for Different Coupons

Coupons (%)	Yield Levels		Change in Price
	14%	12%	
8	66–05	75–06	9–01
12	88–05	99–16	11–11
16	110–26	124–15	13–21

how many futures contracts must be sold for every $100,000 of face value requiring protection.

A GNMA CDR futures contract can be satisfied by the delivery of any GNMA national coupon. The Chicago Board of Trade has issued constants for each coupon which must be used to calculate an invoice amount. To determine the face amount of the substitute coupon, which is equivalent to $100,000 principal of GNMA 8s, divide the constant into 1. The result will indicate how many GNMA CDR futures contracts must be sold to hedge $100,000 face value of any substitute coupon. Exhibit 12–9 is a listing of CBOT constants for current actively traded GNMA coupons.

These constants have been computed in a linear manner. Therefore, the results from their employment are not exactly the same as those generated by a yield maintenance technique. At high yield levels, the difference can be pronounced.

Factors Causing a Basis Change

Yield Curve. A shift in the yield curve is the most common reason for a basis change. The yield curve is a plot of current yield levels for Treasury securities at various maturities. It is usually described as being normal, flat, or inverted. A normal curve depicts a moment in time when short-term yields are lower than long-term yields. When this relationship is inverted, the yield curve becomes inverted. A normal and inverted yield curve is illustrated in Exhibit 12–11.

Psychology. An additional cause for a shifting yield curve is related to expectations. When yield levels are expected to go down and prices go up, investors rush to buy cash. Owning cash securities enables them to earn interest income. At such times, cash prices often advance faster than futures prices. An inverse phenomenon can be experienced in a bear market when funds are withdrawn

EXHIBIT 12–11

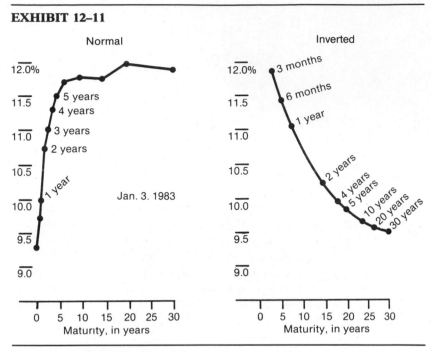

Source: Technical Data Corporation.

from investments with long maturities. Since futures contracts can be shorted with a minimum amount of dollars, they generally trade below the equivalent cash market at the outset of a bear market.

GNMA II CONTRACT OVERVIEW

To simplify and increase the efficiency of hedging GNMA securities and other mortgage-backed bonds, the CBOT began trading a new contract in early 1984, referred to as GNMA II. Its primary distinctive features are:

— Allows delivery of GNMA II certificates in addition to GNMA Is.

— Restricts allowable coupons for delivery purposes to current national coupons—in effect, when a contract expires and those issued within the six-month period prior to and including the delivery month.

— Permits physical delivery of GNMA securities. This eliminates the need for a mortgage originator to register as a "regular originator" with the CBOT.

— Has a price cap of 102.5. This will eliminate the delivery of most premium bonds and stabilize the futures contract price more closely to the cash price of a current coupon GNMA.

As of March 1985 this contract has attracted insufficient open interest to warrant consideration for use in major hedging programs.

SUMMARY

The financial futures markets began in October 1975 with the introduction of GNMA futures contracts. These contracts permitted the hedging of residential originations and standby commitments. For instance a mortgage banker may issue a forward commitment to purchase a mortgage at a future date at a specified rate. Financial futures permit the mortgage banker to hedge this commitment against an unexpected rise in rates.

Of course the decision to hedge is never simple and must be entered carefully. Forward commitments still offer an alternative to futures markets. If futures are used, decisions must be made on the appropriate contract, when the hedge should be initiated, the hedge ratio to be employed, as well as a determination of cash flow exposure. A final decision on the proper futures position to take requires an analysis of GNMA pricing fundamentals and the basis relationship between cash and GNMA CDR futures contracts. Once the anticipated yield relationship can be forecast hedge ratios can be implemented. Finally the emergence of the adjustable rate mortgage (AMR) has created a new challenge for hedging. Several studies are now being conducted on how to hedge both the liability costs associated with their acquisition and their value. It appears that the liability cost can be hedged by the use of short term contracts but little progress has been made in determining the value of the mortgage in the secondary market.

NOTE

[1] Considerable academic discussion has centered on the effect of GNMA futures on the price variability of the spotmarkets. For a discussion of opposite views see Figlewski [1981] and Simpson and Ireland [1982].

SELECTED REFERENCES

Bookstaber, Richard. "Interest Rate Hedging for the Mortgage Banker: The Effect of Interest Rate Futures and Loan Commitments on Portfolio Return Distributions." *Review of Research in Futures Markets* 1, no. 1 (1982), pp. 22–51.

Dunn, Kenneth B., and John J. McConnell. "Valuation of GNMA Mortgage-Backed Securities." *Journal of Finance.*

_____. " A Comparison of Alternative Models for Pricing GNMA Mortgage-Backed Securities." *Journal of Finance*

Figlewski, Stephen. "Futures Trading and Volatility in the GNMA Market." *Journal of Finance*, May 1981, pp. 445–56.

Froewiss, Kenneth. "GNMA Futures: Stabilizing and Destabilizing." Federal Reserve Bank of San Francisco *Economic Review*, Spring 1980, pp. 20–29.

Hill, Joanne, and Thomas Schneeweis. "The Use of Interest Rate Futures in Corporate Financing and Security Investment." *Proceedings* VII, International Futures Trading Seminar. IBJ: 1981.

Liro, Joseph, Hill, Joanne, and Thomas Schneeweis. "Hedging Performance Under Rising and Falling Interest Rates." *Journal of Futures Markets*, Winter 1983, pp. 403–44.

Simpson, W. G., and Timothy C. Ireland, "The Effect of Futures Trading on the Price Volatility of GNMA Securities." *Journal of Futures Markets*, Winter 1982, pp. 357–66.

CHAPTER 13

Applications of Futures for Corporate Finance

WORKING CAPITAL MANAGEMENT
LONG–TERM CAPITAL MANAGEMENT
INTERNATIONAL CAPITAL MANAGEMENT
CORPORATE MANAGEMENT
SUMMARY

In contrast to financial institutions such as banks, brokerage firms, and investment management firms, most corporations are not primarily engaged in the business of managing or trading financial assets. Corporations are both suppliers and borrowers of financial capital. As borrowers they issue securities to obtain funds for investments in real assets. As suppliers of financial capital they lend acquired cash balances and in return obtain financial assets. These financial assets are held until used for inventory accumulation or capital projects.

The price uncertainty associated with anticipated purchases or sales of financial assets can be partially eliminated by purchases and sales of financial futures contracts in related securities. A financial position that leaves a firm exposed to unexpected price declines in financial assets can be hedged with the sale of financial futures. The risk of unexpected price increases can be hedged with the purchase of financial futures. Corporations involved in international business operations may also choose to use currency futures markets as an alternative to the forward market to hedge their currency exposure.

Financial management has generally separated capital decisions into two areas: (1) long-term financing and (2) working capital management. Long-term financing is principally concerned with obtaining funds to purchase long-term fixed assets. Working capital management deals primarily with cash, marketable securities, receivables, and inventories. Within these two areas of capital management, financial futures provide alternatives to other available methods of risk management. In the following sections, we review the use of financial futures in working capital management as well as in long-term capital budgeting.[1]

WORKING CAPITAL MANAGEMENT

Working capital management deals with short-term sources and uses of funds such as Treasury bills, Certificates of Deposit, commercial paper, bank loans, and Eurodollar deposits. Corporations have shown a steadily increasing demand for short-term funds (Exhibit 13–1). In recent years, however, interest rates on short-term corporate funds have been volatile (see Exhibit 13–2). Financial futures provide protection against unexpected price changes in corporate short-term borrowing and investment.

For example, assume that in June a corporation decides to lock in the cost of borrowing for a prospective $10 million 90-day commercial paper sale in August. Commercial paper discount rates are currently 10 percent. As shown in Exhibit 13–3, the corpo-

EXHIBIT 13–1
Assets and Liabilities of Nonfinancial Corporations

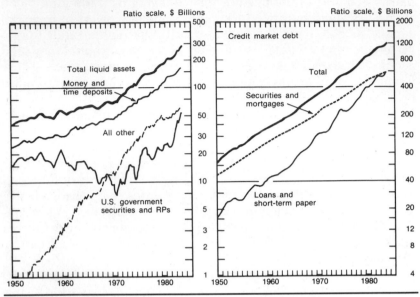

Note: Amount outstanding; End of year, 1950–51; Seasonally adjusted, end of quarter, 1952–.

Source: 1984 Historical Chart Book, Federal Reserve Board of Governors.

ration may sell 10 90-day September Treasury bill futures contracts with a maturity value of approximately 9.77 million. The discount rate on the futures contracts is 9 percent. By August interest rates have risen unexpectedly. The treasurer issues the firm's 90-day commercial paper at a discount of 10.5 percent. He or she offsets the earlier futures sale by buying $10 million in Treasury bill futures contracts, which carry a discount of 9.30 percent. The resulting profit on the hedging transaction is $7,583. If the hedge was not conducted, the cost of borrowing would have been $265,410. Since the hedge was conducted, the effective cost of borrowing was $257,827 ($265,410 less the hedge profit of $7,583). The discount was reduced from 10.5 percent to 10.2 percent. The increased cost of issuing the commercial paper was partially offset by an increase in the profit from the hedge.

In Exhibit 13–3, the discount rate on the issue is set at the time of the sale. The rate will not be readjusted during the life of the contract. A loan or a note is often written so that the interest rate is tied to a particular market rate (e.g., prime rate). If the market rate increases, the yield on the variable rate note or loan

EXHIBIT 13–2
Short-Term Interest Rates, Business Borrowing

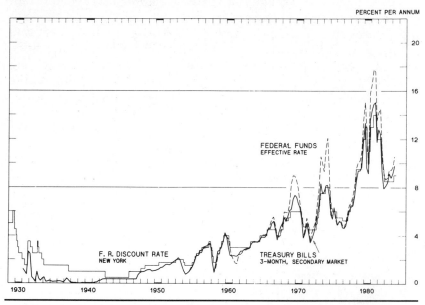

Note: Prime rate, effective date of change; commerical paper, quarterly averages.
Source: 1984 Historical Chart Book, Federal Reserve Board of Governors.

EXHIBIT 13–3

Cash Market	*Futures Market*
June 1:	
Anticipated selling of $10 million 90-day commercial paper in September (current discount 10%)	Sold 10 September Treasury bill contracts at 9% ($9,772,500)
August 1:	
Sold $10 million of commercial paper at 10.5% ($9,734,583)	Bought (offset) 10 September Treasury bill contracts at 9.30% ($9,764,917)
Interest cost: $265,417	Gain: $7,583

Effective interest cost: $257,834 (discount 10.2%)

will also increase. As shown in Chapter 3 (see Exhibit 3–5) variable rate loans or floating notes can also be hedged against changes in interest rates.[2] In hedging a variable rate loan it is important that the interest rate change has an equal dollar effect on the loan and futures contract. The dollar effect of a 1 percent interest rate change on a 90-day futures contract is $2,500 per $1 million principal, while each 1 percent increase in the cost of a one-year loan is $10,000 per $1 million. As the loan approaches maturity, the value of each 1 percent interest rate change in the 90-day futures contract remains $2,500 per million, while the dollar value of a 1 percent interest rate change on the one-year loan declines. Throughout the life of the loan, adjustments would have to be made in the number of outstanding futures contracts in order for rate changes to have equal dollar impact on the futures contracts and the loan.

Several alternatives exist to matching the dollar value change of the futures contract with the expected dollar value change in the variable rate loan. For example, the firm may sell Treasury bill futures in the nearby contract month. As the maturity of the Treasury bill contract nears, the hedge could be rolled over into the next contract month. The number of contracts rolled over each time would fall as the term of the loan decreases. Contracts could be sold throughout the hedge if a closer interest rate sensitivity is desired.

In addition to the above rollover strategy for financial futures, a firm may (1) sell a series of future contracts in consecutive contract months and offset the futures contracts as the loan approaches maturity or (2) sell futures contracts that mature after the loan matures and offset contracts as the loan ages. The best approach depends on the specification of the variable rate contract and the expected shifts in the yield curve. For instance, if the corporation sells futures contracts that mature after the loan matures, it is possible that short-term prime rate increases which affect the loan rate may not affect the value of the futures contract. Likewise, the alternative of selling futures contracts that mature during the year may also result in little correspondence between short-term rate increases affecting the loan and the futures contracts.

In addition to the use of financial futures to hedge the uncertainty of short-term capital costs, financial futures provide corporate managers a means to hedge the value of existing short-term capital investments as well as the investment rate on future short-term investments. For instance, a corporate official with short-term funds already invested faces the risk of an unexpected rise in rates (lower prices). If rates rise (prices fall) unexpectedly and one is forced to sell the securities before maturity, he or she would suffer an unexpected capital loss. If the corporate manager had sold futures contracts previous to the unexpected rise in yields (fall in prices) the gain in repurchasing the futures at lower prices would partially offset the loss on the investment.

A corporation that forecasts future excess cash receipts may guarantee a purchase price for short-term securities prior to the cash receipt through the purchase of a futures contract. The futures contract purchase fixes the return at a value close to today's existing forward rates. Upon receipt of the cash, the investment may be made and the futures position offset. The actual rate on the investment will be adjusted by the profits or losses from the futures contracts.

It is important to point out that in determining the risk exposure for short-term assets and liabilities, a decision must be made to hedge specific asset or liability positions or to reduce overall (net) exposure. The process of evaluating net interest rate exposure for corporations is similar to the gap management discussed for banks in Chapter 9. Interest-sensitive liabilities should be subtracted from interest-sensitive assets. Net exposure at any point in management's working capital cycle would be positive if there is net money to invest and negative if interest-sensitive liabilities exceed interest-sensitive assets. For positive gaps a fall in interest rates would lower working capital profits.

In order to hedge net positive exposure, the corporation would purchase a financial future. A long future position would profit from an unexpected fall in rates. For a negative gap a rise in interest rates would reduce a firm's working capital profit. In order to hedge net negative exposure, the corporation would sell a financial future. A short futures position would profit from an unexpected rise in rates.

The corporation should be careful to insure that the estimated loss from a change in interest rates is correlated with the price movement on the futures contracts. If the net exposure is due to a mix of short-term assets, a direct hedge is not possible. The corporate manager should also be aware that a firm's cash flows may contain seasonal net exposure patterns. A company may have a positive exposure at some periods and negative exposure at other periods. Futures positions therefore should also be seasonal. In addition, the anticipated net exposure is often merely an estimate rather than an exact measure. A hedged position placed to reduce overall exposure may result in increasing net exposure if expected investments or borrowings do not occur.

LONG-TERM CAPITAL MANAGEMENT

In the previous sections, financial futures were shown to offer opportunities to hedge the risk of unexpected interest rate changes in working capital management. Futures can also be useful in managing the risks of long-term funds. Long-term debt and equity issues provide a large portion of corporate net funds requirements. The principal risk in corporate financing is that debt and equity prices will fall unexpectedly before the security issue can be sold. By selling futures contracts, a firm could hedge against a decline in stock or bond prices associated with changes in overall economic conditions. Assume that on March 1, a firm decides to hedge a planned corporate $10 million bond issue (see Exhibit 13–4). At present interest rates on a seven-year corporate bond are 12 percent. Earlier the firm had posted the necessary registration material (under Rule 415).[3] The firm was ready to enter the market as conditions permitted.[4] The firm sold 100 June Treasury note futures contracts at a yield of 10.4% to hedge against a rise in rates. Soon after, rates began to rise unexpectedly. Fearful of further rate rises the firm decides on April 1 to issue the securities. Over the 30-day period interest rates on corporate notes have risen to 12 percent. Yields on Treasury note futures also rose to 11.01%. The gain from closing out the futures position held the cost of the new debt issue to under 11 percent.

Stock index futures offer similar protection against unanticipated equity price changes.[5] Corporations planning a stock issue may reduce risk of loss in equity value by selling equity futures contracts. If equity prices fall before the issue is sold, the losses on the stock issue are reduced by repurchasing the futures at a lower price. The number of futures contracts purchased depends on the sensitivity of the security's returns to those of the index used as a base for the futures contract (see Chapter 7).

EXHIBIT 13–4

Cash Market	*Futures Market**
March 1:	
Decides to issue $10 million in 7-year corporate notes. (Current yield: 11%)	Sells 100 June Treasury note futures contracts at 86.60 ($8,660,000) (Yield 10.84)
April 1:	
Issues $10 million 7-year corporate notes at par at a yield of 12.0%.	Buys 100 June Treasury note contracts at 81.07 ($8,107,000) (Yield 11.01%)
Increase in interest cost $100,000 in each of 7 years; present value $456,375	Gain $553,000

* Yield equivalents are based on 8% 10-year Treasury notes.

In hedging new stock issues it is important to be familiar with the effectiveness of the alternative stock index futures. For some firms the S&P 500 futures contract offers the best correlation between changes in the value of the futures contract and a firm's unexpected equity price change. Depending on market correlations, futures contracts based on the NYSE, Value Line Index or the MMI may be more appropriate hedging vehicles. For instance, for large firms whose price movements are highly correlated with the Dow Jones Index, the MMI futures contract may offer the best potential hedge.

There is no guarantee for either stocks or bonds that the cash market gain or loss will be exactly offset by the futures trade. Hedging will not insure against losses or assure gains.[6] For hedging corporate bond and stock issues, a cross-hedge is required and substantial basis risk is present. The degree of basis risk depends on the firm. Hedge ratios are more stable for firms that have eliminated much of the unsystematic price movement associated with basis risk. For instance, compared to Baa-rated corporate bonds, the price movement of Aa-rated corporate bonds is more highly correlated with the price movement of U.S. Treasury bonds (see Hill and Schneeweis (1982)). Likewise well-diversified firms whose equity price movement is highly correlated with stock index price movements may be easily hedged. In contrast, equity issues for small, undiversified firms may show instability in their basis relationships with stock index futures (see Figlewski (1984)).

Basis risk may be especially high for security issues that are hybrid bond/stock issues. For instance, as convertible bonds reach their conversion value, their prices will behave like an equity security. When convertible bonds are near their floor value, their prices will react similarly to a firm's long-term bonds. Likewise, preferred stock may normally react to information as if it were a bond. When dividend payment is in doubt, however, the price of preferred stock may not follow the pricing patterns of a corporation's bonds.

To the degree that financial futures offset unexpected changes in a firm's cost of debt or equity, financial futures may provide a hedge against a corporation's error in estimating the firm's cost of capital. If the cost of capital can be estimated with greater certainty, a manager may be more willing to enlarge the firm's capital budget. To the extent that futures reduce variability in earnings, investors can reduce the necessary risk premium on a firm's cost of capital. Financial futures may therefore be instrumental in reducing a firm's cost of capital.[9]

INTERNATIONAL CAPITAL MANAGEMENT

Corporations invest and borrow funds in foreign capital markets as well as U.S. capital markets. Foreign funds are available both in U.S. dollars (Eurodollars and Eurobonds) and foreign currencies. Foreign banks do not face many of the restrictions imposed on financial institutions in the United States. As a result, foreign banks can offer higher returns on U.S. dollar deposits and lower rates on U.S. dollar denominated loans. The higher yields on investment and lower yields on loans have resulted in corporations' increased use of the Eurodollar and Eurobond markets. Since 1980 new issue volume of Eurodollar floating rate notes alone has increased from 3 billion to over 10 billion (see Exhibit 13–5). Eurodollar futures can be used to hedge short-term rates of return and cost of funds in the Eurodollar market.

Consider a corporation that has a $10 million floating rate loan based on the three-month LIBOR rate. Eurodollar futures could be used to hedge the risk that the LIBOR rate may rise over the anticipated one-year length of the loan. The dollar effect of a 1 percent change in the LIBOR rate is four times greater on the one-year floating rate note than on the three-month Eurodollar rate. A corporation with a 1 year $10 million floating rate note may therefore initially sell $40 million in three month Eurodollar futures contracts. As the maturity of the loan decreases, the Eurodollar contracts would be repurchased to keep the relative dollar effect of yield changes similar.

Just as Eurodollar futures contracts can be used to hedge interest rates in the U.S. market, U.S. Treasury bond futures contracts can be used to hedge the value of Eurobond investment and the yield on new Eurobond issues.[7] Eurobond issues have become increasingly popular as a financing mechanism for multinational corporations. However, caution is advised for any Eurodollar or Eurobond cross-hedge. The corporate manager must be aware of

---

EXHIBIT 13–5
New Issue Volume of Eurodollar Floating Rate Notes

	Number of Issues	Dollar Amount
1980	45	$ 2,970,000,000
1981	84	$ 6,380,000,000
1982	90	$11,490,000,000
1983 (through October)	46	$10,150,000,000

the possibility of basis risk. Several studies have shown that Euro-dollar and Eurobonds may have weak correlation with the U.S. Treasury bill or Treasury bond yields.[8]

Even though dollar-denominated foreign assets are an important part of international investment, international investment and trade often occur in foreign currencies. In recent years foreign exchange rates have fluctuated widely (see Exhibit 13–6). Currency futures provide the corporate officer with another vehicle to reduce the risk of changes in exchange rates on foreign investment or interest costs on foreign borrowings.[10] As shown in Exhibit 13–7 an exporter selling a good to a German customer in March but not expecting delivery (payment) until April may wish to sell a June Deutschmark futures contract. If the value of the D mark falls in the interim, the loss in the spot market would be balanced by a gain in the futures. It is important to note that opposite price movements would result in similar final values. A fall in exchange rates would result in spot gains but losses in the futures market. A rise in foreign currency values would result in a gain in the spot market but a loss in the futures.

EXHIBIT 13–6
Spot Exchange Rate Indexes (dollar and weighted-average prices)

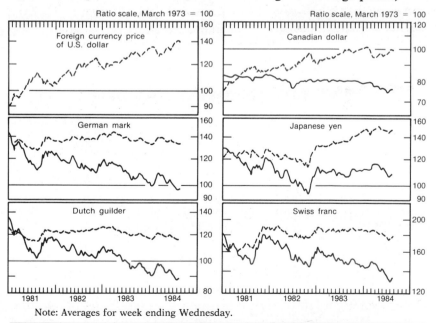

Note: Averages for week ending Wednesday.

Source: *1984 Historical Chart Book,* Federal Reserve Board of Governors.

EXHIBIT 13-7

Cash Market	*Futures Market*
March 1:	
Have commitment to receive in June $5 million in D marks at an exchange rate .35 (14.28 million D marks)	Sell 100 June D mark futures (contract size 125,000 D marks) at .33 ($4,125,000)
April 1:	
Receives D marks and converts to dollars at .34 ($4,855,200)	Buy 100 June D mark futures at a price of .32 ($4,000,000)
Loss: $144,800	Gain: $125,000

CORPORATE MANAGEMENT

This chapter has dealt primarily with the applications of financial futures in corporate management. Corporations should be also aware of the applications for the commodity futures markets in corporate risk management. For instance, a firm may wish to use financial futures to hedge the risk of a rate increase on an anticipated inventory loan. At the same time, a commodity futures contract could be used to hedge the risk of an unexpected increase in price of the inventory to be purchased.

Financial and commodity futures can both affect a firm's growth and production (see Holtausen (1979)). Firm investment decisions are based primarily on expected cash flows and cost of capital. Financial and commodity futures provide corporate managers with a futures market forecast of expected prices. These forecasts enable managers to estimate future firm earnings and costs with greater confidence. Financial research has also established a link between reduced variability in firm earnings and a lower required return by investors.[10] Commodity futures reduce the risk of unexpected changes in real asset costs as well as insuring adequate real asset returns. Financial futures reduce the risk of unexpected changes on financial asset return and cost. Financial and commodity futures can lower the variabilty in a firm's revenue and capital costs.

The use of futures to reduce the risk of unexpected price changes must be viewed in context of the overall exposure of the firm. Management must decide if hedging is to be conducted on a project or on a net exposure basis. An analysis of net exposure requires a highly integrated information, control, and accounting system. Management must establish a hedging plan as well as a means to evaluate its effect on corporate profits. It is not necessary that a firm follow a hedging policy that calls for systematically taking futures positions opposite to a net exposed position or an open position in a single asset. Recent studies have suggested that firm decisions are affected by management policy and hedging costs.[11] For instance, the cost of hedging (e.g., opportunity cost on holding variation margins) must be less than the expected hedging profit. The transaction costs of hedging will also affect how often a hedge is revised. In addition, management may not act to maximize shareholder wealth but to increase their own personal welfare. A corporation's success with financial futures can depend on whether the managers' or stockholders' wealth position is of greater corporate concern.

SUMMARY

Financial management has generally divided the responsibility of capital decisions of the corporate and municipal manager into long-term financing and working capital management. In the area of working capital management, financial futures markets have been shown to be of use in (1) hedging the rise of rates on the issuance of short-term commercial paper and (2) locking in yields on anticipated cash flows as well as on existing investments. Financial and equity futures also permit the corporation to hedge the cost of issuance for long-term debt, preferred stock, and common stock. In addition to the cost of capital and security return, the financial futures markets, in tandem with the foreign currency markets, also permit corporate officials to hedge the exposure of these foreign earnings, interest rates, and asset values against unexpected price changes.

There is, of course, no guarantee that the cash market loss will be offset by a gain in the futures markets. Over repeated business cycle financings, however, the use of futures to hedge portfolio values and new financings should reduce the variability in portfolio return as well as the cost of capital.

NOTES

[1] The hedging applications described in this chapter for corporations can also be applied to municipalities. If successful, the Chicago Board of Trade's introduction of a municipal bond futures contract in 1985 will even further enhance the use of financial futures in municipal capital management.

[2] The principle of purchasing an outstanding amount of futures contracts and reducing the positions relative to the interest rate exposure on a variable rate loan has other uses. In addition to variable loans based on the prime rate, loans have been indexed to inflation and other variables (e.g., business indexes). Since the

bill futures may also be used to hedge the risk of inflation indexed loans. Before the use of Treasury bill futures to hedge such loans, however, the relative yield effect should be considered.

[3] The introduction of shelf registration has made it easier for individual firms to sell securities. This increased flexibility in sales, however, has also introduced a new source of volatility into markets. Old benchmarks, such as corporate supply and stock calendars, are less useful. Futures enable firms to hedge the risk of rapid price changes following their decision to enter the market.

[4] Eligible firms have more than $150 million in stock held by investors unaffiliated with the company. For more details about shelf registration, see Kidwell, Marr, and Thompson (1984).

[5] A firm can also hedge debt securities with options on Treasury bond futures and options on Treasury bonds, though the latter trade in a very thin market. A firm can hedge equity securities with stock index futures, options on stock index futures, stock index options, or options on the equity itself if such options are listed.

[6] Financial futures, however, are not the only tool to reduce the risk of unexpected price changes on the sources and uses of funds; other techniques are also available. Duration techniques discussed in Chapter 7 have been used to fix expected return on financial asset investments. Interest rate swaps have been another popular means of reducing interest rate exposure. An interest rate swap is normally executed through a market maker or a broker. The parties sign a legal contract which dictates the exchange of cash flows at a future date. Simply put, two parties exchange payment schedules which better fit their particular cash flow requirements. The swap is not tied legally to the assets or liabilities of either firm, and normally no principal is exchanged. If one side defaults the other simply stops its own payment schedule. Unlike financial futures little management is required on interest rate swaps. There are no worries over marking-to-market. In addition, swaps can often be conducted for longer periods than those available in the futures markets. Swaps and similar diversification strategies have the additional benefit of structurally changing the asset liability structure of the firm. Swaps, however, are not without their problems. No central marketplace exists for the trading of swap commitments. Equally as important no central clearinghouse exists to guarantee the payment of contracted debt.

[7] Just as interest rate futures are not the only means of managing corporate interest rate risk (e.g., interest rate swaps), currency futures are not the only means of hedging currency risks. For instance, currency swaps between firms can be conducted. A firm may diversify across various currencies and thereby reduce the risk of any one currency moving unexpectedly. Contract forms could be established to take into account the risk of unexpected changes in currency value. Forward contracts can be made in the interbank markets. Financial futures, however, do offer the convenience of an open auction market place. The preferred means of managing exchange risk is therefore dependent on the particular circumstances surrounding the business operation and the firm's familiarity with the particular currency risk reduction method.

[8] See Finnerty, Hegde, and Schneeweis (1980) and Finnerty and Schneeweis (1981) for relationships among U.S., Eurodollar, and Eurobond rates.

[9] See Kolb, Morin, Gay (1983) for an expanded discussion of the possible effects of financial futures on reducing a firm's cost of capital. They also discuss

the use of financial futures to reduce the negative impact of regulatory lag on a public utility's revenue stream.

[10] Earnings volatility has been found to be strongly related to a firm's cost of capital, see Kolb, Morin, and Gay (1983). For an expanded discussion of the use of financial futures and foreign exchange rate futures to hedge foreign interest rates, see Kolb (1982).

[11] Stulz (1984) and Howard and D'Antonio (1984) both review alternative hedging strategies that call for an active management of futures position.

SELECTED REFERENCES

Dale, C. "The Hedging Effectiveness of Currency Futures Markets." *Journal of Futures Markets*, Spring 1981, pp. 77–88.

Ederington, L. H. "The Hedging Performance of the New Futures Market." *Journal of Finance*, March 1979, pp. 157–70.

Finnerty, J., and T. Schneeweis. "Structure of Eurodollar Interest Rates." *Nebraska Journal of Economics and Business*, Autumn 1981, pp. 51–62.

Finnerty J., S. Hedge, and T. Schneeweis. "Interest Rates in the Eurobond Market." *Journal of Financial and Quantitative Analysis*, September 1980, pp. 743–56.

Hill, J., and T. Schneeweis. "The Hedging Effectiveness of Foreign Currency Futures." *Journal of Financial Research*, Spring 1982, pp. 95–104.

Hill, J., and T. Schneeweis. "International Multi-Asset Diversification" French Finance Association, INSEAD, 1985.

Hill, J., and T. Schneeweis, "Risk Reduction Potential of Financial Futures for Corporate Bond Positions." In *Interest Rate Futures: Concepts and Issues*, eds. G. D. Gay and R. W. Kolb. Richmond, Va: Dame, 1982.

Holtausen, D. A. "Hedging and the Competitive Firm Under Price Uncertainty," *American Economic Review*, December 1979, pp. 989–95.

Howard, C. T., and L. J. D'Antonio. "A Risk-Return Measure of Hedging Effectiveness." *Journal of Financial and Quantitative Analysis*, March 1984, pp. 101–12.

Kidwell, D. S., M. W. Marr, and G. R. Thompson. "SEC Rule 415—The Ultimate Competitive Bid." *Journal of Financial and Quantitative Analysis*, June 1984, pp. 183–96.

Kolb, R. W. *Interest Rate Futures*. Richmond, Va.: Dame, 1982.

Kolb, R. W., Roger A. Morin, and Gerald Gay. "Regulation, Regulatory Lag, and the Use of Futures Markets," *Journal of Finance*, May 1983, pp. 405–18.

Kolb, R. W., and R. Chiang. "Improving Hedging Performance Using Interest Rate Futures." *Financial Management*, Autumn 1981, pp. 72–74.

McCabe, G. M., and C. T. Franckle. "The Effectiveness of Rolling the Hedge Forward in the Treasury Bill Futures," *Financial Management*, Summer 1983, pp. 21–29.

McEnally, R. W., and M. L. Rice. "Hedging Possibilities in the Flotation of Debt Securities." *Financial Management*, Winter 1979, pp. 12–18.

Stulz, R. "Optimal Hedging Policies," *Journal of Financial and Quantitative Analysis*, June 1984, pp. 127–140.

Arbitrage and Speculative Strategies

The primary motive for an arbitrageur is profit. Trades are made based on observations and expectations. The observations attempt to identify apparent temporary value discrepancies between two like, or somewhat alike, instruments. Graphs and mathematical routines are used to recognize price abnormalities. The expectation of a trader is enhanced by historical data, a grasp of the supply and demand for particular issues, and an educated guesstimate of future interest rate levels. The latter is improved through an understanding of the alternatives available to the Open Market Committee of the Federal Reserve Board, a knowledge of economics and current events. Finally, an appreciation of the impact on pricing, caused by a change in the shape of a yield curve, is imperative.

The oldest form of arbitrage or spreading is trading cash bonds against similar cash bonds. The only difference between these bonds may be the coupon or maturity dates. Other common arbitrage transactions occur between cash and futures contracts, or futures contracts versus other futures contracts. The latter may be between intermarket contracts or intramarket contracts. Intramarket trades occur when one expiration month is purchased and a different month is sold in identical quantities within the same futures contract. Intermarket transactions are usually made between two futures contracts that have similar price behavior. Buying the NYFE Composite Stock Index futures contract and selling the S&P 500 contract is illustrative of this technique. The number of contracts purchased or sold and the expiration months of these contracts may or may not be the same. Intramarket arbitrage trades are the most popular since the price difference between expiration months of financial futures contracts are normally related to short-term interest rate movements.

INTERMARKET TRADING

A common intermarket trade is the U.S. Treasury bond futures versus GNMA CDR futures transaction. Both futures contracts represent instruments with an 8 percent coupon and $100,000 face value. However, the respective maturities and credit of the underlying collateral differ. In addition, the computation of the cheapest deliverable instrument at a future time is uncertain for both the GNMA and the U.S. Treasury bond contract. The GNMA security that will be delivered at a future date will depend on the FHA rate in existence when a contract expires. The cheapest deliverable bond will depend in part on Treasury financing requirements that may have occurred between the time a position was opened and the time the contract expires. This phenomenon is associated with quarterly government auctions which are used to refinance maturing debt and to raise new funds. If such an auction is scheduled at a time when yield levels for 20-year bonds are unlike the coupon of a current bond issue, the government will issue a new coupon which is reflective of current market conditions. This will enable the Treasury to sell the instrument at a price close to par. These variables make it difficult to forecast which bonds will be available for delivery at future delivery dates.

EXHIBIT 14–1
The Growth of Government Security Trading

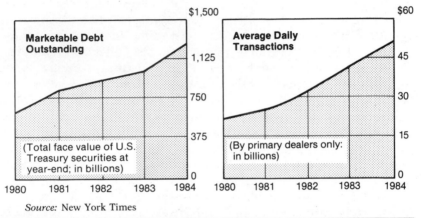

Source: New York Times

Another popular trade is between the 90-day Treasury bill and 90-day CD futures contract. Their relationships vary with private loan demand, prime rate levels, and the immediate desire for investment safety by the public. The 90-day Eurodollar futures contract can also be used as a speculative arbitrage trading vehicle.

Arbitrage is also common in stock index futures markets. Most trading occurs between the S&P 500 Index and the NYFE Index. The positions must be weighted since the dollar values of each contract differ.

INTRAMARKET POSITION

Buying and simultaneously selling different delivery months of one futures contract is the simplest and least risky speculative trade. This trade is called spreading. Delivery months of the same contract generally exhibit similar direction in price changes, but their magnitude often differs. In financial futures, this anomaly is primarily related to yield curve expectations. If the financing cost of a security temporarily exceeds the income that can be earned by owning the security, the future value of the security will reflect this financing loss. This occurs when the yield curve is inverted. During these periods futures contracts for bonds and notes expiring in six months will generally trade at a higher price than the nearby contract. This reflects a negative carry. This price relationship will change rapidly if the yield curve begins to shift, and a negative carry becomes a positive carry. (See Chap 7.) The front month will then be priced higher than the back month. This is the more common relationship.

When trading stock index contracts, a spreader must also be aware of dividend changes in addition to short-term financing costs. Stock splits and new equity capital may affect a contract price if the index is weighted to reflect such activity.

TRADING TECHNIQUES

Every "arb," as traders who specialize in trading spreads are commonly called, has a unique technique for recognizing money-making opportunities. Some arbitrageurs use standard deviations, correlations, and regression analysis. Other traders develop probability models in addition to their mathematical algorithms. Many traders merely depend on intuition or their interpretation of current events. No system is foolproof. Judgment on the value of these methods must be reserved until a system has proven itself over a sustained period of time. The mean, standard deviation, and other time series statistics change rapidly in volatile business climates. If a model is not sensitive to changes, yesterday's success will become tomorrow's disaster. Case studies in this chapter illustrate some successes and failures.

Positions are opened when a price or yield basis appears abnormal. In stock indexes, the term *basis* is synonymous with premiums. The basis or premium can be plus or minus. When a trader is ready to implement a position, thought must be given to the number of contracts that should be bought and sold. Frequently, these are not the same. The face value of one contract may be larger than the face value of the other contract. This is illustrated with the S&P 500 and NYFE Composite futures contracts. A second reason for varying the number of contracts is the ".01 effect." It measures the change in the dollar value of a security or contract if its yield level is altered by .01 percent. As an example of this concept, the 90-day Treasury bill contract traded on the IMM will have a $25 change in value for each basis point move. The face value of this contract is $1,000,000. The U.S. bond contract traded on the CBOT will vary by $31.25, or $\frac{1}{32}$, for approximately a one-third (0.0038) basis point change in the yield level of a $100,000, 8 percent U.S. Treasury bond.

When a trader decides to initialize an arbitrage position, speed is important. A small change in price levels on either side of the contemplated trade may make the exercise unprofitable. Generally, the more difficult leg of the spread is •ransacted first. It is usually the contract with the least liquidity. Confirmation must be received accurately and rapidly in order for the second leg to be positioned. If the trader is not on the floor of an exchange, direct telephone lines to the floor are a necessity. When a spread position is unwound, the least liquid position is lifted first. If trading positions are large, the arbitrageur may choose to lift a position in increments in order to avoid upsetting existing price levels.

RISKS

Even after careful analysis, spread or speculative positions contain risk. Normal relationships may be altered by numerous events. The most common factors causing unexpected changes are related to yield levels and shifts in the yield curve. In addition, the liquidity of the cash market can temporarily be affected by government auctions, unforeseen sizable purchases of specific issues, rapid FHA rate changes, and numerous other governmental actions. International monetary crises or a prominent corporate failure can also temporarily upset existing basis relationships. Although many of these obstacles have only a momentary effect on a position, they could require large lines of credit to sustain a short-term negative cash flow, as futures positions are marked to the market. If credit lines cannot be obtained, the trade must be closed out with a loss.

COSTS OF SPREADING

Every time a trade is executed, two transactions take place. One side is purchased and the other sold. Both sides must be reversed at a later date. When a cash instrument is traded, it is usually bought on the offered side and sold on the bid side of the market. The spread between these quotations is earned by a dealer. For active Treasury bond issues, this might be $\frac{1}{32}$ or $\frac{1}{16}$. For less liquid sectors like GNMA pass-through securities, the bid-ask spread may be ¼ point. A quarter of a point on a million dollar trade is equal to $2,500. When a bond futures contract is traded, the spread between the bid and offered side is normally $\frac{1}{32}$ or $312.50 per million. In addition, the futures broker will charge a commission when the position is closed. Commission rates are dependent on trading volume and credit of the customer. They may vary from $10 to $100 per round turn. To absorb these expenses, a trader must be knowledgable and quick to limit losses. A break-even trade would not be enough to generate a profit, since commissions must be absorbed.

Most trading departments are limited in their exposure to losses by restricted lines of credit or open trading positions. Each trader may be assigned dollar limits for purposes of maintenance margin calls. When these are exceeded, trading positions must be reduced or closed out. Since the risk-and-profit potential of spread trades is usually less than that associated with outright positions, their impact on credit lines must be constantly evaluated.

A second restriction used by some trading departments limits a trader in the number of gross or net positions that may be open at any time. When positions limits are reached, no further opening trades are permitted. These controls may restrict a trader from capitalizing on new opportunities.

When a cash position is one side of a strategy, the cost to finance this position must be evaluated. Professional trading desks can finance 95 percent or more of a Treasury bond or bill position. Should this cost increase abruptly, trading profits will quickly disappear. This will occur if cash positions are financed using overnight repos instead of term loans.

ARBITRAGE—SPREAD CASE STUDIES

The following historical case studies are presented to illustrate the success and failure of classic arbitrage or spread trades. The data are real and represent daily closing prices or yields. The format used will preface the statistics with the assumptions that were made before a trade was initialized. In addition, the mathematical and economic representations that were available to the trader are shown. Standard deviations were employed to evaluate trading opportunities. The case studies were selected for contents and the time the transactions took place. The author is desireous to provide the reader with an insight into price behaviors during volatile periods. Trade dates are identified with sequential numbers on accompanying tables.

U.S. Treasury Bond Futures versus GNMA CDR Futures Spread

Given. On October 7, 1982, an analysis of the Treasury bond versus GNMA futures spread was conducted by the arbitrage desk of the Stratton National Bank. The following economic environment prevailed:

— The U.S. Treasury will run a unified budget deficit of $60 billion during the first quarter of 1983. This represents an all-time high.

— For the fourth quarter of 1982, the U.S. Treasury projected a reduction of income of $5 billion below the same period in 1981, a decline of 3 percent.

— Total employment, hours worked, and overtime was dropping rapidly on a nationwide basis.

— Corporate income was down from the last quarter. Private loan demand was slackening.

— Federal expenditures are up 11.3 percent over the comparable period last year.

— U.S. Treasury's fourth quarter marketable debt requirement is estimated to be $45 billion, of which $10 billion is new money.

— Weekly auctions to average $11.8 billion.

— Treasury yield curve on October 7, 1982 (bond equivalent).

1-year	2-year	5-year	10-year	20-year
10.4%	11.47%	12.87%	12.07%	11.69%

— Other data:

Fed funds	10.12%
Discount rate	10%
Prime rate	13.5%
Current FHA rate	13.5% (changed last on September 24, 1983)

— Price spread distribution (in decimals) between the nearby Treasury bond and GNMA futures contracts for past 91 days from June 1, 1982 to October 3, 1982:

Min	Max	Mean	Std. Dev.
−0.72	5.53	1.33	1.25

Assumptions. Based on this information it was assumed that inflation would continue at a lower rate, prime rates and money market rates would be under downward pressure, and the FHA

EXHIBIT 14–2
Supporting Data: Bond Futures versus GNMA Futures

```
1) BILL:DATE
2) TBONDF:BTBD1    CBOT FIRST TBOND CONTRACT
3) GNMA:BGNI1      CBOT FIRST GNMA CONTRACT (CDR)
4) SPREAD2    BTBD1-BGNI1
```

Seq #	DATE	BTBD1	BGNI1	SPREAD2
1737	1013.82	78.09	69.28	8.81
1738	1014.82	76.97	68.16	8.81
1739	1015.82	76.16	67.50	8.66
1740	1018.82	77.28	68.13	9.16
1741	1019.82	77.53	68.63	8.91
1742	1020.82	77.09	68.22	8.88
1743	1021.82	77.13	68.97	8.16
1744	1022.82	76.34	69.59	6.75
1745	1025.82	74.66	68.41	6.25
1746	1026.82	75.25	68.50	6.75
1747	1027.82	74.81	67.72	7.09
1748	1028.82	75.53	68.34	7.19
1749	1029.82	76.53	69.25	7.28
1750	1101.82	77.78	69.84	7.94
1751	1103.82	78.59	70.28	8.31
1752	1104.82	79.09	70.41	8.69
1753	1105.82	78.44	70.06	8.38
1754	1108.82	78.00	69.78	8.22
1755	1109.82	77.97	69.69	8.28
1756	1110.82	78.03	69.72	8.31
1757	1112.82	77.56	70.25	7.31
1758	1115.82	77.06	69.78	7.28
1759	1116.82	76.31	68.78	7.53
1760	1117.82	77.03	68.94	8.09
1761	1118.82	78.19	69.84	8.34
1762	1119.82	78.19	69.88	8.31
1763	1122.82	77.56	69.56	8.00
1764	1123.82	77.16	68.94	8.22
1765	1124.82	77.00	68.59	8.41
1766	1126.82	76.75	68.13	8.63
1767	1129.82	75.09	67.25	7.84
1768	1130.82	75.41	67.41	8.00
1769	1201.82	75.69	67.41	8.28
1770	1202.82	75.91	67.66	8.25
1771	1203.82	77.22	68.38	8.84
1772	1206.82	77.41	68.41	9.00
1773	1207.82	77.16	68.47	8.69
1774	1208.82	76.31	67.97	8.34
1775	1209.82	76.50	68.38	8.13
1776	1210.82	75.44	67.50	7.94
1777	1213.82	76.00	68.00	8.00
1778	1214.82	76.78	68.72	8.06
1779	1215.82	76.41	68.59	7.81
1780	1216.82	75.66	68.09	7.56
1781	1217.82	75.94	67.94	8.00
1782	1220.82	75.63	67.78	7.84
1783	1221.82	76.06	67.81	8.25
1784	1222.82	75.78	67.66	8.13
1785	1223.82	76.28	68.28	8.00
1786	1227.82	77.13	68.97	8.16

Source: Street Software Technology, Inc.

rate would decline. Since the 10-year maturity was cheap on the yield curve, GNMA prices might begin to improve more rapidly than those of 20-year bonds. On October 13, 1982 (day 1737), the Treasury bond versus GNMA spread jumped to 8.81 or $8^{27}/_{32}$. This was greater than any recent observation and outside of two standard deviations. The trading desk sold 100 December 1982 Treasury bond futures contracts at $78^{03}/_{32}$ and bought 100 GNMA December 1982 futures contracts at $69^{9}/_{32}$. The spread was $+8^{26}/_{32}$. Trading policy established a maximum downside loss of two points, or $200,000, for these positions. (See Exhibit 14–2).

Result. The position was closed out on December 20, 1982 (day 1782) at a spread of $7^{26}/_{32}$ or a gross profit of $100,000. During the past 46-day period, the positions were exposed to a maximum loss of $31,250. This occurred on October 18, 1982 (day 1740). The direct costs associated with this trade were:

Futures commissions   = $ 2,500
Initial margin requirement = $40,000

The initial margins were $400 per spread position. The initial margin would have been increased to $200,000 if only one side of the trade had been futures contracts. On most commodity exchanges, initial margins can be met by using Treasury bills or cash.

Cash versus Futures Arbitrage

Given. On March 14, 1983, the basis trader for the Westport Security Corporation reviewed the following available economic information:

— Unemployment at 10.3 percent.
— Housing industry still struggling to reach 1.6 million starts per year.
— Short-term private sector loan demand down at money center banks.
— Annualized inflation running at 5 percent.
— Inventory/sales ratio near all-time high of 1.75.
— Nonborrowed reserves above $40 billion.
— The Conference Board's Consumer Confidence Index increased seven points in February.
— Industrial production rose by 0.3 in February. This was below expectations.
— M–1 money supply growing at annual rate of 10 percent.

— Heavy Treasury borrowing predicted for April/June 1983 quarter.

— Treasury yield curve on March 14, 1983 (bond equivalent):

1-year	2-year	7-year	30-year
9.26%	9.64%	10.42%	10.00%

— Prime rate = 8.50%.
— Fed funds = 8.75%.
— Price spread distribution between the 10⅜ percent of '12 and the nearby Treasury bond futures contract based on the most recent 48 days (in decimals).

Min	Max	Mean	Std. Dev.
20.66	22.41	21.43	.50

The following is an explanation of the calculations involved used to compute spreads: If the price for the offered side of the 10⅜ percent of '12 is 97.25 or $97^{08}/_{32}$, and the March 1983 futures bond contract is trading at $76^{08}/_{32}$, then the spread is 21–00. This Treasury bond was issued during the February '83 refunding cycle.

The cash price of the 10⅜ percent of '12 could have been divided by 1.2517 to reduce this spread to a smaller number. This constant would have been used for invoicing purposes by the CBOT should the 10⅜ percent of '12 have been delivered to satisfy a March 1983 Treasury bond futures short position. This did not occur since at the time the 14 percent of 11/11 were the cheapest bonds for delivery purposes.

Assumptions. Both long- and short-term rates will continue to improve during the next 30 days. The security company was offered $10 million 10⅜ percent of 11/12 at 97–00 on March 17, 1983. This was $\frac{7}{32}$ below other offers available at that moment. Their yield to maturity was 10.71 percent. The offering was good for five minutes. The March 1983 bond futures contract was trading at 76–10. The trader hits the offer and buys the bonds. The trader knows that if necessary the position could be hedged with bond futures since on March 17, 1983 that spread relationship was within a normal range. The maximum permissible loss for this trading position was one point or $100,000.

One hundred percent of the bond position will be financed using overnight repos. Currently, they are trading at 8.9 percent.

Results. The bonds were sold on April 14, 1983 (day 1862), at par. The trading ledger for this transaction follows:

EXHIBIT 14–3
Supporting Data: Cash versus Bond Futures

SPR1

Date Range: Obs.   1794 - 1841

	N	MIN	MAX	MEAN	VARIANCE	SDEV
ALL	48	20.66	22.41	21.43	0.25326E+00	0.50

1844	318.83	97.16	76.25	20.91
1845	321.83	97.03	76.28	20.75
1846	322.83	97.03	76.06	20.97
1847	323.83	97.78	76.50	21.28
1848	324.83	97.78	76.47	21.31
1849	325.83	97.03	75.75	21.28
1850	328.83	97.16	75.84	21.31
1851	329.83	97.63	76.25	21.38
1852	330.83	97.56	76.25	21.31
1853	331.83	97.22	75.97	21.25
1854	404.83	97.41	76.22	21.19
1855	405.83	98.44	77.22	21.22
1856	406.83	98.69	77.31	21.38
1857	407.83	98.31	77.13	21.19
1858	408.83	98.28	77.00	21.28
1859	411.83	99.25	77.81	21.44
1860	412.83	99.22	77.63	21.59
1861	413.83	99.44	77.94	21.50
1862	414.83	100.06	78.66	21.41

March 17, 1983
Bought $10,000,000   10⅜% of 11/12 at 97–00
   $ 9,700,000.00   Principal value
   +   349,654.70   Accrued interest from November 1982
  $10,049,654.70   Invoice amount

April 14, 1983
Sold $10,000,000   10⅜% of 11/12 at 100–00
  $10,000,000.00   Principal value
  +   492,903.30   Accrued interest from November 1982
  $10,429,903.30   Invoice amount

  $10,429,903.30
 − 10,049,654.70
  $ 380,248.60   Gross profit
Overnight interest expense to finance 100% of position, at 8.9%
for
28 days is $69,656.90.
    $ 380,248.60
    −   69,656.90
    $ 310,591.70   Net profit

The trader was not forced to hedge this position, since the value of the bonds never fell below 97–01 during the time the position was held.

An additional technique that is used to determine when to hedge a position is the use of the .01 effect. The dollar value of a one basis-point change for the 10⅜ percent of 11/12 at a price of 97–00 is $854.64 per million dollars face value. Therefore, a one basis-point move results in a price change of approximately $8,500 for a $10 million position. Since it was agreed upon that the total trading position could not lose more than $100,000, a futures hedge would have been executed before the yield to maturity of the 10⅜ percent of 11/12 increased by 12 basis points to 10.83 percent.

Intramarket Treasury Bond Futures Spread

Given. Armed with the economic information presented in the cash versus futures case study, it was assumed that short-term interest rates would decrease quickly and long-term rates improve slowly. The yield curve would steepen. Therefore, the nearby bond contract could be purchased and the second contract month sold. This would enable the trader to profit from a widening price spread resulting from lower short-term interest rates. On March 17, 1983 (day 1843), the following price spread distribution was available based on the most recent 60-day price observation for the nearby Treasury bond futures contract minus the second Treasury bond futures contract (in decimals).

Min	Max	Mean	Std. Dev.
0.56	0.78	0.67	0.05

The trader decided to simultaneously buy 100 March and sell 100 June bond contracts. When the front month is bought, the position is referred to as a bull spread. March was bought at $76^{01}\!/_{32}$ and June sold at $75^{11}\!/_{32}$. In the jargon of the trade, this spread was bought at plus 22, or plus $^{22}\!/_{32}$. Since the bond spread is affected by overnight repo rates, the trader computed the current implied rate using the following formulas.

Implied Repo =

$$\frac{8}{\text{Nearby price}} \times \frac{360^*}{365} + \left(\frac{\text{Deferred price} - \text{Nearby price}}{\text{Nearby price}} \right) \times \frac{360}{\text{Number of days between deliveries}}$$

EXHIBIT 14-4
Supporting Data: Spread Analysis of Nearby
Treasury Bond Contract versus Second Treasury
Bond Contract

```
1) BILL:DATE
2) TBOND:BTBD1     CBOT FIRST TBOND CONTRACT
3) TBOND:BTBD2
4) SPR10    BTBD1-BTBD2
```

Seq £	DATE	BTBD1	BTBD2	SPR10
1835	307.83	76.88	76.25	0.63
1836	308.83	76.31	75.63	0.69
1837	309.83	76.34	75.69	0.66
1838	310.83	75.97	75.28	0.69
1839	311.83	75.66	74.97	0.69
1840	314.83	76.25	75.56	0.69
1841	315.83	76.75	76.03	0.72
1842	316.83	76.22	75.53	0.69
1843	317.83	76.03	75.34	0.69
1844	318.83	76.25	75.56	0.69
1845	321.83	76.28	75.59	0.69
1846	322.83	76.06	75.50	0.56
1847	323.83	76.50	75.97	0.53
1848	324.83	76.47	75.94	0.53
1849	325.83	75.75	75.25	0.50
1850	328.83	75.84	75.34	0.50
1851	329.83	76.25	75.72	0.53
1852	330.83	76.25	75.72	0.53
1853	331.83	75.97	75.44	0.53
1854	404.83	76.22	75.72	0.50
1855	405.83	77.22	76.69	0.53
1856	406.83	77.31	76.75	0.56
1857	407.83	77.13	76.59	0.53
1858	408.83	77.00	76.44	0.56
1859	411.83	77.81	77.19	0.63
1860	412.83	77.63	77.06	0.56
1861	413.83	77.94	77.34	0.59
1862	414.83	78.66	78.06	0.59
1863	415.83	78.41	77.84	0.56
1864	418.83	78.78	78.22	0.56

$$IR = \frac{8}{76.03} \times \frac{360}{365} + \left(\frac{(75.34 - 76.03)}{76.03} \times \frac{360}{90} \right)$$

$IR = .105 \times .986 - .0363$

$IR = .1034 - .0363$

$IR = .0672$ or 6.72%

* Used to compute bond equivalent yield.

The above calculation is approximate. It assumes a 20-year bond maturity in addition to no accrued interest.

Since the March contract will expire in less than two weeks, the trader expected to hold this position for only several days. If the position had to be rolled forward, the commissions would be doubled.

Results. On March 28, 1983, the trade was offset at plus $^{16}\!/_{32}$. The March contract was sold at $75^{28}\!/_{32}$ and June purchased at $75^{12}\!/_{32}$. Based on 100 spreads, the trade lost $^{6}\!/_{32}$ per spread position or $18,750.

An analysis of the transaction revealed that the spread on March 17 was already too wide compared to the available repo rates in the cash market. The implied overnight financing rate of 6.7 percent was already 200 points below the current Fed funds rate. The expectations of still lower short-term rates had already been adequately reflected in the futures contract prices on March 17. (See Exhibit 14–4).

90-Day CD Futures versus 90-Day Treasury Bill Futures

Given. On July 2, 1982 (day 1667), the money market trader of the Dependable Brokerage Company studied historical spread information pertaining to this trade. This trader recognized that the basis was now at 216 points. This was the difference between the yield equivalent of the 90-day Treasury bill contract subtracted from the yield equivalent of the 90-day CD futures contract. This was close to the maximum range observed over the past 118 days. The following economic data was available:

— Short- and long-term interest rates appear to be coming off their highs.
— The yield curve is almost flat.
— Real gross national product expanded at a rate of 1.7 percent during the second quarter. The gain was somewhat larger than expected.
— GNP was boosted by $8.5 billion in the second quarter.
— Retail sales fell sharply.
— Federal government debt still running at 200 percent of 1981. The current quarter is forecasted to run at a $40 billion deficit.
— Tax receipts down as Reagan's second round of tax cuts become effective.
— Short-term credit demand remains high from the private sector so long as the bond market reflects high inflationary expectations.
— Slope of Treasury yield curve on June 28, 1982 (bond equivalent).

1-year	3-year	7-year	10-year	20-year
14.61%	14.97%	14.91%	14.73%	14.47%

— Other Data:

Overnight Fed funds	14.17%
90-day Treasury bill	13.18%
Discount rate	12.00%
Prime rate	16.50%

— Yield Spread Distribution based on 118 days of observations.

Min	*Max*	*Mean*	*Std. Dev.*
1.18	2.43	1.81	.21

Assumptions. Continuing lack of demand for commercial loan and inventory purposes should accelerate lower interest rates for 90-day CDs. A similar price trend is forecasted for 90-day Treasury bills. However, the Treasury bill price improvement should occur more slowly based on the existing price and yield spreads. Exhibit 14–5 depicts a review of historical Treasury Bill–CD relationships.

On July 12, 1982 (day 1672), the trader sold 100 September

EXHIBIT 14–5
Supporting Data: Spread Analysis of Nearby CD and Treasury Bill Contract

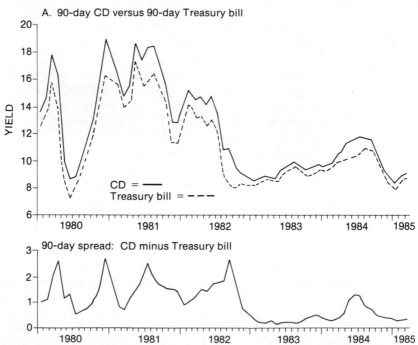

EXHIBIT 14–6
Supporting Data: Spread Analysis of Nearby CD
and Treasury Bill Contract

```
1) BILL:DATE
2) RATE:IMMCD1    IMM C/D FIRST  CONTRACT
3) BILL:M3TBL1
4) SPREAD3    IMMCD1-M3TBL1
```

DAY	DATE	IMMCD1	M3TBL1	SPREAD3
1672	712.82	14.04	11.99	2.05
1673	713.82	14.32	12.24	2.08
1674	714.82	14.42	12.27	2.15
1675	715.82	14.24	12.07	2.17
1676	716.82	13.73	11.59	2.14
1677	719.82	13.72	11.57	2.15
1678	720.82	13.43	11.36	2.07
1679	721.82	13.66	11.64	2.02
1680	722.82	13.28	11.26	2.02
1681	723.82	13.16	11.22	1.94
1682	726.82	13.46	11.55	1.91
1683	727.82	13.53	11.60	1.93
1684	728.82	13.69	11.84	1.85
1685	729.82	13.48	11.62	1.86
1686	730.82	13.18	11.33	1.85
1687	802.82	12.50	10.73	1.77
1688	803.82	12.82	11.07	1.75
1689	804.82	12.64	10.86	1.78
1690	805.82	12.72	10.91	1.81
1691	806.82	12.99	11.19	1.80
1692	809.82	12.73	10.83	1.90
1693	810.82	12.83	11.04	1.79
1694	811.82	12.86	10.99	1.87
1695	812.82	12.42	10.48	1.94
1696	813.82	12.17	10.22	1.95
1697	816.82	11.69	9.82	1.87
1698	817.82	11.19	9.40	1.79
1699	818.82	10.83	9.35	1.48
1700	819.82	10.77	8.90	1.87

```
     SPREAD3

Date Range: Obs.    1672 - 1700
```

	N	MIN	MAX	MEAN	VARIANCE
ALL	29	1.48	2.17	1.92	0.23189E-01

*

1982 90-day Treasury bill futures contracts and purchased 100
90-day September 1982 CD futures contracts at the following
prices:

Sold September 1982 Treasury bill futures at 87.71
Bought September 82 CD futures at   85.73
                          Basis 1.98

Results. The spread was offset on August 18, 1983 (day 1699),
at the following prices:

Bought September 1982 Treasury bill futures at   90.65
Sold September 1982 CD futures at   89.17
                                        Basis   1.48

This generated a profit of $125,000 based on the narrowing of the spread from 198 to 148 basis points. This occurred because Treasury bills improved by 294 basis points and CDs by 344 basis points during the time the trade was open. Each point has a value of $25 per spread. Commissions and financing cost must be subtracted from gross profit to arrive at a net profit.

S&P 500 versus NYFE Index

Given. On April 14, 1983 (day 1862), the following information was available to the equity trading desk of a securities company:

— Congress had not acted on a budget for 1983–84.
— Support was strong for a $30 billion tax increase for 1984.
— OPEC oil was still at $29 per barrel, but spot prices continue to soften.
— Industrial production was at a five-year low—133.5.
— Consumer spending was down, especially in automobiles and other durable goods. Nondurable spending was up 1.5 percent.
— Unemployment was over 10 percent although total employment up.
— Money supply stable but worrisome being watched closely.
— DJIA achieved a record high of 1240 on April 4, 1983: now 1164.
— More speculative stocks beginning to heat up as judged by Value Line Index, closing above 200.
— Percentage of NYSE stocks above 100-day moving average, 92 percent.
— OTC volume as a percent of NYSE volume 91 percent.
— P/E ratio of NYFE Composite Index: 19.5
   P/E ratio of S&P 500 Index: 11.9
— Other data:

Fed funds	8.74%
91-day Treasury bills	8.49%
91-day CD	8.75%
30-year Treasury bonds	10.68%

— Price spread between seven NYFE Index futures—four S&P 500 futures based on 72 consecutive observations.

Min	Max	Mean	Std. Dev
−9.15	1.08	−5.42	−2.22

— On April 14 (day 1862) the S&P 500 closed at 158.2 and
the NYFE Composite Index at 91.2. Therefore, to equalize
the dollar value of an arbitrage trade, most professional
traders use four S&P contracts versus seven NYFE contracts. This case study will use this weighted average. The
price spread is computed by multiplying the NYFE Composite Index by seven and subtracting four times the S&P 500
Index.

Assumptions. It was assumed that a correction is overdue and
that the highly capitalized issues would be affected quickly. On
April 14, the spread was −4.8. This range is within one standard
deviation of the mean. If the Dow Jones Composite Index retreats
by 10 percent to a range of 1080–1100, the spread might increase
to 6, since the NYFE index should retreat more slowly. This assumption was based on the concept that highly capitalized stocks
have a greater effect on the S&P Index since the NYFE index reflects 1500 stocks, many of which are second-tier securities.

The traders buy 70 NYFE June 1983 futures contracts at 91.20
and simultaneously sell 40 S&P 500 June 1983 contracts at 158.20
or a 5.6 basis. A stop-loss limit of $250 per spread, or 50 points,
was established by management.

Result. The positions were reversed on May 19, 1983, at a
spread of −8.0 and a profit of $12,000. The initial logic for entering
this trade was erroneous, since the stock market steadily improved
during the time the positions were open. However, on a percentage
basis, the NYFE contracts increased more rapidly in value compared to the S&P contracts. This difference was magnified by the
respective multipliers. This example is illustrative of the vagaries
of markets. Profits and losses are often made for the wrong reasons.

Exhibit 14–7 on the following pages provides the data for this
case study.

EXHIBIT 14–7
Supporting Data: Weighted Spread Analysis between S&P 500 versus NYFC Contracts

A.

```
BILL:DATE
SPR3   (4*SP3)-(7*NYC)
SPR4   (4*SP51)-(7*NYC1)
```

DAY	DATE	SPR3	SPR4
1791	103.83	-5.17	-5.05
1792	104.83	-3.59	-4.70
1793	105.83	-4.52	-5.90
1794	106.83	-4.89	-6.15
1795	107.83	-4.77	-5.60
1796	110.83	-5.26	-6.50
1797	111.83	-5.73	-6.90
1798	112.83	-5.91	-7.40
1799	113.83	-6.24	-7.85
1800	114.83	-6.09	-8.20
1801	117.83	-6.65	-7.15
1802	118.83	-6.89	-6.50
1803	119.83	-6.85	-6.50
1804	120.83	-6.33	-6.50
1805	121.83	-6.74	-6.45
1806	124.83	-6.56	-5.30
1807	125.83	-5.78	-5.90
1808	126.83	-5.95	-5.75
1809	127.83	-5.11	-5.25
1810	128.83	-5.41	-5.55
1811	131.83	-5.05	-6.20
1812	201.83	-6.43	-5.90
1813	202.83	-5.77	-5.85
1814	203.83	-5.74	-5.60
1815	204.83	-5.47	-5.25
1816	207.83	-5.67	-5.35
1817	208.83	-6.32	-6.90
1818	209.83	-6.53	-6.55
1819	210.83	-5.70	-6.55
1820	211.83	-5.78	-6.10
1821	214.83	-5.51	-6.60
1822	215.83	-6.60	-7.05
1823	216.83	-6.54	-6.55
1824	217.83	-6.15	-6.85
1825	218.83	-6.08	-6.75
1826	222.83	-6.61	-6.50
1827	223.83	-6.02	-8.30
1828	224.83	-5.35	-7.80
1829	225.83	-5.45	-8.15
1830	228.83	-6.02	-6.60
1831	301.83	-4.99	-9.15
1832	302.83	-6.34	-7.90
1833	303.83	-5.44	-7.90
1834	304.83	-5.73	-7.70
1835	307.83	-5.94	-5.80
1836	308.83	-6.76	-6.35

EXHIBIT 14–7 *(concluded)*

B.

1837	309.83	-6.13	-7.40
1838	310.83	-6.35	-5.55
1839	311.83	-6.07	-6.45
1840	314.83	-5.61	-4.90
1841	315.83	-5.06	-5.45
1842	316.83	-5.77	-2.75
1843	317.83	-5.18	-2.94
1844	318.83	-4.99	-2.35
1845	321.83	-3.95	-0.50
1846	322.83	-4.33	-1.10
1847	323.83	-3.71	0.35
1848	324.83	-3.92	0.25
1849	325.83	-3.99	-1.30
1850	328.83	-4.02	-0.60
1851	329.83	-4.32	-1.20
1852	330.83	-3.56	1.08
1853	331.83	-4.37	-5.25
1854	404.83	-4.38	-4.60
1855	405.83	-4.69	-4.80
1856	406.83	-4.59	-5.35
1857	407.83	-4.16	-6.00
1858	408.83	-3.69	-5.80
1859	411.83	-2.93	-4.35
1860	412.83	-2.94	-3.75
1861	413.83	-3.20	-3.20
1862	414.83	-3.40	-4.80
1863	415.83	-3.26	-4.20
1864	418.83	-3.01	-4.30
1865	419.83	-3.42	-3.80
1866	420.83	-3.19	-3.90
1867	421.83	-3.45	-4.30
1868	422.83	-3.37	-4.45
1869	425.83	-3.79	-4.05
1870	426.83	-2.61	-3.45
1871	427.83	-3.00	-3.05
1872	428.83	-2.70	-3.71
1873	429.83	-2.17	-4.15
1874	502.83	-2.84	-2.65
1875	503.83	-2.62	-4.15
1876	504.83	-3.08	-3.65
1877	505.83	-3.72	-4.20
1878	506.83	-3.89	-4.80
1879	509.83	-4.21	-5.35
1880	510.83	-4.56	-6.05
1881	511.83	-5.09	-5.55
1882	512.83	-5.55	-7.20
1883	513.83	-5.85	-7.55
1884	516.83	-5.73	-6.60
1885	517.83	-6.52	-6.45
1886	518.83	-7.65	-7.90
1887	519.83	-7.73	-8.00
1888	520.83	-7.45	-7.75
1889	523.83	-7.01	-8.15
1890	524.83	-6.90	-8.10

SUMMARY

Speculation and arbitrage are necessary for the existence of a successful futures market. Since there are not always the same number of hedgers willing to take opposite positions in the market, speculators insure a liquid market. In addition speculators assist in the process by which all market information is quickly reflected in the price of futures contracts. Arbitrageurs insure that related assets between markets are fairly priced. This improves the efficiency of a market (e.g. that capital will flow to that market offering the highest return for a level of risk).

Speculation can take many forms. Speculators can take open positions in a single contract or take spread positions between contract months of futures instruments. The decision is based on expectations for future spot or cash prices and those implied by a futures contract.

While in the academic literature arbitrage is normally defined as a riskless position that requires zero investment and generates positive profits, an arbitrage position among traders refers to a position in which a trader attempts to capitalize on discrepancies in the normal price relationship between two risky assets. Profits are not assured.

SELECTED REFERENCES

Elton, E.; M. Gruber; and J. Rentzler. "Intra-Day Tests of the Efficiency of the Treasury Bill Futures Market," *Columbia Center For the Study of Futures Markets* No. 38 (October, 1982).

Jones, Frank. "Spreads: Tails and Turtles, and All That," *The Journal of Futures Markets* (Winter, 1981), 565–596.

Hoag, James W.; and K. Peterson LaBarge. "Quasi-arbitrage Opportunities in the Treasury Bond Futures Market," Paper presented at Eastern Finance Association Meeting (New York, 1983).

Kolb, R.; G. Gay; and J. Jordon. "Are There Arbitrage Opportunities in the Treasury Bond Futures Markets," *Journal of Futures Markets* (Fall, 1982), pp. 217–30.

Rendleman, R., and C. Carakine. "The Efficiency of the Treasury Bill Futures Market," pp. 211–12, in C. Gay and R. Kolb. *Interest Rate Futures Concepts and Issues*, Richmond, VA: Robert F. Dame, Inc., 1982.

PART 3

Special Topics

In the final section, topics necessary for a fuller understanding of the financial futures markets are presented. In Chapter 15, the delivery procedures of active futures contracts are described. While most futures positions are offset prior to delivery, it is the prospect of delivery that insures a correlation between spot and futures price movement. The continued expansion of financial futures markets is fueled by the information explosion fostered by the computer revolution. In Chapter 16, the use of the computer in financial futures trading is explored. Security markets have also experienced growth in using options and options on futures. In Chapter 17 the financial markets for options on futures are reviewed. Together the options and futures markets offer the corporate and investment managers a selection of financial tools necessary to solve their financial problems in a superior manner.

Delivery Procedures

The act of making or taking delivery of a futures contract remains one of the great mysteries associated with futures trading. Historically, fewer than 2 percent of all contracts traded are offset by deliveries. The possibility of delivery, however, remains the major factor in keeping the basis between cash and futures in their proper relationship.[1]

Financial futures contracts that are not offset by an opposite trade must be closed out by delivering an approved cash instrument or making cash payments. Instruments eligible for delivery on a contract expiration date are carefully defined in delivery manuals which can be obtained from the appropriate exchange. Deliveries against the Treasury bond, Treasury note, and GNMA contracts will likely be satisfied with other than 8 percent coupons. The maturity dates of securities selected for delivery may also differ. Since the deliverable instruments may vary in both coupon and maturities, they are often called, market-basket contracts. These contracts were fully described in Chapter 6. On the other hand, money market cash instruments can differ only in their remaining maturities as permitted by contract specifications.

Since the short, or seller, initializes a delivery action, it is obvious that a delivery will not take place unless it is profitable compared to offsetting a position. To maximize profits, the short will deliver the cheapest eligible instrument. This will only occur if the short can purchase a suitable security for less than the invoice amount that can be received from the futures exchange when a delivery is made. This occurs infrequently since the futures price of a contract theoretically reflects the value of the cheapest deliverable security. During the duration of a contract, the identity of the least expensive issue may change many times. Traders should be able to identify and track the cheapest security at all times, since the price of the nearby futures contract will likely reflect its value. After identifying the issue, a trader will be able to compute the implied carrying profit or loss associated with a contemplated future delivery transaction. By adding the carrying cost to the acquisition price of the cheapest cash instrument, a comparison can be made to a futures contract price to determine whether it is trading rich or whether it is cheap to cash. As the expiration date approaches, the price basis will become smaller and less volatile.[2]

On some occasions, the decision to deliver may be a last minute choice dictated by cash market prices. On the CBOT, this can occur in bonds, GNMAs, and notes, because a short can give a delivery notice until 5 P.M., EDT, two hours after the financial futures markets have closed. This gives the short an opportunity to shop for cheap bonds in the cash market which could be used to deliver against a 3 P.M. closing futures price. Although this type of opportunity seldom occurs in size, it is referred to as the "wild card" in the industry.[3]

HOW TO DELIVER A FUTURES CONTRACT

When a short wishes to trigger a delivery, the clearing broker, who is also called a clearing futures commission merchant, is notified. All positions not offset during the last day of trading are automatically satisfied with deliveries. When a short position will be closed by a delivery, the clearing corporation is notified by the clearing broker. Most clearing corporations select a recipient by matching the short position with the oldest long position. Some clearing corporations use a random number generator to select the long position that will receive delivery. The procedure used for each contract is explicitly defined in a delivery manual.

When a clearing broker is notified of an impending delivery by the clearing corporation, the broker contacts the selected client holding the long position. It is the responsibility of a clearing broker to make certain that all customers who have long positions in a delivery month have the financial means to accept delivery. Normally, financing can be arranged for deliveries. The cash instrument used to transfer title may be a Treasury bond, note, money market instrument, or warehouse receipt. For Eurodollar and stock index contracts, settlement is in cash requiring no exchange of title.

After taking delivery, the long has several alternatives. The buyer can sometimes redeliver the cash instrument into the same contract before it expires. If it is profitable, the security can be held, financed, and redelivered into the next nearby contract. In some instances, the long may elect to sell the cash instruments immediately. If a warehouse receipt is involved, it can be surrendered. These decisions are ordinarily deferred until a description of the specific issue being delivered is available. In market-basket contracts, like U.S. Treasury bonds, this will not be provided until the Notice of Intention Day. Although each contract has a slightly different delivery procedure, Exhibit 15–1 is representative of a typical financial contract delivery timetable.

EXHIBIT 15–1
Principles of Delivery

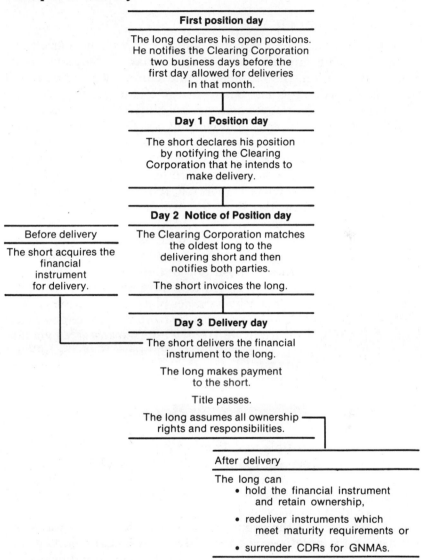

First position day

The long declares his open positions.
He notifies the Clearing Corporation
two business days before the
first day allowed for deliveries
in that month.

Day 1 Position day

The short declares his position
by notifying the Clearing
Corporation that he intends to
make delivery.

Day 2 Notice of Position day

Before delivery

The short acquires the
financial
instrument
for delivery.

The Clearing Corporation matches
the oldest long to the
delivering short and then
notifies both parties.

The short invoices the long.

Day 3 Delivery day

The short delivers the financial
instrument to the long.

The long makes payment
to the short.

Title passes.

The long assumes all ownership
rights and responsibilities.

After delivery

The long can
  • hold the financial instrument
    and retain ownership,

  • redeliver instruments which
    meet maturity requirements or

  • surrender CDRs for GNMAs.

Source: CBOT Delivery Manual.

LONG–TERM TREASURY BOND DELIVERY PROCEDURES

General Information

The delivery of a Treasury bond contract can be initialized by the short during any allowable business day of the expiration month. In addition, the customer could commence the delivery cycle on the second to last business day of the previous month since the delivery window opens at that time. The term delivery window defines when and for how long a delivery notice can be initiated by a customer who owns a short position. When the yield curve is steep, deliveries usually take place on the last permissible day since overnight financing costs are less than the coupon income. When the yield curve is inverted, most deliveries are made on the first permissible day since the overnight financing cost exceeds the coupon income.

To be deliverable, a contract grade Treasury bond must have a minimum of 15 years to maturity remaining on the date it is delivered against a futures position. If the bond is callable, as are most U.S. Treasury bonds, it must have 15 years to the call date remaining at the time delivery takes place. All securities deliverable against a single contract must be from the same issue. The actual deliveries occur using book entry bonds transferred via the Federal Reserve wire transfer system. On January 1984, the following issues were eligible for delivery to and including the indicated dates. See Exhibit 15–2.

Invoicing Calculations

It is currently impossible to deliver an 8 percent Treasury bond. All outstanding 8 percent U.S. Treasury bonds were issued many years ago. Therefore, their remaining life-to-maturity, or call date, is now less than 15 years from a futures contract expiration date. Using a yield-to-maturity basis, the Position Day settlement price must be adjusted to the coupon rate and remaining maturity or call date of the bond selected for delivery. It is assumed that the bonds have semiannual coupons. Semiannual compounding is also assumed in the computation of yields. Premiums or discounts are amortized over the life of the issue. For ease of operation, conversion factors are provided by the CBOT, which are used for invoicing purposes. Publication no. 765, revised March 1983, published by Financial Publishing Company of Boston, is used to select the appropriate factor. Exhibit 15–3 is representative of this publication,

EXHIBIT 15–2
Deliverable Treasury Bond Conversion Factors

Coupon	Maturity	Sep 84	Dec 84	Mar 85	Jun 85	Sep 85	Dec 85	Mar 86	Jun 86
8¼	May 15 2000-05	1.0220	1.0216	1.0216	—	—	—	—	—
7⅝	Feb 15 2002-07	0.9651	0.9655	.9655	.9660	.9660	.9665	.9666	.9670
7⅞	Nov 15 2002-07	0.9882	0.9881	.9883	.9882	.9885	.9884	.9887	.9885
8⅜	Aug 15 2003-08	1.0359	1.0359	1.0355	1.0355	1.0350	1.0350	1.0346	1.0345
8¾	Nov 15 2003-08	1.0726	1.0720	1.0718	1.0711	1.0709	1.0702	1.0700	1.0693
9⅛	May 15 2004-09	1.1102	1.1093	1.1089	1.1081	1.1077	1.1068	1.1064	1.1055
10⅜	Nov 15 2004-09	1.2350	1.2336	1.2326	1.2310	1.2300	1.2284	1.2273	1.2257
11¾	Feb 15 2005-10	1.3727	1.3711	1.3689	1.3672	1.3649	1.3631	1.3608	1.3589
10	May 15 2005-10	1.1999	1.1987	1.1979	1.1967	1.1958	1.1945	1.1937	1.1923
12¾	Nov 15 2005-10	1.4794	1.4768	1.4748	1.4722	1.4701	1.4673	1.4651	1.4623
11¾	Feb 15 2001	1.3374	1.3351	1.3322	1.3298	1.3267	1.3242	—	—
13⅛	May 15 2001	1.4650	1.4612	1.4580	1.4541	1.4507	1.4466	1.4431	—
13⅞	May 15 2006-11	1.5984	1.5954	1.5930	1.5898	1.5873	1.5840	1.5814	1.5780
13⅜	Aug 15 2001	1.4910	1.4877	1.4837	1.4804	1.4762	1.4727	1.4684	1.4647
15¾	Nov 15 2001	1.7134	1.7080	1.7032	1.6976	1.6926	1.6867	1.6816	1.6755
14	Nov 15 2006-11	1.6165	1.6135	1.6111	1.6080	1.6056	1.6024	1.5998	1.5965
14¼	Feb 15 2002	1.5790	1.5753	1.5709	1.5671	1.5625	1.5585	1.5538	1.5496
11⅝	Nov 15 2002	1.3427	1.3402	1.3383	1.3357	1.3337	1.3311	1.3289	1.3262
10⅜	Nov 15 2007-12	1.2480	1.2468	1.2461	1.2448	1.2440	1.2427	1.2419	1.2406
10¾	Feb 15 2003	1.2614	1.2600	1.2581	1.2566	1.2546	1.2532	1.2511	1.2495
10¾	May 15 2003	1.2632	1.2614	1.2600	1.2581	1.2566	1.2546	1.2532	1.2511
12	Aug 15 2008-13	1.4221	1.4209	1.4190	1.4177	1.4158	1.4144	1.4124	1.4110
11⅛	Aug 15 2003	1.3006	1.2991	1.2970	1.2954	1.2933	1.2916	1.2894	1.2877
11⅞	Nov 12 2003	1.3753	1.3728	1.3709	1.3683	1.3663	1.3637	1.3616	1.3589
12⅜	May 15 2004	1.4284	1.4258	1.4237	1.4209	1.4187	1.4159	1.4136	1.4107
13¼	May 15 2009-14	1.5602	1.5580	1.5564	1.5541	1.5524	1.5500	1.5482	1.5458

which provides all factors for coupons ranging from 7 percent to 15¾ percent and terms to maturity up to 40 years by quarters.

There are numerous software packages available to identify the cheapest deliverable bonds on any trading day. The programs multiply the 3 P.M. closing prices in decimals, by the selected conversion factor, and the contract value. This principal amount is compared to the offered side of the cash market price of a specific issue. If the simulated futures invoice price is greater than the cash market price, the short will buy the cash bonds and inform the clearing broker of his intention to deliver. An arbitrary invoice price is calculated in the following manner:

EXHIBIT 15–3

Coupon rates

Term	8%	8⅛%	8¼%	8⅜%	8½%	8⅝%	8¾%	8⅞%
15	1.0000	1.0108	1.0216	1.0324	1.0432	1.0540	1.0648	1.0757
15-3	.9998	1.0107	1.0216	1.0325	1.0434	1.0543	1.0652	1.0761
15-6	1.0000	1.0110	1.0220	1.0330	1.0440	1.0550	1.0660	1.0769
15-9	.9998	1.0109	1.0220	1.0330	1.0441	1.0552	1.0663	1.0774
16	1.0000	1.0112	1.0223	1.0335	1.0447	1.0559	1.0670	1.0782
16-3	.9998	1.0111	1.0223	1.0336	1.0448	1.0561	1.0673	1.0786
16-6	1.0000	1.0113	1.0227	1.0340	1.0454	1.0567	1.0681	1.0794
16-9	.9998	1.0112	1.0226	1.0341	1.0455	1.0569	1.0683	1.0798
17	1.0000	1.0115	1.0230	1.0345	1.0460	1.0575	1.0690	1.0805
17-3	.9998	1.0114	1.0230	1.0346	1.0461	1.0577	1.0693	1.0809
17-6	1.0000	1.0117	1.0233	1.0350	1.0467	1.0583	1.0700	1.0817
17-9	.9998	1.0115	1.0233	1.0350	1.0468	1.0585	1.0702	1.0820
18	1.0000	1.0118	1.0236	1.0355	1.0473	1.0591	1.0709	1.0827
18-3	.9998	1.0117	1.0236	1.0355	1.0474	1.0592	1.0711	1.0830
18-6	1.0000	1.0120	1.0239	1.0359	1.0479	1.0598	1.0718	1.0837
18-9	.9998	1.0118	1.0239	1.0359	1.0479	1.0600	1.0720	1.0840
19	1.0000	1.0121	1.0242	1.0363	1.0484	1.0605	1.0726	1.0847
19-3	.9998	1.0120	1.0241	1.0363	1.0485	1.0607	1.0728	1.0850
19-6	1.0000	1.0122	1.0245	1.0367	1.0490	1.0612	1.0734	1.0857
19-9	.9998	1.0121	1.0244	1.0367	1.0490	1.0613	1.0736	1.0859
20	1.0000	1.0124	1.0247	1.0371	1.0495	1.0619	1.0742	1.0866
20-3	.9998	1.0122	1.0247	1.0371	1.0495	1.0620	1.0744	1.0868
20-6	1.0000	1.0125	1.0250	1.0375	1.0500	1.0625	1.0750	1.0875
20-9	.9998	1.0124	1.0249	1.0375	1.0500	1.0626	1.0751	1.0877
21	1.0000	1.0126	1.0252	1.0378	1.0505	1.0631	1.0757	1.0883
21-3	.9998	1.0125	1.0251	1.0378	1.0505	1.0632	1.0758	1.0885
21-6	1.0000	1.0127	1.0255	1.0382	1.0509	1.0637	1.0764	1.0891
21-9	.9998	1.0126	1.0254	1.0382	1.0509	1.0637	1.0765	1.0893
22	1.0000	1.0128	1.0257	1.0385	1.0514	1.0642	1.0771	1.0899
22-3	.9998	1.0127	1.0256	1.0385	1.0514	1.0643	1.0772	1.0901
22-6	1.0000	1.0130	1.0259	1.0389	1.0518	1.0648	1.0777	1.0907
22-9	.9998	1.0128	1.0258	1.0388	1.0518	1.0648	1.0778	1.0908
23	1.0000	1.0131	1.0261	1.0392	1.0522	1.0653	1.0783	1.0914
23-3	.9998	1.0129	1.0260	1.0391	1.0522	1.0653	1.0784	1.0915
23-6	1.0000	1.0132	1.0263	1.0395	1.0526	1.0658	1.0789	1.0921
23-9	.9998	1.0130	1.0262	1.0394	1.0526	1.0658	1.0790	1.0922
24	1.0000	1.0132	1.0265	1.0397	1.0530	1.0662	1.0795	1.0927
24-3	.9998	1.0131	1.0264	1.0397	1.0530	1.0663	1.0795	1.0928
24-6	1.0000	1.0133	1.0267	1.0400	1.0534	1.0667	1.0800	1.0934
24-9	.9998	1.0132	1.0266	1.0399	1.0533	1.0667	1.0801	1.0935
25	1.0000	1.0134	1.0269	1.0403	1.0537	1.0671	1.0806	1.0940
25-3	.9998	1.0133	1.0267	1.0402	1.0537	1.0671	1.0806	1.0941
25-6	1.0000	1.0135	1.0270	1.0405	1.0540	1.0676	1.0811	1.0946
25-9	.9998	1.0134	1.0269	1.0405	1.0540	1.0675	1.0811	1.0946
26	1.0000	1.0136	1.0272	1.0408	1.0544	1.0680	1.0816	1.0951
26-3	.9998	1.0134	1.0271	1.0407	1.0543	1.0679	1.0816	1.0952
26-6	1.0000	1.0137	1.0273	1.0410	1.0547	1.0684	1.0820	1.0957
26-9	.9998	1.0135	1.0272	1.0409	1.0546	1.0683	1.0820	1.0957
27	1.0000	1.0137	1.0275	1.0412	1.0550	1.0687	1.0825	1.0962
27-3	.9998	1.0136	1.0274	1.0411	1.0549	1.0687	1.0825	1.0963
27-6	1.0000	1.0138	1.0276	1.0415	1.0553	1.0691	1.0829	1.0967
27-9	.9998	1.0137	1.0275	1.0414	1.0552	1.0691	1.0829	1.0968

Source: Financial Publishing Company, Boston, Mass. 02215. Publication No. 765.

Nominal contract size	$100,000.00
Future settlement price (in decimals)	.9575
Settlement price	95,750.00
Conversion factor from publication No. 765	× .975
Invoice price per contract	93,356.25
Number of contracts =	× 1
Total invoice price	$ 93,356.25

The accrued interest is added to the invoice price.

Daily interest	$ 20.72
Number of days elapsed	× 60
Total interest per contract	$ 1,243.20
Number of contracts	× 1
Total accrued interest	$ 1,243.20
Invoice price	$ 93,356.25
Accrued interest	1,243.20
Total invoice amount	$ 94,599.45

It is generally a safe assumption that the cheapest bonds for delivery are those with the highest coupon and longest maturities. Due to bond duration and current yield levels, lower coupon bonds with shorter remaining terms to maturity can become the more desirable issues for delivery. These bonds are usually available at a discount price below 90. The environment surrounding the September 1982 Treasury bond future is an example of this phenomenon. Over $1.25 billion bonds were delivered and most were 8¾ of 11/08 or 9⅛ of 5/09. All but 10 of the contracts delivered were settled on the last permissible day. When the March 1983 contract expired, the 14s of 2011 once more became the cheapest issue for delivery.

In summary, bond deliveries into the futures market are possible but cumbersome for the nonprofessional. A trained staff and/or a sophisticated computer system is required to keep track of a large matrix of variables. In addition, if financing rates change rapidly, a profitable projection can readily turn into a loss. Because of the factors associated with making deliveries in size, few participants utilize the delivery option.

10–YEAR NOTE DELIVERY PROCEDURES

General Information

The delivery procedures and invoicing routines are identical to those described for the long-term Treasury bond contract. The remaining maturity of notes eligible for delivery must be not less than 6½ years or more than 10 years. A list of notes that could be delivered as of November 1984, is shown in Exhibit 15–4 on the next page.

In computing the cheapest note to deliver, the one with the longest remaining maturity appears to be the candidate. Deep discount notes have not yet been attractive to deliver. This is a devia-

EXHIBIT 15–4
Deliverable Treasury Notes

Coupon	Maturity	Amount (in billions)	DEC 84	MAR 85	JUN 85	SEP 85	DEC 85	MAR 86
14-7/8	Aug 15, 1991	$1.7	1.3433	-	-	-	-	-
14-1/4	Nov 15, 1991	$1.9	1.3208	1.3121	-	-	-	-
14-5/8	Feb 15, 1992	$2.5	1.3499	1.3401	1.3308	-	-	-
13-3/4	May 15, 1992	$9.0	1.3114	1.3037	1.2951	1.2871	-	-
10-1/2	Nov 15, 1992	$4.0	1.1421	1.1390	1.1353	1.1320	1.1282	1.1248
10-7/8	Feb 15, 1993	$4.5	1.1675	1.1634	1.1598	1.1556	1.1518	1.1475
10-1/8	May 15, 1993	$4.75	1.1263	1.1238	1.1207	1.1181	1.1150	1.1122
11-7/8	Aug 15, 1993	$5.25	1.2357	1.2305	1.2258	1.2204	1.2154	1.2098
11-3/4	Nov 15, 1993	$6.0	1.2325	1.2281	1.2231	1.2185	1.2132	1.2085
13-1/8	May 15, 1994	$5.26	1.3302	1.3244	1.3178	1.3117	1.3049	1.2986
13-3/4	Jul 15, 1991	$5.51	1.2871	-	-	-	-	-
12-5/8	Aug 15, 1994	$5.5	1.3037	1.2980	1.2927	1.2868	1.2813	1.2751
12-1/4	Oct 15, 1991	$5.51	1.2181	1.2122	-	-	-	-
11-5/8	Nov 15, 1994	$5.75	1.2419	1.2381	1.2335	1.2284	1.2247	1.2205

Source: Chicago Board of Trade.

tion from the bond calculations and is probably associated with a built-in conversion factor bias toward maturity differences.

GNMA CDR Delivery Procedures

The delivery subtleties of this contract are materially different from the Treasury bond contract since delivery can only be made with a collateralized depository receipt (CDR). The CDR resembles a warehouse receipt and behaves like a perpetual bond. The CDR has no maturity date and may remain outstanding for perpetuity unless surrendered by the holder, replaced with another CDR by the issuer, or used to offset another short GNMA CDR position. The CDR holder will receive $635 per month. This instrument is unique in the marketplace and suffers from illiquidity when used for purposes other than delivery against an open GNMA CDR futures contract.

Only originators registered with the CBOT may issue CDRs. The registration procedure requires approximately 10 business days and is documented in the contract delivery manual. If a trader is not a regular originator but wishes to deliver a CDR in satisfaction of a short position, he may purchase an outstanding certificate.

Most speculators would find it unwise to take delivery of a CDR. Upon surrender of a CDR, the issuer will deliver the cheapest available GNMAs. These will probably be odd-lot denominations of premium bonds. These are difficult to resell at favorable prices in the commercial marketplace. The actual CDR delivery procedure is similar to the Treasury bond contract. Three days elapse from notification of intent to deliver until payment is received.

Invoicing for GNMA CDR

The invoice amount for a GNMA contract is the settlement price multiplied by $100,000, plus any accrued interest. Since 8 percent GNMAs issued in the late 70s are paid down, discounted, and expensive compared to current coupons, it is unlikely that they would be used as collateral for CDRs or delivered if a CDR is surrendered. If a coupon other than an 8 percent GNMA is delivered, the equivalent principal balance is computed by using factors provided by the CBOT. The factors in Exhibit 15–5 can be used to calculate the equivalent balances.

To compute the invoice amount of a transaction involving a current GNMA coupon, follow these directions:

Assumption: Short chooses to deliver 16 percent GNMAs. Currently, he owns a certificate whose principal balance is $62,800.

EXHIBIT 15–5
GNMA Equivalent Principal Balance Factors and Principal Balance Equivalents

GNMA Interest Rate	Factor*	Amount Equivalent to $100,000 Principal Balance of GNMA 8s
6½	1.121233	$112,123.30
7	1.078167	$107,816.70
7¼	1.058201	$105,820.10
7½	1.038062	$103,806.20
7¾	1.018675	$101,867.50
8	1.000000	$100,000.00
8¼	.982198	$ 98,219.80
8½	.965018	$ 96,501.80
9	.931677	$ 93,167.70
9¼	.916031	$ 91,603.10
9⅜	.908403	$ 90,840.30
9½	.900322	$ 90,032.20
9¾	.885609	$ 88,560.90
10	.871460	$ 87,146.00
10¼	.857143	$ 85,714.30
10½	.843289	$ 84,328.90
10¾	.830450	$ 83,045.00
11	.817439	$ 81,743.90
11¼	.804829	$ 80,482.90
11½	.793021	$ 79,302.10
11¾	.781250	$ 78,125.00
12	.769724	$ 76,972.40
12¼	.758534	$ 75,853.40
12½	.747664	$ 74,766.40
12¾	.736920	$ 73,692.00
13	.726744	$ 72,674.40
13¼	.716846	$ 71,684.60
13½	.707214	$ 70,721.40
13¾	.697350	$ 69,735.00
14	.688231	$ 68,823.10
14¼	.679117	$ 67,911.70
14½	.670578	$ 67,057.80
14¾	.661888	$ 66,188.80
15	.653595	$ 65,359.50
16	.622084	$ 62,208.40
17	.593472	$ 59,347.20

* Multiply the factor by $100,000 to obtain the equivalent principal balance to $100,000 of GNMA 8s for the corresponding coupon.
Source: Chicago Board of Trade Rules and Regulations.

$$\frac{\text{Principal balance of GNMA}}{\text{Factor for 16\% GNMA}} = \frac{\text{Equivalent principal balance of GNMA}}{}$$

$$\frac{\$62,800}{.622084} = \$100,951$$

If the originator delivers this certificate, the long will have to pay $100,951. The delivery rules permit a short to deliver a principal balance equivalent to $100,000 plus or minus 2½ percent. This eliminates the use of any certificate whose invoice value would be below $97,500 or above $102,500. The over- or underamount is called a tail. Usually, a tail will only be delivered if the issue selected for delivery is selling for less than par. Since FHA/VA rate changes occur frequently during the periods of interest volatility, it becomes difficult to correctly project a current GNMA coupon for distant option months. This makes the calculation for profitable deliveries risky.

The delivery activity represented by the GNMA CDR contract is small in percentage to its open interest. As of April 1984, only 2,760 CDRs were registered with the CBOT, and 2,723 were outstanding.

Cash Settlement Contracts

The concept of cash settlement has become popular with the public acceptance of stock index contracts. However, it was first employed by the Chicago Mercantile Exchange in December 1981 when it began trading the Eurodollar contract. This technique eliminates the need to transfer a physical commodity when delivery takes place. Instead, a trader is debited or credited a dollar amount that reflects the difference between today's closing price and yesterday's closing price of an expired contract.

Eurodollars and equities are volatile and are traded in liquid regulated markets. An efficient delivery mechanism had to be developed in order to design an acceptable contract that closely reflects the value of the underlying security. The Eurodollar market is in excess of $1 trillion and geographically dispersed throughout Europe and the Caribbean basin. Since the yield of a Eurodollar loan is tied to the London Interbank offered rate, price manipulation is of little concern. The continuous availability of large denominations of fixed maturity paper from a specific international banking institution is questionable. The rule of sovereign risk can momentarily restrict one major lending institution from conducting business with another regardless of credit considerations. Therefore a trader of Eurodollar contracts does not wish to make or take delivery of paper associated with a specific international lending institution. The delivery mechanism would become inefficient and be reflected in the price of a contract. These potential political barriers made the delivery of negotiable instruments impossible to administer and necessitated the use of cash delivery contracts.

During 1983, various stock index futures contracts began trading actively on the Chicago Mercantile Exchange, the New York Futures Exchange, and the Kansas City Board of Trade. All contracts track indexes which are recomputed continuously during the day. Costs and logistics would make the actual delivery of the stocks which comprise these indexes impractical, if not impossible. Investors who buy or sell stock index futures contacts do not wish to make or take delivery of one share of all securities represented by any index. Since a stock index is composed of well-defined securities whose cash value is determined daily, a cash settlement is feasible and practical.

The size of the cash-to-futures premium over the life of a contract will depend on interest rates, dividends, market psychology and transactions costs to purchase or sell comparable cash and futures positions. In addition, expectations will have a major bearing on the premium. In terms of transaction and interest opportunity costs, it is much cheaper to short a futures contract than to short a portfolio of stocks.

With the receipt of a favorable tax ruling in the Technical Corrections Act of 1982, stock index deliveries became more prevalent. It qualified cash settlement contracts for equal tax treatment with other commodity contracts. In addition, the enactment of the 32 percent flat tax treatment of commodity profits and losses in the Economic Recovery Act of 1981 provide some unique tax trading strategies for active stock traders.

In summary, the basis risk associated with market-basket contracts is eliminated by the use of cash settlements during the final trading days. Unforeseen costs related to storage, insurance, and delivery of a physical commodity are also removed.

EURODOLLAR DELIVERY PROCEDURES

Last Day of Trading

Trading will cease on the second London bank business day immediately preceding the third Wednesday of the contract month at 3:30 P.M., London time. If this is a New York or Chicago bank holiday, the last day of trading is the first London bank business day immediately preceding the Wednesday of the contract month.

Final Settlement Price

Cash settlement is determined by the IMM Clearing Corporation. Twelve of 20 London participating banks are polled for their

LIBOR rate for three-month Eurodollar time-deposit funds both at the close of trading and at a randomly selected times within the last 90 minutes of trading. The actual settlement price will be 100 minus the average of the two observations.

Clearing brokers holding open positions at the termination of trading will make or receive payments to the clearing corporation in accordance with regular maintenance margin procedures. The final settlement price will be used to determine the debits and credits generated on the last day of trading.

STOCK INDEX DELIVERY PROCEDURES

Last Day of Trading

The S&P 500 contract ceases trading on the third Friday of the contract month. The expiration date of the NYFE Index contract is also the third Friday of the contract month. The Value Line contract stops trading on the last business day of the contract month.

Final Settlement Price

The actual cash settlement of these contracts is simple, fast, and inexpensive. The difference between the closing price of the last day of trading and the preceding trading day is transferred to or from the clearing corporation by clearing members the following morning. All open positions of the expiration month are then offset.

The following accounting transactions would occur if a NYFE Composite Stock Index position established at 96 remained open after 4 P.M. on December 19, 1984, the last day of trading for the December 1984 contract. If the contract closed at 96.40, the long would be credited with $200 and the short debited for $200 per contract. After deducting commissions, all remaining margin funds in the account would be returned.

After two years of trading, industry acceptance of the cash settlement procedure seems high. Futures to cash price convergence has been good at the moment of expiration, and the surprises associated with delivery of market-basket contracts have been eliminated. Those traders who have developed skills in recognizing wild card opportunities will undoubtedly mourn the passing of market-basket deliveries. The majority of traders and clearing brokers will probably support more cash delivery contracts.

90–DAY TREASURY BILL PROCEDURES

The procedure is simple, the invoicing calculation is fundamental, but this exercise generates more errors than other financial instruments. The tripwire is the IMM delivery regulation which requires deliveries to be completed to clearing banks by 1:45 P.M., EDT. This is 30 minutes before the Federal Reserve normally closes its window. If this deadline is missed, the short is charged one or more days of interest. This expense may easily offset the potential profit generated from a delivery transaction.

Last Day of Trading

The first delivery day in a nearby contract month is a variable date related to outstanding one-year Treasury bills. The actual date is determined by the first day of the month on which an outstanding one-year Treasury bill has 13 weeks remaining to maturity. The last day of trading will normally fall on Wednesday since Treasury bills mature on Thursdays. Delivery can be made during three business days following the last day of trading. If one of these days falls on a holiday, deliveries will be extended by one day. Eligible instruments must have 89 to 91 days remaining when delivery is made. The December 1983 cycle had December 22, 1983, as its first delivery day. Since Friday, December 23, 1983, was a holiday, the last delivery day occurred on Tuesday, December 27, 1983.

Delivery on a 90-day Treasury bill commences after the close of trading of the current month. Delivery commitment forms, executed by the short and long, must be received by the IMM Clearing Corporation on the last day of trading. The short's form must include the identity of the Chicago or New York bank that has been registered with the IMM and is a member of the Federal Reserve System. It must also include the name and account number at the designated bank from which the security will be transferred in book entry form. The long must provide similar information as to how and where payment will take place. A list of approved banks is available from the clearing corporation. The clearing broker normally completes these documents for the customer.

The clearing corporation will match buyers with sellers, notify the appropriate clearing brokers, and monitor the delivery process. Payment must be made by wire transfer using Fed funds.

Interest calculations are unnecessary since Treasury bills are discount instruments. The following calculation is used to determine an invoice amount.

Dollar value $= DV$

$DV = \$1$ million $-$

$$\frac{(\text{Days to maturity} \times \text{Treasury bill yield} \times \$1 \text{ million})}{360}$$

Treasury bill yield $= \$1$ million
$\qquad\qquad\qquad\qquad - \text{IMM Index at contract settlement}$

In summary, delivery is uncomplicated but requires attention to timing. If a trader's bills are financed by a repurchase agreement, consideration should be given to arranging an overnight bank loan on the last day to assure timely delivery.

90–DAY CERTIFICATE–OF–DEPOSIT (CD) DELIVERY PROCEDURES

The invoicing mechanism for this contract is sufficiently sophisticated to restrict most deliveries to the CD dealer community. Deliverable securities must have a fixed maturity value of $1–1.2 million dollars. CD's must mature between the 16th and last day of a month 90 days after the current month. In addition, they may have no more than 185 days of accrued interest payable at maturity. The security must have been issued by an approved bank on the current no-name approved list.

The invoicing is based on add-on yield-to-maturity mathematics. This differs significantly from discount yield computations used to quote Treasury bills. The buyer of a CD which is sold prior to maturity earns the offered yield on the total investment principal plus interest. The seller receives the proceeds, plus accrued interest which can be used to make an additional investment at current yield levels.

Formula *(a)* is used to compute the invoice price for a $1 million 90-day Treasury bill:

(a)

$$\text{Invoice price} = \left(1 - \frac{90}{360}\,[\text{Treasury bill yield}]\right) \text{million}$$

Treasury bill yield $= 100$
$- \text{IMM Index on last day trading (LTD)}$

This formula results in an invoice price of less than $1 million.

Formula *(b)*, which is used to compute the add-on yield CD invoice amount, results in a total in excess of $1 million.

$$(b) \ \text{Invoice price} = \frac{(\text{maturity value})}{1 + \dfrac{90}{360} \ [\text{CD yield}]}$$

NOTES

[1] This is especially true during the expiration month of a futures contract. At the maturity of the contract, the futures price must approach the price of the deliverable.

[2] Considerable debate exists on the contract maturity effect for futures prices. Samuelson has shown that auto regressive or price series, variance sold increases as maturity approaches. In contrast, Anderson and Danthane have maintained that futures price variability increases as maturity approaches.

[3] The opportunity to deliver cheap bonds against a closed futures price gives advantage to the short. However, futures invoice prices, even at delivery, may not equal the cheapest-to-deliver cash bond prices. The value of the wild card option is primarily a function of the supply the variance individuals and the time to delivery notice. Various option models are presently being used to price the wild card value.

SELECTED REFERENCES

Anderson, R. W.; and J. P. Danthine. "The Time Pattern of Hedging and The Volatility of Futures Prices." Columbia Center for the Study of Futures Markets, no. 7 (April, 1981).

Financial Futures: The Delivery Process in Brief. Chicago: Chicago Board of Trade, 1982.

Jones, F. "The Economics of Futures and Options Contracts Based on Cash Settlement." *Journal of Futures Markets,* Spring 1982, pp. 63–82.

Kilcollin, Thomas. "Different Systems in Financial Futures Markets." *Journal of Finance,* December 1982, pp. 1183–98.

Samualson, P. A. "Proof that Properly Anticipated Prices Fluctuate Randomly." *Industrial Management Review* (Spring 1965), pp. 41–49.

Yardini, Edward. "Managing Interest Rate Risk with Bond Futures." *Columbia Center for the Study of Futures Markets,* June 1981.

Computer Modeling for Financial Futures

Recent advances in computer technology have revolutionized analysis of financial futures markets. In addition to permitting more efficient internal recordkeeping at trade member and corporate offices, computer-based technology has resulted in a more systematic approach to active futures trading. While most of the hedging procedures and futures trading activities discussed in this book do not require computer support, a computer-based support system greatly eases the decision and analysis process. Computer systems have therefore become an integral part of managing financial futures trades and developing financial futures strategies. Given the complexity and effort required to set up a computer-based financial modeling system, many individuals may choose to defer the actual management of financial futures to recognized professionals. Other individuals, however, may wish to establish their own computer-based financial futures modeling system or depend on externally designed computer software.

Numerous software packages exist for the analysis of financial futures (see Appendix). These programs provide educational training, portfolio management and tracking (monitoring profits and loss of futures position), trading (fundamental and technical) analysis, and access to market trade data.[1] Certain financial futures modeling systems are offered by governmental organizations, private firms, and trade organizations for public use. Other programs have been devised for specific firms' internal use and are presented here in order to provide the reader with an appreciation for the range of computer applications in financial futures.[2]

Educational Software

One way to become more familiar with financial futures trading is to practice decision making using the concepts discussed in the previous chapters. Trading exercises in a simulated market environment help one to become more familiar with financial futures markets. Most futures trading exercises are essentially accounting programs that record trading activity. The user decides the choice of contracts, margins, commissions, and initial accounting balances. Users can institute a variety of realistic market orders, including buy or sell at market, stop-loss, and market-if-touched. Profits and losses from completed buy (sell) and sell (buy) trades are added and subtracted from the account balances. Margins and margin calls on open positions are subtracted from the account balance. Transaction fees are also reflected. All orders for execution during a particular trading session are collected before a deadline and processed. The trading report summaries provide a complete and cumulative record of the user's final position. A hypothetical example of a report is given in Exhibit 16–1.[3] For Exhibit 16–1 the trading activity is as follows:

1. Trader 1 received a report on actions taken through the second price quote of July 11. The traders initial account balance is $100,000.
2. Under the section, Transaction to Open, the report listed all orders that opened positions for trader 1.
3. The various subheadings (such as Commodity, Date, and Action) show the requisite details of each order executed. The last subhead, Margin, shows the total amount of margin posted to date for the specific contract.
4. The section under Transaction to Close lists all buy or sell orders executed in closing a position for trader 1. The subheads indicate the details of each closing transaction.
5. The Transaction to Open shows that this individual bought (MBUY) four September 1984 Treasury bond contracts on July 7, 1984.
6. The Transaction to Close section indicates that two of these contracts were offset by subsequent sell orders on July 9, 1984. (The other two contracts remain open as of the report date of July 11, 1984.)
7. Two sell orders for September 1984 Treasury bonds were cancelled due to limit price moves of July 10, 1984.
8. Note that the open Treasury bond contracts were each subject to a margin call on July 10, 1984.
9. The margin account for the open Treasury bond contracts reflects the initial margin of $1,500, plus the $500 margin call required by the adverse price movements.
10. Trader 1 has realized a $2,900 profit on the two roundturns undertaken to date.
11. Trader 1's account balance of $98,900 reflects a profit of $2,900. Adding the $98,900 to the $4,000 margin account still posted yields a final account balance of $102,900.

Repeated use of a manual or computer-based trading game will enable the user to feel comfortable when trading financial futures in practice. The next step is to begin actual financial futures trading. Regardless of whether one is a hedger, speculator, or arbitrageur, decisions to trade are made on the basis of expected price movements. The advent of the computer has permitted a quick

EXHIBIT 16-1*

Trader 1 Report Date 7/11/84

1

7 MSEL ORDER TBOND SEP84 7/10/84 VOID DUE TO LIMIT PRICE MOVE
MSEL ORDER TBOND SEP84 7/10/84 VOID DUE TO LIMIT PRICE MOVE

8 MARGIN CALL $500.000 TBOND SEP84 7/10/84
MARGIN CALL $500.00 TBOND SEP84 7/10/84

3

| | | | 2 | TRANSACTION TO OPEN | | | | 4 | TRANSACTION TO CLOSE | | | |
COMMODITY	DATE	ACTION	PRICE	TRADE VALUE	MARGIN	DATE	PRICE	REASON	TRADE VALUE	COMMISSION	PROFIT
5 TBOND SEP84	7/ 7/84	MBUY	$ 0.79500	$79500.0	$ 0.00	7/ 9/84	$0.81000	MSEL	$81000.0	$50.00	$1450.00
TBOND SEP84	7/ 7/84	MBUY	$ 0.79500	$79500.0	$ 0.00	7/ 9/84	$0.81000	MSEL	$81000.0	$50.00	$1450.00
TBOND SEP84	7/ 7/84	MBUY	$ 0.79500	$79500.0	2000.00						
TBOND SEP84	7/ 7/84	MBUY	$ 0.79500	$79500.0	2000.00						
					$ 4000.00						

9

11 ACCOUNT BALANCE $98900.00   10 $2900.00

* The actual program and descriptive material are available from the Chicago Board of Trade.

and accurate review of market conditions. Most trading systems can be classified as either technical or fundamental. Technical trading systems rely on discovering repeating patterns in past price series. In contrast, fundamental analysis attempts to uncover and forecast the underlying economic factors which are the source of futures price changes and then to forecast the impact of these factors on futures prices.

TECHNICAL TRADING SYSTEMS

The basic reason for studying past price behavior is the belief that patterns of price movement are often repeated over time. To the degree that individuals react to price changes in a consistent fashion, analysis of price movements may be a guide to successful trading strategies.

Trading rules based on technical analysis are widely used by floor traders, brokers, and speculators. They are particularly popular with active futures traders and are less frequently used in hedging strategies. The popularity of technical analysis is partly due to the fact that the data required (e.g., price, volume, open interest) are easy to obtain and to store for computer analysis. Technicians generally use one or a combination of the following techniques.

Charting. Computer output is not limited to lists of numbers. Computers have facilitated the visual analyses of pricing patterns. The user need only decide on how the data should be presented. Many software and data products available for futures analysis include a wide range of charting and graphing options. Two popular pricing charts are bar charts and point and figure charts.

Bar Charts. In Exhibit 16–2, a typical bar chart is presented. The top line marks the point of the day's highest price. The bottom line marks the day's lowest price. The closing price is shown by a short horizontal tick mark extending to the right. The data may, or course, be presented over various time periods: daily, hourly, or over even shorter periods of time. From the chart, the trader may observe price movements which he or she believes may forecast upcoming market moves. Chartists try to identify both support and resistance areas. They believe resistance areas represent fundamental trading pressure. For instance, if a price touches an upper level without breaking through that price range, a contract's resistance area has been reached. However, if that area is then penetrated on the upside, a significant price improvement may be expected. In contrast, if a price continues to bounce off a price-level

EXHIBIT 16–2
Basic Bar Chart Formations

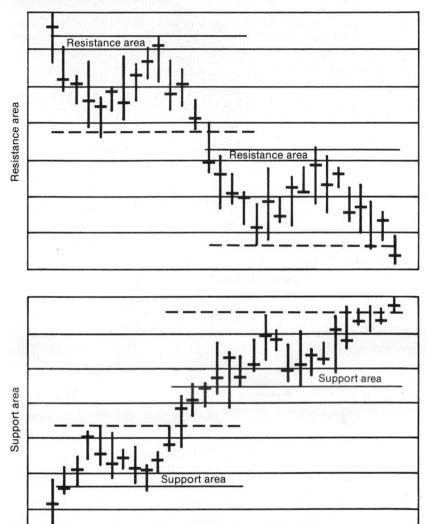

Source: Commodity Trading Manual, © 1977, Chicago Board of Trade.

floor, the downward penetration of that area may be considered a sell signal.

Channels and Trends. In addition to offering information on resistance areas, charting trend lines permits one to estimate potential price movements. An uptrend occurs when periodic lows are made at increasing price levels. When these lows are connected, they form a trend line. Closing prices may occur at random above the line, but none should occur below the trend line. A downward trend is usually identified by successive daily highs that are continually lower than the previous ones. If the lines connecting the daily lows and those connecting the daily highs are parallel, a channel has been created. Exhibit 16–3 illustrates uptrend and downtrend channels. A breakout from a channel is often regarded as a forecast for a major uptrend or downtrend.

Head-and-Shoulder Formations. In addition to an analysis of trend lines and channels, a chartist's review of head-and-shoulder formations is considered an accurate technical barometer for predicting a reversal in the market. A trend line often consists of four distinct moves: the left shoulder, the head, the right shoulder, and an abrupt penetration of the neckline as in Exhibit 16–4. If prices fall below the neckline, a bear market is forecasted. In contrast, a breakout from an inverted head-and-shoulder formation is regarded as a positive signal for a price improvement.

Moving-Average Charts. The moving-average chart places a moving-average line over a bar chart. The line may be based on varying time periods (e.g., a 10-, 30-, or 360-day moving average). The principal advantage of a moving-average chart is that moving averages reduce the effect of short-term price fluctuations. When a moving average reaches a predefined low, the market may be ready for an upturn. Likewise, when a moving average reaches a forecasted high, the market may have peaked.

Point and Figure Charts. As with bar charts, point and figure charts enable the trader to visually review pricing patterns in the underlying commodity. A point and figure chart is shown in Exhibit 16–5. For a point and figure chart, price is generally plotted on the vertical axis and time on the horizontal. Daily plots are not recorded at regular horizontal intervals. Rather, daily closing prices are recorded vertically until they overlap an already occupied mark. When this occurs, the plot or mark is moved to the column on the immediate right. No importance is attached to the time element. The chart is used to identify the direction and potential of a price change.

In developing a point and figure chart, the scale must be equal to or larger than the minimum move of the contract being charted.

EXHIBIT 16–3
Channels

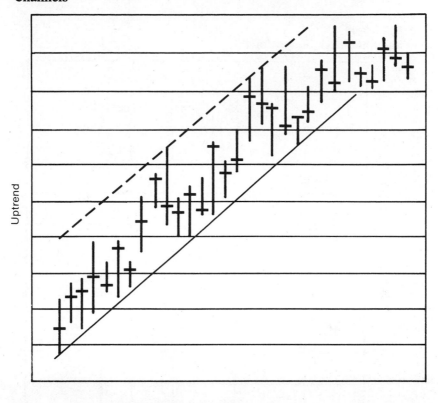

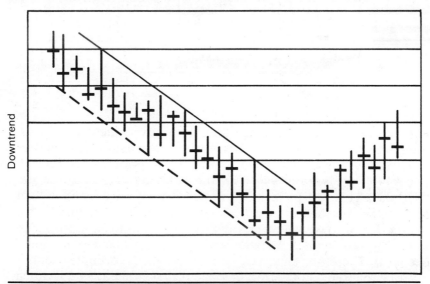

Source: Commodity Trading Manual, © 1977, Chicago Board of Trade.

EXHIBIT 16–4
Head and Shoulders Formations

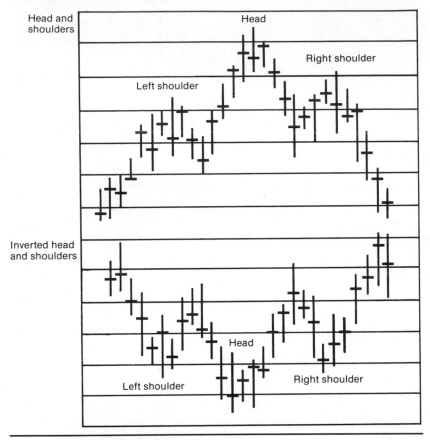

Source: *Commodity Trading Manual*, © 1977, Chicago Board of Trade.

For instance, if one charts the long-term government bond contract, one could use a scale of $\frac{2}{32}$ for each vertical increment selected. The contract charted in Exhibit 16–5 began trading on Day 1 at 94–14. It closed at 94–16 on the next day and 94–20 on the third day. This last price move required two marks, one on top of the other on the same vertical axis, since the price jumped $\frac{4}{32}$. On the fourth day, the price for this contract closed once more at 94–20. The space associated with this price had already been occupied. Therefore, the space to the right of the occupied square must be marked. On the fifth day, the price closed at 94–21. Since the scale for this chart requires a $\frac{2}{32}$ price move, no action was required.

EXHIBIT 16–5
Point and Figure Chart

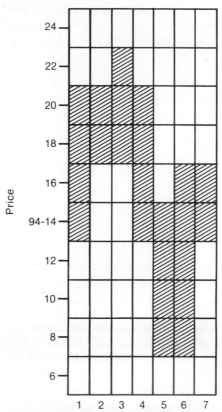

The basis for analyzing charts is that one may be able to visually perceive patterns of price movement that cannot be discovered by numerical analysis. Individuals may make more accurate decisions from graphical representations of data than from statistical representations of data. Some analysts, however, favor reviewing price patterns in a statistical framework. Through statistical modeling of the price, volume, and open interest data, they believe that the underlying price movements can be forecasted.

In statistical analysis, technicians have used a wide range of forecasting methods, including (1) moving averages, (2) exponential smoothing (3) simple regression, and (4) decomposition methods. As with charts, these alternative forecasting techniques are available on most on-line computer services. The alternative forecasting methodologies are briefly summarized as follows:

Naive Forecasts. A naive forecast is a simple trend extrapolation. Past data may indicate an average weekly increase of 5 percent. A naive forecast for next week would then also be a 5 percent increase.

Moving Averages. A moving average forecast is one in which the number of observations averaged remains constant, with the oldest data being removed as new data become available.

Exponential Smoothing. Exponential smoothing is a form of a moving average. Exponential smoothing produces a forecast that equals the previous forecast minus a portion of the error in that forecast.

Multiple Regression. Multiple regression assumes an equational relationship of the form $Y = a + b_i X_i \ldots b_n X_n$.
The independent variable, X, can be any factor affecting Y.

Decomposition. Decomposition breaks a time series into the various components that determine its value: trends, seasonals, and cycles. A forecast is made by predicting each factor separately and then adding them.

Whether or not one believes in the technical approach to trading, trading rules based on technical analysis do have influence on the price movement of futures contracts. Since technical traders respond to technical signals instead of fundamental information, technical trading will have the greatest influence in the market when trading by fundamental-oriented market participants is low.

FUNDAMENTAL ANALYSIS

In contrast to technical analysis, fundamental analysis attempts to forecast price movements by finding economic factors which affect actual price movements. For financial futures, fundamental analysis is based on the valuation models of financial futures and forecasts of the models underlying factors. Prices in futures markets react to new economic information in a similar fashion to prices of the underlying instruments. Hence forecasting stock dividends, interest rates, and economic trends is key to fundamental analysis of financial futures in the same sense as it is to the analysis of stocks and bonds.

Most tests of the value of fundamental analysis have determined that financial markets are efficient in the sense that they reflect all publicly available information. In order to forecast price movements other than those already implied in the market, one would have to have additional private information or correctly interpret the public information differently than the market. For instance, to forecast interest rate changes from a money supply forecast, the fundamental analyst would have to determine if his or her forecast of the money supply differs from the expected money supply. Forecasts of money supply form the basis of supply for credit; forecasts of new debt offerings form the basis of the demand of credit. Analysts who concentrate on stock index futures may focus their attention on forecasting expected stock dividends.[4]

EVALUATING FORECASTING TECHNIQUES

Given the alternative technical and fundamental methods available for futures price forecasting, the methods used to analyze futures prices depend on several criteria: (1) patterns in the data, (2) type of model desired, (3) time horizon, (4) cost of obtaining a prediction, and (5) the accuracy of the forecast. For instance, if price data contains a seasonal pattern, a simple moving average would be sufficient. Causal models depict expected relations among variables, but the magnitudes of all independent variables must be predicted in order to forecast the dependent variable. If the decision must be made weekly, models requiring monthly data or extensive modeling are not usable.

Three types of costs are associated with computerized forecasting methods: developmental, storage, and operating. Developmental costs include expenditures for writing or modifying a computer program to obtain a working model. A computerized trading method entails costs for storing the program and data in a computer's memory. Operating costs consist mainly of processing costs on computers. In addition, there are personnel costs involved. These are often more difficult to compute and larger than the computer costs.

The value of a forecasting method, therefore, depends on more than the accuracy of its predictions. Accuracy, however, is important. There are at least three ways to measure accuracy: the mean-squared error, the mean-percentage error, and the mean absolute-percentage error. The mean-squared error gives substantially more weight to large errors than to small errors, whereas the mean absolute-percentage error reflects only the average deviation. The mean-percentage error is a measure of bias.

Forecast error is usually defined relative to the actual price to facilitate comparison across securities and over time. This percentage forecast error is measured as follows:

$$E_{t,n} = (S_{t+n} - F_{t,n})/S_{t+n} \tag{16-1}$$

where

S_{t+n} = Price observation in period $t + n$
$F_{t,n}$ = Forecasted price in period t for cash price in period $t + n$
$E_{t,n}$ = Percentage forecast error.

The mean-squared forecast error *(MSE)*, mean-absolute error *(MAE)*, and mean forecast error *(MFE)* are calculated as follows:

$$MSE = \sum_{t=1}^{n} (E_{t,n})^2/n \tag{16-2}$$

$$MAE = \sum_{t=1}^{n} |E_{t,n}|/n \tag{16-3}$$

$$MFE = \sum_{t=1}^{n} E_{t,n}/n \tag{16-4}$$

The mean-squared error *(MSE)* gives a greater weight to extreme forecast errors than the mean absolute error *(MAE)*. However, for both, the greater the error, the lower the forecast effectiveness. The *MSE* and *MAE* indicate relative levels of forecast error but do not give the direction of the forecast error. The mean forecast error *(MFE)* is used to detect the presence or direction of the bias in forecasts of future prices. The mean forecast error will be (1) zero in the case of average unbiased forecasts, (2) significantly negative in the case of upward biased forecasts, and (3) significantly positive in the case of downward biased forecasts.

SUMMARY

Computer modeling is rapidly becoming the accepted way of teaching, recording, and trading financial futures. Properly established computer systems permit the transmittal and analysis of financial futures with speed and accuracy. In this chapter, examples of computer technology in tutorial, accounting, and trading activity were presented. Although the trading of financial futures remains as much an art as a science, the trading systems described in this chapter offer the user alternative means of analyzing market trends.

Many new computer-based trading systems will contain multiple functions for receiving up-to-the-minute prices covering all markets, the ability to display graphically any price movement, and the capability for order entry, contract analysis, and accounting monitoring.

APPENDIX

Computer Software for Financial Futures Traders*

Software programs for futures and options traders continue to pour out, making it almost impossible to keep on top of this market. This listing, compiled from a survey of software suppliers, is an attempt to describe briefly some of the current offerings. We do not pretend that it is a complete listing of all programs available. The fact that a software firm is not listed here should not be taken as any reflection by the magazine on the firm's integrity or reliability. Nor does inclusion mean the magazine endorses or recommends a particular package.

Abacus Software
Box 7211, Grand Rapids, Mich. 49510.
(616) 241-5510.
TAS-64
Sophisticated technical analysis system; manual input or automatic input through Dow Jones or Warner Computer Service. $85. Commodore 64.

ADP Comtrend
1345 Washington Blvd., Stamford, Conn. 06902. (800) 243-2556.
Videcom Graphic Quotations System
Real-time and historical commodities data from around the world.
Videcom Plus
Videcom service on personal computer.
TrendSetter System
Real-time commodity and stock trading data via satellite on personal computer.
AutoQuote
Real-time quotes on IBM PC.

Agribusiness Computing Solutions
130 McCormick Ave., Suite 100, Costa Mesa, Calif. 92626. (714) 966-1572.
Tradecom
Computing solutions optimized for cash markets organized into front-office (trading and management) and back-office (traffic and finance) operations. $15,000. DEC PDP 11/23 "look-alike."

Agri-Commodities Inc.
811 Turnpike St., North Andover, Mass. 01845. (617) 681-1105.
Meat Analyzer
Meat Hedging Decision Matrices
Identifies opportunities to buy and store cash meats and/or hedge in livestock futures. Apple II+.

Analytic Investment Management Inc.
Bay 214 Union Wharf, Boston, Mass. 02109. (617) 523-0620.
Portfolio Manager
Futures, including currencies, stock indexes and debt instruments, portfolio manager; uses probability theory and expectations, $1,000/mo. Time-share for any personal computer.
Inventory Manager
Mathematically sophisticated hedging program for companies exposed to inventory risk; applies to currencies and stocks as well. $300/mo. plus connect and start-up fee. Time-share basis.

Anidata Inc.
7200 Westfield Ave., Pennsauken, N.J. 08110. (609) 663-8123.
Market Analyst
Charts basic studies and user formulas. Portfolio manager. Automatically retrieves daily and historical data from two data bases. $495. Apple II, II+, IIe; IBM PC/XT.

* "Software for Traders" *Futures Magazine*, December, 1984. Reprinted with permission from *Futures Magazine*, 219 Parkside, Cedar Falls, Iowa 50613.

Applied Decision Systems
37 W. 228 Route 64, St. Charles, Ill.
60174. (312) 377-7280.
MarketView
MarketView/Lm
Color graphics, real-time tick charts,
spreads and ratio charts, technical analysis, trendlines. Live intraday and historical charts, time and sales, limits and
alerts. MarketView $600/mo.; Market-
View/LM $2,500. IBM PC, PCjr, XT.

BearClaw Software Systems Inc.
16044 Napa St., Sepulveda, Calif. 91343.
(818) 894-8790.
MarkeTrader
Real-time quote processor providing bar
charts, time and sales, stop alerts. Interfaces several quote vendors. $500. IBM
PC, Pcjr, XT, AT and compatibles.

Bishop Camp & Dewey
600 Madison Ave., 11th Floor, New
York, N.Y. 10022. (212) 838-4811.
Programs with daily output to determine government bond and mortgage-
backed security values used to forecast
interest rates. $24,000–$60,000. All computers.

Briar Software Services Inc.
Box 1390, 10 Oak St., Southampton, N.Y.
11968. (516) 283-5569.
Customized Configurations
Designs modular financial application
software, structures hard disk configurations of directories and subdirecto-
ries. $25,000 and up. Lisa; IBM PC, XT,
AT.

Brokerage Communications Inc.
Box 365, Somonauk, Ill. 60552. (800)
435-4385; (312) 552-4168.
Trademaster
On-line charting system for intraday and
interday charts, time and sales. Quotes
monitor. $195/mo. IBM PC.

Brokerage Systems Inc.
2 N. Riverside Plaza, Chicago, Ill. 60606.
(312) 559-0250.
TRACS—Trade Reporting and

Accounting Control System
FCM back-office accounting suitable for
institutional traders, cash market dealers and regional brokers as well as clearing members. $40,000 and up. IBM
S/36, Baby 36, S/34.

CalcShop Inc.
Box 1231-U, W. Caldwell, N.J. 07007.
(201) 228-9139.
OpVal
Evaluates stock, index and futures options: 96 Black-Scholes forecasts in 18
seconds. Graphs, Dow Jones interface,
newspaper-like electronic book operations. Basic $65; advanced $250. IBM
PC; Apple II, II+, IIe, IIc, III and compatibles.

Chart Engineering Group
216 Clanton Park Road, Downsview,
Ontario, Canada M3H 2G1. (416) 630-
3107.
Analytical Quality Graphs
Full vertical screen mode for precision
charts. Changes intraday screens in one-
third second. Overnight $150; intraday
$900. Apple II+ (64K), IIe, IIc; Franklin,
and compatibles.

Chronometrics Inc.
327 S. LaSalle St., Chicago, Ill. 60604.
(312) 461-9434.
Compact
Comprehensive tool for nonstock options. Option evaluation, risk analysis,
opportunity scanning. $750/mo.; settle-
ment-only data $250. Time-shared via
ASC II 300/200 baud terminal or personal computer with modem.
Price/Stress
Daily electronic newsletter presents ad-
visories on debt instruments, precious
metals, currencies and S&P 500 futures.
Over $330/turn average profit. Telerate
$300/mo. dial-up; $250/mo. plus computer charges. Telerate, ASC II 300/1200
baud terminal or personal computer
with modem.

Citicorp Information Services
850 Third Ave., New York, N.Y. 10022.

Citiquote Investor
Access to five years of pricing data, complete dividend history and other descriptive and analytical information on over 60,000 securities. $395. IBM PC, XT and compatibles.

Comm Basic Associates Inc.
7920 Chambersburg Road, Dayton, Ohio 45424. (513) 233-9904.
Hedger System Software
Trader System Software
Systems tailored to customer trading and hedging needs, including training, service and support. Vector Graphic, NCR, other computers.

Commodity Accounting Systems
777 N. First St., #205, San Jose, Calif. 95112. (408) 295-3304.
CFATS
Time-sharing solutions to pooled and managed account reporting and record-keeping problems. HP 3000 time-share host. Dial-up user needs only a terminal.

Commodity Advisory Corp. of Texas
7603 Bellfort, Suite 420, Houston, Texas 77061. (713) 644-5277.
Cybercast
Real-time and historical technical analysis programs. 25 tested indicators; 6 years of five-minute tick data; 10 years long-term data. $250,000. Hewlett-Packard desk top 9845B opt 270.
Cybercast Electronic Update Service
Evening update services for Cybercast Chart Service. All material necessary to update and interpret chart service. 15 markets standard. $1,000 upfront, $300/mo. TRS-80, Apple IIe.

Commodity Communications Corp.
420 Eisenhower Lane North, Lombard, Ill. 60148. (800) 621-2628.
FutureSource
Real-time information system for futures traders. Instant quotes, technical analysis, news, charts, price alerts, programmable screens. $250–$395/mo. IBM PC, Televideo, COMPAO, Appple, IBM compatible computers.

Commodity Information Services Co.—CISCO
327 S. LaSalle St., Suite 800, Chicago, Ill. 60604. (312) 922-3661.
Futuresoft
Open design, completely self-contained futures analysis system. Includes data base, utility programs to maintain data base and five analysis programs. $695. IBM PC and compatibles.

Commodity Quote-Graphics
Box 758, Glenwood Springs, Colo. 81602. (303) 945-8686.
TQ 20/20 System
Charts and technical studies based on real-time price quotes. $1,600. Epson QX-10.

Commodity Systems Development Associates
20863 Stevens Creek Blvd., Suite B2-A, Cupertino, Calif. 95014. (408) 255-5533.
Contract research and system testing for technical traders who do not have access to sophisticated research facility.

Commodity Systems Inc.—CSI
200 W. Palmetto Park Road, Boca Raton, Fla. 33432. (800) 327-0175; (305) 392-8663.
Quicktrieve, Quickmanager, Quickplot, Quickstudy
Retrieves, manages, graphically reviews and studies futures, stocks, bonds, bills, financial indicators and economic data from CSI's MARSTAT data base. $135 for software and 1 mo. service; $29/mo. and up thereafter; Apple II+, IIe, IIc; IBM PC, XT; Columbia; Commodore 64; TRS-80 III.

Commodity Trading System
18311 Spellbrook, Houston, Texas 77084. (713) 859-5449.
Computer-Aided Trading System
Real-time quotes, graphics display (5-minute intervals). Shows profits in real time with complete transaction log audit. $895. IBM PC/XT.

Commonwealth National Co. Ltd.
1045 Curlew Drive, Virginia Beach, Va. 23451. (804) 422-8809.
Golden Waves
Reduces market price action into easily understood symbols, including risk stop points, oversold-overbought indicators, highs, lows, etc. $3,450. IBM PC.

Compu-Cast Corp.
1015 Gayley Ave., Suite 506, Los Angeles, Calif. 90024. (213) 476-4682.
Stock Market Securities Program
Program indicates probable price moves. Dow Jones-CompuServe input auto file. Creates DIF files for spreadsheets. $325. IBM PC and compatibles, TRS-80 III.

Computer Application Services
Box 1091, Los Alamitos, Calif. 90720. (213) 493-2411.
IMIS—Investors Management Info System
Tracks client portfolios and valuation. Output on disk or print. $295. IBM PC.

Computer Asset Management
Box 26743, Salt Lake City, Utah 84126. (801) 964-0391.
Market Mood Monitor
Graphic charting of over 20 stock market technical indicators. Manual or modem updating. Includes five years of data. $185; modem updating $120/yr. Apple II+, IIe; IBM PC, XT and compatibles.
The Technician
Stock market timing and analysis program graphically charts more than 70 tape, sentiment and monetary indicators. Automatic modem updating. $395; modem updating. $120/yr. IBM PC, XT and compatibles.

Computer Evaluations Inc.
333 St. Charles, Suite 1111, New Orleans, La. 70130. (504) 466-5540.
Silver/Gold Trading Program
Trading signals and historical simulations for silver and gold futures contracts. $200. IBM, Apple, TRS-80.

SP500/NYSE Stock Index Trading Program
Trading signals and historical simulations for S&P 500 and NYSE stock indexes. $200. IBM, Apple, TRS-80.

Computer Workshop Inc.
1626 Ogden Ave., Downers Grove, Ill. 60515. (312) 971-0004.
Compucage
Position control and accounting for government securities trading. Calculates traders profit and loss, settlement, generates confirms. $12,500. IBM XT.

Compu Trac Inc.
Box 15951, New Orleans, La. 70175–9989. (800) 535-7990.
Compu Trac
Technical analysis, data retrieval and optimization of stock and commodity prices on daily, weekly or monthly basis. $1,900. IBM PC, XT, AT; Apple; Franklin.
Intra-Day Analyst
Real-time, on-line technical analysis of futures and options using 16 different studies and numerous charting tools. IBM PC, XT, AT; Apple; Franklin.
Trade Plan
Advanced computerized technical analysis program in conjunction with Compu Trac-d computer. Compu Trac-d.

Compuware
15 Center Road, Randolph, N.J. 07869. (201) 366-8540.
Stock and Options Analysis
Four programs (Option, Opgraph, Newprem, Portval) aid hedging in listed options against common stocks and assist in portfolio management. $99.95. Apple II+, IIe; TRS-80 III, IV.

Com-Tech Software
141 W. Jackson Blvd., Suite 1531 A, Chicago, Ill. 60604. (312) 341-7557.
Futures OptionMaster
Compute fair market value, delta, vega, common spreads, time decay and implied volatility for options on futures plus personal account management. $295. Apple (80 column), IBM.

Crawford Data Systems
Box 705, Somis, Calif. 93066. (805) 484-4159.
OPTIONX
Calculates fair value, risk-reward ratio and expected return for stock options, taking dividends and commissions into account. $145. Apple II+, IIe.

CyberEngineering Corp.
Box 4143, Huntsville, Ala. 35815. (205) 881-8542.
CyberBox and Jenkins
Analyzes and forecasts time series using Box and Jenkins modeling philosophy. Uses ARIMA techniques to identify, estimate and forecast univariate series. $500. Hewlett-Packard 200, 150; IBM PC.
Cyber4ier
Analysis and forecasting of cyclic time series models via cyclic descent procedure that adjusts frequency and amplitude to minimize squared error. $750.
CyberKalman
Analysis and forecasting of time series using Kalman filtering techniques to continuously fit and update chosen Box and Jenkins model. $1,000.

Cyber-Scan Inc.
Box 250, Winsted, Minn. 55395. (612) 485-4233.
Cyber-Scan
Technical analysis programs for commodity, stock and option markets (Market-Aid, Technical-Charter, Cyber-Scan, Scanner, Mini-Tic, Super-Tic). Standard software and custom programming services. $195–$1,695. Apple II+, IIe.

Cytrol Inc.
4620 W. 77th St., Edina, Minn. 55435. (612) 835-4884.
CyLock PC Access and Data Protection
Protects PCs from unauthorized access. Allows authorized users to encrypt files for private and shared use and produce an audit trail. $449. IBM PC, XT.

Datalab Inc.
5135 Elkmont Drive, Rancho Palos Verdes, Calif. 90274. (213) 375-0182.

Options Analyst Plus
Stock version ($450) analyzes stock options; nonstock version ($350) analyzes index and futures options. Strategies from simple call purchases to complex combinations analyzed. IBM PC, Apple II.

Decision Economics Inc.
14 Old Farm Road, Cedar Knolls, N.J. 07927. (201) 539-6889.
Stockcraft
Portfolio management (profit and loss, tax accounting and performance monitoring), technical analysis and trading strategy optimized for after-tax returns. $118. Apple II+, IIe, IIc, III.

Distek Inc.
Box 1108, Lake Mary, Fla. 32746. (305) 322-3835.
ProfitTaker
Analytic software generates precise trading recommendations based on user-controlled technical indicators. Fully disclosed logic. Includes ProfitAnalyst historic testing simulator. Apple II+, IIe ($795; with ProfitAnalyst, $1,495); IBM PC/XT ($995; with ProfitAnalyst, $1,995) and compatibles.

Dunn & Hargitt
22 N. Second St., Box 1100, Lafayette, Ind. 47902. (317) 423-2624.
Dunn & Hargitt Commodity Data Bank
Computerized data bank for all major commodity futures; daily price and volume data since July 1959. $100–$3,500. All diskettes, magnetic tapes and data cards.

FBS Systems
P.O. Drawer 248, Aledo, Ill. 61231. (309) 582-5628.
Market Window
Chart program for farmers. User does not have to be present to access daily price quotes. $795. TRS-80 (2, 12, 16); IBM PC; TI PC.

FCI Invest/Net
99 N.W. 183rd St., N. Miami, Fla. 33169. (305) 652-1710.

The Insider Trading Monitor
Tracks buys, sells and option exercises of corporate insiders for all U.S. stocks. Updated within 24 hours of filing at Securities and Exchange Commission. Dial-up $1/minute. All computers.

The 500 Group Inc.
3610 S. Ocean Blvd. #605, S. Palm Beach, Fla. 33480. (305) 588-3888.
Marketrac
Short-term system with graphics. Includes envelope projection, custom indicators, precise buy-sell signals, 50 or more Dow Jones Industrial Average points potential per signal. $195 (with manual); manual alone, $40. Apple II+, IIe, IIc; IBM PC, XT and compatibles.

Futures Arbitrage Inc.
2290 Zephyr St., Lakewood, Colo. 80215. (303) 232-3701.
Historical Tick Data
Futures time and sales data, cleaned and compressed onto floppy disk. Graphics, listing software and strategy modeling available. $10–$20 per contract month for data; $200 for graphics and listing software. IBM PC and compatibles, Apple, Tandy.

Futures Software Associates
Box 263, Lima, Pa. 19037. (609) 983-4636.
FRL
Comprehensive research language to manipulate and analyze any number series in arbitrary complex ways by forming simple English sentences. $585. Apple, IBM, most other computers.

Nelson George & Co. Inc.
Box 219, New York, N.Y. 11363.
Futures Commod-Analyzer
Scientifically measures market motion in commodities. $495. IBM, Apple.

Glenco Engineering Inc.
3920 Ridge Ave., Arlington Heights, Ill. 60004. (312) 392-2492.
Data Padlock
Encrypts and decrypts files with password. $150. IBM PC and compatibles.

Padlock II
Prevents software from being copied. Call for price. IBM PC and compatibles.

Hale Systems Inc.
Marketing Group, 1044 Northern Blvd., Roslyn, N.Y. 11576. (800) 645-3120; (212) 895-3810.
PEAR Portfolio Management System
Includes portfolio appraisal, realized and unrealized capital gains and losses, security cross-reference, statement of investment income and complete audit trail for stocks and indexes. $600 (Apple II, IIe); $695 (IBM PC, XT).
The Organizer
Fills all back-office requirements for CTAs, CPOs and brokerage firms. $10,000 micro; time-sharing costs on request. Apple, IBM PC.
Wall Street Wizard
More than 7,000 pages of information a day on major stocks and commodities, S&P groups and markets as a whole. $35/hr. Any micro with communications package or dial-up terminal.
Dial/Data
Automatic pricing for microcomputer users. Tracks daily, weekly and monthly prices for stocks, options and commodities. $30 for software; 3¢–10¢ per price for data accessed. IBM PC, XT; Apple II, IIe, III.

Halliker's Inc.
2508 Grayrock St., Springfield, Mo. 65807. (417) 882-9697.
Max:Chart
Creates large, hard copy Gann method charts using Commodity Systems Inc. data. $149.95.
Max:Tables
Creates hard copy Gann tables. $49.95.
Max:Format
Changes data into any form for charting—weekly, monthly, quarterly or user format. $49.95. Apple II, IIe, IIc.

Harvard Investment Service Inc.
Box 319 Glenview Drive, Harvard, Mass. 01451. (617) 772-5950.
Easy Trader
Software trading system for all futures,

stocks and options. Free five-year track record available for every trade. $2,800. IBM, Apple, all MS-DOS computers.

H&H Scientific Inc.
13507 Pendleton St., Fort Washington, MD. 20744. (301) 292-2958.
Stock Option Analysis Program
Uses Black-Scholes model to calculate fair market price for options. $250 (Apple II, II+, IIe); $350 (IBM PC).
Stock Option Scanner
Scans list of 3,000 stock options and ranks in order top 50 and bottom 50. $350 (Apple II, II+, IIe); $400 (IBM PC).

Hooper, Gold
2121 San Diego Ave., Suite 301, San Diego, Calif. 92110. (619) 298-4651.
Marketime
Fully automated long-term investment program for gold and silver. 90% profitable trades over 6½ years. $95/mo. All Apples, IBMs, popular models.

C.R. Hunter & Associates Inc.
1527 Northwood Drive, Cincinnati, Ohio 45237. (513) 761-9322.
The Permanent Portfolio Analyzer
Tracks portfolios and analyzes their purchasing power in several inflation scenarios. Gives suggested portfolio for each scenario. $295. Apple II+, IIe, IIc, III: IBM PC, XT, PCjr; all compatibles.

Interactive Software Research Inc.
7940-2 Airpark Drive, Gaithersburg, Md. 20879–4127. (301) 840-0417; (514) 931-0201.
Tickwatcher
Stockwatcher
Real-time analysis direct from exchanges. Portfolio alarms to screen, pager or satellite transceiver; electronic mail. $495. Apple, IBM and compatibles.

Intermountain Technical Services Inc.
Box 6062, Bellevue, Wash. 98007. (206) 627-5029.
(Intermountain programs below available for Apple II+, IIe, IIc, III: IBM PC, XT, AT.)

Datapac
Eight programs for price data file management. $65.
Graphics I
Six separate charting programs, each supplied in BASIC and in compiled machine language. $50.
Graphics II
One machine-language charting program in seven different studies. $90.
Technical Analyst Package
Includes Graphics II, Datapac and a choice of 1 of 10 trading systems. $190.
Trading Systems
Includes two programs (auto-run historical testing and optimization and auto-run trading signal generation) for 10 systems. $80/system; $600/all 10 systems.

Internation Software Centre
10 Speen St., Framingham, Mass. 01701. (617) 879-8585.
PEMS Market Trend Analyzer
Tracks and summarizes technical stock indicators, discerns strengths and weaknesses. $395–$595. IBM PC/XT, Eagle, others.

Investment Analysis Systems
1936 N. Clark #219, Chicago, Ill. 60614.
Options Portfolio Analyst
Values individual and multiple options to the market and to their theoretical values. Determines net delta and other position evaluations. $250. IBM PC.
Investor Graphics I
Collects and graphs price or other data; calculates and displays several indicators. Quicktrieve compatible format. Real-time updates optional. IBM PC.

Investment Growth Corp.
(Same as Distek Inc. listing.)

Investment Software
Box 2774, Durango, Colo. 81301. (303) 563-9543.
Technical Indicator Program
Calculates and plots 18 widely used technical stock market indicators. Stores values in yearly files for immediate recall. $69.50. IBM PC; Apple II+, IIe, IIc.

Investment Support Systems Inc.
1455 Broad St., Bloomfield, N.J. 07003.
(201) 338-0321.
(Futrak programs below available for
IBM PC, XT, AT and compatibles. Prices
upon request.)
Futrak/Portfolio
Full line of accounting, management
and operations reporting capabilities
and performance monitoring.
Futrak/LME
Portfolio service plus features to handle
transactions at London Metal Exchange
and U.S. metals exchanges.
Futrak/Broker
Management reports, profit and loss
statement, equity by customer and registered representative, and commission.
Futrak/Graphics
Intraday and historical charts on all
commodity price movements.

Investor's Micro Software
(Same as Harvard Investment Service
Inc. listing.)

Kidder Reports Inc.
114 Liberty St., Suite 303, New York,
N.Y. 10006. (800) 457-5577.
Kidder Trade Evaluator
Sophisticated analysis of cash-futures
arbitrage opportunities so user can eval-
uate relative value. $450/mo. IBM PC,
Apple II+, other MS-DOS compatibles.

Kinsey's Kommodity Kapers
2318 Second Ave. MS803, Seattle, Wash.
98121. (206) 325-0719.
Kapers'
Generates multiple buy-sell signals automatically or manually for fast trading
funds and pools. Provides analyses, forecasts, charts, files, account management.
$5,000 plus override percentage. Com-
patible with any system.
Swinger 7 Mark II*
Anticipates, identifies and confirms
profitable price reversals, tops and bot-
toms. Forecasts upcoming objectives,
support, resistance. Indicates early en-
tries, exits for swing or position traders.
$995. Commodore, IBM PCs, Apple,

TRS-80, Kaypro, Osborne, TI, Victor or
any MS-DOS system. Modifications
available for others.
Swinger 7 Mark III*
Advanced version for professional traders, brokers, advisors, research and development firms. Multipath analyses
with permanent storage and recall, hard
copy and networking. $1,995. All com-
puters.

K-Wave Financial Services
Box 1675, Sausalito, Calif. 94965. (415)
388-9474.
Advisor Portfolio Management
Portfolio management of multiple accounts. Designed for money managers,
brokers, traders. $1,250. All PC-DOS
(IBM compatible), MS-DOS, CP/M 86,
CP/M 80.
Analyst Graphics Program
High-end technical analysis program for
creating formulas, macroprocessing, all
kinds of point-and-figure and bar charts,
volume, moving averages and price
monitoring. $4,995. IBM PC (compati-
bles), MS-DOS, CP/M 86, CP/M 80. Requires high-resolution graphics capability.

Lambert-Gann Publishing
Box O, Pomeroy, Wash. 99347. (509)
843-1094.
Gann Trader I
High-resolution charts (on dot matrix
printers) that follow methods of W. C.
Gann. Computes Gann's price and time,
square of 9 and hexagon points. Apple
II, IIe, II+ ($498); Apple hard disk ver-
sion ($529); IBM PC Quicktrieve or
Compu Trac data versions ($549 each).

Lambert Programming Service
434 N. Crescent Heights Blvd., Los
Angeles, Calif. 90048. (213) 658-6284.
EIGHT
All calculations needed for the book,
*New Concepts in Technical Trading Sys-
tems*, by J. Welles Wilder Jr., with varia-
ble parameters. $600. IBM PC, PCjr, XT,
IBM clones; TRS-80 III, IV; HP-41 CV,
CX.

LaSalle Capital Management
141 W. Jackson Blvd., Suite 1740A, Chicago, Ill. 60604. (312) 663-5610.
Hedging program
Generates futures or options hedge for given cash position for novice or experienced user. Interactive feedback on hedge design. $3,500. IBM PC and compatibles.

Lotsoff Systems Inc.
20 N. Wacker Drive, Suite 3200, Chicago, Ill. 60606. (312) 368-1442.
Fixed-Rate Lending Manager
Integrated microcomputer program for tracking assets, funding sources and futures positions. Designs hedges, executes deferred accounting and reports hedge performance. $1,500. IBM PC/XT and some compatibles.
Futures Transaction Manager
System for tracking futures positions and margin flow. Specifically developed for financial hedging operations. $3,500. IBM PC/XT and some compatibles.

Macro-Trend
7420 Westlake Terrace #1009, Bethesda, Md. 20817. (301) 365-3737.
Macro-Trend
Automated commodity system generates entry and exit points, reversals, protective stops. Daily trading data, retrieved after market close via phone. $2,500/yr.; demo diskette $25. Apple II+, IIe, IIc.

Market Data Systems
3835 Lamar Ave., Memphis, Tenn. 38118. (901) 363-0500.
Model 65—Futures Price Quotation Service
On-line service provides volume, open interest, net change, open, high, low and close. Instantly updates trades, bids and asks. Over 100 pages in variety of formats and 10 pages of bar charts. $295/mo. plus exchange fees. Most personal computers.

Marketfax Info Services Ltd.
12 Sheppard St., Suite 500, Toronto, Ontario, Canada M5H 3A1. (416) 365-1728.
Marketfax
User can create charts of 7,000 equities for technical analysis interpretation. Prime time $600/mo. minimum for 12 hr.; nonprime time $100/mo. and communications charge. Commodore 64, Apple II MacIntosh, IBM compatibles.

Market Information Inc.
11414 W. Center Road, Suite 100, Omaha, Neb. 68144. (402) 333-6633.
Long-term and short-term chart analysis choices of IDA, Compu Trac, Futrak and Comtrax on IBM XT; Apple II+, IIe.

MBA Information Corp.
5100 Poplar Ave., Suite 3000, Memphis, Tenn. 38137. (901) 767-3970.
Wall Street Analyst
Tool allows computation and graphics of up to 13 different technical studies. $199 (Apple and compatibles); $299 (IBM PC and compatibles); $119 (Commodore).

McGraw-Hill Book Co.
1221 Avenue of Americas, New York, N.Y. 10020. (212) 512-2345.
Investpak
Twenty-five interactive programs for handling investment problems, questions and decisions. $250. Apple II+; TRS-80I, III; IBM VM/CMS (mainframe); DEC VAX 11/780 (mainframe).

Memory Systems Inc.
5212 Hoffman, Skokie, Ill. 60077. (312) 674-4833.
Technical Trader
Advanced technical analysis allowing individual combination of technical indicators. $450. Apple, IBM PC, Apple and IBM compatibles.

MFX Commodities Inc.
Box 869, Presque Isle, Maine 04769. (207) 764-4433.
Commodity
Futures technical analysis, accounting and bookkeeping for FCM. $80. IBM.

Micro Futures
Box 2765, Livonia, Mich. 48154. (313) 422-0914.
(Micro Futures programs below available for IBM PC, Apple II, TRS-80.)
Comdata
Menu-oriented commodity data management system creates, updates and edits any data file. Includes quotes, weekly, monthly and spread programs. $125.
Data on Disk.
Provides current and historical data on 45 commodities starting in 1969. $5/contract.
MJK Access
Warner Access
Telephone retrieval of current or historical commodity/securities data. Menu-operated, automatic log-on/log-off, local call, 24-hour access. $75 each.
Maband, Macross, OS, MO
Four programs for technical trading using moving averages. Automatic daily signal reports plus "rollover" simulations on selected variables over any series of contracts with summary. $75 each.

Micro-Investment Software Inc.
9621 Bowie Way, Stockton, Calif. 95209. (209) 952-8833.
Stockchart-II
Stock analysis including on-balance volume analysis. Communications and charting capabilities. $350. IBM PC, COMPAQ.

Micro Systems Services Inc.
5205 Abelia Drive, Orlando, Fla. 32811. (305) 298-3134.
Futures Analyst
Provides daily and historical market data from MJK Associates. Includes data base editing and management. $75. Apple II+, IIe, IIc.

Micro Team
12401 W. Olympic Blvd., Los Angeles, Calif. 90064. (213) 207-5330.
Commtrader
Real-time display of futures prices. $1,200. IBM PC, PCjr.

MicroVest
Box 272, Macomb, Ill. 61455. (309) 837-4512.
Profit Optimizer
Automatically finds profitable stop strategy and profitable parameters for 20 trading techniques to optimize user's strategy. $395; demo disk $5. Apple II series.
High-Tech
Thirty different technical analyses on daily or weekly stocks and commodities. Auto-run feature and graphic displays. $395. Apple II series.

MJK Associates
122 Saratoga Ave., Suite 11, Santa Clara, Calif. 95051–2926. (408) 257-5102.
Commodity Data Information Service
Daily futures and cash data for 57 major commodities. Micro data retrieval. Charting. Local phone access. Apple II, IBM PC, TRS-80 and other micros.
POISE—Portfolio Opportunities Investigated through Simulated Executions
Commodity trading model programming, simulation, evaluation and optimization. Use any terminal to access MJK's HP 3000 Series III.

Monchik-Weber Corp.
11 Broadway, New York, N.Y. 10004. (212) 269-5460.
Specialize in computer systems and information services for financial industry. Products in three functional areas include data base, portfolio management and system development.

National Computer Network
1929 N. Harlem Ave., Chicago, Ill. 60635. (312) 622-6666.
COMDAT
More than 20 traditional technical analyses plus custom programming possibilities. $150/mo. plus $10/hr connect and $3/CPU minute. Any computer with modem.
Nite-Line Communications Program
Automatically updates Compu Trac, Chart Trader, Investor's Tool Kit files

with minimum effort and error checking. $45. Apple II+, IIe; IBM PC, XT.

Nite-Line
Historical end-of-day data on all stocks, bonds, options, futures traded in United States and Canada. $30 introduction and hourly charge ($9 local, 300 baud). Any computer with modern.

OPTDAT
System analyzes option spreads, deltas, theoretical values; evaluates various positions. $250/mo. or $15/day plus charges. Any computer with Asynch modem.

NewTEK Industries
Box 46116, Los Angeles, Calif. 90046. (213) 874-6669.

Compu/CHART
Generates and displays charts from 73 points of value with three moving averages for stock trend analysis. Compares up to four stocks at a time; graphics capability not required. $99.95. General CP/M, Kaypro, Televideo 950, Osborne, Xerox 820-II, 860.

NEXUS Research Inc.
Box 1024, Dillon, S.C. 29536. (803) 774-7006.

Chartist
Technical analysis program with graphics to screen, printer and plotter. Bar charts and technical indicators. Auto-run unattended operation. $695. IBM PC, XT, AT; Zenith 151, 161; COMPAQ; Columbia Data Products.

Northwest Analytical Inc.
520 N.W. Davis St., Portland, Ore. 97209. (503) 224-7727.

NWA Statpak
Multifunction statistics and trend analysis. Interfaces with other software— word processors, spreadsheets, data bases. $495. CP/M, MS-DOS, PC-DOS, CTOS, BTOS, MacIntosh.

N-Squared Computing
5318 Forest Ridge Road, Silverton, Ore. 97381. (503) 873-5906.

Market Analyzer
Manipulates, plots and compares any type of numerical data. Provides unlimited experimentation with indicators. $295. Apple II+ (64K), IIe, IIc; IBM PC (128K).

Stock Analyzer
Creates indicators and plots bar and point-and-figure charts for on-screen analysis. Reads Dow Jones MA, Compu Trac and N-Squared data disks. $295. Apple II+ (64K), IIe, IIc; IBM PC (128K).

Market Illustrator
Combination of Market and Stock Analyzer programs but less powerful. $195. Apple II+ (64K), IIe, IIc.

O.C.O. Software Inc.
1120 Mar West, Suite A, Tiburon, Calif. 94920. (415) 435-5001.

Comm-Vue
Technical trading system provides buy and sell recommendations along with recommended stop-loss positions for up to 35 commodities. Draws bar charts. Apple.

Speculator
Game with 15 days of actual market data and news headlines; 22 commodities, 3 contract months each. Player can enter trades, watch fills and check equity. $79. IBM PC and compatibles.

OptiManagement Resources Inc.
CN851 1000 Herrontown Road, Princeton, N.J. 08452. (609) 924-8957.

Technical Trader Service
Service implements user-defined trading systems and analyses. Responsive to user needs; allocations for managed accounts.

Options-80
Box 471-FM, Concord, Mass. 01742. (617) 369-1589.

Stock Option Analyzer
Analyze option transactions for maximum return. Indexed manual; 80A includes Black-Scholes. $125–$170. IBM PC, XT and compatibles; Apple II series, Apple III; TRS-80 series.

Options Research Inc.
256 Sutter St., Fourth Floor, San Francisco, Calif. 94108. (415) 981-0964.

(Options Research programs below available on time-sharing basis on any terminal with communications software and 300/1200 baud modem.)

Trador
Produces theoretical value, risk and profit reports for portfolio of stocks, futures and options on stocks, indexes and futures.

History
Produces historical report of several measures of volatility including monthly, annual and implied volatilities.

Scannor
Searches for trade opportunities, spreads, covered call writes, conversions, overvalued and undervalued options for given criteria.

Port
Portfolio accounting system keeps record of options transactions. Produces close-open profit reports, position summaries and cross-reference tables.

TVF
Displays real-time theoretical values and implied interest rates for index futures.

Pardo Corp.
515 N. Sheridan Road, Evanston, Ill. 60202. (312) 866-9342.

Swing Trader
Sophisticated software to enhance and maintain profitability and usability. Incorporates Gann, Elliott and pattern recognition in proprietary trading model. Optimization, simulation and testing capabilities. $1,440. Apple II, II+, IIe, III; IBM PC.

Advanced Chartist Plus
Technical analysis graphics program for traders. Produces daily, weekly or user-defined bar charts with full price and data scaling. $325–$445. Apple II, II+, IIe, III; IBM PC, XT, AT.

Long Distance Runner
Designs, optimizes, tests and monitors trading models with up to four moving averages. Compound trading signals with crossovers. $995. Apple II, II+, IIe, III.

Trackman
Tracks, calculates and produces a report

including profit-loss, open equity, margin and order status. Produces analysis and summary. $295. Apple II, II+, IIe, III.

Passage Technologies
Box 58162 Station L, Vancouver, B.C., Canada V6P 6C5.

Smart Chart
Technical analysis for stocks and commodities includes color graphics, chart printouts and data base communications. $65. IBM PC, TRS-80 III.

The Pennsylvania Group
2 Bala Plaza, Bala Cynwyd, Pa. 19004. (800) 772-7638.

Penn Point
Advice on selection of computer-based investment research product best suited to customer's needs.

Andrew Pepper
250 E. 65th St., New York, N.Y. 10021. (212) 239-4360.

Stock Market Analysis and Trading
Three-part program includes market direction, stock selection and evaluating stocks in relation to others. $250. Apple II+.

Powers Research Inc.
30 Montgomery St., Jersey City, N.J. 07302. (201) 434-8181.

Hedge Management Back-Office System
Complete record-keeping system reports flow-of-funds, audit trail, margin calls, option premium earned and paid by broker, by profit center, by hedge. IBM PC, XT.

Asset/Liability Hedge Management System
Complete program for analysis of balance sheet risk. Generates net gaps, projected gaps, duration adjusted gaps, hedge ratios, projected income statement with hedges, scenario analysis.

Micro Hedge Management System
Analyzes risk by asset portfolio or liability portfolio, generates hedge ratios, futures position, number of contracts, daily hedge effectiveness, monitoring reports.

Princeton Research Inc.
122 S. Robertson Blvd., Suite 300, Los
Angeles, Calif. 90048. (213) 274-8785.
Matrix/Guardian System
Total futures trading and money man-
agement system with real-time trading
record. $3,250. Apple II+, IIe, IIc, III;
IBM PC, XT; TRS-80 III, IV; HP-41CV,
CX.

Professional Farm Software
219 Parkade, Cedar Falls, Iowa 50613.
(319) 277-1278; (800) 553-2910; (800)
772-2106 in Iowa.
Chart Analyst
Charting system for stocks and commodities generates high-low-close bar,
point-and-figure, moving averages and
spread charts. $275; rental $90/mo.;
demo $14.95. IBM PC, XT, AT.

Programmed Press
2301 Baylis Ave., Elmont, N.Y. 11003.
(516) 775-0933.
(Programmed Press programs below
run on IBM, Apple, Radio Shack, Com-
modore, Sanyo, Kaypro, DEC, CPM, MS-
DOS computers and cost $119.95 each.)
Investment Software Package
Fifty investment programs forecast and
evaluate price, risk and return on stocks,
bonds, options, futures.
Statistical Forecasting Package
Twenty interactive programs; includes
multiple regression, time series analysis,
exponential smoothing for forecasting.
Foreign Exchange
Interactive programs forecast and evaluate price, risk, return for currencies.
Commodities Futures
Interactive programs, including option
valuation models, forecast and evaluate
price, risk and return on options, futures.
Options, Futures and Arbitrage
Seven option models forecast and evaluate price, risk and return on options, futures and arbitrage.
Bonds and Interest Rates
Interactive programs forecast future
values of bonds and annuities and evaluate investment.

Stock Market Software
Interactive programs forecast profits,
evaluate price, risk, return for stocks.

QFS Inc.
Box 565, Ardsley, N.Y. 10502. (914) 591-
6990.
Data Connection
Updates and maintains data on stocks,
bonds, options, commodities, mutual
funds and market indexes. $110. IBM
PC/XT and compatibles.

Quote-Edge Systems
29 S. LaSalle St., Suite 420, Chicago, Ill.
60603. (312) 263-4864.
Comtrax
Real-time trade tool stores tick by tick
and daily price information on all U.S.
commodities. Technical analysis, graphs
and quotes. $995. IBM PC/XT, AT.

Raden Research Group Inc.
Box 1809, Madison Square Station, New
York, N.Y. 10159. (212) 732-0871.
*PRISM—Pattern Recognition
Information Synthesis Modeling*
Develops forecasting model from histor-
ical data on up to 500 indicators. Pro-
gram learns functional form without as-
sumptions. $25,000–$100,000. IBM PC.

Roberts-Slade Inc.
Box 610, 1570 N. Main, Spanish Fork,
Utah 84660. (801) 798-8102.
*OCTOOL—On-line Commodity Trading
Tool*
Charting and technical analysis in both
interday and intraday format. Intraday
programs (including accounting) in
real-time. $995; yearly renewal $200.
IBM PC, XT and compatibles.

Rolfe & Nolan Computer Services
194–200 Bishopsgate, London, England
EC2. 01–623–6941.
Futures Accounting System
Real-time system provides full documentation accounting, control and analysis for all futures and option markets
worldwide.

RTR Software Inc.
444 Executive Center Blvd., Suite 225,
El Paso, Texas 79902. (915) 544-4397.
RTR Point and Figure Charting
Standard point-and-figure charting and
analysis. $125. Apple II, II+, IIe, IIc.
TechniFilter
Stock screening and selection according
to user-defined technical analysis crite-
ria. Buy-sell strategy testing and optimi-
zation. $300. IBM PC, XT; Apple II+, IIe,
IIc; Texas Instruments PC.

Satellite Syndicated Systems Inc.
8252 S. Harvard Ave., Tulsa, Okla.
74137. (918) 481-3275.
Data Quote
Allows personal computer to respond to
stock and commodity data stream from
seven exchanges. Transmitted via satellite. $50. IBM PC and compatibles.

Savant Corp.
Box 440278, Houston, Texas 77244,
(800) 231-9900; (713) 556-8363.
(Savant programs below available for
IBM PC, XT, AT and compatibles.)
The Technical Investor
Up to four independent windows to plot
various technical analyses. Updates
prices automatically. Includes point-
and-figure charting. $395.
The Technical Databridge
Allows users of Technical Investor to
transfer data into and out of spread-
sheets such as Lotus 1–2–3. $145.
Optioncalc
Calculates theoretical value of stock op-
tions using Black-Scholes model for
calls and puts. $89.

Software Options Inc.
19 Rector St., New York, N.Y. 10006.
(212) 785-8285.
Futures Margin System
Monitors futures positions, client and
broker margin accounting, daily trade
confirmations. Provides daily and
monthly open position statements for up
to 500 accounts. $8,000–$16,000. IBM
PC/XT.

COTS/FairValue
Option pricing, risk management and
portfolio system for futures options.
$2,950. IBM PC and compatibles.

Spiral Enterprises
308 Crown Road, Willow Park, Texas
76086. (817) 441-8901.
Stock Market Advisor System
Evaluates market trend and gives advi-
sories for action. $172.95. TRS-80 (1, 3
and 4), LNW, Max-80 and compatibles.

Star Value Software
12218 Scribe Drive, Austin, Texas 78759.
(512) 837-5498.
OptionVue Plus
Comprehensive maintenance and analysis system for serious private investors
in options. Includes Dow Jones data capture. $495. IBM PC and compatibles.
Professional OptionVue
Manages extensive positions for market
maker in options. Graphic analysis and
variety of tabular reports. $895. IBM PC
and compatibles.

Street Software Technology Inc.
40 Wall St., Suite 6003, New York, N.Y.
10005. (212) 425-9450.
GAASS System
Six months on-line historical data base
of daily closes on U.S. Treasury cash and
futures securities. More than 100 analytical programs plus applications for cash-
futures arbitrage evaluation. $600/mo.
Time-sharing, any terminal with modem.
Time Series
Daily quotes of financial futures contracts and cash deliverables on-line from
contract inception. Model capable of
manipulating data. $400/mo. Time-
sharing.
Pricing Service
Daily bid and asked prices for all U.S.
Treasury bills, notes, bonds, GNMAs and
complete agencies on-line by 5:30 P.M.
(EST) for same day position valuations.
$300/mo. Time-sharing.

Summa Software Corp.
Box 2046, Beaverton, Ore. 97075. (503) 644-3212.
Winning on Wall Street
Fully integrated three-module system. Data base and automatic data retrieval, interactive charts, 23 technical analysis tools, complete portfolio accounting with simulation mode. $700. IBM PC, XT and compatibles; Apple II, II+, IIc, IIe.

Supported Software
100 S. Ellsworth, Ninth Floor, San Mateo, Calif. 94404.
Options Evaluator
Integrates Black-Scholes and arbitrage-parity strategies with options analysis. $100 plus $50/mo. license.

Sydney Development Corp.
600–1385 W. Eighth Ave., Vancouver, B.C., Canada V6H 3V9. (604) 734-8822.
Stox C
Nine types of charts, three major data base services, price-volume quotes, historical quotes, index activity, fast analysis and decisions. $99. IBM PC.
Stox M
Personal portfolio management system for managing up to 30 active portfolios on one diskette. Geared to new tax act. $199. IBM PC.

Technical Analysis of Stocks and Commodities
Box 46518, Seattle, Wash. 98146. (206) 938-0570.
Volume 1
Subroutines only for Compu Trac. Fast Fourier Transform (FFT) with data preprocessing, Finite Impulse Response (FIR) filter, momentum oscillator of triple exponential smoothed data (TRIX), market direction indicator plus six utilities. $30 for magazine subscribers. Apple II+, IIe, IIc, III.

Technical Data Corp.
45 Milk St., Fourth Floor, Boston, Mass. 02109. (617) 482-3341.
(Technical Data programs below available for IBM PC, XT and compatibles.)

Fixed Income Portfolio Manager
Manages and analyzes multiple fixed-income portfolios. $2,850.
The Bond Swap Analyzer
Evaluates profitability of bond swap. $1,700.
The Mortgage Calculator
Calculates and analyzes all kinds of mortgaged-backed securities. $1,500.
The Rate of Return Analyzer
Computes and graphs total rates of return for up to 14 issues. $1,375.
The Yield Calculator
Performs calculations on all kinds of fixed-income securities. $375.
The IDC Data Link
Automatically prices portfolio of securities via phone dial-up. $250.

Technicom Inc.
736 N.E. 20th Ave., Fort Lauderdale, Fla. 33304. (305) 523-5394.
(Technicom programs below available for Apple and IBM PC computers.)
Datafile
Allows user to enter and store all price data for use in other Technicom trading programs. $300.
The Master System
Reversing system keeps trader in market at all times to catch every move. $600.
The Dynamic Wave System
Channel breakout system with separate entry and exit channels. $600.
The Dual/Dynamic Wave System
Similar to previous program but channels change dynamically with price action over predetermined user-adjustable range. $700.
Moving Averages
Allows up to three moving averages with user-selected parameters. $500.
Accudex
Computerized version of Commodex system with user-adjustable moving averages. $600.
Profit Catcher and Profit Catcher II
Similar to Larry Williams' Trend Catcher system using principle of measuring price volatility for adjustable number of days. Programs identical but II includes Autoanalyzer feature. $500 and $700.

Daytrader/1 and Daytrader/2
Generates daily buy/sell orders and calculates target price to exit. Both include Autoanalyzer and are identical except for different calculation formula. $500 each.

Relative Strength and Momentum
Generates RSI and momentum figures. Number of days variable. $200.

The Spring/Reverse System
Improved version of Larry Williams' Floor Trader System. $500.

Grant Renier's Advanced Dual Accord
Computerized version eliminates manual calculations. $400.

Wilder's 8 Programs
Six systems plus Relative Strength and Momentum above, programmed from J. Welles Wilder's book, *New Concepts in Technical Trading Systems.* $200/each; $700/all eight.

Autorun
Runs Wilder's 8 Programs above automatically and unattended, offering printed list of daily trading recommendations for each system for each contract. $300.

Tradecenter Inc.
25 Hudson St., New York, N.Y. 10013. (212) 226-4700.

Tradecenter
Real-time graphic price information with five-year data base covering stocks, options, futures. Professional trading tool. $1,500–$2,500/mo. HP 150, IBM PC.

Troy-Folan Productions Inc.
29 Miller Road, Wayne, N.J. 07470. (201) 694-0424.

Stock Momentum Studies
Measures price momentum, relative strength, exponential moving averages and regular moving averages for any stock, futures contract or index. $325. Apple II, IIe, IIc.

Ultimate Data Systems Limited
26 Broadway, Suite 1257, New York, N.Y. 10004. (212) 943-0171.

Tuffs Hedging Module
Integration of cash items, futures and options with hedge reporting, delta neutral positions, overall profitability, mismatch analysis, spread analysis. $12,000. VAX.

Tuffs FCM Module
FCM/broker processing system with accounting, customer statements, commission billing, NFA reporting. $40,000. VAX.

Tuffs Futures Module
Full back-office and accounting for futures with ledger, broker reconciliation, profitability, positions, limits. $25,000. VAX.

Tuffs Options Module
Full back-office and accounting for options with general ledger, broker reconciliation, pricing models, integration of options and cash. $12,000. VAX.

Wall Street Graphics Inc.
Box 562, Wall Street Station, New York, N.Y. 10268. (212) 495-4488.

Market Eas-alyzer
Stock market timing. $695; demonstration $10. Apple IIe, II+; IBM PC.

WSI Corp.
41 North Road, Bedford, Mass. 01730. (617) 275-5300.

Real-Time Weather Information System
Access to data base of real-time weather data and information. Accessible via dialup at 1200 and 300 baud. Price varies with usage.

Worley Commodities Inc.
16010 Barkers Point Lane, Suite 675, Houston, Texas 77079. (713) 497-7787.

QuickBroker
Issues specific trades and defined risk twice a day. $25/mo. All microcomputers.

Zacks Investment Research
2 N. Riverside, Suite 1900, Chicago, Ill. 60606. (312) 559-9405.

Microanalyst
Maintains personal financial data base with downloading capabilities from Zacks estimates. Value Line, Computstat and DRI. Investment analysis language allows user to do fundamental analysis

and generate reports. $10,000–$25,000. IBM XT, COMPAQ, Leading Edge XT. *Zsearch* Screening data base of 90 current fundamental, estimate and price data items for 3,000 companies. Data provided weekly on diskettes. Interfaces with Lotus 1–2–3. $8,000–$16,000. IBM XT, AT; AT&T 6300; COMPAQ; Leading Edge.

NOTES

[1] In order to analyze the fundamental factors of futures prices or the benefits of technical rules, the underlying price data must first be collected. Many services provide on-line data bases and analytical analysis of economic information. Since obtaining price information on a timely basis is necessary for traders, it is often advisable to subscribe to a real-time data base service. Several of these analytical services and data sources are listed in the Appendix. Most real-time services provide only current data. In order to establish trading rules historical data is also necessary. To foster greater understanding and use of financial futures, governmental and trade organizations (e.g., CBT and CME) have made available low-cost, historical trade data. Periodicals (e.g., *Intermarket, Futures Magazine, Computer Review*) also provide a source of current information on new computer-based data and trading programs.

[2] Computer support software is now available on a real-time basis. See L. Nathans, "Programs for Real-Time Analysis of Stock Index Futures Trading," *Wall Street Computer Review*, August/September, 1984, pp. 59–63.

[3] This report is taken from a computer-based futures trading exercise offered by the Chicago Board of Trade.

[4] For instance, a general rule of thumb for S&P 500 futures is that a 10 percent change in dividend expectations is worth about a .2 index point change in the fair value of the futures premium.

SELECTED REFERENCES

Barnes, Robert M. *Commodity Profits Through Trend Trading.* New York: John Wiley & Sons, 1982.

Burns, Joseph. "Electronic Trading in Futures Markets." *Financial Analysts Journal,* January–February 1982, pp. 33–41.

Cornell, Bradford. "The Relationship Between Volume and Price Variability in Futures Markets." *Journal of Futures Markets,* Fall 1981, pp. 302–16.

Darrow, Joel W., and James R. Belileve. "The Growth of Databank Sharing." *Harvard Business Review,* November–December 1978, pp. 180–89.

Moriarity, Shane. "Communicating Financial Information Through Multidimensional Graphics." *Accounting Research,* Spring 1979, pp. 205–24.

Neftci, Salih N., and Andrew Policano. "Can Chartists Outperform the Market? Market Efficiency Tests for Technical Analysis," no. 53, *Center for the Study of Futures Markets,* April, 1983.

Wheelwright, Steven C., and Makridakis, Spiros. *Forecasting Methods of Management.* New York: John Wiley & Sons, 1980.

CHAPTER 17

Options and Options on Futures

THE OPTIONS MARKETS

Options, options on futures, and futures contracts are all called "derivative securities." They share the characteristics of having a limited life and of being derived from an underlying instrument (e.g., bonds, stock indexes, stocks, or currencies. However, in contrast to futures contracts, options represent a *right* rather than an *obligation* to buy or sell a specific quantity of an underlying asset at a given price on or before a specified delivery date. At delivery the holder of a futures contract is required to purchase or sell the underlying instrument. The holder of the option may decide to let the option expire at delivery without purchasing or selling the underlying instrument. The decision that the option holder must make to exercise the option or not will depend on the relationship between the exercise price of the option contract and the price at which the same transaction can be carried out in the marketplace. The "optionable" exercise feature and the fixed exercise price of options provide option users with unique alternatives to futures contracts for risk management, arbitrage, and speculation.

Exchange-traded options and options on futures in financial instruments have developed largely within the last 12 years.[1] The Chicago Board of Options Exchange (CBOE) introduced exchange-traded common stock options in April 1973. Today stock options are traded at five exchanges: the CBOE, American Stock Exchange, Philadelphia, Pacific, and Midwest Stock Exchanges. Over 350 stocks have both put and call options traded on these exchanges. In the last few years many new types of option contracts have been introduced. The most successful new options are those on stock indexes and on Treasury bond futures. Dealer markets in U.S. government bond options, GNMA options, and foreign currency options have also developed. These dealer or over-the-counter (OTC) options are offered by most major U.S. government securities and foreign exchange dealers. Various exchange-traded options on stocks, stock indexes, fixed income securities, and currencies are listed in Exhibit 17–1.

Options and futures markets are often grouped together under the term *speculative markets*. They both serve as a means of speculating on the future price of the underlying instrument. They both can be employed in a variety of risk management or arbitrage strategies that capitalize on the option or futures contracts price correlation with the price of the contract's underlying instrument. In this chapter, we discuss the differences and similarities between

---

EXHIBIT 17–1
Options Traded in Financial Instruments and Currencies

	*Exchanges**
Stock and stock index options	
Stock options	CBOE, AMEX, PCE, PHX, MWE
S&P 100 Index options	CBOE
S&P 500 Index options	CBOE
Major Market Index (MMI) options	AMEX
NYSE Composite Index options	NYSE
Value Line Index options	PHX
Market Value Index options	AMEX
Computer Technology Index options	AMEX
Technology Index options	PCE
Gold and Silver Index options	PHX
Options on S&P 500 futures	CME
Options on NYSE futures	NYSE
Debt instrument options	
Options on U.S. Treasury bond futures	CBT
Options on U.S. Treasury note futures	CBT
Options on Eurodollar futures	CME
U.S. Treasury bond options	CBOE
U.S. Treasury note options	AMEX
OTC Treasury bond options	—
OTC GNMA options	—
Currency options	
British pound options	PHX
Canadian dollar options	PHX
West German mark options	PHX
French franc options	PHX
Swiss franc options	PHX
Options on West German mark futures	CME
OTC currency options	—

Option Exchanges:
AMEX—American Stock Exchange
CBOE—Chicago Board Options Exchange
MWE—Midwest Stock Exchange
NYSE—New York Stock Exchange
PCE—Pacific Coast Exchange
PHX—Philadelphia Stock Exchange

Option on Futures Exchanges:
CBT—Chicago Board of Trade
CME—Chicago Mercantile Exchange
COMEX—Commodity and Metals Exchange

---

options and futures as financial instruments and as investment tools. Since the subject matter of this book is financial futures, we primarily focus on options and options on futures as alternatives to financial futures.[2]

CHARACTERISTICS, VALUATION, AND STRATEGIES

An option is an agreement between two parties in which one party is given the right to buy (sell) an asset while the other party assumes an obligation to sell (buy) that asset. This obligation of the seller is contingent upon the option holders' exercise of the right to buy or sell. The party that purchases the right to exercise the option is termed the option buyer. The party who sells the right to buy or sell an asset is called the option seller (writer).

As with futures contracts, all exchange-traded options contracts involve the clearinghouse on one side of the trade. In addition, options contracts on financial instruments and currencies are also made directly with other parties "over the counter." These OTC options are less standardized and less liquid than exchange-traded options, but they may be more tailored to the particular risk management strategy of the investor.

There are two basic types of options: *calls* and *puts*. The purchaser of a call option has the right to buy or "call away" a specified amount of the underlying security at a specified price up to a specified date. The purchaser of a put option has the right to sell or "put to" a writer a specified amount of the underlying security at a specified price up to a specified date. The price at which the security may be "called away" or "put to" is called the *exercise price* or *striking price*. The last day on which the option may be exercised is called the *expiration date*. The price of an option contract is often referred to as its *premium*.

For most put and call options (e.g., stocks, currency), the option is based on a specified asset. The buyer of a call option on a futures contract (e.g., U.S. Treasury bond future), however, obtains the right to purchase a futures contract at a specified price at any time prior to the option's expiration. Thus, the buyer of a call option on a future has the right to acquire a long futures position at the option exercise price. The purchaser of a put option on a futures contract obtains the right to sell a futures contract at a specified price at any time prior to expiration. Thus, the buyer of a put option on a future has the right to acquire a short futures position.

Anyone selling an option on a futures contract has the firm commitment upon exercise to a acquire futures position. That is, if the option buyer exercises his or her option to assume a long futures position, a call option writer must assume the opposite short position. Conversely, if the put option buyer exercises his

---

EXHIBIT 17–2
Put and Call Options on Futures
Contracts

	Put	Call
Buyer assumes	A short futures position	A long futures position
Seller assumes	A long futures position	A short futures position

---

or her option to assume a short futures position, a put option writer will be assigned the opposite long futures position (see Exhibit 17–2).

Valuation of Call Options

The use of options in various risk management, speculation, and arbitrage applications should be based on an understanding of the pricing fundamentals of call and put options.[3] Exhibit 17–3 contains examples of price quotations for exchange-traded options. Each put or call option is identified by its exercise or strike price and by an expiration month. Each option premium has two components to evaluate: time value and intrinsic value. The intrinsic value of a call option is the greater of zero or the difference between the price of the underlying contract security and the exercise price. For example, if a security is trading at $88, an investor holding a call option with an exercise price of $80 could exercise the option for a gain of $8 per share. In this case, the option has a positive intrinsic value of $8 and is said to be in-the-money. If the asset's price were $70, or $10 less than the exercise price, the option would have no intrinsic value and would be out-of-the-money. The call option price is always equal to or greater than its intrinsic value (net of trading costs.) If the option price were below the intrinsic value, one could buy the option, exercise it to obtain the security and resell the security in the market for a riskless profit.

The time value or time premium of a call option is the difference between the option price and its intrinsic value. This time premium captures the amount that the option purchaser is willing to pay for the chance that the option will become profitable prior

EXHIBIT 17–3
Selected Quotations on Options and Options on Futures

FUTURES OPTIONS

Wednesday, March 13, 1985

T-BONDS (CBT)–$100,000; points and 64ths of 100%.

Strike Price	Calls–Last June	Calls–Last Sept	Calls–Last Dec	Puts–Last June	Puts–Last Sept	Puts–Last Dec
64	4-22	4-15	....	0-16	0-60	1-35
66	2-46	2-59	3-01	0-38	1-35	2-20
68	1-32	1-60	2-08	1-17	2-32	....
70	0-44	1-12	1-30	2-29	3-44	....
72	0-18	0-45	0-61	3-61	5-07	....
74	0-07	0-26	0-40	5-49	6-49	....

Est. vol. 25,000; , Tues. vol. 11,376 calls, 11,941 puts
Open interest Tues.; 132,356 calls, 97,531 puts

GOLD (CMX)–100 troy ounces; dollars per troy ounce.

Strike Price	Calls–Last Jun	Calls–Last Aug	Calls–Last Oct	Puts–Last Jun	Puts–Last Aug	Puts–Last Oct
280	21.00	27.00	32.00	4.40	6.40	8.00
290	13.60	19.90	25.70	7.50	9.20	11.00
300	7.80	14.00	18.80	11.60	13.30	15.00
320	2.00	5.70	11.00	25.60	25.00	26.00
340	0.50	2.30	5.80	41.10	41.00	40.00
360	0.30	1.20	3.00	64.00	59.50	56.00

Est. vol. 8,500, Tues. vol. 13,022 calls, 3,003 puts
Open interest Tues.; 41,994 calls, 29,595 puts

SILVER (CMX)–5,000 troy ounces; cents per troy ounce.

Strike Price	Calls–Last May	Calls–Last Jly	Calls–Last Sep	Puts–Last May	Puts–Last Jly	Puts–Last Sep
475	101.0	117.0	126.0	1.8	8.5	12.0
500	78.0	96.0	106.0	3.7	12.5	18.0
550	38.0	59.0	73.0	12.5	25.0	31.0
600	11.0	32.5	48.0	35.0	48.0	53.0
650	3.0	17.0	31.0	77.0	83.0	83.0
700	1.0	9.0	19.0	125.0	125.0	119.0

Est. vol. 3,000, Tues. vol. 891 calls, 1,198 puts
Open interest Tues.; 19,405 calls, 16,644 puts

NYSE COMPOSITE INDEX (NYFE)–$500 times premium

Strike Price	Calls–Settle Mar	Calls–Settle June	Calls–Settle Sept	Puts–Settle Mar	Puts–Settle June	Puts–Settle Sept
100	3.20	6.85	9.20	0.01	0.65	1.05
102	1.25	5.30	7.70	0.10	1.05	1.50
104	0.15	4.00	6.35	0.90	1.70	2.10
106	0.02	2.95	5.10	2.80	2.55	2.85
108	0.01	2.05	4.10	4.80	3.65	3.75
110	0.01	1.40	3.20	6.80	4.95	4.75

Est. vol. 2179, Tues vol. 1086 calls, 115 puts
Open interest Tues.; 7404 calls, 4,363 puts

S&P 500 STOCK INDEX (CME)–$500 times premium.

Strike Price	Calls–Settle Mar	Calls–Settle Jun	Calls–Settle Sep	Puts–Settle Mar	Puts–Settle Jun	Puts–Settle Sep
170	8.70	13.30	....	0.00	0.80	1.35
175	3.05	9.30	12.90	0.05	1.55	2.25
180	0.25	5.95	9.60	2.20	3.20	3.80
185	0.00	3.75	7.10	6.95	6.10	....
190	0.00	2.25	5.00	....	9.20	....
195	0.00	1.25	3.25	....	....	....

Est. vol. 9,608; Tues. vol. 4,975 calls; 906 puts
Open interest Tues.; 23,059 calls; 30,686 puts

SUGAR–WORLD (CSCE)–112,000 lbs.; cents per lb.

Strike Price	Calls–Settle Jly	Calls–Settle Oct	Calls–Settle Mar	Puts–Settle Jly	Puts–Settle Oct	Puts–Settle Mar
2.00	....	....	....	....	....	....
3.00	1.50	1.91	....	0.09	0.12	....
4.00	0.60	1.00	1.90	0.30	0.29	0.25
5.00	0.20	0.55	1.30	0.95	0.85	0.60
6.00	0.13	0.30	0.88	1.80	1.60	1.15
7.00	0.06	0.19	0.62	2.80	2.50	1.88

Est. vol. 24; Tues. vol. 44 calls; 3 puts
Open interest Tues.; 2,352 calls; 225 puts

W. GERMAN MARK (CME)–125,000 marks, cents per mark

Strike Price	Calls–Settle Jun	Calls–Settle Sep	Puts–Settle Jun	Puts–Settle Sep
28	2.14	....	0.26	0.49
29	1.44	1.98	0.55	0.78
30	0.93	1.43	0.98	1.22
31	0.55	1.03	1.60	1.79
32	0.33	0.75	2.34	2.48
33	0.17	0.52	3.15	3.07

Est. vol. 6,042, Tues. vol. 4,665 calls, 1,258 puts
Open interest Tues.; 27,004 calls, 13,949 puts

SOYBEANS (CBT)–5,000 bu.; cents per bu.

Strike Price	Calls–Settle May	Calls–Settle Jly	Calls–Settle Nov	Puts–Settle May	Puts–Settle Jly	Puts–Settle Nov
525	....	....	....	¼	....	4¾
550	37	46¼	....	1	4	10
575	15¼	29	36½	6	10¼	18½
600	4¾	16	25	20¼	21¾	29½
625	1	8¼	16½	40½	37½	45½
650	¼	3¾	11½	65¼	57	63½

Est. vol. 3,500, Tues. vol. 2,169 calls, 387 puts
Open interest Tues.; 17,805 calls, 6,399 puts

CATTLE–LIVE (CME) 40,000 lbs.; cents per lb.

Strike Price	Calls–Settle Apr	Calls–Settle Jun	Calls–Settle Aug	Puts–Settle Apr	Puts–Settle Jun	Puts–Settle Aug
60	....	....	....	0.02	0.07	0.12
62	....	....	0.35	0.12	0.22	0.35
64	0.45	....	0.87	0.77	0.55	0.87
66	0.05	1.80	1.50	2.35	1.30	1.70
68	0.00	0.95	0.82	4.30	2.42	2.90
70	0.00	0.47	0.40	6.32	3.92	....

Est. vol. 568, Tues vol. 608 calls, 150 puts
Open interest Tues.: 10,236 calls. 5,280 puts

FOREIGN CURRENCY OPTIONS

Wednesday, March 13, 1985

Philadelphia Exchange

Option & Underlying	Strike Price	Calls–Last Mar	Calls–Last Jun	Calls–Last Sep	Puts–Last Mar	Puts–Last Jun	Puts–Last Sep
12,500 British Pounds-cents per unit.							
BPound	100	s	r	10.25	s	1.00	r
108.63	.105	3.70	5.30	6.50	0.05	2.40	r
108.63	.110	0.35	2.80	4.20	s	4.85	r
108.63	.115	r	1.40	2.50	r	8.75	r
108.63	.120	r	0.60	r	11.30	12.50	r
108.63	.125	r	r	0.90	r	17.50	r
108.63	.130	r	r	s	21.00	r	s
50,000 Canadian Dollars-cents per unit.							
CDollr	..71	s	r	r	s	0.67	1.22
71.61	...72	s	0.93	r	s	r	1.51
71.61	..73	s	0.60	r	s	r	r
71.61	...74	r	0.40	r	1.88	2.55	3.02
71.61	...75	r	r	r	2.91	3.20	r
71.61	...76	r	r	r	4.00	r	r
71.61	...77	r	r	s	4.85	r	s
62,500 West German Marks-cents per unit.							
DMark	..28	s	r	2.82	s	0.28	r
29.70	...29	0.81	1.60	0.79	0.02	0.58	0.80
29.70	...30	0.10	0.98	1.50	0.42	0.94	1.32
29.70	...31	0.01	0.65	1.10	1.20	1.56	r
29.70	...32	r	0.35	0.75	r	r	r
29.70	...33	r	r	0.50	r	r	r
29.70	...34	r	0.12	r	r	r	r
29.70	...35	r	0.07	s	r	r	s
125,000 French Francs-10ths of a cent per unit.							
FFranc	.100	0.05	r	r	r	r	r
6,250,000 Japanese Yen-100ths of a cent per unit.							
JYen	... 37	r	r	r	r	0.26	r
38.42	..,38	0.48	r	r	r	0.58	r
38.42	...39	0.03	0.79	1.28	0.55	r	r
38.42	...40	r	0.43	0.85	r	r	r
38.42	...41	r	r	0.54	r	r	r
38.42	...42	r	0.11	0.36	r	r	r
62,500 Swiss Francs-cents per unit.							
SFranc	..33	s	r	r	s	0.31	0.50
34.99	...35	0.18	1.40	1.92	0.14	0.89	1.20
34.99	...36	0.02	0.90	1.43	r	r	r
34.99	...37	r	0.50	r	r	r	r
34.99	...38	r	0.31	0.80	r	r	r
34.99	...39	r	0.16	r	r	r	r

Total call vol. 9,495 Call open int. 236,063
Total put vol. 2,698 Put open int. 105,930
r–Not traded. s–No option offered. o–Old.
Last is premium (purchase price).

INTEREST RATE OPTIONS

Wednesday, March 13, 1985
For Notes and Bonds, decimals in closing prices represent 32nds; 1.1 means 1 1/32. For Bills, decimals in closing prices represent basis points; $25 per .01

Chicago Board Options Exchange

U.S. TREASURY BOND–$100,000 principal value

Underlying Issue	Strike Price	Calls–Last Mar	Calls–Last Jun	Calls–Last Sep	Puts–Last Mar	Puts–Last Jun	Puts–Last Sep
12½% bond	102	....	2.13	....	..	1.25	
due 8/2014		....	....	...	..	..	.
11¾% bond	98	....	1.21	....	...	....	
due 11/2014	100	....	1.05	...	1.17	...	
	102	....	0.18	...		...	
	104	...	....	...	5.14	...	
11¼% bond	96	....	1.10	...		...	
due 2/2015							

3 p.m. prices of underlying issues supplied by Merrill Lynch: 13¼% 110 26/32; 12½% 103 18/32; 12% 99 16/32; 11¾% 98 14/32; 11¼% 95 8/32.
Total call vol. 192 Call open int. 9,093
Total put vol. 31 Put open int. 8,534

INDEX OPTIONS

Wednesday, March 13, 1985

Chicago Board

S&P 100 INDEX

Strike Price	Calls–Last Mar	Calls–Last Jun	Calls–Last Sep	Puts–Last Mar	Puts–Last Jun	Puts–Last Sep
150	....	....	....	....	1/16	...
155	23	....	....	....	....	....
160	16½	19¼	21	1/16	1/16	⅛
165	11	13	....	1/16	1/16	5/16
170	5¾	8¼	10⅛	1/16	½	1
175	1¼	5	6⅝	9/16	1 13/16	2⅝
180	1/16	2½	4	4⅝	4¾	5⅛
185	1/16	15/16	2¼	9½	9½	9½
190	1/16	5/16	1 1/16	....	...	14
[illegible]	....	1/16	7/16	....	....	....

Total call volume 236,929 Total call open int. 895,275
Total put volume 168,118 Total put open int. 478,890
The index: High 177 74: Low 175.28; Close 175.42, –1 97

American Exchange

MAJOR MARKET INDEX

Strike Price	Calls–Last Mar	Calls–Last Apr	Calls–Last May	Puts–Last Mar	Puts–Last Apr	Puts–Last May
235	19	21½	....	1/16	1/16	....
240	14¾	18⅜	....	....	3/16	....
245	9¾	13	....	1/16	13/16	1¼
250	3⅜	7¾	...	⅛	2	2⅞
255	11/16	5	7	2⅛	4⅛	5
260	1/16	2¾	5	6⅝	7¼	7½
265	1/16	1⅜	2⅝	11¼	10½	....
270	....	9/16	....	....	....	....

Total call volume 29,467. Total call open int. 94,538.
Total put volume 23,954. Total put open int. 58,083.
The index: High 256.20; Low 253 17: Close 253.36, –2.20.

N.Y. Stock Exchange

NYSE OPTIONS INDEX

Strike Price	Calls–Last Mar	Calls–Last Apr	Calls–Last May	Puts–Last Mar	Puts–Last Apr	Puts–Last May
85	10⅛	....	....	...	....	...
90	13⅜	14¾	....	...	....	...
95	½	10¾	....	....	...	....
100	3⅜	5	6⅞	....	¼	7/16
105	1/16	1¾	2¾	1 13/16	2 1/16	2 9/16
110	....	7/16	⅞	6 7/16	6 11/16	....
115	....	1/16	¼	....	....	....

Total call volume 10,122. Total call open int. 72,195.
Total put volume 4,757. Total put open int. 49,091.
The index: High 104.17; Low 103.15; Close 103.24, –0.79

to the expiration date. In our example, if the asset's price is $70, the call option may still have a value of above zero even though the underlying asset is trading at less than $80.

For an in-the-money call option, the time premium reflects the amount that the option purchaser is willing to pay for the chance that the option will become even more profitable should the underlying security appreciate further prior to option expiration.

Black and Scholes (1973) have provided a widely used formula for calculating the value of European call options on nondividend-paying stocks.[4] In contrast to an American option, a European option can only be exercised at the expiration date. In their model as shown in Exhibit 17–4, the price of a call option on a nondividend-paying stock depends on five factors: the price of the underlying security *(S)*, the strike or exercise price of the option *(E)*, the volatility of the price of the underlying security *(σ)*, the time remaining to maturity *(t)*, and the level of interest rates *(r)*. Certain modifications must be made to the Black-Scholes model to make it suitable for use in valuation of options on other financial instruments. Exhibit 17–5 shows the effect of changes in value of each of the above factors in the valuation of different types of call options.

EXHIBIT 17–4
The Black-Scholes Formula for Call Options

The Black-Scholes formula is based on the following assumptions:
1. Frictionless capital markets: No transactions costs of taxes and all information simultaneously and freely available to all investors.
2. No short-sale restrictions.
3. All asset prices following a continuous stationary stochastic process.
4. A constant risk-free interest rate over the period to expiration.
5. No dividends.

The resulting formula:

$$C = S \times N(d_1) - \frac{E \times N(d_2)}{e^{rt}} \qquad (17\text{-}1)$$

$$d_1 = \frac{\ln(S/E) + (r + 1/2\,\sigma^2)\,t}{\sigma\sqrt{t}}$$

$$d_2 = \frac{\ln(S/E) + (r - 1/2\,\sigma^2)\,t}{\sigma\sqrt{t}}$$

where

C = option value
r = continuously compounded riskless interest rate
S = price of stock
E = strike or exercise price of option
e = 2.718
t = time to expiration of option as a fraction of a year
$σ$ = the standard deviation of the continuously compounded annual rate of return
$\ln(S/E)$ = natural logarithm of S/E
$N(d)$ = value of the cumulative normal distribution evaluated at d

---

EXHIBIT 17–5
Effects of Changes in Valuation Factors on Pricing of Call Options*

Option Type	Security Price (S)	Exercise Price (E)	Volatility of the Security (σ_s)	Time to Expiration (T)	Level of Interest Rates (r)
Conventional equity or stock index	+	−	+	+	+
Foreign currency	+	−	+	+	?
Fixed deliverable debt instrument (e.g. Treasury bills)	+	−	+	?	−
Variable deliverable debt instrument (e.g., Treasury bonds and Treasury notes)	+	−	+	+	−
Futures contract	+	−	+	?	−

* This table should be read as follows: a plus sign indicates that an increase in the value of a factor will increase the value of a call option and an instrument, a minus sign indicates a decrease in the option value, and a question mark indicates an ambiguous effect.

Source: L. S. Goodman, "The New Option Markets," Federal Reserve Bank of New York *Quarterly Review*, Autumn 1983, p. 42.

For call options on all classes of financial instruments, the price of the option increases as the price of the underlying security increases. Likewise the effect of increased volatility is similar for options on stocks, fixed-income securities, and stock indexes, as well as for options on financial futures.[5] All else being equal, the more volatile the price of the underlying security, the greater the price of the call option. Investors are willing to pay more for an option whose underlying asset price is more likely to exceed its exercise price. A high probability of a large loss when the asset price is below the exercise price has less impact since the investor would not exercise the option in this situation.

Changes in interest rates and time to expiration do not affect all call options prices similarly. For call options on stock and stock indexes, increases in short-term rates are generally associated with increases in call option prices. First, the present value of the exercise proceeds declines as interest rates increase. Second, as interest rates rise, the lower leverage of the call option will raise its value relative to the cost of carrying the actual stock.

When futures contracts are the underlying security, there is no initial investment (margin is held in interest-bearing securities), while the option cost is an outright capital expense. As a result, an interest rate increase will lower the value of the call option relative to its underlying future contract. For options on fixed-income futures contracts, the negative impact of an interest rate increase is compounded, since a rise in interest rates normally causes a fall in the price of the underlying futures contract.

Call options on actual debt securities are generally inversely related to interest rate changes.[6] For call options on Treasury bonds and Treasury notes (variable deliverable debt options), interest rate levels have an effect on the price of the underlying security as well as on the relative advantage of owning the options versus owning the debt security. The effect on option values of the fall in the price of the underlying debt security from an upward shift in interest rates is larger than the positive marginal effect on option values associated with the higher carrying cost of the debt instrument. For foreign exchange options, the effect of interest rate changes is generally indeterminant. As with debt instruments, a rise in interest rates affects both the carry cost differential between the option and the underlying security as well as the value of both the spot exchange rate and forward currency value. The relative impact of interest rate changes on these components of option value will determine the final effect.[7]

Time to expiration has a positive impact on the price of a call option on an underlying equity security or currency. All else being equal, a call option with a longer time to expiration will be worth more than an option with a shorter time to expiration, since the longer maturity option has value even after the shorter term options have matured. For call options on futures, however, the positive relationship between time to expiration and option value may not hold. Call options on futures with different expiration months have different underlying instruments because they call for purchase or sale of futures contracts expiring in different months. Thus, depending on the time series of futures prices, option prices may increase or decrease with time to expiration.

Certain modifications must also be made to the Black-Scholes model to make it suitable for use in valuation of options on dividend paying stocks.[8] The payment of a dividend causes the value of the underlying stock to fall because the purchaser of the stock is no longer entitled to the dividend. Offsetting this lower underlying stock value for the call option holder, is the fact that the disadvantage of holding the call option versus the stock has been reduced since the stock holder is no longer entitled to something the option holder is not.

In fact, the assumption of no dividends in the Black-Scholes model may be part of the basis for findings that the Black-Scholes model prices differ from actual options prices.[9] Black reports that the Black-Scholes model underprices (overprices) deep out-of-the-money (in-the-money) call options. Macbeth and Merville found biases that were opposite those reported by Black. Recent empirical studies indicate that the direction and degree of the bias may depend in part on the magnitude of the dividend on the stock.[10] Out-of-the-money options on stocks with low dividends tend to be underpriced by the Black-Scholes model. In-the-money options on stocks with small dividends tend to be overpriced. As dividends increase, out-of-the-money options seem to be overpriced and in-the-money options underpriced. Thus, dividend levels may explain the contrasting results of Black and Macbeth and Merville.

When dealing with stock-based options one is also faced with the uncertainty associated with timing and level of dividends.[11] For stock index options, however, errors in the prediction of a single stock's dividends flows will have less of an impact on an index option value than on that of a stock option. Moreover, the volatility of an index or a portfolio of stocks is considerably less than that of the average stock. Index volatility is typically in the 10–25 percent range, whereas the average volatility of optionable stocks is generally 25–35 percent. This means that index option prices will tend to be a smaller percentage of the price of the underlying index than will the average price of an option on an individual stock.[12]

Valuation of Put Options

As with call options, the put option has two components to evaluate: time value and intrinsic value. The intrinsic value of a put option is the difference between the exercise price and the price of the underlying security. If a security is trading at $88, an investor holding a put option with an exercise price of $90 could exercise the option for a gain of $2 per share. In this case, the option has a positive intrinsic value of $2 and is said to be in-the-money. If the security's price was $92, or $2 more than the exercise price, the put option would have no intrinsic value and would be out of the money. The underlying security can be sold in the open market at a higher value than $90.

Like call options, a put option usually sells for more than its intrinsic value. The time value of a put option is the difference between the option's price and its intrinsic value. For an in-the-money put, the time premium reflects the chance that the option will become even more profitable prior to the expiration date. When the put option is out-of-the-money, the premium or market price consists entirely of its time premium and reflects the chance that the option will become profitable prior to expiration.

Black and Scholes have provided a formula for calculating
the value of a European put option on non-dividend paying stocks.
(A European put option can only be exercised on the expiration
date). The valuation formula for European put options on common
stocks is shown below:[13]

$$P = \frac{E \times N(-d_2)}{e^{rt}} - S \times N(-d_1) \qquad (17\text{-}2)$$

where all notation is as previously defined in Exhibit 17–4.

Put option prices are influenced by the same factors that play
a role in call option prices: the price of the underlying security
(S), the strike price of the option *(E)*, the volatility of the price
of the underlying security (σ), the time remaining to maturity
(t), and the level of interest rates *(r)*. A put option's price, however,
will be inversely rather than positively, affected by changes in
the price of the underlying financial instrument. Volatility and
time to expiration have the same relationship to put prices as they
do to call option prices.

A put option gives one the right to sell the underlying instrument and hence *receive* funds. The longer the time to expiration,
the greater the probability of large price changes in the underlying
asset and hence the value of the put. However, the longer the
time to option expiration, the lower is the present value of the
proceeds of exercising the put giving the put a lower value. The
net effect of time to expiration on put prices depends on the relative
value of the stock price to the exercise price. An increase in volatility increases the probability of a large difference between exercise
price and security price. The higher probability of large loss when
the asset price is above the exercise price has less impact because
the put holder will not exercise the option.

There exists a relationship between the value of a put and a
call option, called *put-call parity*, that also can be used as a means
of arriving at the value of a put option. The prices of puts, calls,
and futures on the same underlying asset and the risk-free interest
rate are related such that prices of any three of the instruments
determine the price of the fourth. Put-call parity arises from the
fact that the payoff of a stock protected by an at-the-money put
option and financed by a borrowing of the present value of the
exercise price equals the value of a long call position.

$$C = P + (S - E/e^{rt}) \qquad (17\text{-}3)$$

EXHIBIT 17–6
Put-Call Parity

	Initial Value	Value At Expiration		
		$S^* < E$	$S^* = E$	$S^* > E$
Portfolio 1:				
Buy a put	P	$E - S^*$	0	0
Buy spot asset	S	S^*	S^*	S
Borrow amount	$-Ee^{-rt}$	$-E$	$-E$	$-E$
Net Flow	$P + S - Ee^{-rt}$	0	0	$S^* - E$
Portfolio 2:				
Buy a call	C	0	0	$S^* - E$

This parity relationship holds exactly for European puts only, but it still establishes a floor for the price of an American put. It implies that the price of a put will be at least equal to the call price minus the difference between the current stock price and the present value of the exercise price of the option or:

$$P \geq C - (S - E/e^{rt}) \qquad (17\text{--}4)$$

Exhibit 17–6 demonstrates put-call parity by showing that the final values are the same for two portfolios for various terminal values of the option's underlying asset. In equilibrium, the initial values of the two portfolios must be the same; if the costs of establishing the two portfolios differed, arbitrage opportunities would exist.

Exhibit 17–7 extends the analysis to a portfolio containing futures, as well as puts and calls, on the same underlying asset. Here the portfolio contains a written call, a purchased put, and a long futures position—all three instruments having the same expiration dates and the options having the same exercise price.[14]

EXHIBIT 17–7
Put-Call-Futures Parity

	Initial Value	Value at Expiration		
		$S^* < E$	$S^* = E$	$S^* > E$
Sell a call	$-C$	0	0	$-(S^* - E)$
Buy a put	P	$E - S^*$	0	0
Buy a future	0	$S^* - F$	$S^* - F$	$S^* - F$
Net Flow	$P - C$	$E - F$	$E - F$	$E - F$

Since the terminal value of this risk-free portfolio is set when the portfolio is established, in equilibrium the end value should equal the initial value of the portfolio continuously compounded at the risk-free rate over the term of the options and futures:

$$(P - C)e^{rt} = E - F \tag{17-5}$$

Since in equilibrium, P and C are related by Equation 17-3, we have

$$(Ee^{-rt} - S)e^{rt} = E - F \tag{17-6}$$

or

$$F = Se^{rt} \tag{17-7}$$

That is, in equilibrium the futures contract is priced at a continuously compounded carrying charge of r percent (risk-free rate) relative to the price of the underlying asset. A futures contract could be substituted for the asset in forming arbitrage portfolios of puts, calls, and a risk-free security of maturity t.

Option Strategies

Options can be held alone or in combination with other assets for purposes of risk minimization, risk reduction, or return enhancement.[15] As shown in Exhibit 17–8a, when the price of an asset underlying a call option increases above the exercise price, a purchase of a call option provides considerable profit potential. Likewise, as shown in Exhibit 17–8b, if the price of an asset underlying a put option decreases below the exercise price, the purchased put option can achieve a positive return. Moreover, since a purchased put or call option is exercised only at the buyer's discretion, a purchased option can be considered a limited risk. However, as shown in Exhibit 17–8c, a call option writer who does not own any of the underlying asset has a potential loss that is theoretically unlimited since the assets price could rise to any price.

Options can be used like futures to minimize the exposure to the price risk of an underlying asset. The hedge ratio or delta of an option represents the change in the option price for small changes in the value of the underlying security.[16] For instance, if a $1 change in a security's price is associated with a 50-cent change in the call price, the option has a delta of .5 and one could construct a fully hedged position by writing calls on twice as many securities as are bought or held. If the investor is short two calls, a $1 increase (decrease) in a stock price would be matched by a

EXHIBIT 17–8
Profits and Losses from Various Strategies

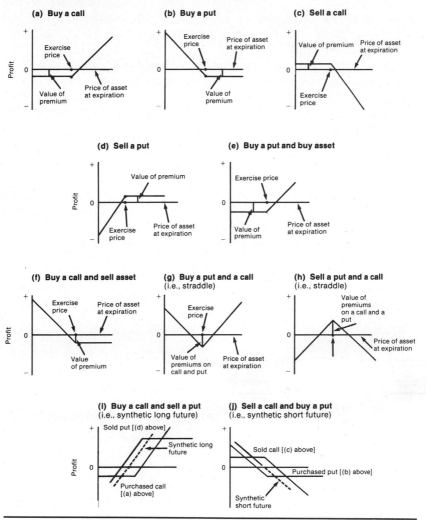

$1 decrease (increase) in the call position's value. A fully hedged position may be maintained by adjusting the ratio of the security position to the option position.

This use of options to eliminate all price risk is comparable to a fully hedged position with futures. The hedge ratio for a deep out-of-the-money security is near zero, while the hedge ratio for a deep in-the-money security is near one. This is expected. If an option is deep enough in the money, the option price will track price changes in the underlying security on a dollar for dollar basis. If an option is far enough out of the money, it may not follow the price of the underlying security at all and will have a hedge ratio close to zero.

Many potential option strategies exist that alter the pattern of profits or returns depending on the price behavior of the underlying security. To derive the profit for a combined asset and option position one should add the cost and profits of the combined positions. The risk of price decreases on a long security position can be reduced by purchasing a put option, or the risk of an increase in prices on a short position can be reduced by buying a call. The purchased put option would limit downside risk but not upside potential (Exhibit 17–8e). A purchased call option when combined with a short position in an asset would limit the risk of a price rise but not limit the downside potential (Exhibit 17–8f).

By combining options with other options as well as with futures contracts, even more specialized forms of portfolios can be constructed. For instance, an option spread is a portfolio of calls (or puts) on the same underlying asset where profits on one or more calls (or puts) offset losses on the other calls (or puts). There are two basic types of option spreads. A *price spread* (or vertical spread) involves buying the call option for a given time, and price, and then selling a call option for the same expiration date at a different strike price (e.g., buy an October option at 80 and sell an October option at 90). A *time spread* (or horizontal spread) involves buying and selling an option for the same asset and strike price but at a different expiration date. The spread strategy chosen usually depends on one's forecast of the option's underlying security.

By combining puts and calls, even more option strategies can be created. To purchase a *straddle,* one buys a put and a call option with the same strike price (Exhibit 17–8g). The profit of this strategy, if the two options are held to expiration, is the sum of the profits for the put option and the call option. The strategy is profitable if the final price of the underlying asset is sufficiently higher or lower, than either exercise price. The profit pattern for a short straddle is just the negative of that for the buyer. The seller profits if the final price is sufficiently close to the exercise price (Exhibit 17–8h). It should be noted, however, that the seller may face early exercise and thus may not have the choice of maintaining the position until expiration.

Futures positions can also be constructed from various combinations of calls and puts. For instance, a *synthetic long futures position* is created through the purchase of a call and the sale of a put having the same terms (e.g., same exercise price and expiration). If the value of the underlying security rises (falls), the value of the long call will rise (fall to zero) while the value of the short put falls to zero (rises). In effect, for relevant portions of the graph in Exhibit 17–8i the positions will cancel out. Likewise, a long put and a short call create a *synthetic short futures position*. As the value of the underlying security falls (rises), the value of the long put increases (decreases to zero) and the value of the short call decreases to zero (increases). In practice, differences in premiums paid for options positions and margin requirements may result in the value of the position not being identical to futures positions.

Options may also be used to convert established long or short futures positions into synthetic long and short calls or puts. For instance, the purchase of a put will hedge the possible loss on a long position while leaving unlimited rewards. Likewise, by buying a long call in combination with a short position in futures, the risk of a price rise is limited since the call can be exercised. The number of security positions are endless. A list of possible synthetic positions are given in Exhibit 17–9.

The equilibrium relationships between options and futures requires various restrictive assumptions on the degree of substitutability between markets. These include equality in transaction costs; ability to transact simultaneous transactions at stated parity levels; and institutional, tax, and government regulations that do not bias investor choice. Structural similarities and differences between options and futures markets, as well as their unique applications in risk management, are discussed in the following section.

EXHIBIT 17–9
Synthetic Options Positions

Synthetic long futures = Long call + Short put
Synthetic short futures = Long put + Short call
Synthetic long call   = Long put + Long futures
Synthetic short call   = Short put + Short futures
Synthetic long put   = Long call + Short futures
Synthetic short put   = Short call + Long Futures

OPTIONS AND FUTURES: SIMILARITIES AND DIFFERENCES

The choice between options and futures on financial instruments depends in part on the similarities and differences between the two markets, some of which are given in Exhibit 17–10. Certain similarities in the factors affecting options and futures prices are evident. First both options and futures prices are linked to the prices of the underlying security. Moreover, the prices of options and futures contracts are related to other common factors such as short-term interest rates and the income of the underlying instrument. Both options and futures have a limited life, and both have contracts have been established by an exchange and are guaranteed by a clearinghouse.

Options and futures also have important structural differences that make them each uniquely suitable for different types of traders and investors. The initial cash outflow is greater when buying options, representing the maximum loss on the position. For futures a security deposit is required when a position is initiated. One reason for the existence of a security deposit for futures contracts is that in the futures markets losses and gains are realized daily. In contrast, for purchasers of option contracts, gains and losses are not realized until the positions are offset or exercised. For futures, delivery is only possible on specific dates in the delivery month depending on contract specifications, whereas option delivery can occur at any time in the life of the option.

Options and futures can be further evaluated by considering both the expected return and the expected risk.[17] Exhibit 17–11a compares the hypothetical return distribution of a bond (stock) portfolio in a stable and in a volatile interest rate (price) environment. Although the expected return of the portfolio is higher in

---

EXHIBIT 17–10
Similarities and Differences between Futures and Options

Similarities	Differences
Link to underlying security	Different initial cash flows
Prices related to common factors (e.g., interest rates)	Futures are mark-to-market daily
Limited life	Option prices are a function of volatility of the underlying security
Contracts available expiring in different months	Option strategies can change the pattern of portfolio returns in a unique way
Contracts created and guaranteed by clearinghouse	
Used for risk management purposes	

EXHIBIT 17–11
Hedged and Unhedged Return Distributions

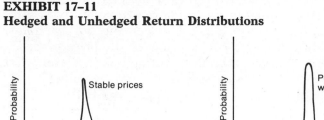

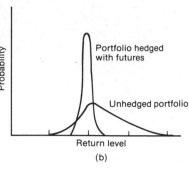

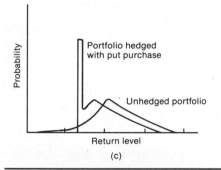

Hypothetical return distribution for an asset portfolio: *(a)* not hedged; *(b)* hedged by selling futures; and *(c)* hedged by purchasing put options.

a volatile environment, the standard deviation of return (i.e., the risk) is also greater. Futures cannot change the fundamental nature of the portfolio's return distribution. The distribution of returns of a fully hedged portfolio is similar to that of a short-term money market position.

Buying put options, on the other hand, can not only protect the value of a bond or stock position, but also change the distribution of returns favorably. Put protection eliminates large losses while retaining the possibility of gains. This insurance, however, has a cost: the put premium. The payment of this premium adds a cost to the stock or bond position that effectively reduces returns relative to those of an unprotected position. As Exhibit 17–11b demonstrates, this strategy establishes an acceptable minimum return in advance.

In a similar fashion, selling call options limits the return distribution of the upside, but increases the probability of returns close to the average or expected return. Most options strategies alter the upside return potential or downside return volatility in some way. They thus give investors a risk management tool that allows them to take advantage of a correct view of the price prospects for the underlying instrument while adjusting risk to a level below what it would be if only the underlying security were held.

Options, like futures, also present an opportunity to use a high degree of leverage to speculate on expected price movements in the underlying security. The cost of options is higher than futures initially, but the speculator does not need to mark-to-market and can never lose more than the initial cost. For example, as shown in Exhibit 17–12, assume a three-month, at-the-money option on a security is available for $3 on a $60 security. If the stock moves up to $72 at exercise, the option will be worth $12. The security holder would have a capital return of 20 percent (12/60); the option holder will have made 300 percent (9/3) return on his or her investment. The long futures position shows a profit of $10 on a zero investment for an infinite percent return with maximum leverage. (The cost of the futures position should, in fact, be considered the opportunity cost of keeping funds in the Treasury bill used as margin.)

The holder of a short futures position would have realized the same $10 as a loss. Alternatively, the put option holder, who also presumably has a bearish outlook, would have a much lower realized loss of $2, the initial investment. It is obvious from this example that the potential risks and rewards from options and futures are quite different in nature.

The options markets currently attract interest on the part of the retail stock and bond investor and institutional money manager because most widely used options strategies expose the holder to limited risk at a cost that is known at the start. This situation

---

EXHIBIT 17–12
Leverage Potential of Futures and Options

	Beginning Price	Ending Price	Initial Investment	Amount of Profit (loss)	Capital Return
Security	$60	$72	$60	$12	20%
At-the-money call option	3	12	3	9	300
At-the-money put option	2	0	2	(2)	(100)
Long future	62	72	0	10	—
Short future	62	72	0	(10)	—

differs from that for futures positions with their mark-to-market requirement. Options contracts also tend to be available in smaller units than futures contracts, which makes options more suitable for investors with limited capital. Futures markets, on the other hand, are popular among brokerage and dealer firms because of their liquidity and low trading cost per transaction.

Options are particularly well suited for hedging the risk of *potential* transactions or for cashing in on potential returns of the underlying security. For example, in placing a bid for a Treasury bond one would like to guard against the possibility that the bid may not be accepted, yet protect oneself from unexpected rises in yields on which the bid is outstanding. The purchase of a put option provides this protection against a bond price decline, yet it need not be exercised if the bid is not accepted. If one had hedged the bid with a short futures position, one could be exposed to losses on the futures position if the bid was not accepted and interest rates fell. The value of the put would also decline with rising bond prices but could only fall as low as zero.

Covered call option writing represents the sale of some potential returns on a security holding. If the price of the underlying security is below the exercise price at expiration, the call writer gets to keep the call premium as well as the security. The call writer thus earns some of the potential returns that were possible given the past volatility of security but were not realized over the period that the option was in effect. The final choice between a futures or options strategy depends on an investor's personal evaluation of their relative costs and benefits. Individuals with little experience in options or futures trading may wish to contact a qualified expert before initiating a trading strategy.

SUMMARY

Security markets have experienced a rapid increase in trading activity in options and options on futures as well as in financial futures. Two types of options exist: calls and puts. A call (put) option gives the buyer the right to purchase (sell) a specific asset at a specified price and up to a specified date. In contrast to futures, an option represents a right rather than an obligation to buy or sell a specific quantity of an underlying instrument at a given price on or before a specified date. Since an option need not be exercised, the option limits a buyer's risk.

Option prices are like futures prices in that they are linked to the value of the underlying security. However, they are also influenced by the expected volatility of the underlying security, a factor that adds an element of uncertainty to the valuation of options.

Options offer many of the opportunities available with futures: hedging, arbitrage, and speculation. Options also provide unique strategies unavailable with futures. With options, the investor can alter the distribution of returns by selling potential upside returns or buying insurance against downside losses. Also, the options buyer is not required to post margin upon purchasing a put or call or to mark-to-market while the option position is open. Options do require a larger initial cash investment than futures. These differences make options a valuable addition to the investment tools available to institutional money managers and individual investors.

NOTES

[1] For a recent review of option markets see Andrew Rudd, "Option Markets," in *Handbook of Modern Finance*, ed. D. Logue (New York: Warren, Gorham, Lamont, 1984).

[2] For a more complete treatment of options and option trading strategies, readers are advised to consult books devoted solely to this topic. These books include Robert A. Jarrow and Andrew Rudd, *Option Pricing* (Homewood, Ill.: Richard D. Irwin, 1983); Richard M. Bookstaber, *Option Pricing and Strategies in Investment* (Reading, Mass.: Addison-Wesley, 1983); John C. Cox and Mark Rubenstein *Option Markets*. Englewood Cliffs, N.J.: Prentice Hall, 1985.

[3] Laurie Goodman, "New Option Markets," *Quarterly Review, Federal Reserve Bank of New York*, Autumn 1983, pp. 35–47, contains a very readable and informative summary of new option markets and the valuation concepts appropriate to them.

[4] Fischer Black and M. Scholes, "The Pricing of Options and Corporate Liabilities," *Journal of Political Economy*, May/June 1973, pp. 637–54.

[5] For a mathematical presentation of the effect of each of these factors on call option prices see Jarrow and Rudd (1983).

[6] Options on debt generally take one of two forms: fixed deliverable options or variable deliverable options. The fixed deliverable option requires that a debt instrument with fixed characteristics be delivered (e.g., a three-month Treasury bill). A variable deliverable option requires that a specified existing debt issue be delivered. Thus the maturity of the delivered issue changes as the option expires. The fixed deliverable option has generally been used for Treasury bills and the variable delivery option has been adopted for Treasury bonds and Treasury notes. For options on fixed deliverable debt instruments (Treasury bills), the effect of interest rates changes may be indeterminate. For short-term securities the fall in price due to a rise in interest rates may not outweigh the positive marginal effect on option values associated with the higher carrying cost of the debt instrument.

[7] The valuation of currency options also requires some modifications in the standard Black-Scholes pricing model. Mark B. Garman and Steven W. Kohlhagen have shown in *Foreign Currency Option Values* (Berkeley: University of California), December 1982, that two interest rate inputs are required: the interest rate in the

underlying currency and the interest rate in the currency in which the option is denominated. The choice of a foreign currency option buyer can be viewed as that of buying the currency today and depositing it to earn the interest rate available for deposits in the currency; or alternatively, buying the option today in dollars and investing the difference between the currency value and option price at the dollar denominated risk-free rate. Hence, the decision of whether or not to buy the currency option or the currency, and thus the option value, will depend in part on the differential between these two sets of interest rates.

[8] Various alternative models exist for adapting the Black-Scholes model for dividends. See R. Geske, "The Pricing of Options with Stochastic Dividends Yields," *The Journal of Finance,* May, 1978, pp. 617–25; R. W. Whaley, "On the Valuation of American Call Options on Stocks with Known Dividends," *Journal of Financial Economics,* June, 1981, pp. 207–11; and Richard Roll, "An Analytic Valuation Formula for Unprotected American Call Options on Stocks with Known Dividends," *Journal of Financial Economics,* November, 1977, pp. 251–58.

[9] F. Black, "Fact and Fantasy in the Use of Options," *Financial Analyst Journal,* July/August 1975, pp. 36–72; J. Macbeth and L. J. Merville, "An Empirical Examination of the Black-Scholes Call Option Pricing Model," *The Journal of Finance,* December 1979, pp. 11–73–86; and N. B. Gultekin, R. J. Rogalski, and S. Tinic, "Option Pricing Estimates: Some Empirical Results," *Financial Management,* Spring 1982, pp. 58–69.

[10] W. E. Sterk, "Tests of the Two Models for Valuing Call Options on Stocks with Dividends," *The Journal of Finance,* December 1982, pp. 1229–1238. Sterk, "Option Pricing Dividends and the In-and-Out of the Money Basis," *Financial Management,* Winter 1983, pp. 47–53.

[11] The effect of changes in dividend amounts and timing of dividend payments has been recently estimated to alter the estimate of S&P futures fair values by roughly .10 index points per quarter. See "Significance of Error in Estimating Dividends," *Stock Index Strategist* (Donaldson, Lufkin, and Jenrette) June 1984, p. 9.

[12] For additional discussion of option pricing for options on stocks, options on futures, and options on stock index futures see M. Brenner, G. Courtadon, and M. Subrahmanyam "Options on Stock Indices and on Stock Index Futures," Working Paper, New York University, March 1984; M. Assay, "A Note on the Design of Commodity Option Contracts," *Journal of Futures Markets* 2, no. 1 (1982), pp. 1–8; and E. Moriarty, S. Phillips, and P. Tosini, "A Comparison of Options and Futures in the Management of Portfolio Risk," *Financial Analyst Journal,* January–February 1981, pp. 61–67.

[13] The valuation formula for put options on other financial instruments is given in Goodman [1983].

[14] James Meisner and John W. Labuszewski, "Modifying the Black-Scholes Option Pricing Model for Alternative Underlying Instruments," *Financial Analyst Journal,* November–December 1984, pp. 23–27, also provides modified Black-Scholes option models for analyzing underlying instruments.

[15] For examples of alternative strategies with options see Basic Spread Strategies Strategies in Buying and Writing Options on Trading Bond Futures, (Chicago Board of Trade).

[16] In the Black-Scholes call option model, the minimum risk hedge ratio is equal to $n(d_1)$, the cumulative normal probability associated with d, standard deviations from the mean. For further examples of the application of the Black-Scholes model, see W. Sharpe, *Investment.* (Englewood Cliffs, N.J.: Prentice-Hall, Inc., 1985.)

[17] In evaluating the performance of asset positions hedge with options, tradi-

tional risk return performance measures based on mean and variance may not be applicable. Unlike futures, performance methods based on variance reduction are not sufficient since variance is not a suitable proxy for risk in options strategies because options reduces variance asymmetrically. See Richard Bookstaber, "Problems in Evaluating the Performance of Portfolios with Options," *Financial Analyst Journal*, January/February 1985, pp. 48–62. For an alternative method of evaluating performance on managed options see Andrew Rudd, "Option Markets," in *Handbook of Modern Finance*, ed. D. Logue (New York: Warren, Gorham, and Lamont, Inc., 1984).

SELECTED REFERENCES

Black, Fischer, and M. Scholes. "The Pricing of Options and Corporate Liabilities." *Journal of Political Economy*, May/June 1973, pp. 637–54.

Black, F. "Fact and Fantasy in the Use of Options." *Financial Analyst Journal*, July/August 1975, pp. 36–72.

Bookstaber, Richard. *The Complete Investment Book*. Glenview, Ill.: Scott, Foresman, 1985.

————. *Option Pricing and Strategies in Investment*. Reading, Mass.: Addison-Wesley, 1983.

Bookstaber, Richard, and Roger Clarke. "Option Portfolio Strategies: Measurement and Evaluation." *Journal of Business*, October 1984, pp. 469–92.

————. "Problems in Evaluating the Performance of Portfolios with Options," *Financial Analyst Journal*, January/February 1985, pp. 48–62.

Brenner, M.; G. Courtadon; and M. Subrahmanyam. "Options on Stock Indices and on Stock Index futures." Working Paper, New York University, March 1984.

Brenner, M., and Dan Galai. "Implied Interest Rates." Working Paper, Hebrew University, February 1984.

Cox, J., Ingersoll, J. and Ross S. "The Relationship Between Forward and Future Prices." *Journal of Financial Economics*, December 1981.

Cox, J. C.; S. A. Ross; and M. Rubenstein. "Option Pricing: A Simplified Approach." *Journal of Financial Economics* 7 (1979), pp. 229–63.

Cox, J. and M. Rubenstein. *Option Markets*. Englewood Cliffs, N.J.: Prentice Hall, 1985.

Garbade, Kenneth D., and Monica M. Kaicher. "Exchange-Traded Options on Common Stock." *Quarterly Review, Federal Reserve Bank of New York*, Winter 1978–79, pp. 26–40.

Garman, Mark B., and Steven W. Kolhagen. *Foreign Currency Option Values*. Berkeley: University of California, December 1982.

Goodman, Laurie. "New Options Markets." *Quarterly Review, Federal Reserve Bank of New York*, Autumn 1983, pp. 35–47.

Gultekin, N. B.; R. J. Rogalski; and S. Tinic. "Option Pricing Estimates: Some Empirical Results." *Financial Management*, Spring 1982, pp. 58–69.

Jarrow, Robert A., and Andrew Rudd. *Option Pricing*, Homewood, Ill.: Richard D. Irwin, 1983.

Macbeth, J., and L. J. Merville. "An Empirical Examination of the Black-Scholes

Call Option Pricing Model." *The Journal of Finance,* December 1979, pp. 1173–86.

Meisner, James F., and John W. Labuszewski. "Modifying the Black-Scholes Option Pricing Model for Alternative Underlying Instruments." *Financial Analyst Journal,* November–December 1984, pp. 23–27.

Modest, D. M., and M. Sundaresan. "The Relationship between Spot and Futures Prices in Stock Index Futures Markets: Some Preliminary Evidence." *Journal of Futures Markets* 3, pp. 15–42.

Moriarty, E.; Susan Phillips; and Paula Tosini. "A Comparison of Options and Futures in the Management of Portfolio Risk." *Financial Analyst Journal,* January–February 1981, pp. 61–67.

Rudd, A. "Option Markets," in *Handbook of Modern Finance,* ed. D. Logue. New York: Warren, Gerham, Lamont, 1984).

Sterk, W. E. "Tests of the Two Models for Valuing Call Options on Stocks with Dividends." *The Journal of Finance,* December 1982.

Sterk, W. E. "Option Pricing Dividends and the In-and-Out of the Money Basis." *Financial Management,* Winter 1983, pp. 47–53.

Glossary

FINANCIAL INSTRUMENT FUTURES

Every profession or trade has its own jargon, and futures trading is no exception. Its language is not difficult to understand, but it can be confusing if one interprets the terms as they are used on a stock exchange. Several expressions that are used interchangeably in equity and futures transactions have totally different meanings in their respective contexts.

Arbitrage. A trading strategy designed to take advantage of differences between two investments with identical payoffs. One is purchased, and the other is sold. The objective of the transaction is to profit from a temporary price discrepancy between the two instruments when they return to a normal price relationship. In futures trading, arbitrage usually refers to a trade based on a price discrepancy between futures and cash whereby the cash security can be purchased (sold) and the futures contract sold (purchased) for a profit.*

Associated Person. A CFTC registration that is a necessity for everyone handling futures customer orders.

Basis. The difference in price or yield between the financial futures contract and the cash market for the underlying instrument. In the equity market, the basis is often referred to as a premium or discount.

Basis Point. A measurement of the change in yield levels for debt and money market instruments. One basis point equals $\frac{1}{100}$ of 1 percent.

Bid. An offer to purchase at a specified price. (See *Offer.*)

Broker. A person who earns a commission for transacting the sale of a futures contract. A floor broker executes customer orders in a pit

---

* In pure arbitrage, the trader bears no risk during the duration of the trade. The term risk arbitrage is often used to refer to trades that attempt to profit from price discrepancies between two investments that are very similar, but not identical.

located on the floor of a commodity exchange. A CFTC license is required to practice as a broker.

Brokerage Fee. The same as a commission in the stock market; however, the fee charged per contract is paid only once when the position is closed-out by an offsetting transaction or delivery.

Buy-In (Offset). An equal and opposite transaction to an earlier short position.

Cash Forward Market GNMAs. A market made by GNMA dealers who trade in GNMA mortgage-backed securities 30–180 days in the future.

Cash Instrument. The actual security, bill, or note that would be eligible for delivery if one wished to satisfy an open futures obligation without offsetting the position. Only a small percentage of contracts are ever satisfied by delivery.

CFTC. Commodity Futures Trading Commission—an independent government agency whose members are appointed by the president of the United States with responsibility for regulating U.S. futures exchange activities.

Cheap. A traders' vernacular describing a security that is underpriced in relation to other securities. An overpriced security is referred to as "rich."

Clearinghouse. A corporation closely associated with a futures exchange through which all futures contracts are made, offset, and delivered. All financial obligations related to the margins associated with a trade are monitored and enforced by this organization. A clearinghouse is owned by its membership and is self-regulating.

Clearing Member. A member firm of the clearinghouse or organization. Each clearing member must also be a member of the Exchange. Not all members of the Exchange, however, are members of the clearing organization. All trades of a nonclearing member must be registered with, and eventually settled through, a clearing member.

Collateralized Depository Receipts (CDRs). The CDR GNMA mortgage interest rate futures contract traded on the CBOT does not allow for direct delivery of GNMA certificates in the settlement of a futures position. Instead, the contract calls for the delivery of a negotiable instrument called a collateralized depository receipt. A CDR is a document prepared, signed, and dated by a depository bank to reflect the fact that a seller has placed a $100,000 minimum principal balance for GNMAs with an 8 percent coupon or equivalent for safekeeping on the date so indicated. It is similar to a warehouse receipt.

Commission (or Round-Turn). The one-time fee charged by a broker to a customer when a position is liquidated either by offset or delivery.

Contract Month. The month in which futures contracts may be satisfied by making or accepting a delivery. (See **Delivery Month.**)

Contract Regulations. A knowledge of contract regulations is imperative for participants in the futures markets. These regulations define which securities can be delivered to satisfy a position, when delivery can be made, and who can make it. This is especially important to GNMA and Treasury bond traders, since most contracts permit premium bonds to be delivered. When persons with a long position stand for delivery, they should expect to receive the cheapest commodity that can be purchased to satisfy an obligation.

Correlation Coefficient. Correlation is the degree to which yield or price fluctuations of one security or money market instrument are associated with those of another such security or money market instrument. A correlation coefficient of 1.0 implies that prices move in perfect synchronism. A 0.0 indicates no interrelationships between the series.

Cross-Hedge. The buying or selling of financial futures contract to protect the value of a cash position of a similar, but not identical, instrument or portfolio. This type of hedging is a measured risk, since the outcome of such a transaction is a function of the price correlation of unlike securities. It is conceivable that a negative correlation could exist between two instruments at any moment despite the presence of a strong positive correlation over an extended period of time.

Current Delivery (month). The futures contract that is closest to expiration. This contract is sometimes referred to as the nearby month.

Day Trades. Trades that are opened and closed on the same day. These are usually conducted by scalpers or customers who are active speculators. Day trades may occur at lower brokerage fees than overnight trades.

Delivery Month. Most contracts are posted every quarter for periods of two years. The delivery month is the calendar month during which these contracts mature and "go off the board." It is also called the spot month.

Delivery Notice. A formal procedure that must be followed if an open position in the delivery month is to be satisfied by a delivery of a permissible security as defined in the contract.

Delivery Points. Those points designated by futures exchanges at which the financial instrument covered by a futures contract may be delivered in fulfillment of such contract.

Discount Price. The price of a bond trading at less than par. (Par is 100 cents on a dollar of its face value.)

Discretionary Account. An account over which any individual or organization, other than the person in whose name the account is carried, exercises trading authority or control.

First Day of Notice. The first day on which a seller can notify a buyer that he or she wishes to deliver a cash commodity against an open futures position. This procedure is regulated by the clearing corporation.

Futures Commission Merchant (FCM). A firm or person engaged in soliciting or accepting and handling orders for the purchase or sale of futures contracts, subject to the rules of a futures exchange and who, in connection with such solicitation or acceptance of orders, accepts any money or securities to margin any resulting trades or contracts. The FCM must be licensed by the CFTC.

GNMA. Government National Mortgage Association—an agency under the Department of Housing and Urban Development that has the jurisdiction to approve the issue of mortgage-backed securities that are fully guaranteed for repayment of principal and interest by the U.S. Treasury as described in the standard prospectus for HUD 1717, 3/73.

Hedging. A technique used by institutions that substitutes the sale (purchase) of a futures contract for the sale (purchase) of the actual cash security. Success is related to the price correlation of the futures contract with that of the security being hedged. Hedging can also refer to a purchase transaction in which the actual purchase of a security in the cash market is deferred by purchasing a futures contract for a temporary period. (See **Cross-Hedge.**)

Last Trading Day. Day on which trading ceases for an expiring contract.

Limit Bid or Limit Sell Moves (daily trading limits). Refers to the maximum price move a contract can experience during one trading session before it is stopped from trading as explicitly defined in the contract. After a contract stops trading, it can be reopened if someone is willing to trade above or below the daily price limit at a later time during the trading session.

Limit Order. An order in which the customer designates either a price limit or a time limit before execution is possible.

Liquidity. A term used to describe the price sensitivity of a contract. Liquidity can also be measured by the size of an order that can be executed without significantly affecting the execution price.

Local. A member who generally trades only for his own account. Also referred to as "floor trader."

Long. A buyer of a contract. If not offset, the long will take delivery of a contract on its expiration date.

Margins. Several types of margins are used in trading commodities. A security deposit guaranteeing performance is called an initial or original margin. The dollar amount required for a contract varies with its volatility and whether the customer is a speculator or a hedger. Initial margins can be deposited in the form of cash and Treasury bills. Letters of credit are acceptable at some clearing corporations. The minimum amount required for customers is designated by the clearing broker. Initial margins required for clearing members are assigned by the clearing corporation.

Daily price movements are debited or credited to an account. If trading losses or the withdrawal of funds cause an account to drop below a maintenance margin level, it must be restored to the minimum initial margin requirement. The customer maintenance margin level is designated by the Exchange board and is frequently changed. There must be a sufficient amount of cash in an account to meet the daily margin calls of the clearing corporation. Margin associated with daily price movement is often called variation margin, and the process of posting margins is called marking-to-market.

Mark-to-Market. An arithmetic procedure conducted daily by a brokerage house for each open account. The procedure debits or credits the available balance of the account by the sum of the dollar change in value of open contracts resulting from price movements that occurred during the last trading session.

Market Order. An order to buy or sell a contract immediately at the most advantageous price available.

Maximum Price Fluctuation. The maximum amount the contract price can change, up or down, during one trading session as fixed by Exchange rules. Also referred to as a limit move.

Minimum Price Fluctuation. Smallest increment of price movement possible in trading a given contract.

Nearbys. The nearest actively traded month in a selected commodity contract.

Notice Day. A day on which notices of intent to delivery, pertaining to a specified delivery month, may be issued.

Offer. Indicates a willingness to sell a futures contract at a given price. (See *Bid.*)

Offset. See *Buy-In.*

Omnibus Account. An account carried by one Futures Commission Merchant with another Futures Commission Merchant in which the transactions of two or more persons are combined and carried in the name of the originating broker rather than designated separately.

Open Interest. A figure that refers to the total number of contracts not offset or satisfied by a delivery for a given contract. The larger the number, the more liquid the contract. Thus, it would be unadvisable to buy or sell 100 contracts of a specific month if there was only an open interest of 124.

Open Outcry. A technique of public auction used to make bids or offers in a pit. Brokers cannot buy and sell positions they own without availing themselves of this procedure.

Opening, The. The period at the beginning of the trading session officially designated by the Exchange during which all transactions are considered made "at the opening."

Pit. A trading area on the floor of a futures exchange where all trades associated with a product are conducted.

Point. An amount equal to 1 percent of the principal amount of a fixed-income security or mortgage. Points are computed when a bond or mortgage is bought or sold. They are used to alter the yields of bonds or mortgages to current market rates.

Position. An open trade commitment.

Premium. The excess of one futures contract price over that of another. (See *Basis.*)

Pricing. Government bond and note prices are expressed in points and 32nds as in 97–01 with digits to right of the dash being 32nds of a point. The points reflect a percentage of par—thus, 100–00 is 100 percent of par. A price of 94–08 would indicate a price of $94\frac{8}{32}$ percent of par.

Range. The high and low prices recorded during a specified time.

Reporting Limit. Sizes of positions set by an exchange, or the CFTC above which brokerage firms must report all open customer positions to the designated authority. These limits are more stringent for speculative positions than for hedge transactions.

Repurchase Agreement. The selling of a security by a dealer to another party who simultaneously agrees to resell the same securities to the dealer at a predetermined price and date.

Reverse Repurchase Agreement (reverse repo). The sale of security by an investor or mortgage banker to a dealer, while the investor simultaneously agrees to repurchase the security at a specific price and data. It is used to temporarily borrow against collateral.

Rich. See *Cheap.*

Round-Turn. Procedure by which the long or short position of an individual is offset by an opposite transaction, or by accepting or making delivery of the actual financial instrument.

Scalping. Trading for small gains. It normally involves establishing and liquidating a position quickly, usually within the same day.

Settlement Price. The daily price at which the clearinghouse clears all trades. The settlement price of each day's trading is based on the closing range of that day's trading. Settlement prices are used to determine both margin calls and invoice prices for deliveries.

Short. A sale. It is also associated with an open interest rate contract that permits the contract holder to satisfy a position by delivering an appropriate security or collateralized depository receipt. It can be offset through an equal and opposite trade. A short initiates a delivery notice.

Short Squeeze. A situation in which a lack of supply tends to force prices upward.

Speculator. A trader in futures contracts who attempts to profit from anticipated price changes. The term is also used to identify a pit trader who takes very short term positions.

Spread. The simultaneous purchase and sale of different contract months of the same futures contract. This is usually executed when the price relationship between contract months is deemed to be abnormal. The positions are simultaneously offset when the price relationship between contract months return to normal. This trading technique is similar to an arbitrage transaction.

Spot Price. The current cash market price of a security.

Variation Margin. See *Margins*.

Glossary for Options on Futures

Assignment. Notice to an option writer that an option has been exercised by the option holder.

At-the-Money. An option whose strike price is equal—or approximately equal—to the current market price of the underlying futures contract.

Buyer. The purchaser of an option, either a call option or a put option. Also referred to as the option holder.

Call Option. An option which gives the option buyer the right to purchase (go "long") the underlying futures contract at the strike price on or before the expiration date.

Class of Options. All call options—or all put options—on the same underlying futures contract.

Closing Transaction. A purchase or sale that liquidates—offsets—an existing position. That is, selling an option that was previously purchased or buying back an option which was previously sold.

Combination. A position created either by purchasing both a put and a call or by writing both a put and a call on the same underlying futures contract.

Covered Option. An option written against an opposite position in futures.

Delta. The amount by which an option's price is expected to change for a unit change in the underlying futures price. With the exception of deep-in-the-money options, the change in the option premium is usually less than the change in the futures price. The further an option is out-of-the-money, the smaller the change in the premium and the smaller the delta.

Exercise Price. The price of the underlying futures contract at which the option contract gives the owner the right to buy or sell the future.

Expiration Date. The date after which the option contract becomes null and void. Options must be exercised by a specific time on the expiration date.

In-the-Money. An option that has a positive intrinsic value; i.e., for which the futures price exceeds the exercise price of a call option or the exercise price exceeds the futures price for a put option.

Intrinsic Value. The difference between the futures price and the option exercise price for a call option; the difference between the exercise price and the futures price for a put option. The component of option value that is based on the proceeds realized if the option is exercised immediately.

Naked Writing. Writing a call or a put on a futures contract in which the writer has no opposite cash or futures market position. This is also known as uncovered writing.

Opening Transaction. A purchase or sale that establishes a new position.

Out-of-the-Money. A put or call option that currently has no intrinsic value. That is, a call whose strike price is above the current futures price or a put whose strike price is below the current futures price.

Premium. The price of an option—the sum of money, arrived at in the competitive market, which the option buyer pays and the option writer receives for the rights granted by the option.

Put Option. An option which gives the option buyer the right to sell (go "short") the underlying futures contract at the strike price on or before the expiration date.

Seller. Also known as the option writer or grantor. The sale of an option may be in connection with either an opening transaction or a closing transaction.

Series. All options of the same class having the same strike price.

Short. The position created by the sale of a futures contract or option (either a call or a put) if there is no offsetting position.

Spread. A position consisting of both long and short options (all calls or all puts). For example, a long position in a call with one-strike price and expiration and a short position in another call with a different strike price and/or expiration.

Straddle. A combination in which the put and the call have the same strike price and the same expiration date.

Strike Price. The price at which the holder of the call (put) may exercise the right to purchase (sell) the underlying futures contract. Also referred to as the ***Exercise Price.***

Time Value. Any amount by which an option premium exceeds the option's intrinsic value. If an option has no intrinsic value, its premium is entirely time value.

Underlying Futures Contract. The specific futures contract that can be bought or sold by the exercise of an option.

Writing. The sale of an option in an opening transaction.

Questions

CHAPTER 1

1. What conditions led to the creation of the commodity futures, foreign exchange, and financial futures markets?

2. Describe a short hedge. Describe a long hedge. What are their purposes?

3. What are the economic benefits of futures markets?

4. How do speculators differ from hedgers?

5. Contrast futures and forward markets.

6. List the financial futures contracts that are currently traded.

7. Given your knowledge of the evolution of these markets, identify a financial asset that does not now have a futures market that would lend itself to futures trading.

CHAPTER 2

1. What are the differences between floor brokers, scalpers, and position traders?

2. Describe the role of the exchange clearinghouse.

3. What is the difference between initial margin and maintenance margin?

4. Why is the CFTC only a regulator of last resort?

5. Describe the process initiated when one places an order to purchase a futures contract.

6. How does a typical futures market function in terms of trade execution and record-keeping?

CHAPTER 3

1. What is the difference between the discount rate and yield on a Treasury bill?

2. What is the deliverable instrument in each of the short-term financial futures markets?

3. Why are CD and Eurodollar rates above Treasury bill yields?

4. Describe some uses of the CD, Eurodollar, and Treasury bill futures markets.

5. What factors should be considered in choosing between Treasury bill and CD futures for a banker hedging a fixed-rate loan?

6. Describe some uses of the Treasury bond, Treasury note, and GNMA futures markets.

7. What is the role of government security dealers in the cash and futures markets for U.S. Treasury securities?

8. Describe a mortgage pass-through security and a GNMA CDR.

CHAPTER 4

1. What factors would determine which stock futures contract to use?

2. How do the settlement procedures for stock index futures differ from most fixed-income futures contracts?

3. What opportunities do stock market index futures offer investors?

4. Do stock index futures allow an investor to hedge market risk or total risk?

5. What are the special tax considerations of stock futures contracts versus stocks?

6. Why has the S&P 500 future been the most successful of the stock index futures contracts?

7. Identify three applications of stock index futures.

CHAPTER 5

1. What are the principle effects of changing yields on fixed-income security prices, and what determines the magnitude of the effect of changing yields?

2. Explain the role of forward rates in determining the prices of securities with different maturities.

3. Explain the difference between the expectations, liquidity preference, and market segmentation hypotheses.

4. What are some of the problems in valuing securities with multiple cash flows?

5. Briefly describe various techniques of stock valuation.

6. How would the valuation of a bond differ from that of a portfolio of stocks?

7. What causes duration to vary among bonds with different characteristics?

CHAPTER 6

1. What is the principal distinguishing characteristic between futures on short-term and long-term securities?

2. How does security income in the form of interest and dividends affect futures pricing?

3. What are carrying costs?

4. Describe how market-basket delivery criteria may affect futures contract pricing.

5. Explain conversion factors and the concept "cheapest-to-deliver."

6. Why do stock index futures prices often differ by more than 1 percent from their theoretical values?

7. Discuss some of the institutional and market structure influences affecting futures prices.

CHAPTER 7

1. What is the difference between a direct hedge and a cross-hedge?

2. What is basis risk?

3. How does basis risk affect hedging strategy?

4. How is cost of carry related to basis?

5. Explain alternative means of determining hedge ratios.

6. Discuss problems in the measurement of hedge ratios.

CHAPTER 8

1. Describe the various steps necessary for designing a hedging program.

2. What factors should one consider in selecting a futures portfolio contract to hedge long-term corporate bonds?

3. What are the accounting rules and tax treatment for gains and losses on futures contracts for corporations?

4. Describe the difference between continuous hedging and selective hedging.

5. How can variation margin affect the profitability of a futures hedging strategy?

6. Design a hedging plan for a company deciding to use Eurodollar futures as a temporary substitute for short-term investments or as an anticipatory hedge. Be sure to include an objective statement and administrative or organizational plan.

7. Design a futures strategy plan for a pension fund that will be using stock index and Treasury bond futures to adjust their stock–bond allocation over short periods. Be sure to include an objective statement and an organizational plan.

CHAPTER 9

1. What are the principal centers of bank profitability?

2. What is the purpose of asset and liability management?

3. How do futures protect the inventory value of stocks and bonds?

4. What is the difference between micro and macro hedging?

5. Name two ways in which bank investment and trust divisions use financial futures.

6. What are some of the reasons for banks' limited use of financial futures?

CHAPTER 10

1. Describe the principal activities of underwriters, security dealers, and security traders.

2. How has shelf registration resulted in greater risk to the underwriter?

3. How are inventory positions effectively hedged?

4. How would market makers and block traders benefit most from futures?

CHAPTER 11

1. How do financial futures fit into the long-term investment management objectives of pension funds and insurance companies?

2. How do the responsibilities of sponsors of pension funds differ from those of the portfolio manager?

3. Why and how would financial futures be used in asset allocation strategies of a pension fund?

4. Explain how financial futures might be helpful in the following situations. Also identify what other means exist for dealing with these situations and how financial futures would be compared to the alternatives.

  a. Portfolio manager receives a cash contribution from the sponsor at the end of the company's fiscal year that will increase the size of the portfolio by 25%.
  b. The pension sponsor discharges several equity investment managers and divides the funds between two new managers, one of which is an index fund manager.
  c. A pension sponsor with a favorable outlook for interest rates in the short run would like to increase the duration of the fixed income funds she oversees without disrupting the management approach of the portfolio managers handling the investment of the funds.
  d. A portfolio manager wishes to reduce the beta of his portfolio from its current high level of 1.4 down to 1.1 without selling the stocks he has carefully selected.
  e. A life insurer faces the risk of rising funds costs on a growing amount of policy loans outstanding that are earning interest rates well below the current cost of funds.
  f. A property and casualty insurer is having a profitable year with plenty of cash available for new municipal bond investments, but is concerned that this is not a favorable time to purchase long-term bonds because of the risk of increases in interest rates in the next 6–9 months.

5. Explain how the differences in life and property and casualty insurance companies affect their use of financial futures.

CHAPTER 12

1. Describe the price risks facing mortgage investors and originators.

2. What questions should be asked before a hedge action is instituted?

3. Describe the differences between the forward and futures markets in the mortgage industry.

4. Discuss factors affecting basis change in the GNMA futures markets.

5. Under what conditions will a Treasury bond futures contract be a superior hedging instrument to GNMA futures?

6. What aspects must be considered in hedging construction loans?

CHAPTER 13

1. What are the principal uses of futures in working capital management?

2. What risks are involved in hedging net interest exposure?

3. What types of corporate bonds and stocks are best hedged with financial futures?

4. How can futures markets be used to hedge the risk of interest rate fluctuations in countries without futures markets?

5. How can financial futures affect a firm's capital investment decisions?

CHAPTER 14

1. What is the difference between intermarket and intramarket trading?

2. Pure arbitrage (a riskless trade for excessive profit) is not possible. Comment.

3. How do arbitrage and/or speculative opportunities differ between the fixed income and equity futures markets?

4. What are the costs associated with a cash versus futures bond arbitrage trade?

CHAPTER 15

1. How does delivery of market-basket based futures contracts differ from specific issue futures contracts?

2. How does cash settlement differ from physical delivery?

3. How might delivery affect the pricing of futures contracts before the contract month arrives?

4. Why is the invoice price different from the futures settlement price for Treasury bonds?

5. Why is cash settlement used for some futures contracts and physical delivery for others?

CHAPTER 16

1. What major components must be evaluated in designing a computer support system for financial futures trading?

2. Describe several technical trading systems.

3. What is the basis behind technical trading systems?

4. What is fundamental analysis as applied to financial futures?

5. Describe different methods of testing for forecast accuracy.

CHAPTER 17

1. What are the five principal factors affecting the pricing of security options? How do they affect the pricing of stock options? How do they affect the pricing of interest rate futures?

2. Explain the concept of put-call parity.

3. How do options differ from futures in reducing risk of the cash security?

4. What is a synthetic options position? A synthetic futures position?

5. Discuss the similarities between options and futures contracts and the markets in which they are traded.

6. In what ways do options alter the return distribution of a stock or bond position?

7. Compare the risk and potential return from speculating with options, futures, and the underlying security.

Bibliography

Introduction to Financial Futures Markets

Anderson, Ronald W. "The Industrial Organization of Futures Markets: A Survey." *Center for the Study of Futures Markets* 66 (July 1983).

Arak, Marcelle, and Christopher McCurdy. "Interest Rate Futures." *Federal Reserve Bank of New York Quarterly Review*, Winter 1980, pp. 33–46.

Besant, Lloyd, and Thomas Schneeweis. "Financial Futures Markets." In *Handbook of Modern Finance*, ed. D. Logue. New York: Warren, Gorman, and Lamont, 1985.

Black, F. "The Pricing of Commodity Contracts." *Journal of Financial Economics*, January/March 1976, pp. 167–78.

Burns, Joseph M. *A Treatise on Markets, Spot, Futures and Options*. Washington, D.C.: AEI Institute for Public Policy, 1979.

Carleton, Dennis. "Futures Markets: Their Purpose, Their History, Their Growth, Their Successes and Failures." *Center for the Study of Futures Markets* 78 (April 1984).

Chalupa, Karl V. "Foreign Currency Futures: Reducing Foreign Exchange Risk." *Federal Reserve Bank of Chicago Economic Perspectives*, Winter 1983, pp. 3–11.

Chrystal, K. A. "A Guide to Foreign Exchange Markets," *Federal Reserve Bank of St. Louis Review*, March 1984, pp. 5–18.

Commodity Futures Trading Commission. *Annual Report*, 1983.

Commodity Trading Manual. Chicago Board of Trade, 1982.

Edwards, Franklin. "Futures Marketing Transition: The Uneasy Balance between Government and Self-Regulation." *Center for the Study of Futures Markets* 46 (January 1983).

Edwards, Franklin. "The Clearing Association in Futures Markets: Grantor and Regulator." *Journal of Futures Markets*, Winter 1983, pp. 369–92.

Fitzgerald, M. Desmond. *Financial Futures.* London: Euromoney, 1983.

Fabozzi, Frank, and Irving Pollack, eds. *The Handbook of Fixed Income Securities.* Homewood, Ill.: Dow-Jones Irwin, 1983.

Gay, Gerald, and Robert Kolb. *Interest Rate Futures: Concepts and Issues.* Richmond, Va.: Robert F. Dame, 1981.

Goldstein, Henry N. "Foreign Currency Futures: Some Further Aspects." *Federal Reserve Bank of Chicago Economic Perspectives,* Winter 1983, pp. 3–13.

Gray, Roger W., and David Rutledge. "The Economics of Commodity Futures Markets: A Survey." *Review of Marketing and Agricultural Economics* 39 (1971) pp. 57–108.

Houthakker, H. "The Regulation of Financial and Other Futures Markets." *Journal of Finance,* May 1982, pp. 481–91.

Jaffee, Dwight M. "The Impact of Financial Futures and Options on Capital Formation." *Center for the Study of Futures Markets* 84 (April 1984).

Kane, Edward. "Market Incompleteness and Divergence between Forward and Futures Interest Rates." *Journal of Finance,* May 1980, pp. 221–34.

Kemp, D. "A Monetary View of the Balance of Payments." *Federal Reserve Bank of St. Louis Review,* April 1975, pp. 14–22.

Kilcollin, Thomas. "Different Systems in Financial Futures Markets." *Journal of Finance,* December 1982, pp. 1183–98.

Kipnis, G. M. and F. J. Fabozzi (ed) *Stock Index Futures.* Homewood, Ill: Dow Jones-Irwin, 1984.

Kolb, Robert. *Understanding Futures Markets.* Glenview, Ill.: Scott Foresman, 1985.

Kyle, A. S. "A Theory of Market Manipulations." *Center for the Study of Futures Markets* 64 (July 1983).

Merrick, J., and S. Figlewski. "An Introduction to Financial Futures." *Salomon Brothers Center for the Study of Financial Institutions,* No. 6., 1984.

Phillips, Susan M. "Regulation of Futures Markets Theory and Practice." *Review of Futures Market Research* 3, no. 2 (1984), pp. 150–58.

Powers, Mark, and David Vogel. *Inside the Financial Futures Markets.* New York: John Wiley & Sons, 1981.

Rebell, Arthur L., and Gail Gordon with K. B. Platnick. *Financial Futures and Investment Strategy.* Homewood, Ill.: Dow Jones-Irwin, 1984.

"Regulation of Futures Markets." Proceedings of *Center for the Study of Futures Markets* Conference. *Journal of Futures Markets,* Summer 1981.

Rosen, Jeffrey S. "The Impact of the Futures Trading Act of 1982 upon Commodity Regulations." *Journal of Futures Markets,* Fall 1983, pp. 235–58.

Rothstein, Nancy, and James M. Little, eds. *The Handbook of Financial Futures.* New York: McGraw-Hill, 1984.

Sandor, Richard. "The Interest Rate Futures Markets: An Introduction." *Commodities* 5, no. 9 (September 1976), pp. 14–17.

Schneider, Howard. "Regulation of Futures Trading." In *Handbook of Financial Markets,* ed. Frank J. Fabozzi and Frank C. Zarb. Homewood, Ill.: Dow Jones-Irwin, 1981.

Schwarz, E. W. *How to Use Interest Rate Futures Contracts.* Homewood, Ill.: Dow Jones-Irwin, 1979.

Telser, Lester G. "Why There Are Organized Futures Markets." *Journal of Law and Economics* 24 (1981), pp. 1–22.

Telser, Lester G., and H. N. Higinbotham. "Organized Futures Markets: Costs and Benefits." *Journal of Political Economy* 85 (1977), pp. 969–1000.

Characteristics of Spot, Futures, and Options Markets

Arnold, Tanya S. "How to Do Interest Rate Swaps." *Harvard Business Review,* September–October 1984, pp. 69–101.

Arak, Marcelle, and Christopher McCurdy. "Interest Rate Futures," *Federal Reserve Bank of New York Quarterly Review,* Winter 1979, pp. 33–46.

Arrow, Kenneth J. "Futures Markets: Some Theoretical Perspectives." *Journal of Futures Markets,* Summer 1981, pp. 107–16.

Bennett, Dennis, Deborah L. Cohen, and James E. McCulty. "Interest Rate Swaps and the Management of Interest Rate Risk." Presented at the Financial Management Association Meetings, Toronto 1984.

Black, F., and M. Scholes. "The Pricing of Options and Corporate Liabilities." *Journal of Political Economy,* May–June 1973, pp. 637–58.

Bookstaber, Richard M. *The Complete Investment Book.* Glenview, Ill.: Scott Foresman, 1985.

Bookstaber, Richard M. *Option Pricing and Strategies in Investment.* Reading, Mass.: Addison-Wesley, 1981.

Conroy, Robert M., and Richard J. Rendleman, Jr. "Pricing Commodities when Both Price and Output Are Uncertain." *Journal of Futures Markets,* Winter 1983, pp. 439–50.

Cox, J. C., J. E. Ingersoll, and S. A. Ross. "The Relation between Forward and Futures Prices." *Journal of Financial Economics,* December 1981, pp. 321–47.

Figlewski, Stephen. "Futures Trading Volatility in the GNMA Market." *Journal of Finance,* May 1981, pp. 445–56.

Garbade, Kenneth. *Securities Markets.* New York: McGraw-Hill, 1982.

Garbade, Kenneth D., and Monica M. Kaicher. "Exchange-Traded Options on Common Stock." *Federal Reserve Bank of New York Quarterly Review,* Winter 1978–79, pp. 26–40.

Gay, Gerald D., and Steven Manaster. "Implicit Delivery Options and Optimal Delivery Strategies." Working Paper, Georgia State University and University of Utah, 1984.

Goodman, Laurie S. "New Option Markets." *Federal Reserve Bank of New York Quarterly Review,* Autumn 1983, pp. 35–47.

Granito, Michael R. *Bond Portfolio Immunization.* Lexington, Mass.: Lexington Books, 1984.

Gray, R. W., and D. S. Rutledge. "The Economics of Commodity Futures Markets: A Survey." *Review of Marketing and Agricultural Economics* 34 (1971), pp. 57–108.

Gulteken, N. Bulent, and Richard J. Rogalski. "Alternative Duration Specifications and Measurement of Basis Risk: Empirical Tests." *Journal of Business,* May 1984, pp. 241–64.

Hill, J., B. Mayerson, and T. Schneeweis. "An Analysis of Variation Margin in Hedging Fixed-Income Securities." *Review of Research in Futures Markets* 2 (1983), pp. 136–59.

Jones, Frank J. "The Integration of the Cash and Futures Markets for Treasury Securities." *Journal of Futures Markets,* Spring 1981, pp. 33–57.

Kamara, A. "The Behavior of Futures Prices: A Review of Theory and Evidence." *Financial Analysts Journal,* July–August 1984, pp. 16–29.

Kaufman, George G. "Measuring and Managing Interest Rate Risk." *Federal Reserve Bank of Chicago Economic Perspective,* January/February 1984, pp. 16–29.

McCurdy, Christopher J. "The Dealer Market for U.S. Government Securities." *Federal Reserve Bank of New York Quarterly Review,* Winter 1977, pp. 35–47.

Moriarty, Eugene, Susan Phillips, and Paula Tosini. "A Comparison of Options and Futures in the Management of Portfolio Risk." *Financial Analysts Journal,* January–February 1981, pp. 61–67.

Nunn, K., J. Hill, and T. Schneeweis. "Corporate Bond Price Data Sources and Return/Risk Measurement." *Journal of Financial and Quantitative Analysis,* forthcoming.

Rosenbloom, Richard H. "A Review of the Municipal Bond Market." *Federal Reserve Bank of Richmond Economic Review,* March/April, 1976, pp. 10–19.

Silber, William L. "Market Maker Behavior in an Auction Market: An Analysis of Scalpers in Futures Markets." *Journal of Finance,* September 1984, pp. 937–55.

Telser, Lester, and Harlow N. Higinbotham. "Organized Futures Markets: Costs and Benefits." *Journal of Political Economy* 85 (1977), pp. 969–1000.

Tosini, P. A., and E. J. Moriarty. "Potential Hedging Use of a Futures Contract Based on a Composite Stock Index." *Journal of Futures Markets*, Spring 1982, pp. 83–103.

Zwick, Bruton. "The Market for Corporate Bonds." *Federal Reserve Bank of New York Quarterly Review*, Autumn 1977, pp. 27–36.

Basic Hedging and Arbitrage Strategies

Anderson, R., and J. Danthine. "Hedging and Joint Production." *Journal of Finance*, May 1980, pp. 487–98.

————. "Time Period Hedging and The Volatility of Futures Prices." *Review of Economic Studies*, April 1983, pp. 249–66.

————. "Cross-Hedging." *Journal of Political Economy*, December 1981, pp. 1182–96.

Bacon, P. W., and Williams, R. "Interest Rate Futures: New Tool for the Financial Manager." *Financial Management*, Winter 1976, pp. 32–38.

Baesel, J., and D. Grant. "Optimal Sequential Futures Trading." *Journal of Financial and Quantitative Analysis*, December 1982, pp. 683–95.

Branch, B. "Testing the Unbias Expectations Theory of Interest Rates." *The Financial Review*, Fall 1978, pp. 51–66.

Capozza, D. R., and B. Cornell. "Treasury Bill Pricing in the Spot and Futures Markets." *Review of Economics and Statistics*, November 1979, pp. 513–20.

Chance, D. "An Immunized-Hedge Procedure for Bond Futures." *Journal of Futures Markets*, Fall 1982, pp. 231–42.

Conroy, Robert M., and Richard J. Rendleman. "Pricing Commodities when Both Price and Output Are Uncertain." *Journal of Futures Markets*, Winter 1983, pp. 439–50.

Cornell, Bradford. "The Relationship between Volume and Price Variability in Futures Markets." *Journal of Financial Markets*, Fall 1981, pp. 303–16.

Ederington, L. H. "The Hedging Performance of the New Futures Markets." *Journal of Finance*, March 1979, pp. 157–70.

Franckle, C., and A. J. Senchack. "Economic Considerations in the Use of Interest Rate Futures." *Journal of Futures Markets*, Spring 1982, pp. 107–16.

Gay, G. D., and R. W. Kolb. "The Management of Interest Rate Risk." *Journal of Portfolio Management*, Winter 1983, pp. 65–70.

Hill, J., and T. Schneeweis. "Risk Reduction Potential of Financial Futures for Corporate Bond Positions." In *Interest Rate Futures: Concepts and Issues*, ed. G. D. Gay and R. W. Kolb. Richmond, Va.: Robert F. Dame, 1982.

————. "The Use of Interest Rate Futures in Corporate Financing and

Security Investment." *Proceedings International Futures Trading Seminar,* VII, Chicago Board of Trade, 1983.

_____. "Reducing Volatility with Financial Futures," *Financial Analysts Journal,* November/December 1984, pp. 34–40.

_____. "On the Estimation of Hedge Ratio for Corporate Bond Positions." In *Advances in Financial Planning and Forecasting,* ed. C. F. Lee. JAI Press, forthcoming.

Hilliard, J. "Hedging Interest Rate Risk with Futures Portfolios under Term Structure Effects." *Journal of Finance,* December 1984, pp. 1547–69.

Ho, Thomas. "Intertemporal Commodity Futures Hedging and the Production Decision." *Journal of Finance,* June 1984, pp. 351–76.

Howard, Charles T., and Louis J. D'Antonio. "A Risk Return Measure of Hedging Effectiveness." *Journal of Financial and Quantitative Analysis,* March 1984, pp. 101–12.

Johnson, L. "The Theory of Hedging and Speculation in Commodity Futures." *Review of Economic Studies,* March 1960, pp. 139–51.

Jones, F. S. "Spreads: Tail, Turtles, and All That," *Journal of Futures Markets,"* Spring 1981, pp. 33–58.

Kolb, R. W., and R. Chiang. "Improving Hedging Performance Using Interest Rate Futures." *Financial Management,* Autumn 1981, pp. 72–79.

Kolb, R., and G. Gay. "Are There Arbitrage Opportunities in the Treasury Bond Futures Markets." *Journal of Futures Markets,* Summer 1982, pp. 211–30.

Kuberek, Robert C., and Norman G. Pefley. "Hedging Corporate Debt with U.S. Treasury Bond Futures." *Journal of Futures Markets,* Winter 1983, pp. 345–54.

Lang, R. W., and R. H. Rasche. "A Comparison of Yields on Futures Contracts and Implied Forward Rates." *Federal Reserve Bank of St. Louis Review,* December 1978, pp. 21–30.

Little, Patricia K. "Negative Cash Flows, Duration, and Immunization: A Note." *Journal of Finance,* March 1984, pp. 283–88.

McCabe, G. M., and C. T. Franckle. "Effectiveness of Rolling the Hedge Forward in the Treasury Bill Futures Market." *Financial Management* 12, Summer 1983, pp. 21–29.

Pitts, Mark, and R. Kopprasch. "Hedging Short-Term Liabilities with Interest Rate Futures." Presented at the Financial Management Association Meetings, San Francisco, 1982.

Poole, W. "Using T-Bill Futures to Gauge Interest Rate Expectations." *Federal Reserve Bank of San Francisco Economic Review,* Spring 1978, pp. 7–19.

Puglisi, D. J. "Is the Futures Market for Treasury Bills Efficient?" *Journal of Portfolio Management,* Winter 1978, pp. 64–67.

Rendleman, R. J., Jr., and C. E. Carabini. "The Efficiency of the Treasury Bill Futures Market." *Journal of Finance*, September 1979, pp. 895–914.

Silber, W. "Market Maker Behavior in an Auction Market." *Journal of Finance*, September 1984, pp. 937–54.

Stein, J. "The Simultaneous Determination of Spot and Futures Prices." *American Economic Review*, December 1961, pp. 1012–25.

Stein, J., M. Rzepczynski, and R. Selvassio. "A Theoretical Explanation of the Empirical Studies of Futures Markets in Foreign Exchange and Financial Instruments." *Financial Review*, February 1983, pp. 1–32.

Stulz, Rene M. "Optimal Hedging Policies." *Journal of Financial and Quantitative Analysis*, June 1984, pp. 127–40.

Toevs, A. and D. Jacob, "Interest Rate Futures: A Comparison of Alternative Hedge Ratio Methodologies," Morgan Stanley, June 1984.

Trainer, Franics H. "The Uses of Treasury Bond Futures in Fixed-Income Analysis. *Financial Analysts Journal*, January–February 1983, pp. 27–34.

Turnovsky, S. "The Determination of Spot and Futures Prices with Storable Commodities." *Econometrics* 51 (1983).

Wardrep, Bruce, and James F. Buck. "The Efficacy of Hedging with Financial Futures: A Historical Prospective." *Journal of Futures Markets*, Fall 1982, pp. 243–54.

Working, H. "Futures Trading and Hedging." *American Economic Review*, June 1953, pp. 514–33.

————. Hedging Reconsidered." *Journal of Farm Economics* 35 (1953), pp. 544–61.

Financial Futures: Applications

Arditti, Fred D. "Interest Rate Futures: An Intermediate Stage toward Efficient Risk Reallocation." *Journal of Bank Research*, Autumn 1978.

Asay, Michael R., Gisela A. Gonzalez, and Benjamin Wolkowitz. "Financial Futures, Bank Portfolio Risk, and Accounting." *Journal of Futures Markets*, Winter 1981, pp. 607–18.

Baker, James. "A Beginner's Guide to Proper Use of Interest Rate Futures." *ABA Banking Journal*, February 1982, pp. 129–35.

————. "Statistical Relationships Are Key to Bank's Use of Interest Rate Futures." *ABA Banking Journal*, March 1982, pp. 88–95.

Batlin, Carl Alan. "Interest Rate Risk, Prepayment Risk, and the Futures Market Hedging Strategies of Financial Intermediaries." *Journal of Futures Market*, Summer 1983, pp. 177–84.

Black, Fisher. "The Investment Policy Spectrum: Individuals, Endowments, and Pension Funds." *Financial Analysts Journal*, January–February 1976, pp. 23–31.

Blanton, Kimberly. "Tool for Sponsors Overrides Advisor, Asset Allocations." *Pensions and Investment Age*, November 28, 1983, pp. 23–24.

Bookstaber, Richard. "Interest Rate Hedging for the Mortgage Banker." *Review of Research in Futures Markets* 1, no. 1 (1982), pp. 22–51.

Daane, Kenneth E., and Albert J. Fredman. "How Banks Can Use Interest Rate Futures." *Bankers Monthly Magazine*, April 1979.

Dew, James Kurt, and Terrence F. Martell. "Treasury Bills Futures, Commercial Lending, and the Synthetic Fixed-Rate Loan." *The Journal of Commercial Banking Lending*, June 1981, pp. 27–38.

Drabinstott, Mark, and Anne O'Mara McDonley. "The Impact of Financial Futures on Agricultural Banks." *Federal Reserve Bank of Kansas City Economic Review*, May 1982, pp. 19–30.

————. "The Effect of Financial Futures on Small Bank Performance," *Federal Reserve Bank of Kansas City Economic Review*, November 1982, pp. 15–31.

Etter, Wayne E., and Donald R. Fraser. "Mortgage Bankers and the GNMA Futures Market." *The Mortgage Banker*, August 1979, pp. 27–29.

Figlewski, Steven, and Stanley J. Kon. "Portfolio Management with Stock Index Futures." *Financial Analysts Journal*, January–February 1982, pp. 52–59.

Goodman, L., and M. Langer. "Accounting for Interest Rate Futures in Bank Asset Liability Management." *Journal of Futures Markets*, Winter 1983, pp. 415–28.

Hill, Mark. "How a Commercial Bank Trader Uses the Treasury Bond Market for Various Hedging Applications." *Review of Research in Futures Markets* 1, no. 3 (1982), p. 204–9.

Hill, Joanne, and T. Schneeweis. "The Use of Interest Rate Futures in Corporate Financing and Security Investment." *Proceedings International Futures Trading Seminar* VII, Chicago Board of Trade, 1981.

————. "Risk Reduction Potential of Financial Futures for Corporate Bond Positions." In *Interest Rate Futures: A Comprehensive Anthology*, ed. G. Gay and R. W. Kold. Richmond, Va.: Robert F. Dame, 1983.

Hill, J., J. Liro, and T. Schneeweis. "Hedging Performance of GNMA Futures under Rising and Falling Interest Rates." *Journal of Futures Markets*, Winter 1983, pp. 403–14.

Ho, Thomas, and A. Saunders. "Fixed Rate Loan Commitments, Take-Down Risk, and the Dynamics of Hedging with Futures." *Journal of Finance and Quantitative Analysis*, December 1983, pp. 499–576.

Keen, Howard. "Interest Rate Futures: A Challenge for Bankers." *Federal Reserve Bank of Philadelphia Business Review*, November–December 1980, pp. 13–22.

Koch, Donald, D. Steinhauser, and Pamela Whigham. "Financial Futures as a Risk Management Tool for Banker and S&Ls." *Federal Reserve Bank of Kansas City Economic Review*, September 1982, pp. 4–14.

Kolb, Robert, Roger Morin, and Gerald D. Gay. "Regulatory Lag and the Use of Futures Markets." *Journal of Finance*, May 1983, pp. 405–18.

Koppenhauer, G. D. "Selective Hedging of Bank Assets with Treasury Bill Futures Contracts." *Journal of Financial Research*, Summer 1984, pp. 105–70.

Lev, B., and S. Kunitsky. "On the Association between Smoothing Measures and the Risk of Common Stocks." *Accounting Review*, April 1974, pp. 259–70.

Levich, Richard. "The Efficiency of Markets for Foreign Exchange: A Review and Extension." In *The Efficiency of Foreign Exchange Markets*, ed. D. Lessard. Boston: Warren Gorham and Lamont, 1979.

Owens, Patricia. "How a Pension Fund Manager Uses Financial Futures to Hedge A Portfolio." *Review of Research in Futures Markets* 3 (1982), pp. 218–26.

Pan, F. S., and James Hoag. "The Pricing of GNMA Futures Using Dealer Quotations and Spot Transactions." *Review of Research on Futures Markets* 3, no. 3 (1984), pp. 244–55.

Parker, Jack W., and Robert T. Daigler. "Hedging Money Market CDs with Treasury-Bill Futures." *Journal of Futures Markets*, Winter 1981, pp. 597–606.

Rzepczynski, Mark S. "The Behavior of Primary Government Security Dealers and Their Use of Financial Futures." *Review of Research in Futures Markets* 3, no. 3 (1984), pp. 282–317.

Schweser, Carl, Joseph Cole, and Lou D'Antonio. "Hedging Opportunities in Bank Risk Management Programs." *Journal of Commercial Bank Lending*, January 1980, pp. 29–41.

Viet, E. Theodore, and Wallace W. Reiff. "Commercial Banks and Interest Rate Futures: A Hedging Survey." *Journal of Futures Markets*, Fall 1983, pp. 283–94.

Tax and Accounting Issues

Accounting for Interest Rate Futures. Chicago: Arthur Andersen & Co, 1985.

Asay, M. R., G. A. Gonzalez, and B. Wolkowitz. "Financial Futures, Bank Portfolio Risk, and Accounting." *Journal of Futures Markets* 1, no. 4 (Winter 1981), pp. 607–18.

Beaver, W. H. "Accounting for Interest Rate Futures Contracts." *Center for the Study of Futures Markets* 11 (March 1981).

Goodman, Laurie, and Martha J. Larger. "Accounting for Interest Rate

Futures in Bank Asset–Liability Management." *Journal of Futures Markets,* Winter 1983, pp. 415–28.

Miller, E. "Tax-Induced Bias in Markets for Futures Contracts." *Financial Review* 15, no. 2 (Spring 1980), pp. 35–38.

Mortgage Bankers Association of America, International Management Committee. *Accounting for GNMA Mortgage Interest Rate Futures Market Transactions:* A statement of opinion approved by the International Management Committee, Mortgage Bankers Association of America. Washington, D.C., n.d.

O'Brien, J. "Tax Topics: Interest Rates Futures—Commercial Banks." In *Interest Rate Futures: Concepts and Issues,* ed. G. D. Gay and R. W. Kolb. Richmond, Va.: Robert F. Dame, 1981.

Rice, M., and P. Peterson. "Financial and Tax Accounting Treatment for Hedging with Financial Futures Contracts." *Proceedings International Futures Trading Seminar,* VI, Chicago Board of Trade, 1979, pp. 1–10.

Index

*This book has been set VideoComp in 10 and 9 point
Aster, leaded 2 points. Part numbers are 24 and 42
point Compano Italic and part titles are 36 point
Compano Bold. Chapter numbers are 18 and 48
point Compano Italic and chapter titles are 24 point
Compano Bold. The size of the type page is 26 by
47 picas.*